Great Australian
CRICKET STORIES

Great Australian
CRICKET STORIES

Ken Piesse

The Five Mile Press

The Five Mile Press Pty Ltd
1 Centre Road, Scoresby
Victoria 3179 Australia
www.fivemile.com.au

First published 2010

Printed and bound at Griffin Press. Only wood grown from sustainable regrowth forests is used in the manufacture of paper found in this book.

Designed and typeset by Shaun Jury.
Front cover photographs: From top left Golden Age hero Warwick Armstrong, Don Bradman & Jack Fingleton at the MCG, Kerry O'Keeffe (picture courtesy of Patrick Eagar), Shane Warne (Patrick Eagar) and the historic Member's Pavilion at the Sydney Cricket Ground.
Back cover photographs: The Ken Piesse Collection.
Internal photographs: The majority of the photographs included in this book are from the Ken Piesse Collection. The author would like to thank the following for their generosity in also providing photographs: Jack Atley, The Beldam Collection (UK), Cricket NSW, Cricket Victoria, *Cricketer* magazine, David Munden/Sportsline (UK), Chris Nevins, John O'Sullivan, Marylebone Cricket Club, Melbourne Cricket Club, Patrick Eagar (UK), Scotch College Melbourne and the Warne family.

National Library of Australia Cataloguing-in-Publication entry:
   Great Australian cricket stories / Ken Piesse.
   ISBN: 9781742482408 (hbk.)
   Cricket – Australia – Anecdotes.
   Other Authors/Contributors:
   Piesse, Ken.
   796.3580994

CONTENTS

FOREWORD

Charles Darwin, with his exquisite theory of 'The Evolution of Species', gave a greatly enhanced significance and meaning to the word 'evolution'.

The game of cricket has certainly not been through such an exacting evolution but nevertheless has had a wonderful transformation, from a simple pursuit played with sticks and a ball on any old paddock, into the sophisticated and many-facetted operation that we know today. An amazing and continuing evolution but with one common and unchanging factor throughout: a continuing fund of delightful stories that could only emerge from a game with entrancing characteristics. National heroes and far more modest practitioners are involved, a period of over a century is covered and the stories have their birth in both the past and evolving forms of the game.

The heroes range from Victor Trumper through Monty Noble, Charlie Macartney, Bill Ponsford, Bill O'Reilly, Don Bradman, Arthur Morris, Keith Miller, Neil Harvey, Richie Benaud, Alan Davidson and, of course, the more modern superstars including Steve Waugh, the Chappell brothers, Glenn McGrath, Adam Gilchrist and perhaps the greatest bowler of all time, Shane Warne.

It was my good fortune to have played with and to have lasting memories of a number of them.

One was Keith Miller, a superlative cricketer and free spirit, who whether enthralling prime ministers, royalty or those more humble was a singularity from which a multitude of stories emerged. A cricket match in which he participated was for him, and those watching, a joyous, stress-free event. Keith was a World War II fighter pilot and who has not heard of his definition of stress as 'a Messerschmitt up your arse'? I have mentioned his free spirit, but whilst he took his cricket seriously perhaps his field placing instructions to the NSW state teams touring country regions was typical. 'Scatter,' he'd order and somehow or other the field was set!

Lasting Memories:
Colin McDonald treasures his
time as a Test player.
Scotch College, Melbourne

Much more about 'Nugget' Miller is revealed in the stories. I particularly enjoyed his irreverence towards Lord Tedder. 'Thank you, boy,' together with a one-penny tip when accepting a cup of tea from his former commander and Air Marshal of the Royal Air Force. Enough said.

Neil Harvey, whom I consider to have been the greatest Australian batsman since World War II, features automatically in the stories. Whilst I played with him in more than 40 Test matches, my favourite and first memory of him is as 12-year-old schoolboys captaining our respective schools in a grand final cricket match. It was also the first occasion in which either of us had played on a turf cricket pitch. My team batted first and scored about 200. In reply Neil, without any effort, had accelerated to 75 when his batting partner hit the ball to me in the covers and ran. I threw the ball to our wicketkeeper, and the bails were removed with Neil short of his ground. The umpire at square leg, one of my teachers and our cricket coach, raised his finger in a paroxysm of delight. It was not noticed in all the excitement that the wicketkeeper had not actually taken the ball – it had continued on its way to fine leg, but Neil was on his way. We would never have got him out any other way. His team was dismissed for the grand total of 105. We all knew we had witnessed a future master. In my experience it was always wonderful to bat with him. The bowling would suddenly become less forbidding due to his mastery over whomever he faced.

I could go on about playing with Richie Benaud, Alan Davidson, Arthur Morris and Ray Lindwall amongst others, but Ken Piesse, one of the greatest lovers of the game, has brought together an excellent and wide-ranging collection of cricket stories which includes them all.

I commend his collection to all prospective readers.

Colin McDonald
Beaumaris, 2010

INTRODUCTION

'If you find something you really love you will never work again.'
– MARK TWAIN

Cricket has been my passion ever since I can remember. Every day is a joy, surrounded by my books and cricketing knick-knacks. A new world opened when I happened across a copy of *Playfair Cricket Monthly* from England. Enticing advertisements included three or four for specialist cricket book dealers, who quickly garnered a new teenage client from faraway Australia. A once-a-week paper round was never going to satisfy this young man's fancies, so I started delivering papers daily, and once every two or three weeks Dad would spend part of his lunchtime lining up at the bank on the corner of Collins and Queen for a sterling draft to fund my latest acquisitions.

We'd go to the local library in Parkdale and I would borrow the entire 15 books devoted to cricket and sit them up on a small wooden bookshelf in my bedroom and imagine they were mine. *Bradman the Great* by BJ Wakley and *Cricket's Secret History* by Walter Hammond were among my favourites. The run feats of those two ultimate Ashes heroes were truly staggering.

Bradman's remarkable Ashes series of 1930 was the subject of many a school essay, both written and verbal. Hammond's book including all his four tours to

Dream On: Ken Piesse in a borrowed baggy green.

Australia and the famous players he opposed before and after World War II became new heroes.

As my library started to expand, Dad built one set of shelves and then another. Soon every wall of my bedroom was enveloped by books or cricket posters. Having been given a copy of *Wisden* one Christmas and been amazed by the run-scoring feats of the leading Australian players such as Bobby Simpson, who began one year in Brisbane with 359 and followed with two more double-centuries in the next two weekends, I began the first of a run of first-class stats books as well as newspaper scrapbooks, lovingly pasting in cricket cuttings and stories from around Australia courtesy of Dad who each night would bring home *all* the morning papers from around the country. Mum taught me how to make clag and away I went, cutting and pasting to my heart's content.

It didn't matter how tired he was after a day in town, Dad would often leave his car in St Aubin Street and bowl to me in the carport. Off would come his jacket and away he'd go with his little seam-ups while the light held.

At the weekends we'd go to the cricket and I'd keep score, ball by ball, in my NSW Cricket Association 'Official' Scorebook while Dad took himself off into the MCC's 'Cigar Stand' to meet a few of his mates before returning with a sandwich and a drink. These were blissfully happy days and the Melbourne Cricket Ground a home away from home, in summer and winter.

Mum became as addicted to cricket as us and had the radio permanently on 774 3LO for the direct description of the great matches or for the regular Shield updates from Dick Mason and Peter Booth. When the Australians toured the West Indies in '65, a makeshift bed was set up for me in the lounge room so I could listen to the direct description into the wee hours on our old Healing radiogram.

Mum still proudly recalls the day I carried my bat for Beaumaris in an underage grand final. 'You got 65, the red inks, didn't you?'

'Yes Mum, that's right.'

Being 86 not out herself, she'll occasionally repeat parts of a conversation from five minutes earlier, before stopping to say: 'Have I already told you that?'

'No Mum,' I say. 'You're going fine ... by the way ... what's Don Bradman's batting average?'

'Ninety-nine ... point ... 99.94!'

She still comes to see me play. I was marking centre at the start of one recent match and about to face the first ball when Mum suddenly moved from her vantage spot at straightish mid-off to directly behind the bowler's arm – just as he'd begun his run-up. There are no sightscreens when you play for the Kingston Saints thirds. Hard-pressed to adhere to the Greg Chappell principle of watching the ball out of the hand, this one was fortuitously just wide, which was lucky for me as I was seriously distracted.

'Chopper,' I called to our local umpire and to general laughter from the opposition, 'can you tell my Mum to move?!' Sooner than I wanted, I was back with her on the sidelines, and she explained that I'd always told her the best viewing was directly behind the wicket!

My sister Anne claims to be the least cricket-minded person in the entire Piesse constellation yet at one cricket dinner at Bellerive (Hobart), I asked her to pass the Bill Lawry and she instinctively reached for the opener. Impressive that.

When I'm not playing or practising, I'm in my book room, a little like Mr Bennett from Jane Austen's *Pride & Prejudice,* who was always retiring to his library, with explicit instructions not to be disturbed. I've been promising for years to take my wife Susan to Italy – once they start playing some decent cricket there. Our whole family became used to me commandeering the dinner table for my layouts, copy and pictures for the latest magazine. The television would always be on in the corner tuned into Channel Nine.

Jessie, one of our four beautiful daughters, was being squired by one young man who happened to let drop that he played cricket. He was a bowler. 'Oh,' she said. 'Can you bowl a googly?' Jess will rummage through boxes of books in some of the inner-city second-hand shops, find something which looks promising and immediately ring to see if I have it. Once she secured, with the hard-to-get dust jacket, a nice-condition copy of *Elusive Victory,* EW Swanton's 1950–51 Ashes tour book. A 1940 *Wisden* as yet remains uncovered, despite Jessie's regular requests to bookshop owners up and down Brunswick Street.

Cricket breeds good people and a rare fellowship and rapport. Having landed in Barbados airport one day as co-hosts of an Events Worldwide supporters' tour, Susan and I were about to join a long line for customs inspections when one gentleman called us over. 'You with the cricket? Come this way!' he said, holding open a side gate. Through we bowled, our bags unchecked.

Another time, Ali Bacher, one of the white knights of the 'new' South Africa, met us at Johannesburg Airport. The main contingent of tourists, media and former players had flown in 24 hours earlier, yet here he was making a special trip to Jan Smuts, just for us. I'd explained we'd been unavoidably delayed because I'd been committed back in Melbourne on the Saturday. 'It was the last day of a two-dayer, Ali.'

'I understand Ken, I totally understand.'

Keith Miller and I were friends. He lived at Mornington, the neighbouring bayside town to ours, and we'd chat regularly. One morning he rang and asked if I'd been watching television the previous night. 'My mate Parky [Michael Parkinson] was on,' he said [on Andrew Denton's *Enough Rope*]. 'And guess what? Out of all the actors and actresses, heads of state and ambassadors ... guess who he said was his hero? Me ... little ol' me!' He spoke with the passion of a 16-year-old rather than someone who was 80-something.

I'd visit the old Bodyline batsman Leo O'Brien every week or so and share a cuppa. He'd tell his stories and in me he had a captive audience. I'd just started editing *Cricketer* magazine and I told Leo how I'd love to interview Bill Ponsford, the ultimate record-breaker, before the arrival of DGB. Leo told me how 'Ponny' was an ever-so-private person and since his wife died, saw only his family and a few of his old bowling clubmates where he lived at Woodend. I put it in the too-hard basket, but not before also sounding out Geoff Ponsford, one of Bill's sons, who basically said the same thing. A few days later, Geoff phoned me back and said: 'Dad will see you ... after all.' I almost fell over. Years later, at the reopening of the Western Stand, named after Ponny, I met up with Geoff again and he said our interview was only possible because of Leo. 'He wouldn't let up until Dad said yes.'

Another time Leo and I were discussing evergreen Clarrie Grimmett's amazing bowling figures in the mid-'30s series in South Africa. 'I'll always remember his figures, Leo,' I said. 'He was 44 years old and he took 44 wickets ... surely that should have been enough to get him on the '38 tour of England. Surely he was better than Frank Ward or Ted White.'

We discussed and debated and Leo then said: 'Well ... why don't you ask Don about it? He'll tell you.'

Within a week of my letter, a note came back from Don Bradman on his familiar No. 2 Holden St, Kensington Park letterhead thanking me for news of Leo and wishing me to be remembered to his old mate, with whom he'd first batted during 1932–33. 'As for Grimmett in 1938?' he concluded, 'he was finished ... yours sincerely ... Don Bradman.'

Apparently there had been a dressing-room tiff, where Grimmett had inadvertently made a remark Bradman considered offensive. The Don was captain and a prime selector. Clarrie would have loved to have had those few minutes over again.

I told Keith Miller one day of Bradman's reticence to debate the Grimmett issue and he said how important it was to stay in The Don's good books. 'And that's something which didn't come naturally to a few of us!' he said, his eyes twinkling.

Years earlier, for a lark, 'Nugget' had bowled two bouncers in a row at The Don. It was his Sydney testimonial of 1948–49. The first was hit at the speed of light through mid wicket for 4, Sam Loxton at mid-off calling it to be the most gorgeous cricket shot he ever saw. The second, yards quicker, zeroed past Bradman's right ear. The Don turned white. Sam was beside

Ever-So-Private: Bill Ponsford finally opened up after initially playing an ever-so-straight bat to the early questions.
Cricketer magazine

himself. 'No more, Nug. No more,' he said. He loved The Don like a second father.

Within weeks Miller had sensationally been left out of the touring team to South Africa.

One morning we had a cuppa and Nugget was very emotional, talking of how Bradman had ruined his life; he was jealous of his popularity; he should have captained Australia and it was all Bradman's fault he didn't. 'No, Nugget, he didn't ruin your life,' I said. 'No one has packed more into their life than you. No one … but you would have made a bloody good captain of Australia.'

Even though I didn't see any of them play, Keith, Leo, Ponny and 'Ninna' Harvey remain four of my all-time favourites from yesteryear, alongside boyhood heroes like Greg Chappell and Dennis Lillee through to the 'moderns' such as Adam Gilchrist, Shane Warne and Steve Waugh. I once bowled a six-ball over to Steve, at Royal Ascot. It went for 32. At the end of it, all he did was smile and re-marked his

Invincibles: Ken Piesse with the three remaining Invincibles, Arthur Morris (left), Sam Loxton and Neil Harvey.
Bruce Postle

guard. His 90-odd came in about half an hour. The gulf between Test player and club player was enormous.

More than most, Steve had a keen appreciation of the history of the game and as he walked across the MCG one morning for practice, at a time when he was in his twilight years, he stopped when I suggested to him that age really was only a number and how Jack Hobbs had made 100 of his 191 centuries *after* his 40th birthday. 'There's hope for me yet then,' he said with a grin.

Gilchrist, 'Warnie', Richie Benaud, Bill Lawry, Matthew Hayden and Darren Lehmann have been among many to kindly write forewords for some of my earlier books. So did Billy Brown, then in his 80s and still sharp as a button. We had a lovely few hours together one morning at his home in Brisbane and I rang the following morning to thank him and his lovely wife Barbara for their hospitality: 'Ken Piesse?' he said. 'I remember you. Do I owe you money?!'

Another Test opener of note, Colin McDonald, and his wife Lois are equally delightful. I playfully call him 'Sir Colin' because of his pro-republican views. I'm honoured that he has contributed a foreword for this book. I'd send him one chapter and he'd ask for another. And another. He's still so passionate about the game and loved the read. Twelve months earlier, I'd assisted him in the publication of his autobiography. We'd argue over the usage of a particular word or two. I'd state my case and he'd state his. Occasionally I'd win, but not often. Playing for Australia takes rare skill and vision – and massive determination.

I told him about all the scrapbooks I'd been lucky enough to collect along the way, material from which are included in the pages that follow. I lent Colin the '56 Ashes one, a tour in which he built his reputation as one of the finest batsmen in the world.

He also pored over the entire manuscript and read and re-read the interviews with past greats like 'the King', Jack Ryder and 'the Prince of Umpires' Bob Crockett. He particularly liked the chat with Victor Trumper, still one of Australia's favourite cricketers almost a century after his death. 'I've never seen these stories before, Ken,' he said. 'People will love it.'

I hope you all do. The pleasure has been in the making, I can assure you!

Ken Piesse
Mt Eliza, August 2010

The Don: Averaged 99.94 in a fabulous, unparalleled Test career.

1
99.94

---

*'"Grab him, Acka, grab him," she screamed.
"He can't swim!" As Bradman spluttered and splashed
and began going down for the second time Marks dived
in, grabbed Don and pulled him into the boat ...'*

OUR DON BRADMAN

Who is it that all Australia raves about?
Who has won our very highest praise?
Now is it Amy Johnson, or little Mickey Mouse?
No! It's just a country lad who's bringing down the house.

And he's Our Don Bradman – And I ask you is he any good?
Our Don Bradman – As a batsman he can sure lay on the wood.
For when he goes in to bat
He knocks ev'ry record flat,
For there isn't anything he cannot do,
Our Don Bradman – Ev'ry Aussie 'dips his lid' to you.

Jack O'Hagan (1930)

THE DAY THE DON ALMOST DROWNED

*A casual day of boating on the Hawkesbury almost ends
in tragedy for a young Don 'Braddles' Bradman and
one of his best mates Alec 'Acka' Marks.*

The Hawkesbury River is still one of the most beautiful waterways
in the great city of water, although Berowra is no longer a haven for

koalas and kookaburras but a part of Sydney suburbia; a place where people with four-wheel drives and mobile phones live before they move to Pymble or Hunters Hill. There were, of course, no freeways in those days and once a motorist and his passengers moved past the uninteresting little railway town of Hornsby, they were in the bush. The old Pacific Highway connected Sydney to Brisbane but to call the main route between two capital cities 'a highway' was tantamount to calling your surfboard 'a ship'. The two lanes of the 'highway' [one each way] wound around the ridges, curved sideways, dropped to the gorges and picked up again. Sometimes the road was made of asphalt and tar and sometimes it was made of rolled-out dirt that had been there since before the Dreamtime – and sometimes it wasn't rolled. In those days, carsickness was an ailment of epidemic proportions.

The trip to Berowra did not start auspiciously. Soon after the two cricketers and their girlfriends had passed Hornsby, the car had a flat tyre. Alec Marks, who was about as mechanical as Merv Hughes is suave, somehow managed to remove the wheel but when he looked at the spare, he found it was old and tatty and certainly not a piece of equipment that you would choose to use, except in the direst emergency.

Fortunately, there was a garage [as service stations used to be called] just up the hill, so Marks rolled the tyre up the steep incline to see if it could be repaired. In a few minutes, the mechanic had pulled out a sharp piece of metal from the rubber and patched it, and the tyre was ready to go. Flushed with triumph, Marks gave the thumbs up to his companions down the road and began to roll the tyre down the hill while he ran beside it like those old paintings we used to see of polite young ladies playing with hoops. A hoop, however, was built for polite young ladies – a tyre was built for speed! As Marks began to pick up pace, so did the tyre and, as the road became steeper, suddenly it bolted. Down the road it raced, roaring along with its new patch coming into view every fraction of a second.

'Braddles, grab the tyre!' Marks shouted as the object gained momentum and hurled towards the two 'good sorts' and the world's greatest batsman, who were all leaning against the car near the bottom of the incline. But the tyre had gained its freedom and like the wild bush horses from Snowy River it must have seen its 'well loved mountains full in view', for it bumped left, crossed the road, hit a boulder, jumped high in the air and plunged over the side of a cliff. Down it crashed, sweeping branch, bush and bramble from their moorings. Down, down it continued, a hundred feet and then some, before disappearing forever into the dark undergrowth at the base of a forest that had never heard the sound of a human footstep. Meanwhile, Marks, a top schoolboy sprinter, racing down in pursuit of the rampaging tyre, also couldn't stop and was into his follow-through when he passed the passengers who were leaning on the car watching the drama. He pulled up about 50 yards past the vehicle and walked slowly back. Looking straight ahead, Marks reached into the boot and casually remarked to his open-mouthed companions, 'Okay; now let's see how the spare goes!'

When eventually the four arrived at Berowra, the two men hired a boat. While the girls retired to the boat owner's bathroom to freshen up, Bradman and Marks started up the boat and took it out on the river to 'get the feel'. They were out about a hundred yards when the boat's engine coughed and petered out. Anyone who has tried to start an old-fashioned outboard engine with a leather piece of pulling equipment that looked as if it came from a barber shop knows the frustration of the exercise. *BBBrrr* then silence. *BBBrrr* then nothing again. Jessie and Lillian, having finished their 'freshening', walked down the wharf and stood watching as their men tried with muscle and finesse to get the little craft moving.

'Here, give me a look at the motor, Acka, something might be blocked,' Don suggested and bent over to examine the engine. The sight of the Bradman posterior shoved into the air was too much for an occasional practical joker like Alec Marks and with a quick movement of his left leg, Marks sent his mate over the side and into the Hawkesbury.

On the wharf, Lillian laughed, but not Jessie. 'Grab him, Acka, grab him,' she screamed. 'He can't swim!' As Bradman spluttered and splashed and began going down for the second time, Marks dived in, grabbed Don and pulled him into the boat.

Alec Marks later recounted this story to his playing group at the 19th hole at Pennant Hills Golf Club. One of the group suggested that if Don Bradman had actually drowned, then Marks would still be in Long Bay Jail. Another said that he would never have gone to jail, as the next day the headlines would have read: BRADMAN DROWNS – MARKS LYNCHED AT BEROWRA WHARF.

Alec, however, didn't agree with this. He felt that the headlines would have read: BRADMAN DEAD – MARKS MOVES UP BATTING ORDER.

Great Australian Cricket Stories, Neil Marks (ABC Books, Sydney, 2002)
*Neil Marks is Alec Marks' son. Don Bradman married his childhood sweetheart Jessie
Menzies in 1932 and later described their 45-year marriage as 'the best partnership
of my life'.*

BRADMAN'S METEORIC RISE

*The joy felt throughout all of Australia was considerable
when country boy Don Bradman helped lift Australia
to its only win of the 1928–29 summer.*

New South Wales cricket is greatly indebted to the country for many past champions. [Charlie] Turner, [George] Bonnor, [Tom] McKibbin, Bill Howell from the West, the brothers Moore [Leon and Billy], [Walter] McGlinchey from the Hunter district and James Rainey Munro Mackay of Uralla are a few, but never has the southern district produced a batsman greater than Don Bradman, who has shot so suddenly to the front. Not since 'Sunny Jim' Mackay attracted attention by his many centuries in the north has a greater run-getter been brought to the metropolis from the rural parts.

Sydney, a few years ago, read of a noted feat of a Bowral youngster, just past his middle teens, who made more than 300 for his town against Moss Vale. Enthusiasts were not greatly interested then, but when

Southern Highlander: A young Don Bradman first began to break records in Bowral before shifting to Sydney.

in the final, a season later, the same boy again topped the third century, they paid more attention and there was wonderment that he had not been seen in the city in the annual country week carnival. The committee controlling this made certain that he was not omitted on the next occasion and the youth immediately made good. The [New South Wales Cricket] Association saw that he was given every opportunity and events of the last two seasons, particularly the current one, showed that their foresight has been amply rewarded.

First Time in a Baggy Blue: The New South Wales touring team to Adelaide in 1927–28 included a 19-year-old Don (standing, third from right) who started with the first of his 117 first-class centuries.
Cricket NSW

Dick Jones, one of the state selectors and an official of St George, quickly scented a chance of benefiting his club and giving the Bowral boy a chance of playing in the best of company. Don started with a century against Petersham, so there was further proof that the country reputation was not lightly gained.

He has gone from one success to another in Sydney. His two separate centuries against Queensland followed by 87, 132 not out and 58 not out in successive innings last week show his calibre.

Because he lacked the artistry of some of the other stars and there was just the faintest trace of just a little crudeness in some of his shots, some feared he might not be reliable, but when in the first innings of the recent game against England it was necessary to rely on the good old straight bat, he proved that despite the critics, he was a success where the polished ones failed. And in addition to revealing that his batting was sound, the innings showed he possessed a splendid fighting temperament.

New South Wales suffered a serious loss when Johnnie Taylor dropped out of first-class cricket. His work in the outfield was as classy as has been witnessed on the Sydney Cricket Ground. Don Bradman proves likely to be a worthy successor. He throws himself into the work with zest. And his splendid return to the wicket caps his tireless fielding. The hardest day will never be too hard for Bradman.

Born in Cootamundra and having lived nearly all his 20 years in Bowral, he belongs entirely to the south. Evidently his mind was turned to cricket by the ability of his uncle, for George Whatman is no ordinary batsman himself. He was a partner – running into the double-century – in one of the boy's biggest country triumphs.

Source unknown, 'Rambler' (March 1929)

NOT EVERYONE WAS IMPRESSED

Too cheeky … not safe enough … that was another
old champion's opinion of the young Don.

I remember having dinner with [Don] Bradman after he had scored 252 not out against Surrey – rain on the remaining two days of the match forced the question of how many more he could make to remain unanswered – and talking to him of what the critics had been saying, in humbleness or amazement, about his style.

The critic more especially under discussion was AC 'Archie' MacLaren, who, in the *Evening Standard* that day – writing, of course, before the event – had said that Bradman had apparently modelled his style on Charlie Macartney. 'Bradman,' it seemed to MacLaren, 'was too cheeky at the start of his innings to be regarded as a safe batsman and he cut unnecessarily and dangerously hard.'

'I hope he was at the Oval today,' was Bradman's answer when I showed him the cutting.

With the 1930 Australians: Behind the Scenes in the Fight for the Ashes, Geoffrey Tebbutt (Hodder & Stoughton, London, 1930)

ONE GREAT ON ANOTHER

English batting master Jack Hobbs was full of
acclamation for Bradman's 974 runs at an average
bordering 140 in the five Ashes Tests of 1930.

But what a wonderful thing it was, all the same, to bat as he did on English turf! I would not compare Bradman to George Gunn, Archie MacLaren, Reggie Spooner, Frank Woolley or one of our great classic batsmen. He is more of a run-getting machine, a first kinsman to Phil

Mead of so many years ago. Bradman never hit the ball in the air. He had an exceptionally accurate sense of timing. He had marvellous sight. The pace he got on his hits on the leg side was astounding. He only seemed to place his bat against the ball and yet it flew with the flow of a full-blooded drive. As for Bradman the man, we had heard a lot about him and particularly in relation to his alleged aloofness (it is the easiest thing in the world for any action of a successful man to be construed as 'swollen-headedness' ... I know this, as it is my own experience).

Personally, I always found Bradman an attractive, simple-hearted lad. He has surely done enough to be excused a certain amount of swollen-headedness, which, let me add, I have never observed in him. I must say, however, that it would have pleased me better had he been more demonstrative as he ought to have been to show more of the joy of life when he got his three 100s in the Tests.

The Daily Star, Jack Hobbs (London, August 1930)

A SPECTACULAR TRANSFORMATION
Jack Fingleton says The Don was a huge drawcard everywhere he went after his stunning batting feats in England in 1930.

Some of the older players, possibly resenting the manner in which he [Don Bradman] had turned their cricket world upside down, never went out of their way to be particularly friendly towards him. Bradman did not mind that, because he had enough to engage his attention. Four years before, his world revolved around a village [Bowral] best known as a warning for a refreshment stop on the journey between Sydney and Melbourne.

In 1930, when he was a mere 21 years of age, the whole cricket world revolved around him, and this, to put it without stress, was a most unusual transformation. At his inexperienced age in 1930, Bradman evidently did not think he was doing wrong in cutting himself off from the rest of the team at the end of a game, although he did much the same thing in 1938 when the team of which he was captain in England never saw him again on tour after he had injured himself in the fifth Test.

Nor, when he returned to Australia in 1930, did Bradman think he was leaving himself open to criticism when he left the ship at its first port of call and proceeded across Australia ahead of the team in what was a triumphal and somewhat commercial procession.

He made appearances at city theatres. The original conquering hero had no greater welcome from civic authorities; but for the others, trailing behind like Mrs Murphy's cows, the barriers between Bradman and themselves were built even higher. One said they felt like apologising for themselves when, in the wake of the regal Bradman entry and exit, they came after the champagne into an atmosphere of stale beer.

Bradman did not come home to rest after his English labours. On his return from England, he hit the business front as spectacularly as he had hit the cricket front. Bradman bats, Bradman hats, Bradman boots, Bradman shirts, Bradman suits, Bradman gloves and pads rolled off the assembly line like parts of Spitfires during the English blitz.

This part of his career must be mentioned. It had a connection with his cricket and serves to give an impression of his associations with other players. The manner in which he bestrode the cricket world like a colossus, on and off the field, should be truly assessed, for what more likely than that all this played its part, and a big part, in the trap of Bodyline set for his downfall? The next time Perth saw Bradman after he had hastened away from his teammates of 1930 was when he came to play against [Douglas] Jardine's team ...

No prince could have had a more regal entry into Perth. As the long and dusty eastern train jolted to a stop, thousands crammed the station, the adjoining roofs and buildings, the exits and the streets outside. Police had to force a passage for Bradman, and the Palace Hotel, where we stayed, was in a constant simmer by day and night.

Cricket Crisis, Jack Fingleton (Cassell & Company, London, 1946)

A FIRST GLIMPSE OF THE DON

A hero-worshipping Kirwan Ward was among the
20,000 to pack the WACA Ground for a glimpse of
Don Bradman, playing for the first time in Perth in 1932.

Lord knows when it was that I first clicked through the Hale Street turnstile and went hurrying into the West Australian Cricket Association ground. Memory, eroded by wisdom, or cynicism, has a habit of fixing on some minor recollection and carelessly discarding major ones. But the WACA scene that memory has selected for me is as sharp as if I were watching it at this very minute on a television screen. First, the desperate wriggling and struggling to escape the octopus tentacles of a soulless office where nobody seemed to realise the overwhelming importance of the fact that this was Saturday afternoon, or that the English team was playing in Perth. Then, the breathless race down Barrack Street to swing onto the moving tram like an urbanised Tarzan.

Tram conductors – like the barrackers on the Hill at Sydney – were conscious of their reputation as characters. They felt a responsibility towards their public. As we dropped off the rear platform at Queens Gardens, our bloke held up a tiny toy cricket bat of the kind that very small boys get in those red-mesh Christmas stockings. 'Hey,' he yelled, addressing the backs of a rapidly receding audience, 'the Now of Patord's left 'eez bat in the tram.'

The Nawab of Pataudi was playing in the English team and it was a scream, that any man could have a name like that. We ran on, delighted that our trammie hadn't let us down, that he was a real character. And, as we turned into Hale Street which is that short street running between the eastern fence of Queens Gardens and the WACA's high, red-brick wall, we became at once part of the crowd. For the genuine sports nut, the aficionado, the fan, this is a delicious moment, this moment when one feels the turnstile yield and the buzz from the human bee-swarm in the arena intensifies. I have felt that peculiar clutch at the heart on entering Wembley Stadium, Madison Square Gardens and the Melbourne Cricket Ground. It has been there – that old black magic – at Madrid's Plaza de Toros, at Lenin Stadium in Moscow and in Tokyo's Budokan, but all that came later than the WACA – much later.

Post-war Hero: Don Bradman's comeback to big cricket in 1946 was embraced by the cricketers, the fans, and particularly newspaper editors looking for circulation boosts.

There were 20,000 people at the ground that day and they crackled as if with static electricity. It was more characteristically a football crowd than a cricket crowd; a crowd more likely to roar than to clap politely.

From the pavilion, just as I arrived and found viewing space, there emerged a smallish, almost weedy young man, under a cap that flopped all over his head in the cricketing fashion of the day, like a Scotsman's tam-o'-shanter. The blue cap of New South Wales. He was only a year or two older than I, yet, pressing as close to the members' enclosure as possible, I gazed upon him as if he had just walked across the Swan River without breaking the surface. He had never set foot on the WACA before. I could recall with absolute accuracy all of his cricketing deeds. As he moved at a calm, deliberate pace across the outfield, like a farm labourer plodding to work, they finally got his name hoisted on the scoreboard over by the car-barn ... BRADMAN. It was what we were all there for.

Well, Bradman scored the usual safe single on the leg side that had already become his standard start to a huge score, then two more careful singles. There was never anything of the nervous young beginner about him, never any suggestion that he could possibly be overawed by any occasion. He was simply a self-assured young man who had a definite appointment with a double-century later in the afternoon. He knew it, we knew it. The only person present at the WACA that day who didn't know it was a tall, elegant Yorkshireman named Hedley Verity who now loped in to bowl, slow left-arm, round the wicket from the Causeway end. There had been overnight rain, producing the kind of wicket that English county batsmen play on as often as not, but one such as we Australians seldom encounter. We hadn't, at this point, begun to consider the wicket at all. Sticky wickets were things to worry ordinary mortals, not Bradman. And then a terrible thing happened. We watched the red ball floating absurdly high to Bradman, wondering to which boundary he would thump it. We saw it bounce gently on to the white blade and slide off it towards first slip. At first slip, his broad stern towards us, was Walter Hammond, one of the finest slip fielders who ever lived. He took the catch as nonchalantly as a pelican swallowing a pilchard and there was Bradman, still poker-faced, still with that steady stride, walking back to the pavilion.

There were interesting events after that. Verity had six for 23 by tea, but what we waited for was to see Bradman return to the crease and put these iconoclasts in their place [in the follow-on]. This time the young Don made 10, then hooked one from GOB 'Gubby' Allen hard to none other than the Nawab of Pataudi at square leg. And that was it.

Bradman, of course, was playing for a combined eleven, for

this was the only way we would ever see any of the big name Australian cricketers. We weren't in the Sheffield Shield and no West Australian had the faintest chance of being considered for Test selection. To have suggested then, in 1932, that one day an Australia–England Test match would be played at the WACA would have been as outrageous as suggesting that men would fly to the moon in some crazy kind of Jules Verne job and walk about on its surface ...

The Historic Test, Australia v England, Perth, Western Australia, 11–16 December, 1970, Kirwan Ward (WA Newspapers, Perth, 1970) Western Australia's inaugural Test match was to be noted for a classic century on debut by Greg Chappell and a Test-best 171 from Ian Redpath.

Prolific: One of Don Bradman's signature shots was the off-drive, which he invariably timed with a precision most could only dream about.
John O'Sullivan Collection

BRADMAN'S DILEMMA ... WILL HE PLAY?

Having missed the first Bodyline Test with illness, Don Bradman's tiff with the Board of Control over his employment with Associated Newspapers and desire to write and commentate on the Tests he was due to play in saw him in doubt for the second Test in Melbourne right up until the eve of the game.

No one in Melbourne last night outside the player himself could say with certainty whether DG Bradman, Australia's champion batsman, would be playing in the second Test match against England to begin on the Melbourne Cricket Club ground at 12 today.

The Board of Control last night, in defiance of public opinion, decided to reaffirm its rule which prohibits Test players who are not solely employed as journalists from writing or commenting on any first-class cricket match. This automatically prevents Bradman from following his occupation and throws upon him the responsibility of choosing between Test cricket and his work.

Bradman did not attend practice yesterday with the other Australian players and his friends professed not to know anything of his intentions. It cannot be said definitely until today whether he will be at the Melbourne ground to take his place in the team, although reports from Sydney last night stated that as far as Associated Newspapers Ltd, his part-time employers, were concerned, Bradman was free to play in the Test regardless of the Board's ruling.

The motion before the Board last night was one by New South Wales delegates to amend the player-writer rule by deleting the word 'solely' before the word 'occupation', the effect of which would be to allow Bradman or any player in a similar position to write and play. The proposal was defeated but no information was given as to the voting.

The Board shelved the general question of banning players from broadcasting until the end of the season, but it carried a resolution asking those Australian XI players at present engaged in broadcasting not to make any criticism or statement over the air which might tend to a breach of good relations between the broadcaster and other Australian XI players or players or officials of visiting teams.

Obviously the Board hedged on the broadcasting because it knew that about half a dozen players, including [captain Bill] Woodfull, [Vic] Richardson and [Stan] McCabe, as well as Bradman, have contracts with broadcasting companies, and if it took prohibitory action it might cause a stampede in the team which would be disastrous on the first day of a Test.

A former teammate and close friend of Bradman said last night he had been informed by the champion yesterday that if he

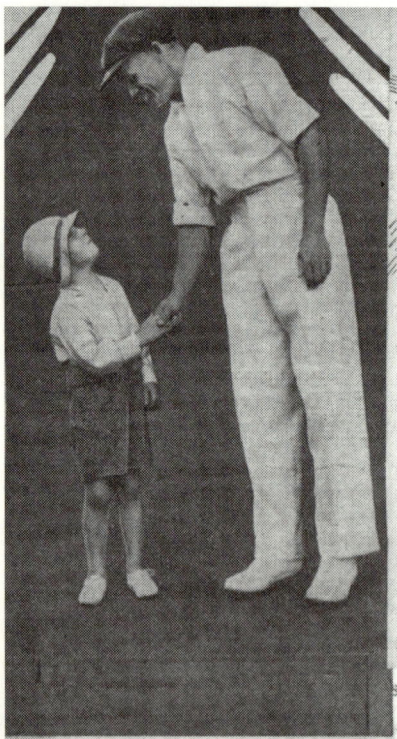

SHAKING HANDS with the great.—A small admirer wishing Don Bradman good luck at the M.C.G. yesterday. Bradman injured his ankle and could not take the field.

Hero of the Masses: Don Bradman meets a young fan at the 1931–32 Melbourne Test with the South Africans.

He's Out: News of Don Bradman's absence, through illness, from the first Test team in 1932–33 was greeted with all-round dismay.

could not write he would not play any more Test cricket. Another Melbourne friend, Mr Schelnack, of Cookson Street, Camberwell, said Bradman told him last night he was sure the decision of the Board would go against him, but he was not worrying about it. He had not made up his mind about playing.

The wicket will be hard and fast at the start. The forecast is for fine weather for at least two hours.

The Age, writer unknown (Melbourne, 29 December 1932)

BRADDLES: THREE PROFILES

1928 D BRADMAN (New South Wales). Bradman is a country man who has played for his club and district, and who, in his first interstate match, against South Australia made a century. He is a right-handed batsman, short build, fairly strong and very active. There is nothing stodgy about either the man or his play. He is a good starter, has plenty of confidence and pluck, is a quick scorer, and puts lots of power into his shots; indeed, one wonders where all the power comes from. He must have a very quick eye, for he is very fleet of foot and walks down the pitch with great daring to make splendid strokes off deliveries which might otherwise provide difficult propositions even to play. His style

DON BRADMAN
ENGAGED

Boy And Girl Romance Of Schooldays

Don Bradman

SYDNEY, Sunday. — The international cricketer, Don Bradman, yesterday announced his engagement to Miss Jessie Menzies, the eldest daughter of Mr. and Mrs. J. Menzies, of Burwood.

Bradman and his fiancee went to school together, and her father and mother once lived in Bowral.

Headliner: Don Bradman's engagement, to Jessie Menzies, in 1930–31 was front-page news.

is somewhat similar to that of Clem Hill and like the famous left-hander, he impresses with the idea that he is thoroughly enjoying himself. He is a most likeable chap and altogether a good type of cricketer.

Test Cricket Certainties and Possibilities for 1928–29, MA Noble (New Century Press Limited, Sydney, 1928)

1938 DG BRADMAN, South Australia (captain). Played formerly for NSW. Age 29. Born 27 August 1908. Probably the greatest batsman and run-getter of all time. Brilliant, dashing and consistent performer under varying conditions. Plays every possible shot, has a quick eye and cleverly uses his feet. Magnificent field in all positions, with deadly return. Slow leg-break bowler, useful as partnership breaker. Holds world record of 452 not out and highest Test score against England of 334. Topped the batting averages of the Australian team in England, 1930 and 1934. Last season [1937–38] he eclipsed [Clem] Hill's Australian record aggregate in first-class cricket of 17,221 on his way to scoring 1822 runs, average 91.52. And in scoring 6771 runs at 100.7 in 47 matches, he passed Hill's Sheffield Shield record of 6274 in 68 matches. A truly prolific record-breaker.

Test Cricket 1938 National Broadcasts (Australian Broadcasting Commission, Sydney, 1938)

1948 DONALD GEORGE BRADMAN, of South Australia, who is now 39 years of age, is making his fourth tour of England as an international player. Many critics consider Bradman today to be below the standard of his peak years, but although perhaps not quite the thrasher of bowlers as in former days, still he is quite capable of compiling any number of runs in a more sedate way. Like the old grey mare 'he is not as young as he used to be', but what little he may have lost in activity he has made up in experience and canniness; and I have little doubt that runs will flow from his bat in sufficient quantity to worry just as much as heretofore the bowlers who present themselves during the coming tour. Bradman does not indulge too frequently in the annihilating stroke play of prewar days, but he is more secure – if that be possible – and just as effective, even if it should take him a little longer to compile a couple of hundred runs in an innings. He will undoubtedly add a few more to the already phenomenal list of records in the statistical book before he finally retires from the game.

Fight for the Ashes, CG Macartney (Findon Publications, London, 1948)
The Don averaged 72 in the Tests and 89 on tour, making 11 centuries in all and leading Australia to a 4–0 victory with one Test drawn. His team became known as 'The Invincibles'.

WHAT IF . . .
Had every catch and half-chance been held,
The Don would still have averaged 75!

Don Bradman gave 24 unaccepted chances in Test matches, including 18 against England. In 13 innings, he gave only one chance, in two innings he gave two chances, in one he gave three and in one he gave four.

Four of these 24 chances (including three v England) were given after he had passed 100 . . .

Of his 29 centuries, 10 included at least one chance, and of these 10, two were chanceless until *after* he had reached 100. Only in eight of his 29 centuries would he have failed to make 100, had every possible chance been taken . . .

Had every chance he gave been accepted, The Don's career record would have been: Tests 52, innings 80, not out 7, highest score 273, runs 5438, average 74.79.

Bradman the Great, BJ Wakley (Mainstream Publishing, London, 1999 edition)

WORDS OF WISDOM

A young Richie Benaud told Keith Miller one day how disappointed he was not to bowl to Don Bradman, who retired the very season Richie debuted. 'Son,' said Miller, 'that was your *good* luck!'

TRULY 'BRADMAN-LIKE'

*Sir Donald Bradman's contribution to cricket
in retirement was phenomenal.*

From September 1935 until June 1986, Sir Donald Bradman served in various capacities on official South Australian Cricket Association committees. The appended list shows only his attendance at properly convened meetings and does not include ad hoc discussions, or meetings connected with the [Australian] Board of Control or any other like body.

When it is considered that Sir Donald was playing until 1948 and also had to travel interstate as a national selector, then this record of his contribution to South Australian cricket puts into its proper perspective how much of his time he devoted to the game.

In 1961–62 when he was chairman of the Board of Control and involved in trying to solve some very contentious cricket matters [like the throwing controversy], Sir Donald was attending cricket meetings (and as always, fully briefed) on at least one day in three. He was still, at this time, deeply involved in his business affairs, too.

Selector: Don Bradman on duty after the war with selection chairman EA 'Chappie' Dwyer.

Don Bradman: the meetings he attended

Season	Meetings attended	Running total	Season	Meetings attended	Running total
1935–36	10	(10)	1961–62	78	(1022)
1936–37	5	(15)	1962–63	50	(1072)
1937–38	6	(21)	1963–64	41	(1113)
1938–39	16	(37)	1964–65	54	(1167)
1939–40	19	(56)	1965–66	47	(1214)
1940–41	6	(62)	1966–67	44	(1258)
1941–42	8	(70)	1967–68	52	(1310)
1942–43	6	(76)	1968–69	59	(1369)
1943–44	30	(106)	1969–70	59	(1428)
1944–45	32	(138)	1970–71	36	(1464)
1945–46	44	(182)	1971–72	31	(1495)
1946–47	26	(208)	1972–73	28	(1523)
1947–48	19	(227)	1973–74	10	(1533)
1948–49	30	(257)	1974–75	14	(1547)
1949–50	55	(312)	1975–76	15	(1562)
1950–51	57	(369)	1976–77	13	(1575)
1951–52	60	(429)	1977–78	21	(1596)
1952–53	36	(465)	1978–79	14	(1610)
1953–54	43	(508)	1979–80	19	(1629)
1954–55	59	(567)	1980–81	15	(1644)
1955–56	57	(624)	1981–82	13	(1657)
1956–57	58	(682)	1982–83	13	(1670)
1957–58	64	(746)	1983–84	11	(1681)
1958–59	74	(820)	1984–85	18	(1699)
1959–60	70	(890)	1985–86	14	(1713)
1960–61	54	(944)			

The History of the South Australian Cricket Association, Chris Harte (Sports Marketing Australia, Adelaide, 1990)

Yesss: Few celebrated with the gusto of Shane Warne, the 'Bradman' of bowling, pictured in 2001 on the third of his four Ashes tours.
Patrick Eagar

2
THE SULTAN OF SPIN

'Watching him [Warnie] I have come to the
conclusion that, given my time over, I would try
to copy him ...' – RICHIE BENAUD

WARNE BY WARNE

*Shane Warne was an aspiring batsman who bowled
just a little when he first drifted into St Kilda.*

It seems like only yesterday that I walked into St Kilda's first practice [in 1987–88] and was asked what I did. Maybe remembering what an old skipper at Brighton [Mike Tamblyn] in the subbies had told me not that long before, I told the practice captain Noel Harbourd that I was a batsman who bowled a bit.

I was shunted down to one of the end nets with the other 17- and 18-year-olds, looking to make the best possible impression. Years later I found out that Shaun Graf [club coach and captain] had approached Noel and asked what the kid with the blond hair did. On being told what I'd said, Shaun smiled and said: 'Not sure about the batting ... but he might be a chance with the ball.'

I played colts, fourths and thirds in that first year and fourths and thirds again the next. Like anyone, it was all about serving an apprenticeship and I was luckier than most to serve mine at the Junction Oval with so many I still number among my closest friends.

Down at the Junction There's a Cricket Ground: St Kilda Cricket Club, the First 150 Years, Ken Piesse (St Kilda Cricket Club, Melbourne, 2006)

DUELLING WITH A CHAMP

*Champion Englishman Graham Thorpe on a memorable duel
with Warnie during his debut Test at Trent Bridge in 1993.*

[Andy] Caddick frustrated Australia awhile longer on the Monday morning and by the time I walked out, the Australians were pretty eager to get stuck into me. They were very chirpy and one of the umpires, Roy Palmer, soon intervened to ask if I wanted him to stop all the swearing. I just said, 'No, I'm enjoying it. Just stop them if they spit at me!'

Steve Waugh and David Boon, both fielding close to the bat, certainly had a lot to say. When I pulled a ball past Boon, crouched at silly point and looking like a Viking with his droopy moustache, he threatened to kill me if I did it again. I kept my mouth shut and got on with the job. As I'd said to Palmer, their words didn't intimidate me but made me all the more determined to give it my best shot. It was just what I needed.

Predictably enough, they tested me out with more short stuff but, by now, the pitch was flat and I dealt with it okay and, eventually, big Merv [Hughes] tried so hard to get rid of [Graham] Gooch and myself, he picked up a strain and hobbled out of the attack. My main memory is of Shane Warne and Tim May's bowling. They were an exceptional partnership and I look back with immense pride at managing to bat against them for what turned out to be almost a whole day (for 14 not out to help force a draw).

Like me, Warne was in his early 20s and hadn't played a lot of Test cricket but he'd already played a big part in the first two Tests and, one reason I'd been picked [was], left-handers were reckoned better able to cope with leg spin. I think it did give me an advantage, particularly once I'd got used to how far he was turning the ball into me. Often, he simply turned it too much and I was able to let it go through and his googly was not that great. But he was incredibly accurate with his leg breaks and I've never seen anyone drift the ball as much as he did in his early days.

He also had a great flipper although, with time, I learned to pick it from the daylight that would show between ball and hand when his arm was at the top of its delivery. Even at this stage, it wasn't hard to work out that this fiery character, with his blond locks, white zinc cream on his face and confrontational attitude, was going to enjoy the celebrity side of the game more than me. Once you had played against him a reasonable amount, you knew what tricks he'd got, but the first few times were difficult. He hadn't played in the one-day internationals and I'd only faced him once before, briefly during Australia's warm-up match against Surrey. I had tried to cut him and missed badly as the ball spun back miles and he soon had me caught down the leg side.

Now, on a slow pitch, I used my pads to kick him away ... a lot. Otherwise, I swept him or went back to try tucking him away on the leg side. Once, I attempted a drive through extra cover but the ball spun straight back past me and I decided against a repeat. In my early encounters with Warne, I found I could stay in but not really dominate. At Edgbaston later in the same series and at Brisbane the following year, I batted around four hours for 60s. In the first innings at the Gabba, I'd tried to take the initiative by going down the wicket but he did me in the flight; I checked the shot and ended up chipping back a return catch for 67 and it was not until much later in the series that I felt confident enough to take more risks against him.

Graham Thorpe: Rising from the Ashes, Graham Thorpe (CollinsWillow, London, 2005)

NEXT TIME AROUND ...
I'LL BOWL LIKE WARNIE
Richie Benaud on the genius of Shane Warne.

Warne is something of a freak bowler. He is unlike other leg spinners I have seen and, in fact, in one or two aspects has rewritten the technique book on over-the-wrist spin bowling. For a start he walks part of the way to the bowling crease; the rest is more of an amble than anything else until the last yard. The ball is only held loosely in his hand but he has exceptionally powerful fingers, wrist and forearm and he utilises sidespin much more than I did. Watching him, I have come to the conclusion that, given my time over, I would try to copy him and use a bit more sidespin, though I found the overspin part of the delivery of immense value bowling in Australia, or anywhere where the pitches are hard and the ball will bounce.

He is a great one for experimenting and, providing his fitness holds up, we will see a variety of different balls, the like of which have not been sighted since Clarrie Grimmett was learning his trade. Best of all, not only are the crowds who watch him bowl enthusiastic about leg-spin bowling, but he is extremely enthusiastic as well. You might be inclined to think he should be, as it is his trade, job and recreation and anything less than enthusiasm would hardly be commonsense. It is very easy though to fall into the trap of becoming blasé, particularly if success has come your way, and to slacken off as regards practice and experimenting.

Warne doesn't do that. The amount he spins the ball tends to inhibit the batsmen, even the good ones, from coming down the pitch at him unless they are absolutely certain they will be to the length of the ball.

The Appeal of Cricket, Richie Benaud (Hodder & Stoughton, Sydney, 1995)

WARNIE V THE DON

Ken Piesse says Shane Warne won more Tests
for Australia than even Don Bradman.

When Shane Warne was a starstruck rookie, wondering if he truly deserved to be in the same dressing-room alongside heroes and icons like Allan Border, he told me how all he really wanted to do was take a timely wicket which changed the match momentum and helped his team win.

His concentration was always towards the team, a key reason why he was so loved by his teammates and adored by the public.

I was sitting with good friend Graham Wilson, the guitar player from The Four Kinsmen, on the balcony seats of the Melbourne Cricket Club's old 'Cigar Stand' in 1992 when Warnie surprised West Indian captain Richie Richardson with his scuttling flipper which hit the base of middle and off. For a lifelong cricket fan like Graham, it was just as memorable a moment as when the Kinsmen won the first of a fleet of 'Mo' awards for being Australia's Entertainers of the Year.

We all jumped with Warnie. It was a key wicket just as the world champion 'Windies' were threatening to take control. Warnie had turned his first Test in Australia and in front of his home-town crowd. He was ecstatic. This was the afternoon in which his career truly blossomed. At only one other Australian venue, Adelaide, was he to be even more potent or consistent a matchwinner.

In all, Warne was chiefly responsible for the winning of 25 of his 144 Tests at a rate of one every five or six Tests, a formidable strike-rate ensuring his status in any elite XI from any era.

Even Don Bradman couldn't claim to have been as important as often, but then again The Don played only 52 Tests and was robbed of some of his finest years by World War II. Analysing his impact on matches, it's little wonder he is held in such exulted status as he was directly responsible for 12 Australian wins in his 52 Tests, at a rate of one every four or five Tests; a slightly superior strike-rate to Warne.

In the last 47 of his 52 Tests, The Don never scored a century for a losing side. Ten of his tons came in matches Australia won by an innings. The most important of those was probably his 232 at the Oval in 1930 and 234 at Sydney in 1946–47.

Statistician Charles Davis says Adelaide 1947–48 could also be added to the list as he made 201, the only double-century in a high-scoring match in which Australia made 674 batting first and India replied with 381 and 277.

Five of The Don's pivotal contributions occurred at the MCG and none in his original home city, Sydney. The Don won nine of his 12 Tests before turning 30, Warnie 15 of his 25 after turning 30.

Brisbane was Warne's most-prolific ground statistically. He was central in three Australian wins there, as he was in Melbourne. But he won four in Adelaide, including the seemingly impossible-to-win second Ashes of 2006–07 after England had declared its first innings closed at 6-551.

Neil Harvey, Australia's finest batsman of the '50s, said Bradman was still an extraordinary player after the war. 'He must have been truly amazing beforehand,' he said.

Warne survived operations to his shoulder and finger and became an even finer bowler late in his career than he'd been when he was at his athletic best in his mid-20s. He breathed fresh life into a dying art.

Former Australian [cricketer] Rodney Hogg says Warne just has to be 'the best bowler of all time. His influence on cricket has been unbelievable.'

Tests The Don 'won'

	Location	Season	His runs
1	Melbourne	1928–29	123 & 37*
2	Lord's	1930	254 & 1
3	Melbourne	1931–32	2 & 167
4	Adelaide	1931–32	299*
5	Melbourne	1932–33	0 & 103*
6	The Oval	1934	244 & 77
7	Melbourne	1936–37	13 & 270
8	Adelaide	1936–37	26 & 212
9	Leeds	1938	103 & 16
10	Melbourne	1947–48	132 & 127*
11	Nottingham	1948	138 & 0
12	Leeds	1948	33 & 173*

* denotes not out

Tests Warnie 'won'

	Location	Season	His wickets
1	Colombo	1992	0-107 & 3-11
2	Melbourne	1992–93	1-65 & 7-52
3	Manchester	1993	4-51 & 4-86
4	Birmingham	1993	1-63 & 5-82
5	Brisbane	1994–95	3-39 & 8-71
6	Melbourne	1994–95	6-64 & 3-16
7	Brisbane	1995–96	7-23 & 4-54
8	Sydney	1996–97	3-65 & 4-95
9	Manchester	1997	6-48 & 3-63
10	Sydney	1997–98	5-75 & 6-34
11	Wellington	1999–2000	4-65 & 3-92
12	Nottingham	2001	2-37 & 6-33
13	The Oval	2001	7-165 & 4-64
14	Adelaide	2001–02	5-113 & 3-57
15	Cape Town	2001–02	2-70 & 6-161
16	Colombo	2002–03	7-94 & 4-94
17	Sharjah	2002–03	5-74 & 3-56

18	Adelaide	2002–03	4-93 & 3-36
19	Galle	2003–04	5-116 & 5-43
20	Kandy	2003–04	5-65 & 5-90
21	Brisbane	2004–05	4-97 & 4-15
22	Adelaide	2005–06	1-77 & 6-80
23	Durban	2005–06	2-80 & 6-86
24	Adelaide	2006–07	1-167 & 4-49
25	Melbourne	2006–07	5-39 & 2-46

On Ya Warnie, Ken Piesse (Wilkinson Books, Melbourne, 2007)

A POSITIVE SPIN
Gideon Haigh's one-on-one interview.

'It is sometimes not a bad thing for a professional sportsman to sit in the crowd and watch from the other side. It is a reminder of how much you miss it when it's not there.'

When Shane Warne confided this reflection in *My Autobiography* in 2001, it was with regard to past incidences of involuntary spectating rather than an expectation of a future exile. But at the end of perhaps the most frustrating year of his career, during which he has seldom been fitter and never less occupied, it is too tempting not to ask him how the thesis stands up.

Pretty well, he reckons: 'I did write that. And it is true. When you're watching, in fact, you tend to pick up other things. Sledging. Style of play. Appealing. Body language. Which, when you're involved in the game, you're less aware of, because you're focused on the match and your opposition;

Exuberant: Shane Warne's victory tango at Trent Bridge in 1997 was triggered by his pivotal seven wickets which ensured Australia the Ashes.
David Munden/SportsLine

because you're emotional. Some of the things I've seen I've learned from. I might even have been guilty of them a few times in my career.'

Not, Warne admits, despite a season behind the microphone in the Channel Nine commentary box while suspended for the heedless popping of a banned diuretic, that he is one of nature's watchers. 'I've enjoyed the commentating,' he says. 'They've all looked after me in the box and I think I'm quite good at it. I love cricket and I've watched more of it than I ever have this summer. But I'm not someone who has to watch it all the time. If someone's been bowling a good spell, one of the quicks, or [Stuart] MacGill, or [Simon] Katich, or one of the batsmen have gotten on top, I've watched it pretty closely. But I prefer doing it. There have been times when Zimbabwe and Bangladesh have played this summer when I've had a bit of a snooze.'

Watching the World Cup, which should have been the crowning glory of Warne's limited-overs career, was particularly difficult; sitting up late at night to follow his mates in the West Indies a little less so, though still frustrating. But Warne operates in a negativity no-fly zone. 'I'm looking at the positive side,' is a phrase he scatters freely in conversation and he manages to make it sound like a creed rather than merely a cliché.

The loss of a year? Think again. Warne regards it as the gaining of two – at least – on the end of what might by now have been a completed career. Positive person? Warne agrees he is: 'Maybe that's why I play cricket the way I do.' Perhaps it's intrinsic to leg spin. Remember how Richie Benaud was nicknamed 'Diamonds', because [HJ] 'Dusty' Rhodes thought that if he put his head in a bucket of shit, he'd come up with a mouthful of gems? Warne would find at least a pile of casino chips.

Learning the Ropes: A young 'Warnie' on the tennis court with father Keith.
Warne family archive

Even the indiscretion that cost him the year has been rationalised away. Warne dismisses it as 'not checking a book' – the book that would have told him that the fluid tablets he took had the potential to act as masking agents for steroids – with the implication that checking a book is something it's a bit hard to expect of people.

The only question that gives him pause, even momentarily, is what night have happened had he received the two-year ban many thought condign: 'Not sure. Don't know. What I would say is that, if I'd been guilty of trying to hide something, if I'd taken the diuretic to cover up a performance-enhancing drug, I should have been rubbed out for life. But I didn't.'

So is there anything he has missed? The answer is interesting. 'I've had a fair bit of contact with the guys over the last year. Darren Lehmann, "Punter" [Ricky Ponting], Damien Martyn, "Binger" [Brett Lee], "Haydos" [Matthew Hayden]. In fact, I'm catching up with Punter tonight. But it's different to when you're playing. You know the thing I really enjoy about walking onto a field for a game – any game, whether it's a Test, or a one-dayer, or a club game – is that you don't know what's going to happen. You don't know whether you're going to knock 'em over, or you're going to get flogged, whether you'll have a bad day, or take a couple of screamers.'

The baggy green? 'Yeah, don't get me wrong. That means a lot to me. But what I miss when I'm not playing is that unpredictability.'

What he would not miss is the unpredictability of his personal life, which reached something of a zenith last August when he was accused of harassment by a South African model and of infidelity by a Melbourne stripper. 'He told me he had an open marriage,' said the latter on television. 'I asked him about his wife and he led me to believe they weren't together.' And for a time, they almost weren't. Simone, whom Warne married in September 1995, took their daughters Brooke and Summer and went to live with her parents; Warne was left with his son Jackson in the palatial 85-square residence that he has spent almost three years turning into a cricketer's Xanadu, complete with cinema and popcorn machine.

Warne is less positive and forthcoming where his marriage is concerned. 'Marriage is a tough job at the best of times,' he says. 'Simone and I have been through a lot together, most of which, unfortunately, has been my fault. But that's in the past now and we're looking forward to getting on with our lives.' If he doesn't invite you [to discuss it] further, that's because the media has tended to welcome itself into Warne's personal life regardless; the extent of intrusion last year startled even a hardened campaigner like Warne. On one

A GREAT SCORE.

In the match Carlton v. Richmond, T. Warne, for Carlton, made 402, only wanting 16 to beat Worrall's 417 record score for Australia. Trying to drive an off ball of Parsons's he made a miss-hit, and Kelly, who had missed him at 40—his one chance—held the catch at extra-cover. Warne had a tremendous reception, for he had got his huge score with fewer lives than usual, hitting 39 fourers and two 5's. He was at the wickets on three successive Saturdays.

The Other Warnie: Tommy Warne, no relation to Shane, was the first Warne cricketing notable, at the turn of the century.

occasion, Warne and his wife agreed to meet for a conciliatory talk in his car in Port Melbourne; within 10 minutes, two Channel Seven vehicles containing film crews had pulled up on either side, boxing them in. 'I still don't know how it happened,' says Warne. 'If you hear anything, let me know.'

Publicly, mind you, Warne handled this imbroglio perhaps better than any other in his career, maintaining his silence and his dignity while all about him were losing theirs and at the height of hysteria rather shrewdly disappearing to Spain and the UK. Whose idea was that? 'Mine. Well, both of ours. I said: "Where would you like to go, Simone?" She said: "Spain." I said: "Let's go."'

It proved a tonic. It turned out that, in this affair, being suspended had advantages, there being no need to create a pretence of normality and continue playing cricket. Observers were also relieved of the unedifying spectacle of Cricket Australia acting as a moral arbiter. Where Warne's indiscretions with a nurse three and a half years ago cost him the Australian vice-captaincy, Cricket Australia CEO James Sutherland this time offered support: 'There are obligations and standards incumbent on players, but there is also a boundary between their public lives and their lives as private citizens.'

Warne appreciated Sutherland's sensitivity; indeed, he thinks highly of the administrator, who is, of course, a former Victorian teammate. But the irony of the situation was not lost on Warne, who commented tartly in *My Autobiography* that Cricket Australia's directors paid too much attention to the media and that the relationship between sins and first stones might profitably be explored: 'I wonder what might happen if the backgrounds of the 14 directors themselves were investigated. If the same rules apply, as they should, then they, too, must have led unblemished lives or they are not fit to do their jobs.'

Top Guns: Captain Steve Waugh with Shane Warne and Glenn McGrath eye a successful Ashes defence in 2001.
Marylebone Cricket Club

'Well, maybe they read my book and took the advice,' Warne jokes now. 'But yes, one minute my personal life was their affair; next minute it was none of their business. Then again, there wasn't really much they could do. I wasn't vice-captain anymore. I was a contracted player but the contract was suspended and I was receiving no money. If that had been their attitude in 2000, then I might have stayed vice-captain and things might be different today. Who knows?'

Who does? If the rigour of his regimen is anything to go by, Warne is certainly planning to be around for a while. In line with Terry Jenner's advice, he did not recommence bowling too early. But since he resumed training on 27 December, his routine has involved three bowling sessions a week of 50 deliveries each, bike rides, swimming sessions, sprint work, weight programs, skipping, boxing and karate. His cross-training has even involved kicks of the football with his friend Aaron Hamill of the St Kilda Australian Rules club, where Warne played in the reserves and under-19s 15 years ago and which over the years has been a favourite haunt.

Nobody seriously doubts that Warne's old Test berth is his for the taking and that he will form part of the team Ricky Ponting leads to Sri Lanka for the tour beginning in March. It might be a year since his last game, but it is only two years since perhaps his best: that 100th Test in Cape Town where he extracted eight wickets from 98 overs, scored 63 and 15 not out and won it almost single-handedly.

The question is not so much about his place in the Australian team as it is about his role in Australian cricket. Times are changing. Warne may have extended his career, but under what circumstances will it be played? On more than one occasion, Warne has said he would have enjoyed playing for Australia during the '70s. He has been thinking primarily of the scrutiny of players' lives, but there is also the issue of the way the game itself is heading.

Warne's approach to cricket suggests a player not completely at ease with Buchananite precepts. In *My Autobiography*, he confessed a preference for using 'the old brain' when he played; computers could only be a 'back-up'. He now goes a little further: too much analysis of cricket can be harmful. 'When you come off the field, I think, you have a bit of a chat, think about the things you got right, what you might do differently, then you move on, and you pick it up the next day. The danger is that if there's too much analysis, people get confused, or bored, or switch off.'

His admiration for the encyclopaedic but intuitive Ian Chappell, with whom he is now tight enough to have played a seven-hour game of backgammon in Darwin during the Test against Bangladesh, is unstinting. 'We check up on him,' says Warne. 'We'll look up a game he's talking about and once or twice what he remembers as a 50 turns out to be a 15, but we hardly ever catch him out. I've never known anyone with his memory for games.'

Warne reckons his mindset is similar. 'I'm pretty good. The one-dayers, they get a bit blurred. I've played seven against South Africa in Johannesburg, for instance, and I have a bit of trouble telling them apart. But I do think I read the game well. I understand it. I've enjoyed my opportunities as a leader. I enjoy the role of a senior player and hopefully my experience can make a contribution to the team in the future.' The opportunity to skipper Hampshire, too, was fundamental to his decision to take up the cudgels there again this season.

What about the end? When we digress, as two Melburnians are wont to do, into the lingua franca of Aussie Rules footy, I remind him of one of St Kilda's best games last season, the finale to the career of its indestructible Nathan Burke. The crowd's salute to Burke at the end of the game was definitely one of the more moving tributes to a player I can remember – the St Kilda fan next to me burst into tears, the Richmond fans who'd seen their team utterly thrashed solemnly shook hands with their counterparts, as though at a funeral. Is this what Warne would like? Something simply spontaneous and demotic in front of a home crowd? Or would he prefer a Waugh-like pageant, in which each city has the opportunity to say farewell and vice versa? Excitement about his career's resumption, it turns out, hasn't curtailed consideration of its conclusion. 'What I would like is to finish on my own terms,' Warne says. 'I think I deserve that.' He doesn't believe that his lost year will tempt him to play more cricket than he should. 'There's plenty of it, though, isn't there?' he says. 'Too much, really. But, at the moment, better too much than not enough.'

The Wisden Cricketer, Gideon Haigh (London, March 2004)

THE WORLD OF SHANE WARNE

'When you've got people telling you how good you are and so forth, it's hard not to be distracted by the whole glossy picture, including money, fame and fortune. It is always the ego – you've got to keep feeding the ego, because you are simply so good and you start getting used to the fact ... the tough lessons to learn are sometimes the ones that involve your own limitations, self-discipline and circumspection – the trick of staying within the safety zone.' – NZ legend Stephen Fleming

Stephen Fleming, Balance of Power, Richard Boock (Hodder Moa Beckett Publishers Ltd, Wellington, 2004)

Journey by Sea: The *Ormuz* transporting the 1899 Australians, including first-timer Victor Trumper (left), took five weeks to reach the Home Country.

3

TRAILBLAZERS

'Most of the New South Wales players wore the famous
cabbage-tree hat of the colony, worth five pounds apiece,
and some of them, in their excitement, took off their
shoes, and played with shoeless feet ...'

GUM TREE GREEN AND GOLD

How Australia adopted its cricket colours.

At a meeting of the Australasian Cricket Council at Adelaide on 8
January 1895, a motion by J Portus [NSW] that the colours be olive
green and the Australian coat of arms be worked into the cap and
coat pocket was not seconded. However, a motion by P Sheridan
[NSW] seconded by JW Colton [South Australia] that the selection of
colours for future Australian elevens be decided by a subcommittee
of HH Budd [Victoria], Portus and Mostyn Evans [South Australia]
was carried. Nothing further was recorded in the minutes and so the
decisions or fate of the subcommittee are something of a mystery.

The next 'official' word on colours appears to have been on 29 May
1908, when the Board of Control, meeting in Melbourne, resolved,
on the motion of H Blinman [South Australia], seconded by J Allen
[Queensland], that the Australian colours be '"Gum Tree" Green and
Gold'. The Board's apparent inability to distinguish a eucalypt from
an acacia aside, it should be noted that Leslie Poidevin was the Board's
representative in London from 1907 to 1911. I don't know sufficient
about his movements to be able to say that he was not in Australia at
the time of the 1908 meeting and, of course, one cannot discount the
possibility that he corresponded with Blinman or Allen. However, it
seems likely that the Board reached its decision without his assistance.

If it had been Poidevin's idea it seems to me more likely that the NSW representative would have put [forward] the motion, not a South Australian or a Queenslander.

Story by Martin Sharp (Melbourne, 1988) based on the Australasian Cricket Council minutes, 8 January 1895, and the Board of Control minutes, 29 May 1908, both held by the Australian Cricket Board; extra research by Stephen Gibbs
In Trumper: The Definitive Biography *(Hodder & Stoughton, Sydney, 1985), author Peter Sharpham says that soon after the 1899 touring party arrived in London, 'a green and gold flag fluttering outside the Inns of Court Hotel in High Holborn proclaimed that the Australian cricketers had arrived for the coming summer.'*

WHY AUSTRALIANS ARE BEST

Globetrotting professional player-umpire Jim Phillips on an important difference in Anglo-Australian cricket.

In generalship the Australians are easily first. They play more in unison, they exchange views in the dressing-room and their captain is thereby assisted materially in many of his plans. A varied past experience in cricket in both countries leads me to attribute much of their success to this.

Off the field an Australian captain receives the benefit of the opinions of his comrades as if he were chairman of a board of directors. The average English captain is more of an autocrat. He rarely seeks advice from his men. If a consultation be held, it is invariably confined to the amateurs and the batsmen, not the professionals and the bowlers. I can recall instances when I have been standing umpire, when able and intelligent professional players on an England side have seen the fallacy of some plan of their captain, but nothing has been said by them, no suggestion made to remedy the mistake.

Another mistake is made in England which does not improve cricket as a science – that is, the system of isolating professionals off the field. Surely, if a man is good enough to play on the same side, he is good enough to dress in the same dressing-room. It is there most useful hints and ideas are exchanged when a game is in progress, which cannot be done so well on the field.

Cricket: A Weekly Record of the Game, Jim Phillips (London, 30 November 1899)

EARLY RICHMOND PLAYERS

In the earlier days of cricket in Melbourne, a cricketers' annual was published in most years. A feature was the somewhat pungent and frank comments of leading Richmond players of the day. The reviews cover a 20-year period from 1856.

WP Barter – Medium-pace, round-arm bowler; not much on the wicket. Not difficult to play. Bats at times with great freedom and very dangerous after an over or two. Weak on the leg stump and more afraid of his fingers than a cricketer ought to be. Not brilliant in the field.

J Boak – Fastest bowler in the colony. When on the wicket very dangerous. Cannot moderate his pace without bowling over his shoulder. A good style of batting, but rather weak in defence. Hits well to square leg. Fields and returns well. A very sure catch. An acquisition to any eleven.

JC Brodie – An elegant but effective bat, medium field.

AM Bruce – Excellent fast round-arm bowler. Has contracted the bad habit of over-bowling himself and if hit about had better be taken off at once. An excellent catch and covers a great deal of ground in the field. Has a tremendous reach and can drive and hit well to leg. Defence rather shy, but on the whole an improving bat.

George Cosstick – An awkward-looking bowler. Bowls a very deceptive ball pretty straight, with good pitch, occasionally approaching the throw. A clumsy but rather effective batsman. Medium field. Returns well.

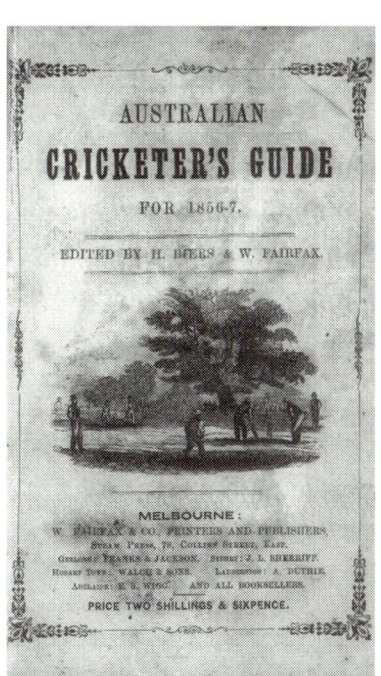

Biers & Fairfax: The first-ever Australian cricket annual, released in September 1857, contained an extensive who's who section on the leading club players of the day.

J Cullen – Stout bat with stubborn defence. Can cut beautifully. Not very energetic in the field but tries hard.

Gideon Elliott – Fastest and straightest bowler in the Australias. Dangerous on lively ground, even to the best bats. Wants headwork in his bowling and is apt to put on unnecessary steam when knocked about or played steadily. Has been underrated as a bat, having as good a style and execution as men ranked above him in that regard. His forte is forward play and Cambridge pokes. He hits 'loose-uns' with great power and freedom. Is not a good field more than five yards away from the wicket. Is again engaged to bowl two days a week for the Melbourne club.

W Elliott – Medium-pace, round-arm bowler, but rather high. No bat and not remarkable in the field. [Although named as Richmond Tradesmen's club, he played for Richmond also.]

RH Fitzgerald – Good bat; fair bowler and field.

J Gillow – Round-arm, moderate-pace bowler. Hangs after the pitch and frequently breaks back. Indifferent field. Wants practice with the bat.

W Hammersley – Medium-pace bowler, straight, but rather low, without 'work'. Has a most peculiar and original way of passing the ball from his left into his right hand when in the act of making the last swing. In batting he has a most brilliant style of driving and cutting, but, in consequence of irregular practice, is more scientific than effective. Appears to have lost, in a measure, the art of hitting. He is one of the few in the colony whose style merits imitation. Capital field in the slips.

HCA Harrison – An improving bat. Fair in the field. The quickest and most elegant runner in the colonies.

John Hodges – Made his debut last season as a bowler (left hand, round-arm) and in several important matches he headed the list of wicket-takers. He is always straight, and has a nasty break-back. He is inclined, however, to pitch the ball a trifle short and thus lets the batsman get a knowledge of his break-back. On several occasions he has proved a useful batsman and has a free and easy style of play. Is not remarkable as a field. [Member of Australia's first Test team in 1876–77.]

Sam Hopkinson – A very steady, painstaking bat. Rather cramped in style and a little shaky about the leg stump. Fields well everywhere and a good thrower. Medium-pace bowler but not particularly straight.

Thomas Huddlestone – A most promising cricketer. Weak in defence and a free, sometimes brilliant hitter. A good field anywhere from the wicket, but rather hasty. Bowls a little.

N Jacomb – Most promising young player, with good defence and nerve.

T Kendall – One of Victoria's best bowlers, who achieved great success last year against the English eleven. Bowls with a nice easy left-hand delivery and, on a wet wicket, is well nigh unplayable; but, at times, his carelessness interferes with his success. Should endeavour to remedy this defect before the bad habit becomes chronic. As a batsman, his determined and resolute hitting against all kinds of bowling has brought him well up in the averages. A good field when he likes to exert himself. [Member of Australia's first Test team in 1876–77.]

John Mace – Has a rather contracted style of play, but very good defence. Weak to the off, but a sure and most powerful leg hitter. Left-hand bowler, low delivery, good pace. Has proved himself most valuable when required in that department. As a wicketkeeper is second only to Marshall. Good in the field and [a] certain catch.

W Manion – A neat left-handed batsman with a nice free style of play.

George Marshall – Captain of Victoria [from 1854 to 1861], and acquitted himself in that difficult post most satisfactorily. As wicketkeeper still unrivalled in the colony. His style of taking the ball, particularly an off one, is neat and good, and has never been equalled here. He fights shy of leg balls, especially on bumpy ground. As batsman his off-hitting [is his] best feature in his play. His defence is rather weak and he dreads a shooter. There is no place in the field where he is not thoroughly at home, although, when not in his own peculiar place, he takes mid-off or long slip. Engaged by Melbourne and is a member of Richmond.

S Morris – Fine, careful batsman, maintains a strong defence; good change bowler; and brilliant field. [A one-Test player with Australia in 1884–85.]

E Mortimer – With practice would make an excellent bowler with very good pace, an admirable pitch and delivery. But hardly straight enough. A good field and promising wicketkeeper. Good steady bat, capital timist. Has the germ of excellence in every department.

GM Nicholls – With practice would make a good batsman. Painstaking and energetic in [the] field.

WH Peryman – Slashing hitter. Excellent point. Can take any place in the field.

James Orr – A most promising player. Bowls round-arm, fair pace and direction. A model in his deportment in the field.

G Smith – An improving cricketer and second only to [Jack] Blackham as a wicketkeeper in Victoria. He did several very smart things last season. A good steady batsman.

JA Smith – A good field out from the wicket. Hits with much power and freedom. A capital field anywhere, very quick and reliable at point. [Played with Richmond Tradesmen also.]

D Sweeney – One of the surest run-getters in the colony with a good but cramped defence. Plays with extreme confidence and great nerve, with a very straight bat. A good wicketkeeper and captain. [Played with Ballaarat also.]

TW Wills – Captain of Victoria [from 1858 to 1876], and, taking him all in all, the best cricketer in Australia. Is a good and deceptive bowler, both fast and medium, round-arm, and slow underhand. Very soon finds out a man's weak points and acts accordingly. Is a beautiful field anywhere, more especially at long slip, and throws unerringly at the top of the wicket. Hits hard and gets runs fast in all sorts of ways. Great at slipping, and has an indescribable but very effective way of getting rid of a ball on the leg stump. Has not an elegant stand at the wicket, nor can his batting be termed graceful. Is liable to be caught at cover point and long off. [Played with a Queensland club also.]

Wilson – A bumping slow round-arm bowler. Pitches the ball short but, getting up considerably, they are difficult to hit away. Is no bat.

Richmond's 100 Years of Cricket: The Story of Richmond Cricket Club 1854–1954,
Percy Taylor (CG Meehan & Co, South Melbourne, 1954)
Team-by-team profiles were a feature of the Victorian cricket annuals from the mid-1850s.

THE FIRST GREAT MATCH, 1856

Politician and cricket tragic Sir David Serjeant, MD opened the batting in Victoria's first intercolonial against New South Wales in 1856.

In the years 1854 to 1857 cricket came boldly to the front and DS Campbell was its great patron. My passport to society, and friendship, was the cricket that I loved. Where now are the boys of that old brigade? Gone, every man jack of them: Bryant, the good sound bowler and steady batsman; Hammersley, of the Cambridge University team and, I think, its Captain, a hard hitter and fair bowler; Marshall, good everywhere, but especially at the wicket, and Wills (the only bowler I ever feared), when in form the hardest hitter (he was, I think, killed by the blacks) ... they're all gone – leaving in one heart, at least, a pleasant memory.

Many a two hours' innings I had on that good Melbourne ground. But I only got in the 50s once. It was in the County of Bourke against the Melbourne Club, in which match, as its highest scorer of 53, I won the prize bat with its silver plate and inscription.

I had persuaded the captain when the match appeared to be lost, to let me try an over with the ball. I was fortunate to secure the wickets of Dr Webster and Captain Hotham and so turned the tide to victory.

There were no long scores – a century in those days I don't remember – the ground was unfavourable. The square might be good, but the ball would not travel in the outer field; one's chance of a 4 was a high drive with all its peril.

In '55 the idea of an intercolonial match, between Victoria and New South Wales, began to be considered. Steam had bridged over the distance and made the voyage between Melbourne and Sydney only four or five days long. At first the idea of playing a match for 500 pounds a side was entertained; but a better sporting spirit won the toss and a home and home match was eventually decided on.

It was on the 27th day of March, 1856, that the intercolonial ball was set a-rolling. Melbourne was excited, and the betting was three to two on the Victorian team. The players had been carefully selected; we had two or three duffers in the lot chosen by social influence, but Mather, Hotham, Philpott and Kingston were sterling 'bats' and Lowe and Elliott were capital bowlers. In the batting nobody came off. The small scores seem marvellous to players of the present day.

Throughout their stay, Victoria held out the hand of welcome, and after a glorious frolic, and with many a hearty cheer, the vanquished bade their visitors farewell.

Scores
Victoria 63 (Mather 16, Kingston 12, Gilbert 4-34, McKone 5-25) and 28 (Philpott 11, McKone 5-11, Murray 3-16) lost to New South Wales 76 (McKone 18, Driver

FIRST·VICTORIAN·ELEVEN.

FIRST INTERCOLONIAL MATCH * PLAYED AT SYDNEY, 1859.
WON BY VICTORIA, BY 2 WICKETS.

By permission of
Messrs Robira & Barbets, Hosie's Café, 307 Bourke St. Melbourne

Immediate Rivals: Victoria narrowly won the first intercolonial against New South Wales in Sydney in 1859.

18, Elliott 7-25, Coulstock 3-30) and 7-16 (Elliott 3-7, Lowe 4-9), in two days, by three wickets.

I record the score – and note with pleasure and with pride, that I played the first over bowled in the first Great Australian Match [involving NSW]. I've always held the opinion that the match was won by the New South Wales underhand bowling, with a moderate break. Most of the New South Wales players wore the famous cabbage-tree hat of the colony, worth five pounds apiece, and some of them, in their excitement, took off their shoes, and played with shoeless feet.

The second innings of the Sydney men was watched with breathless interest. Only once in half a century of cricket have I known its equal in excitement, and that was in the Great Jessop Australian Match when [George] Hirst and [Wilfred] Rhodes, the two last men in, pulled off the English triumph at The Oval [in 1902].

Our Sydney friends required 16 runs to win but Lowe and Elliott bowled so superbly, that seven wickets were taken before the number was secured. This match gave a marvelous stimulus to Australian cricket.

Australia: Its Cricket Bat, Its Kangaroo, Its Farming, Fruit and Flowers, Sir David Serjeant, MD (King & Jarrett, London, 1923)
The very first intercolonial was played five years earlier between Victoria and Tasmania at the Launceston Racecourse.

A NEW CRICKET GROUND FOR MELBOURNE
It was once a south-of-the-Yarra wheatfield ...

The temporary playground at Batman's Hill was found to be in some respects not the best adapted for cricketing and the club selected a more commodious and convenient spot on the south bank of the Yarra, between the river and Emerald Hill. It was a slice of the place that 'Johnny Fawkner' turned into a cultivation paddock in 1835 and grew a crop of wheat there.

Something like the beginning of the Flemington Racecourse, it was 'jumped' by the [Melbourne Cricket] Club, and an unauthorised occupation winked at by the authorities. In 1848, the Superintendent gave a formal permission to use 10 acres of the area as a cricket ground and the cricketers were so elated with their good luck that they proposed to work wonders there in the way of fencing and planting and innumerable other important etceteras. The club happened to be at this time in a condition of comparative prosperity and consequently it effected a good deal of what was so promised. There were 127 members and they went to work with a will. The 10 acres were soon enclosed with a strong four-rail fence, at a cost of 30 pounds, 13 shillings and 4 pence and 1116 yards of the ground turfed for 24 pounds, 13 shillings and 6 pence. September saw them not only out of debt, but when the outstanding subscriptions were got in, they would be 120 pounds in credit. In the beginning of 1849, the Melbourne Club was challenged to play a match against all Van Diemen's Land, but obstacles intervened to prevent its [immediate] acceptance.

The Chronicles of Early Melbourne, 1835 to 1852, Centennial Edition, Vol II, 'Garryowen' (Fergusson & Mitchell, Melbourne, 1888)

Hookesy: One of the great drawcards among the World Series rebels was charismatic South Australian shot-maker David Hookes.

4
TOP GUNS

'Kerry drove at a hundred miles an hour and after he'd gone through a few red lights, I asked him: "Slow down, please, you're frightening the hell out of me!"' – DAVID HOOKES

A LIFE CUT SHORT

David Hookes' tragic death in 2004 outside a South Melbourne hotel prompted a rare outpouring of emotion, including this tribute from his old captain Ian Chappell.

Sometimes the phone would ring at my house and a voice on the other end of the line would say: 'Have you heard so-and-so is not well?' It would be David Hookes telling me about an ex-cricketer's plight because he cared about sportsmen in general and cricketers in particular. Sadly, when the phone woke me at 4.30 am on 19 January, it wasn't 'Hookesy' on the other end but a TV reporter informing me about David's plight.

Hookes loved cricket; he loved playing the game, talking about the game and passing on his knowledge to younger players. It wasn't hard to get into an animated discussion with Hookesy because he had his opinions and he was prepared to voice them. He also thought outside the square when it came to sport. However, he was never a fighter and that is what makes it so hard to cope with the senseless violence that caused his death. Hookes had coped with serious injury on the cricket field, accepted it as part of the game and could even make light of a setback. When an Andy Roberts bouncer broke his jaw in 1977–78 during a World Series Cricket match at the Sydney Showground, he said: 'Sorry, mate' to me as he left the field. As his skipper, I replied: 'You don't have to apologise, Hookesy.'

When it was discovered Hookes had a broken jaw, Kerry Packer didn't wait for the ambulance to arrive. He bundled Hookesy into the back seat of his Jaguar and drove him to hospital. When I visited Hookes the next day, he said: 'I'm okay now.'

'What do you mean now?' I asked. 'Well, the ride to hospital was a nightmare,' he answered. 'Kerry drove at a hundred miles an hour and after he'd gone through a few red lights, I asked him: "Slow down, please, you're frightening the hell out of me!"'

Kerry growled back: 'I'm just taking your mind off the pain of the broken jaw.'

It's not surprising Packer was keen to protect him. Hookes was one of his hottest properties during WSC. He had risen to prominence quickly, in 1975–76 coming into a South Australian side that had finished last the previous two seasons and immediately making important contributions to a team that surprised everyone by winning the Sheffield Shield. He then finished the next season in a blaze of glory by scoring five centuries in six innings.

His run blitz resulted in selection in the Australian side for the 1977 Centenary Test, during which he rose to prominence by belting five successive boundaries off England captain Tony Greig. He grouped blazing cover and square drives with one on-side boundary that took him to a half century and international fame. This was a perfect rejoinder considering that, earlier in the match, the South African–born Greig had moved to silly mid-off while the baby-faced Hookes was batting and asked: 'Have your testicles dropped yet, son?' Hookes, always quick with a retort, responded: 'At least I'm an Australian representing my own country in the Centenary Test.'

The Bulletin with Newsweek, Ian Chappell (Sydney, 3 February 2004)

CAPTAIN NO. 40

*The kid from Sydney's unpretentious working-class west
had inherited the most coveted job in Australian sport.*

On the morning Steve Waugh was named Australia's 40th Test captain, he was in an inner-city Melbourne hotel waiting for the telephone call which would change his life. It was 12 February 1999 and he was watching *Sesame Street,* a breakfast tradition for many parents with littlies.

Just a fortnight earlier, coinciding with his Australian of the Year honor, Mark Taylor had announced his retirement, ending a spectacular 50-match reign in which Australia regained the coveted world Test championship and Taylor guaranteed his enduring popularity by declaring on the same record score as Australia's ultimate sporting icon Don Bradman.

Waugh, then 33, had been Australia's one-day captain for 12 months, his diplomatic and ambassadorial air a comfort to the Australian Cricket Board directors, if not Taylor, who had fought against the role being shared.

Captain No. 40: Sydney's Steve Waugh was selected as captain ahead of his Victorian rival Shane Warne.

The only other genuine contender was spin-star Shane Warne, who had won 10 of his 11 one-day internationals as stand-in for the injured Waugh and at 29 was more than four years his junior. His extroverted ways, however, had not always impressed the conservative elements inherent in the corridors of power at Jolimont.

Waugh may not have been as flamboyant, showy or outwardly dynamic as the colourful Victorian, but his reputation was spotless and qualifications impeccable. In 15 years he had become one of the three top-ranked batsmen in the world. No Australian cricketer, bar The Don, was more respected. And few were more loved.

In 1995, when Australia clinched the world championship at Kingston's Sabina Park, Taylor may have been captain but Waugh was the catalyst, his double-century in the deciding match an extraordinary feat of concentration and focus. Ever since 1991, when he was dropped for the only time in his career, he'd so tightened his game that his Test average had increased from around 30 to in excess of 50. Some may have preferred to watch his artistic brother Mark, but if ever you needed someone to bat for your life, it would always be Steve.

At 8.42 am, Waugh's telephone rang. He'd been overwhelmingly endorsed. A press conference awaited in the Victorian Cricket Association's delegates' room – no room of sufficient size being available at nearby Board headquarters.

Before dressing immaculately in a dark suit, a crisp white shirt, a new floral tie and shiny black shoes, Waugh rang wife Lynnette in

Sydney, his parents and grandparents and Warne, his new deputy. It was a momentous day. The kid from Sydney's unpretentious working-class west had inherited the most coveted job in Australia. It was the extra responsibility and challenge he'd aspired to for years and a title he intended to honour and cherish.

His exhilaration was obvious as he faced a barrage of cameras and microphones. 'I would hope I was picked for the reason I'm the right man for the job – not because I stood in line the longest and had the service,' he said. 'I know I'm ready. My cricket is in good shape. I've done 13 years with the Australian cricket side. It's like when I first was picked for Australia. I was 20 years old, overwhelmed, anxious and a little bit frightened about what was ahead. But this time I'm really excited.'

He spoke with passion about preserving everything good about cricket, playing positively and above all, maintaining Australia's winning streak.

Waugh said Australia had forged a winning formula which required only the most subtle of tweaking. The fundamentals were sound and in Glenn McGrath, Warne and the re-emerging, hungry-to-achieve Jason Gillespie, he had three of the most feared strike bowlers in the world. If anything, with back-up leg spinner Stuart MacGill also making a formidable presence, there was an embarrassment of riches.

'People are going to ask, "Is he as good as Mark Taylor?"' Waugh said, 'but I can only do the job the best that is possible. I don't think I have to change too much. We've had a great five or six years. The team has performed excellently at home and overseas. We're playing aggressive cricket. That's how I always play the game. I play to win. [But] having said that, in Australian cricket we could probably draw a few more games than we've lost over the last couple of years. That is one area I'll be trying to improve – along with chasing [targets] in the second innings.'

Tyros: Steve Waugh with Michael Dimattina during the Australian under-25 tour of Zimbabwe in 1985. *Cricketer*

Under the calm, stable influence of Taylor, Australia had won 52 per cent of its matches and won the world Test championship in the Caribbean in '95. The only other postwar captains with a comparable strike-rate of success were Don Bradman (73 per cent), Lindsay Hassett (58) and Ian Chappell (50).

While he was only nine months younger than the departing captain and had increasingly been hamstrung by leg injuries, he saw no reason why he shouldn't handle both jobs long term. He said age was only a number and the captaincy would increase his appetite for the game. Moreover, he'd served a lengthy year apprenticeship and learned much from his national team predecessors Taylor and Allan Border and at state level, Dirk Wellham, Greg Dyer and particularly Geoff Lawson.

The fanfare upon his appointment was both deferential to Waugh's standing in the world game and to the importance the captaincy is [given] in Australia's sporting psyche. Fans wrote how Waugh's devotion to the baggy green cap and his appreciation of the history of the game were irresistible factors, given the troubled times and allegations against greedy players and captains on the take. From his hometown Sydney, Waugh's father, Rodger, said his son's elevation was five years overdue. Waugh had been Australia's vice-captain since 1996–97 and in all had played 111 Tests.

While Taylor's tactical acumen and ambassadorial flair had been commendable, as a batsman his form over a two-year period since his epic 334 not out in Peshawar had declined markedly. Just weeks after declaring his enthusiasm for one last tilt against old foes Curtly Ambrose and Courtney Walsh, he changed his mind and despite overtures from the Board, declared the Australians would be touring without him. He wanted to go out on top and never again have his place in the team questioned. It was time Australian cricket had a new face.

Test captains and their batting averages [updated to 2010]

Player	Average as non-captain	Average as captain	Captaincy span	Matches as captain
Don Bradman	98	101	1936–48	24
Allan Border	50	50	1984–93	93
Ian Chappell	37	50	1970–75	30
Greg Chappell	51	55	1975–82	48
Lindsay Hassett	45	47	1949–53	24

Bill Lawry	47	46	1967–71	26
Ricky Ponting	55	54	1995–2010	69*
Bob Simpson	33	54	1963–78	39
Mark Taylor	46	39	1994–99	50
Steve Waugh	50	52	1999–2004	57

* To start of winter series v Pakistan, 2010

The Waugh Zone, Ken Piesse (The Book Company Publishing, Sydney, 2003)

PRIDE OF WOLLONGONG

So skilled was Brian Taber with his glovework that
he was often asked if he also played the piano.

You don't have to have a sense of humour as a wicketkeeper, but it helps. Barry Jarman came in one evening during the third Test against the West Indies at the Sydney Cricket Ground, remarking that he had a sore back – 'where 28,000 people have been jumping on it'. That was not Barry Jarman's last rest, but it was the crack of thunder before the deluge. The Australian selectors considered the popular South Australian was entitled to bow out in honourable circumstances and chose him in the fourth Test side for a farewell performance before his own Adelaide people.

The selectors were criticised for that action, for Jarman had kept badly at the SCG, but it was a decision as judicious as it was diplomatic.

Had Brian Taber been appointed Jarman's successor for the fourth Test, it would have meant the delegation of a relatively inexperienced wicketkeeper to a position in a match where there was a danger of crowd hostility towards him in his first Test in Australia, a form of retaliation for the criticism Jarman received in Sydney.

Barry Jarman, now 33, did the job proficiently in Adelaide, though not a catching or stumping offered itself to him throughout the Test.

Tabbsy: Brian Taber, Australia's wicketkeeper in 1972.

The drums had almost stopped beating for Taber by the night of 3 February, the evening of the fifth Test team selection. The feeling was that Jarman would retain his position for the last Test.

But Sir Donald Bradman and Messrs Jack Ryder and Neil Harvey had not forgotten Sydney and the third Test and the abuse the Hill had lavished on Jarman for his errors, and Hedley Brian Taber, 28, at last gained the recognition he had deserved since the third Test at Edgbaston against England in July of last year.

Taber the sportsman is very much like Taber the man: neat and unobtrusive. There is no brashness about him. He is of gentle nature but of firm character, a fact recognised by the New South Wales selectors in their choice of him as state captain before Doug Walters and later by the Australian Board in his surprise promotion as third tour selector for Ceylon, India and South Africa with Bill Lawry and Ian Chappell ... already his dignity and inspiration as NSW captain have made their mark.

Taber is a splendid all-round sportsman. He was a first-division soccer forward as a teenager and he plays 'A'-grade pennant squash with Gordon Rugby Club in the winter. He became Gordon Cricket Club's first-grade wicketkeeper at the age of 16.

But from an early age he sensed his sporting life lay in his own hands. Frequently he's asked: 'Do you play the piano?'

His palms are not exceptionally large, but his fingers are extremely long and well made. There are no scars, no calluses, no visible breaks, a tribute to his ability to position himself to take the ball cleanly, to make light of hard work. As a craftsman, his hands are line references.

When the Indian cricket team was in Australia last summer [1967–68] it was at a disadvantage because it was not accustomed to fast bowling. Graham McKenzie and 'Big Shine' Dave Renneberg had the Indians reaching for adrenalin.

To counteract 'the demons' in the pitch, the Indian batsmen eventually resorted to having their bowlers stand two-thirds of a pitch away and throw the ball at practice. As a schoolboy, Taber adopted the same habit to develop his wicketkeeping.

He was the son of a schoolteacher and the family lived at Fern Hill, three miles from Wollongong. Beside the house was a vacant block of land, flat and tempting to two brothers as devoted to their sport as Brian and Ross, now 31. They managed to procure a spare concrete roller from nearby tennis courts and after clearing and cutting a strip began preparing their own practice wicket. 'We used to get clippings from the bowling green around the corner and roll them into the pitch. When the clippings were wet we got practice for wet wickets. When they dried out, the wicket would roll out into a good track,' Taber recalls. 'We used to cut the grass very close, enough for two wickets, then we'd damp it and roll it. The soil was very like Bulli soil, good dark soil, and it would roll out into a fine strip. That [heavy] roller ... I'll never forget the bloody thing. We would get up and be practising by 6 am and again after school. Quite a few of the first-graders used to come out with us. We also put wire-netting around the wickets. Ross would stand halfway and hurl the ball into the deck for me. That was where I practiced my footwork.'

He began wicketkeeping early in high school. So rapid was his progress that he was chosen for trials in Sydney and won selection in the under-14 state team. Taber would play in the under-16 competition in the morning and then turn out again in the afternoon for the Balgownie first-grade team in the Illawarra District competition.

The Sydney club Gordon made periodic visits south to play Woonona. Young Taber was invited to appear for Woonona, impressed, and the following season, upon the retirement of Bill Englefield, he was asked to attend Gordon's trials. Taber was 16. He was chosen in first grade and has never appeared in a lower grade since. 'Some things come automatically. I always enjoyed it. That's half the battle,' Taber says. 'It's a thankless job at times. You have to concentrate to take every ball. Toward the end of the day you sometimes begin to doze off, to lose concentration. When you're younger, it's harder to concentrate. I attempt to relax between overs and between balls. As soon as the bowler begins coming in, then you prepare yourself. It's a job you have to take up early in life. I adopted a stance early in my career, when I was a schoolboy. I have the same stance now. Footwork and glovework are the essential things, then practice, practice and match play. I used to do a lot of skipping. If your footwork's good, you can get behind the ball and take it easily without any dives.'

For almost a decade his Gordon club captain was that splendid state opening batsman Sid Carroll, now a state selector. Carroll's experience was invaluable to the young wicketkeeper.

Upon the retirement of Doug Ford in 1964, Taber became the state wicketkeeper and within two seasons he was in the Australian team, bound for South Africa.

Australian Cricket, 'Redcap' (Sydney, March 1969)

Phil 'Redcap' Wilkins is one of Australian cricket's most distinguished cricket writers. Taber was to take 56 catches and make four stumpings in his 16-Test career. Twenty of his dismissals came in the 1966–67 South African summer.

ONE OF A KIND
Les Favell had a memory like an elephant, especially
when it came to the bowlers he opposed ...

'When we toured New Zealand in 1957,' Les Favell's long-time South Australian and Australian teammate Barry Jarman said, 'Les was clean bowled first ball [of the tour] by a big, blond fast bowler named [Tony] MacGibbon.

'We'd all forgotten it six years later when the Kiwis passed through Adelaide after a tour of South Africa and had a game against us.

'This bloke MacGibbon opened the bowling and the first ball was about six inches short of a length. Les swung it straight out of the ground where the Victor Richardson Gates are now.

'Then he walked halfway up the pitch and said to the bowler: "Now we're even."'

Les Favell, Alan Shiell (The Les Favell Foundation, Adelaide, 1987)

DEPTHS OF DESPAIR
Neil Hawke's battle to live was front-page news,
all around Australia in the early 1980s.

On Saturday, 6 July 1980, as Beverley and I were preparing for a race meeting, I was suddenly struck with some severe stomach pains. They persisted and were not unlike the pains I had felt with a bowel blockage some five years earlier. Then, I'd also been drinking and eating peanuts the previous night. We cancelled our racing and Beverley called a doctor, who was of little help. Later she took me to see her own doctor who told us to go to the nearby Modbury Hospital if things were no better next morning. We spent a very unsettled night and after attempting an agonising walk at first light, Beverley drove me to the hospital where I was admitted.

Later that day, while resting in bed, I was pleasantly surprised to

Courageous: Neil Hawke endured crisis after crisis.

see Dr Donald Beard enter the ward. Don had been an opening bowler with Sturt when I first played district cricket and is today a very highly regarded surgeon. He was equally surprised to see me and when I described my symptoms he asked me whether I would like him to look after me. I naturally jumped at the opportunity and he decided to wait 24 hours to see whether the blockage would right itself naturally before undertaking surgery.

It did not and with Beverley signing the necessary consent form as next-of-kin, I approached surgery confident in the knowledge that I would soon have relief from the intense pain.

What transpired thereafter now seems like a never-ending nightmare. Back in the ward, things did not go very well. My temperature soared, I was sweating profusely and my blood pressure fell steadily. Beverley arrived at visiting time and could see straight away that I was very ill.

Dr Beard said things were seriously wrong and made plans to have me transferred immediately to the intensive care unit at the Royal Adelaide Hospital, where I was assured of the best possible treatment. He had spoken to Mr Bob Britten-Jones and he was standing by to operate, if necessary.

Beverley was not allowed to accompany me in the ambulance and we found out later that I was not expected to survive the trip through the dense late-afternoon traffic. She followed in her own car and arrived in time to sign a consent form for an operation.

I was introduced to Lindsay Worthley and Dave McCleave, two doctors I was to see a great deal of in the painful months ahead. Calmly Dr Worthley explained that they worked as a team and would do everything they could to help me. I felt terrible, without realising how close to death I was. Somehow this man Worthley exuded confidence and I was quite calm and relaxed when the anaesthetic mercifully took over and put me to sleep.

For the next three months I had very few lucid moments as one crisis followed another. Hallucinations and nightmares clouded my subconscious and only two faces left an impression on my tortured mind. They were Beverley's and Dr Worthley's, affectionately known throughout the medical world as 'Tub', the name coming from some extra poundage he carried as a boy.

I was unaware of what was happening to me, but Beverley saw everything and when the full extent of the happenings was revealed to me, my admiration for her increased ten-fold. Prior to this, the sight of blood was abhorrent to her but now she was hardened to the distressing sight of my abdomen completely open, exposing intestines and other organs. This whole area has subsequently been covered on two occasions by split-skin grafts which greatly improve the appearance! In brief, I had been stricken with septicaemia, gangrene, [and] liver and kidney failure, leading to the removal of a great deal of bowel and leaving me with massive bleeding attacks and blood infections. My heart needed reactivating 12 times and on another occasion I was transfused with 60 litres of blood in one day following a massive bleeding attack. Not for the first time Beverley was sent home by the doctors to await confirmation that my time had come. An *Advertiser* journalist was requested to ring hourly to await the news that would see my obituary published that same day. A large abscess developed on my lower back, and the rest became badly ulcerated. In addition, I required a tracheotomy into my windpipe, which meant I could not speak; nor could I write, as my hands were not strong enough to hold a pen. Beverley, in her usual capable fashion, used a scrabble set and pasted the letters on cardboard. In a crude fashion I could communicate by pointing at letters to make up words, but it was exhausting to try and hold the cardboard and direct shaking fingers at the required letters. I would try and make the sentences as brief as possible, without losing meaning, but this often backfired with new nurses and I was forced to try again, much to my obvious annoyance. My nerves were always on a knife-edge.

Agonising days turned into weeks and then the months started to drag by. Little by little, procedures were undertaken. A small piece of skin taken from my leg 'took' on my exposed stomach, a complete skin-graft was made and, in time, this successfully covered the exposed area.

Eventually I was taken off the respirator and allowed to breathe under my own steam. My voice was given back to me, but I soon showed that I couldn't stand the load and I was returned to the respirator and the silence again.

It was heartbreaking. One step forward and then two backwards.

Many times I wanted to give up the struggle. The pain was endless and because of liver failure they could offer me few pain-killers. I coughed incessantly and required constant suction which left me feeling completely exhausted. Each time I plunged to new depths of despair, Beverley or Tub would pull me out of it and give me the encouragement to keep on fighting. Letters, cards and telegrams arrived daily. The room was covered with cards, hiding the curtains and giving the room a blaze of colour. Beverley would read the mail to me each day and I derived pleasure and hope from the messages of goodwill which came from around the world.

Occasionally, I felt well enough to receive visitors and from their expressions I could tell they were shocked at my condition. Alan Shiell, a former South Australian teammate who once took 202 off an MCC attack, was in tears as he left the room and next day, in his capacity as chief sporting reporter, he wrote a very moving story in the *News*.

I had visits from Barry Jarman, Sir Garfield Sobers, Ian Chappell, Bobby Simpson, Alan McGilvray, Phil Ridings [chairman of the Australian Cricket Board] and Les Favell, my old skipper. We covered a lot of old ground and I always felt better for their company.

Bowled Over, Neil Hawke (Rigby, Adelaide, 1982)
Treating every day as a bonus, Hawke, an ever-so-amiable companion and mate, was to live another 20 years. He died on Christmas Day, 2000, aged 61.

'YOU BASTARD! WAIT 'TIL I GET HOLD OF YOU MILLER!'
Keith Miller was a larrikin hero for tens of thousands,
with mates and contacts on every social stratum.

It was eight o'clock in the morning and Keith Miller stood fortifying himself in the Boulevard Hotel's Hans Heysen reception room with a crystal goblet of champagne, immaculate in his blue AWS Huntington suit and Gloweave Great Shape, his grey-black hair slicked back, his countenance slightly crumpled in the chandeliered first light of day. The gentlemen of the night, representatives of newspaper and radio, were assembled, gorging themselves as wolves on a fallen hind on the grapefruit and pawpaw, the croissants and strawberry pancakes, washed down with wine and black coffee. Overseer for the morning, Harry Beitzel, public relations spokesman for the Australian Soccer Pools, up in the land of the living again after a merciful escape from Melbourne, was painfully hatching an ulcer.

The pools are having a battle down in Melbourne and just when he was to rock Sydney with the most important announcement, with Mr Trevor Thatcher, joint managing director of Vernon's, out from England for a few weeks to run a fatherly eye over the firm's new baby, standing inoffensively at his elbow, there was not a solitary television cameraman in sight, not so much as an entangling lead from a blinding arc light upon which to stumble.

The winner of the prize of $424,338.90 was present, dressed for the occasion in beard and Amcos and glazed eyes, Cabramatta plumber Don Rodley with his wife Christine and 20-month-old son and heir to the fortune, Simon, getting in the mood of things by pouring milk down his chin from a champagne glass and jabbing a finger at the glace cherry on his mother's grapefruit.

The situation was critical. It was an occasion for panic buttons, string-pulling of the most influential order, ringing Hot Line or anything else of an attention-winning nature. Miller was the man for the occasion, the man of the hour. Or, as it eventuated, the man of the half-hour.

He knocked back his champagne and orange juice at a gulp and disappeared, heading for the nearest phone. By 8.30, all four Sydney television stations were represented in the room, interviewers, cameramen, technicians, lights, the lot, to preserve for posterity Don Rodley's moment of massive wealth, the joy, the bliss of discovery that he had won, not $13,000, as he first believed, not $135,000, as he was first informed, but a mere four hundred grand, plus, plus. 'Christ knows how Miller did it. He must have had a few big nobs over a barrel about a bird or something to get those television blokes here so quickly,' one pools man muttered in awe.

Harry Beitzel had a mild attack of hysteria as the television men, a hairy lot with seashell necklaces and bangles, munched the toast and kept Don Rodley waiting half an hour while they breakfasted, but eventually he simmered down to have his bowl of muesli and listen again to the absorbing Rodley biography.

'Well ... Don ... what's it feel like to be a millionaire? Well, half a millionaire?'

'It'll come in very handy. We've been pretty lucky. Retirement? I'd like to, but I might get tired. I put in four entries. Now I wish I hadn't wasted the extra $1.50! I follow Newtown Rugby League team but I thought the pools a good risk. I've been trying to start my own plumbing business, doing odd jobs. I might buy a truck and a few tools. We might take a trip to Switzerland. I had one big win in a daily double a few years ago. I won $25. It's too big to comprehend.'

The pulsating stuff kept coming. Mrs Rodley provided the best line of the morning when a television man reassured her that he would not bite young Simon because he was moving during one of the clips and she responded: 'I'm not worried about *you* biting him. It's just that *he* might bite you.'

Keith Miller prudently retired to the champagne table. It was all too overwhelming. Applying the heaviest corn, Keith Miller is just about the biggest rock that could have dropped in this pool. He revels in being among people, with them, experiencing their jubilation, watching their reactions, the emotion of it all. As a figurehead the organisation could not have a more conspicuous prominence. Fortunately, he knows the blessing of moderation, the moment when to attack and when to rest on his laurels.

He is heaven-sent for the English-based company seeking to establish itself on foreign soil. It means travel to and from Melbourne and Sydney, both stamping grounds during his illustrious sporting career, and, though he will be a grandfather of some 56 summers at the end of this November – 'a grandfather! Oh, easy! Off the back foooot!' – he remains one of Australia's most acceptable, most recognisable sporting heroes, as instantly, overwhelmingly a figure of respect and a man to bring genuine delight to any company to be found anywhere.

This was the first winter Keith has spent in Australia in 20 years and certainly it was most opportune. He was having his hair trimmed at Newport when his barber, John Kape, handed him a newspaper.

Staring from one of the pages was Harry Beitzel, beaming toothily at the expectation of coming to Sydney for a change. Miller knew Beitzel well. He had assisted him with names and numbers for publicity purposes when Harry took the Australian Rules team, the Galahs, to the British Isles in the late '60s.

One phone call and the old cronies met, at West Ryde where a training program for pools agents was being held. The New South Wales marketing manager for the pools heard his name, asked who, and Keith had the job that very afternoon. 'I'm the link man between the pools and the press,' said Keith. 'Instead of sending out reams and reams of publicity handouts each day for editors to say "f**k it, f**k it, f**k it!" and put them on their spikes, I provide the personal touch and go and see them myself.'

The evidence that his methods were successful was there for all to see with the multitude he assembled for the Don Rodley conference and the headlines he obtained in the face of the Canberra ballot in the afternoon newspapers the same day.

The Rodleys left the Hans Heysen room, having been given a $500 cheque in advance to tide them over the fortnight before all complications were overcome and they received their tax-free bonanza.

Miller and Beitzel shanghaied a taxi and set off for Channel Seven at Epping to spread the gospel on television. Miller was a hapless victim. There is no escape from a relentless pressman on a 15-mile car ride. I threw the questions thick and fast.

'[Dennis] Lillee and [Jeff] Thomson? They are as good a pair of fast bowlers as I've seen,' said Keith, 'as good as [Ray] Lindwall and Miller, [Wes] Hall and [Charlie] Griffith, any of my experience. Not of all time, but of my experience, the bowlers I've seen,' he said, immediately enveloping himself in the cricket talk. 'I rate Lillee with any of the great bowlers, one of the real tops. He's getting the Lindwall knowledge now in his bowling. He's the only bowler to come to me and say: "Nugget, what do you think?" And for sheer speed, Thomson is the equal of Frank Tyson and Wes Hall, the fastest bowlers I've seen. And for one year, the forgotten man of Australian cricket, Gordon Rorke. He was tremendously fast. The New South Wales selectors once asked me to help Gordon. He'd been spraying the ball all over the place. I went up to Rawson Oval where he practised and saw him bowl three balls and walked away. I told him I couldn't help him. If I'd started meddling with his style, I might have made him accurate but I'd have ruined his speed. I told him to continue the way he was because he had that rare quality of genuine, great pace.

'This is a really great Australian I attack that we have at the moment, Lillee and Thomson backed up by [Max] Walker and [Gary] Gilmour. Gilmour has to improve. He has great natural talent, as Alan Davidson had during his career. When "Davo" became the spearhead of the Australian attack, look how he matured. What a magnificent bowler he became.

'Nobody likes fast bowling. Nobody likes being hurt. Some batsmen play it better than others, but nobody likes it. Lindwall was in a class of his own because he had nous. He was always thinking, not just bowling for the sake of bowling. Tom Graveney was batting at Lord's in a Test against us and batting bloody well. He was not out at stumps and the next day, Ray said: "Let's limber up quickly. Get into him flat out straight away. He looks a bit sluggish when he starts batting."'

Lindwall and Miller jogged about and did stretching exercises and were raring to go when play resumed. Lindwall yorked Graveney in his first over.

'This is where he shone out above other bowlers,' Miller said. 'He was a student of the game. He thought about his cricket so well. And he could always bowl the ball where he wanted. We were the bulldozers of the Australian team, from 1946 until 1956 when I retired. The first time I saw Ray, he was as yellow as your shirt. Straight after the war, we had a game between the Australian Services and New South Wales. Ray had been up in the Islands and had been taking Atebrin tablets for malaria. He had a hell of a lovely style, even then. He was a slim, lean fellow with a good pair of shoulders, a real athlete. You could see the kid was going to be good. People think of Ray as being a short fellow, but his shoulders made him deceptive in height. He was only an inch or so below six feet. Billy Brown took a side to New Zealand in 1946 and Ray and I were in that team. That was the start of our partnership.'

It was quite a side Brown took to New Zealand on the five-game tour – men like Bill O'Reilly, Lindsay Hassett, Colin McCool, Ken Meuleman, Sid Barnes, Ernie Toshack, Ian Johnson, Don Tallon and Bruce Dooland.

Lindwall and Miller were to become firm friends on that tour. On subsequent tours they were roommates and today they are still as close as in their playing days. Ray is a staunch Catholic, Miller more of a Callithumpian. Each Sunday on tour, Keith would hear Ray

Across the Tasman: The 1945–46 Australians in New Zealand. Back row, left to right: W Watts (scorer), Don Tallon, Keith Miller, Bill O'Reilly (vice-captain), Ernie Toshack, Bruce Dooland, Ron Hamence, EC 'Snowy' Yeomans (manager). Front: Ian Johnson, Colin McCool, Lindsay Hassett, Bill Brown (captain), Sid Barnes, Ken Meuleman, Ray Lindwall.

rummaging about for change to put in the collection plate before going to church and he'd give Ray coins and tell him to say a few Hail Marys for him, too! Each night they'd empty their pockets and toss their change in a heap on a dressing table and Ray would put it in the plate. To this day, they carry out the little ritual. 'Ray was one of the most placid guys I ever met, a gent of gents. I can't remember him blowing his top too often,' said Miller. 'He had a lovely smile and an easy personality. Everything he did seemed effortless. He could hit the ball 10 miles. It was strange but nothing worried him when he was bowling. Yet before he was to go out to bat, he'd be very nervous. His gloves would be trembling.'

Lindwall invariably had the choice of ends and took the downwind duties. Miller bowled into the wind but did not mind the spadework. He found that the extra effort required compelled him to concentrate on swinging the ball and caused him to experiment. With his speed reduced by the wind, he had to master the inswinger and it proved profitable.

Their first Test was in 1946 against Wally Hammond's England side in Brisbane. It was an ill-fated match for Lindwall. Contracting chickenpox, he bowled only 12 overs in the game. In the second innings, Miller took the new ball with Toshack. Don Bradman won the toss, hit 187 and felt obliged, during one of the intervals, to give Toshack a few instructions on how to bowl on a rain-damaged wicket. Miller took seven for 60 in the first innings and Toshack learned so quickly from Bradman that he captured six for 82 in the second to finish with nine for the match. Bill Edrich made 16 runs in the first innings, defying Australia on the most spiteful wicket Miller experienced during his career for just under two hours in a remarkably brave innings. 'Edrich won the DFC [Distinguished Flying Cross] during the war and I felt awful because he was just standing there being hit by the ball. You'd bowl a yorker and it would hit the batsman on the nose. He was a tough little bugger,' Miller said. 'I started to ease up on him. He was black and blue. But the skipper [Don Bradman] came up and said: "Nugget, bowl faster."' Miller eventually had Edrich caught by [Col] McCool, one of his nine wickets for the match. Also in his first Ashes Test, Miller had an innings of 79 before he was trapped leg before wicket by the fast leg-breaker Doug Wright.

During the war, Miller had had three years with the Royal Air Force, flying Mosquitoes from the Norfolk base at Great Massingham, where, coincidentally, Edrich was based. The Mosquito was an extremely versatile plane with two Merlin engines and a plywood fuselage. It was used to bomb Berlin, as well as for photographic reconnaissance purposes and as a day intruder. On one occasion, Miller's Mosquito returned from a raid with only one engine working. He was obliged to crash-land at 180 miles per hour. He crawled out alive but with a back injury which troubled him during his cricket career and which still sticks a sharp knife in him.

Telling Pace: Bill Edrich loses his middle stump to Ray Lindwall during the 1948 tour. Lindwall amassed 27 wickets in five Tests to spearhead Australia's 4–0 victory.

Lindwall ribs him about how he was in the Islands and in New Guinea driving back the Japanese – 'along the Coca-Cola Trail', according to Ernie Toshack, a branch of the Kokoda Trail – while Miller was flying about 'having a ball' in England and beyond! It seems that the natives were referred to by the Australians collectively as 'Jackson'. Lindwall brought it back and applied the sobriquet to Miller. They greet each other still with: 'Hey, Jackson man!' It served to conceal identities on tour, protecting each from the somewhat overwhelming attentions of well-meaning admirers. To be explicit, the nickname kept the 'thumpers' at bay.

Great buddies they may have been, but when they were on opposing sides, their friendship was surpassed only by their rivalry. The two were playing in a Sydney club match on one occasion – St George v Manly – and at lunch they ambled off down to the local boozer. Over a few beers, they made a quiet truce that when each came out to bat, no bumpers would be delivered. Miller bounced back onto Manly Oval and within one or two overs, old pal Lindy came out to bat. He was, of course, no slouch with the bat, having made two Test centuries and 1500 runs in Test cricket.

Miller greeted him with a friendly full-toss and winked down the wicket. Lindy grinned and settled down for a hearty innings. The next ball almost took old mate Lindwall's head off! As the bouncer burned into the wicketkeeper's gloves, Lindwall howled down at Miller: 'You bastard! Wait 'til I get hold of you Miller. I'll skin ya alive!' Friendship never stood in the way of winning a cricket match, especially with a few beers under a man's belt. The flame inevitably burned brighter in those days for the two champions but it almost seems sacrilegious to let drop to Miller's adoring public that the devil-may-care soul of yesteryear was recently at the Hobart-Wrest Point hotel and after a glimpse of the roulette tables, he turned his back on the gamblers and walked out the door. 'After 40 years of being an ardent punter, I have become quickly intelligent. You can't beat them,' he said grinning. Ah ... but the fond memories of the attempts.

Cricketer, Phil Wilkins (Melbourne, November 1975)

CRICKET'S CHARISMATIC CAVALIER

In the mid-'50s Keith Miller was cricket's charismatic cavalier,
a hero for tens of thousands of boys ... and girls ... and
his life story subject to syndication across the globe.

When I was a little shaver learning to play cricket against a lamppost in Melbourne, I never dreamed that one day the game would lead me

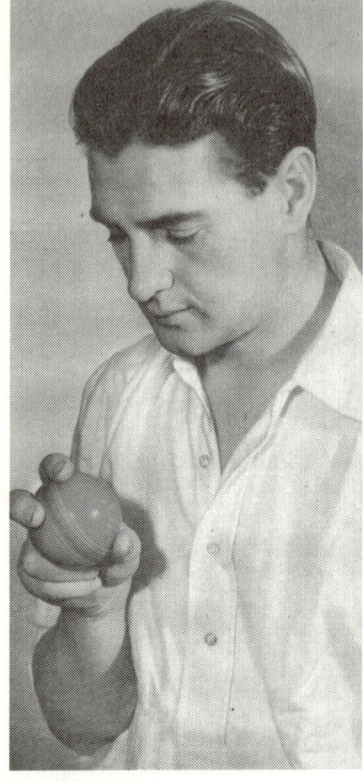

Matinee Idol: Keith Miller was every boy's hero in the '50s. The girls loved him too.

to an informal talk with the Queen at Balmoral Castle. Yet there came a day in 1948 when, with the rest of Don Bradman's first postwar team to tour England, I experienced one of the great thrills of my life – an informal visit to Balmoral. And it was really informal, delightfully so. I remember that Bradman got his knuckles rapped in some quarters because, during one stage of the visit, he had his hands in his pockets. This was rather hard on Bradman, for the Royal family did everything to put us at our ease.

I had a long conversation with the Queen (then Princess Elizabeth) and I remember we discussed the family's beautiful Corgi dogs. I asked her if she had any favourites. She indicated one of the dogs and said: 'That one, I think ... but he's a bit of a devil. The other day I had a piece of cake in my hand and I wanted to do something or other. I put down the cake on the edge of the table and as soon as my back was turned he jumped up and pinched it.'

The Queen was so unaffected that it seemed quite natural for her to use the expression 'pinched it', although I must confess it took me by surprise.

While we were having a look around Balmoral, I spotted a radiogram with a pile of records beside it. I thought immediately of Bach, Beethoven and Mozart. But the record on top of the pile was a modern hit-tune.

In 1953, when the Australians played Middlesex at Lord's, the Queen and the Duke of Edinburgh came to meet the touring party and I happened to be batting. It passed through my mind that I ought to try to enliven their visit. Jack Young [slow] was bowling to me so I jumped out to hit him and 'clocked' him into the Nursery for 6 – just for the Queen's benefit!

We also visited Windsor Castle. Lord Gowrie, Keeper of the Keys and former Governor-General of Australia, showed us around. Lord Tedder, that great airman, was there in mufti, and at afternoon tea he lived up to his reputation for being a bit of a wag. With a full tea-tray in his hand, he came up to me, who had been only a wartime pilot, and said: 'Excuse me, sir; your tea, sir.' The twinkle in his eye gave me the courage to act on impulse. 'Thank you, boy,' I said. And as he turned to leave me, I added, 'Here you are, lad' and handed him a penny. Lord Tedder said: 'Thank yoouuu very much, sir,' and tipped his cap.

But I hadn't always been treated so 'deferentially' by the brass hats. When I was stationed in Gloucestershire during the war, the CO [commanding officer] was a prize 'so-and-so'. He liked neither Australians nor NCOs [non-commissioned officers], and most of the Australians, including myself, were sergeants. Around midnight one night, I was walking along a blacked-out country lane on my way to fly on a mission, busy with my thoughts. A car pulled up beside me and I thought it was someone wanting to be directed. It was the CO. He looked me up and down as if I were something he'd uncovered by turning over a rock in damp soil, and said, 'Miller, you have not got your cap on.'

It was midnight, a deserted lane, a mission on my plate ... I always vowed that if I ever met him after the war, I'd kick his teeth in. Then one day after the war when Keith Miller the cricketer was perhaps better known than had been Sgt Miller, pilot, I was at a pretty swell do, all dressed up to the nines, and afterwards I went for my car. I looked at the attendant. He looked at me ... I need hardly write the next sentence – you are sure to be ahead of me. Yes, it was my old CO! It was the moment I'd have relished years before. Yet I found myself taking him off and buying him a drink. Just as well, I suppose, to let bygones be bygones ...

Cricket ... it has been my life. And once it saved my life. That was in the war. I was almost 20 when the war started. I had my air-crew training in the States. And it was there I met a girl, a secretary, who was later to be my wife. Our training over, I sailed from New York in the *Queen Elizabeth* – playing crown and anchor in the huge school all the way across. One weekend, while stationed at Bournemouth, I was invited to play for the Australian Air Force at Dulwich College. On Sunday night when I got back to camp, I found half a dozen of my friends had been killed in a hit-and-run raid. They were in the bar at lunchtime and it took a direct hit. If I had not been playing cricket, I would have been with them ...

Flying, horse racing, betting – all these have played a big part in the life of Keith Miller, cricketer and I shall have more to say about them.

The Keith Miller Story (Part 1), syndicated in the Adelaide *News* (and elsewhere), Keith Miller (August 1956)

A GOOD SPORT

Few were as noted for their sporting prowess as Ray Lindwall.

This state has had few better all-round athletes than Ray Lindwall, St George full-back and one of the club's hopes for the Tests. Cricket and football come alike to Lindwall who has been running up centuries in football points since his early school days. As Australia's best fast bowler and a member of the team that toured New Zealand recently, Lindwall seems assured of cricket selection against England next summer.

Choices: Ray Lindwall specialised in cricket despite his love of rugby league football.

Absence in the Dominion [however] has jeopardised Lindwall's football prospects for the early matches against England but he will have his chance later in the season. Last Saturday at Hurstville Oval, he played only his second game of the season yet he was in touch almost from the start, despite receiving two injuries.

Apart from being a safe and enterprising full-back, Lindwall is a goal kicker with more than average ability. He ran up 250 points in the 1939 season at Marist Brothers High School, Darlinghurst. Twice that season he kicked 12 goals in a match and in one game he also scored four tries, a total of 36 points.

In 1938, and again a year later, he

received the blazer donated by the NSW Rugby League for the best back in the Catholic Colleges competition.

He played five-eighth then and was coached by Bill Kelly and Jack Redman. In each season he played at school he topped the century, and scored a total of 150 points in 1938.

While still at school that year Ray turned out for St George thirds. His elder brother, Jack, was playing first grade then. Now the brothers play together in St George firsts. Because he was only a lightweight, Ray played full-back with St George then and made such a success of the job that he stayed there.

In 1942, he was the regular first-grade full-back for St George and ran up a total of 186 points for the season – 90 goals and two tries. That included 143 in grade games and the remainder in the Sydney v Country and Cup tie fixtures.

Now 24, Ray Lindwall has built up to 12 stone during his army service and is much more solid than a few years ago. He has the necessary confidence to be a success in big football and his St George clubmates are hoping that this modest player receives an opportunity. Some of the credit must go to his brother Jack. Jack has proved a very handy footballer to the St George club and his clever running has made many tries possible.

The Rugby League News, writer unknown (Sydney, 1 June 1946)
Lindwall specialised in cricket after the 1946 Grand Final in which St George lost 13–12 to Balmain.

BRAVE TO THE VERY END
The story of Bill Newton, the only cricketer awarded the Victoria Cross.

World War II and all its atrocities saw hundreds of young men lose their lives in the service of King and Country. St Kilda Cricket Club was particularly affected with the deaths of Ross Gregory, Stuart King, Teddy Buckland and Victoria Cross–recipient William Ellis 'Bill' Newton.

A first XI player at St Kilda for just eight games in 1939–40, before his enlistment in the RAAF [Royal Australian Air Force] and involvement in the defence of Australia in the south-west Pacific, Newton was the youngest son of a Bourke Street dentist. Newton attended the St Kilda Park Central School and later Melbourne Grammar where in his final year he was central in the school's title-winning season with 37 wickets.

Dark-haired, handsome and outgoing, he was also a prominent footballer with Old Melburnians, being Victoria's vice-captain in the Australian amateur football carnival in Tasmania. At 188 cm (6 ft 2 in) and 89 kg (14 stone) he was an ideal build for a ruckman.

He was also considered such a 'natural' as a fast bowler that he was invited alongside other elite teenagers, including Elsternwick's Keith Miller, to play with the Colts, his dismissal of the iconic Bill Ponsford for four a highlight of his maiden season in 1937–38 in which he claimed 22 wickets at 22.13.

At 19, he represented a Victorian second XI against New South Wales at the MCG in January 1939. He opened the bowling ahead of Testman-to-be Fred Freer and took one for 29 and two for 74, his wickets including Ron Saggers and a 16-year-old Arthur Morris, two of Don Bradman's Invincibles.

For the Colts, he showed improvement, too, taking 29 wickets at 22.72 before joining St Kilda for what proved to be his one-and-only summer in 1939–40.

Teammate Roy Kline said Newton was the fastest bowler at St Kilda, quicker than Tom Leather, but short of the hustling pace of South Melbourne's intimidating expressman Laurie Nash.

With Australia joining the war from September 1939, Newton and dozens of others from the club were to enlist, Newton showing extraordinary courage in serving with the No. 22 RAAF squadron in the battle for the Bismarck Sea. Having learnt to fly in De Havilland Tiger Moths, his low-level assaults in Boston bombers saw him amass 52 enemy raids in a 10-month period from May 1942 to March 1943.

The Victoria Cross, the highest decoration that can be bestowed on an Australian serviceman or woman was awarded posthumously, his citation, in part, praising his 'cool courage, ability, presence of mind and tenacious purposeful resource'.

'Throughout [the sorties],' the citation read, 'he displayed great courage and an iron determination to inflict utmost damage on the enemy. His splendid offensive flying and fighting were attended with brilliant success. Disdaining evasive tactics when experiencing the heaviest fire, he always went straight to his objective. He carried out many daring machine-gun attacks on enemy positions, involving low-flying over long distances in the face of continuous fire at pointblank range. On three occasions he dived through intense anti-aircraft fire to release his bombs on important targets on Salamaua isthmus. On one of these occasions his starboard engine failed over the target but he succeeded in flying back to an airfield 160 miles away.

'When leading an attack on an objective on 16 March 1943, he dived through intense and accurate shellfire and his aircraft was hit repeatedly; nevertheless, he held his course and bombed his target from low-level attack, resulting in destruction of many buildings and dumps, including two 40,000-gallon fuel installations. Although his aircraft was crippled, the fuselage and wing sections having been torn, petrol tank pierced, mainplanes and engines seriously damaged and one of the main tyres flat, Flight Lieutenant Newton managed to fly back to the base and make a successful landing.

'Despite this harassing experience, he returned the next day to the same locality [Salamaua]. His target this time, a single building, was even more difficult but again he attacked with his usual courage and resolution and flew a steady course through a barrage of fire. He scored hits on the building, but at the same moment his aircraft burst into flames.

'Flight Lieutenant Newton maintained control and calmly turned his aircraft away and flew along shore. He saw it as his duty to keep the aircraft in the air as long as he could, in order to take the crew as far away as possible from the enemy position. With great skill he brought his blazing plane down on the water. Two members of the crew were able to extricate themselves and were seen swimming to shore, but the gallant pilot is missing. According to other air crew who witnessed the occurrence, the escape hatch was not opened and his dinghy not inflated. Without regard for his own safety he had done all that a man could do to prevent his crew from falling into enemy hands.

'Flight Lieutenant Newton's many examples of conspicuous bravery have rarely been equalled and will serve as a shining inspiration to all who follow him.'

Newton, 23, was to escape the plane, only to be captured and beheaded on the beach. He was the only airman in the Pacific War to be awarded a VC.

No one had displayed greater bravery in the face of the enemy.

Down at the Junction There's a Cricket Ground: St Kilda Cricket Club, the First 150 Years, Ken Piesse (St Kilda Cricket Club, Melbourne, 2005)

THE NOBLEST ROMAN OF ALL

A profile of Australia's enduring between-the-wars wicketkeeper Bert Oldfield.

'A more polite stumper than Oldfield was never known,' wrote Neville Cardus, after Oldfield's retirement from big cricket. 'It must have been a pleasure to get out to him. Most wicketkeepers roar to high heaven as they seize their opportunities; once I was stumped in a club match by Duckworth and I felt that I had been sandbagged. Oldfield did his fell work stealthily and courteously. A sudden swoop, the flash of a bail in the sunshine – then you saw Oldfield turning to the umpire addressing him quietly but strictly in a point of order: "How was that?" Almost a request for information. And to the fallen batsman Oldfield seemed to say, "I am so sorry, but what could I do? Law 23, you know. Of course it should really be amended. So unpleasant to do anything mean behind one's back. Still, there you are. Better luck, perhaps, next innings …"'

Oldfield was a charming figure in the field, with his upright walk between the wickets, hands flapping – a sprightly walk which always reminded me of Charles Hawtrey as the shy and gentle pirate in *Ambrose Applejohn's Adventure.*

Modest, debonair, invariably considerate and ever willing to advise and help the younger generation – 'a cricketer' in every sense of the term – it's no wonder that Bert Oldfield has long been the idol of Australian cricket enthusiasts and has made hosts of friends all over the world. Without doubt, he is one of the greatest ambassadors Australia has ever sent abroad. And today, having answered the government's call for recruits for

Little Bertie: Modest, debonair and invariably considerate, Bert Oldfield was Australia's first-choice wicketkeeper between the wars.

the militia last April, we find him a sergeant in the 17th Battalion, tackling his new job with keenness and understanding and inculcating the spirit and ideals of the AIF [Australian Imperial Force] into his young charges.

William Albert Stanley Oldfield (to give Bert his full name) was born at Alexandria, Sydney, in September 1890, and was educated at Cleveland Street [Sydney] and Newtown Superior Public Schools. At Cleveland Street he was too young to practise cricket in the luncheon hour with the senior boys on the asphalt playground, though he 'looked on longingly'. But at Newtown, and on his way home, 'on the unprepared grassy patches of the Sydney University flats', he laid the foundation of his glorious cricketing career, though it was not until 1912 when he began playing junior cricket on concrete wickets covered with coir matting that he took seriously to wicketkeeping.

The following season he joined Glebe and very soon won his way into the third-grade team. In his autobiography, *Behind the Wicket,* which is a sheer joy to read, he says: 'Then I resolved to develop my physique (I always have avoided smoking and alcohol), took long walks in the early morning, did a lot of deep breathing and, to my great delight, was accepted in the company of a band of early-morning enthusiasts including none other than the internationals Warren Bardsley and Charlie Kelleway and several interstate men ... who practised on the Jubilee Oval in Glebe during the spring and summer months ... Heavy dew on the grass or even frosts never prevented our keenness for practice. Often we would return home for breakfast with our boots wet through and the ball swollen like a Christmas pudding.'

Towards the end of the 1914–15 season, Oldfield was moved up to Glebe's first-grade team and at the annual meeting of the club, held in July 1915, he was elected to the secretaryship. Two months later, however, on the eve of his 19th birthday, he joined the medical corps of the AIF and, sailing in the *Kanowna* in December, spent eight months in Egypt and another eight months in England with his unit, before getting the chance to transfer to an ambulance in France as a stretcher-bearer. Both in Egypt and England, and later in France, Bert was able to find opportunities to indulge his passion for the grand old game; but probably the weirdest 'practices' that he and his mates in the unit – among them EJ Long, LW Gwynne and Roy Farnsworth, all prominent sportsmen in Sydney – ever had, were on the sand at Heliopolis shortly after their arrival in Egypt. Having no cricketing gear, they played 'imaginary' games, without bat, ball or stumps. In the early evenings these chaps formed the nucleus of the Imaginary team and so realistic did they make the game in respect of the actions of bowling, batting, fielding and wicketkeeping, that one could quite easily imagine that there was a ball and bat and an actual game going on. As an unrehearsed pantomime it was a sheer joy to watch and I have paid good money to see worse turns on the stage.

Needless to say Bert, a bit thinner in body and thicker on top than he is now, but still the same dapper figure, revelled in the fun. His part mostly consisted of being bowler, batsman or fieldsman, for with Ted Long, who was destined to become the AIF team's first wicketkeeper behind the 'sticks', Bert had little opportunity to show that wizardry which was to make him famous.

It was the beginning of June 1917 when Oldfield reached France. A week later, along with some 20 other reinforcements and details, he joined the 15th Field Ambulance (Fifth Division) at Bellevue Farm, outside Albert. The ambulance – which was then under the command of a strict disciplinarian, Lieutenant Colonel JMY Stewart, who had recently been on Surgeon General Howse's staff – was acting as the No. 1 Anzac Corps rest station, but shortly afterwards it moved to Contay to become the 'corps mumps station'. The ambulance remained there for six weeks, when it was entrained for Belgium and went into billets at Sercus to prepare for the part it was to play in the Passchendaele offensive. Until the middle of September, the unit's activities were all strained towards this end, a set program of work being laid down for each day. Physical 'jerks', stretcher drill, section drill, ambulance drill, frequent kit and other inspections, training in anti-gas equipment, numerous route marches over the countryside, through such places as Blaringhem, Renescure, Wallon-Cappel, Morbecque, Thiennes and La Motte, and sports and games brought the unit to a high pitch of efficiency. Writing of this period, Oldfield said: 'If it were not convenient to arrange matches with the infantry, artillery, or other neighbouring units, we played scratch games amongst ourselves ... one match, in particular, stands out in my mind. It took place at Contay ... on a sheltered grassy patch, shaded by tall poplars ... the hessian from the officers' mess was commandeered for the purpose of a wicket and it proved an ideal substitute. Our kit of cricket gear had been sent to us from the war chest and when not in use it was zealously guarded by the quartermaster.'

On 17–18 September, the 15th Field Ambulance moved up, through Reninghelst and Ouderdom, to a position behind Ypres, and on the afternoon of 20 September, 80 of its bearers including Oldfield, went forward to assist in clearing the wounded of the First and Second Divisions, which had that day captured the Menin Road ridge. Camping at the ramparts of Ypres, they lost several men while engaged on this work and were away until the 22nd. Next morning, two officers and 75 bearers – Bertie again among them, and carrying his 48 hours' rations, waterproof sheet, and blanket, as well as other gear – set out in motor lorries for the advanced dressing station on the Menin Road, which was now being run by the 14th Field Ambulance.

From the ADS the bearers moved down the Menin Road, past Hellfire Corner to the Hooge tunnel and Clapham Junction and beyond. By now the Fourth and Fifth Divisions were in the line, in place of the First and Second, and on 26 September they were to attack at Polygon Wood. On the 25th, the Germans nearly forestalled this attack when, assisted by a terrific shell-fire which lasted for hours, they heavily counterattacked the flank of the 33rd British Division, on the right of the 15th Australian Brigade and drove it in. The fighting was desperate and the casualties were heavy, but the British–Australian attack duly went forward next morning and Polygon Wood was captured. During these two days and nights the burden imposed on the stretcher-bearers was a heavy one. Among those great-hearted toilers was young Bert Oldfield, who with his mates, four to a stretcher, carried the wounded back to a collecting post in the Hooge tunnel until, on the morning of the 26th, they were caught in a heavy barrage near Glencorse Wood. A 5.9 [artillery shell] exploding in their midst blew to pieces two of the bearers and their officer patient, and mortally wounded a third bearer. Oldfield, alone of the party to escape death, was yet in a bad way, for he had been wounded between the shoulders and over the eye and had been partly buried, and was now suffering severely from shell shock. He lay there all day and was picked up in a semiconscious condition early in the evening. From Poperinghe he went to the American hospital at Rouen and in the middle of October was transferred to England and sent to the Gloucester City Hospital. It was February 1918 before a medical board pronounced Bert fit to leave hospital, but even then he was to be employed only on light duty. Sent to the AIF kit store at Hammersmith, he was given clerical work to do for the remainder of the war.

Later in the year, when his health improved, he played cricket on Saturday afternoons with the Wattle Club, which consisted of members of the kit store staff. It was in one such match, at Merton, that he made his first century in England. 'My chief recollection at this time,' says one of the Wattle team, 'is the assiduity with which he practised the game. Our depot was very close to the Queen's Club grounds and Oldfield would spend hours each week in the early morning or the evening, having other enthusiasts bowl at him while he practised the art of wicketkeeping.'

Early in 1919, the AIF Sports Control Board came into being for the purpose of encouraging sport in all units and of supervising the organisation and selection of representative teams from the AIF. One of its responsibilities was the AIF cricket team, which toured England and South Africa that year with conspicuous success, and had a far-reaching effect on Australian Test cricket in the postwar years.

Cricketers in the force were invited to submit their name for selection, and eventually about 50 attended Kennington Oval for a week's intensive practice. From these, 16 were chosen for the AIF team. Oldfield, to his great disappointment, was among those passed over, but he got a place in a second AIF XI which left for Oxford to play the various colleges at the University. The week's program included a match against a combined side from New and Trinity Colleges and in that game Oldfield scored a century (as did Ernie Cameron, the manager of the side) and 'was also fortunate in gathering several victims with the gloves'. That night, on returning to the hotel, Bert became 'tremendously excited' when Cameron handed him a wire which he had received from Howard Lacy, the manager of the AIF's No. 1 team. It read: 'Please retain Oldfield as keeper for the AIF match against Oxford.'

'It would be impossible for me (writes Oldfield in his autobiography) to describe my feelings when I realised that I was being given my big chance. This was the beginning of my entry into first-class cricket. During my experience of nearly 20 years of this class of cricket, including 38 Anglo-Australian Test matches, I have had many pleasurable experiences in encountering charming personalities and met with thrilling incidents in the actual playing. Pleasant as those memories are, there still remains paramount in my mind, however, that thrilling moment when I received the invitation to join the official AIF team.'

In the Oxford match, Bert failed with the bat, but took three catches behind the stumps. Thenceforward he had a permanent place in the team, which was reduced from 16 to 14 players. The others were: HL Collins (as captain), CT Docker, [EJ] Long, EA Bull, JM Taylor, WL Trenerry, JT Murray, CS Winning, CB Willis, JM Gregory, CE 'Nip' Pellew, AW Lampard and WS Stirling. Of the 34 matches played in Britain, the AIF team won 15 and lost four, the other 15 being drawn. Oldfield's batting average stood at 32 for 22 innings, his highest score being 80 not out, while behind the wickets he caught 23 and stumped 11.

In October 1919, the team reached South Africa, where it played eight matches, winning six of them. On its return to Australia, it beat Victoria and New South Wales, the match against Queensland being spoiled by rain and ending in a draw.

On 10 March 1920, Corporal WA Oldfield was discharged from the AIF, and, at the age of 23, re-entered civil life. Playing cricket once more for the Glebe club, he was, at the end of the year, chosen for the Australian eleven against England. From then until his retirement from big cricket in 1938, he toured England four times, played twice in South Africa and kept wickets against every visiting international team – the English, South Africans, West Indians and the New Zealanders. He is the only wicketkeeper to score more than 1000 runs in Test cricket and has been responsible for more dismissals in Test cricket than any other wicketkeeper. But, as Harold Heydon wrote in *Reveille* in June 1938, the record of which Bert is probably most proud is his reputation for sportsmanship. He was the last of that wonderful band of Diggers to whom Australian cricket owes so much, and [concluded Heydon] 'one might with justification say, "He was the noblest Roman of them all."'

'Celebrities of the AIF', *Reveille* (No. 111), 'AWB' (London, 1 December 1939)

GOLDEN-AGE GREATS

Fourteen August 1938 saw the passing within hours of each other of two of Australia's golden-age champions, 71-year-olds Hugh Trumble and JJ 'Jim' Kelly, one in Melbourne and the other in Sydney.

Cricketers and followers of the game all over the world will regret to learn of the deaths of Mr Hugh Trumble, a former Test player and

Mates: Melbourne Cricket Club secretary Ben Wardill with the formidable Hugh Trumble.

secretary of the Melbourne Cricket Club, and of Mr JJ 'Jim' Kelly, of Sydney, his contemporary in many Test games.

Mr Trumble had been confined for a few days to his home at Hawthorn, suffering from bronchitis, but his illness took an unexpectedly serious turn on Friday, and he died yesterday morning. Mr Trumble, who was aged 71 years, leaves a widow, six sons and two daughters. The funeral will leave Sleight's chapel at Malvern at 11 am tomorrow for the Springvale Crematorium.

Mr Kelly, who had been ill for some weeks, died in Sydney yesterday. He also was aged 71 years, and was one of the greatest wicketkeepers Australia has produced. He began his Test career in England in 1896 and gave way to H 'Sammy' Carter in the 1907–08 series. In 36 Tests he caught 43 batsmen and stumped 20.

Mr Hugh Trumble, whose death is reported on page one, forsook a banking career for cricket, and as secretary of the Melbourne Cricket Club and a member of many Test teams, he became one of the world's best-known identities in the game. Born on 12 May 1867, he joined the National Bank of Australasia on 22 June 1887 and served in various suburban branches before being appointed accountant at Richmond in June 1903. In 1908, he became manager of the Kew branch, and resigned that position on 30 November 1911, to become secretary of the Melbourne Cricket Club. In that position, which he filled with credit and dignity, he maintained his close association with the game and was the perfect host. He had a reputation as a storyteller, and was ever ready to discuss in a humorous way the many incidents of a long and successful cricket career.

Mr Trumble had a remarkable career in Test cricket. In 16 Test matches in England and 15 in Australia, he took 141 wickets, a record that still stands. The next best was [MA 'Monty'] Noble, with 115 wickets, and for England, [Wilfred] Rhodes, with 109 wickets. He played in 40 interstate games and 220 first-class games altogether in Australia, England, South Africa and America. He first played in Test cricket in 1890 and he finished in a blaze of glory by taking seven for 28 off 41 balls in England's second innings on the Melbourne ground in March 1904, the 'hat-trick' being included in that feat.

In 1902, also on the Melbourne ground, he first took the 'hat-trick' against England. His record in Test cricket was: batting: 31 matches, 55 innings, 70 highest score, 838 runs, average 19.95; bowling: 7895 balls, 2945 runs, 141 wickets, average 21.04. He had five tours to England with Test teams. He did not bowl much on his first tour in 1890, but in the other four he took 120, 148, 142 and 140 wickets respectively, winning the average in the last two tours.

Among his best feats were 15 wickets for 68 runs for Australia against South of England in 1902 and 15 wickets for 199 runs for Victoria against South Australia in 1889. He began interstate cricket in 1887 and took 739 wickets for an average of 21.34. He made 1533 runs in 87 innings, averaging 21.29. His highest score was 107. He made one other century, 105 in England and still holds a Test match record for the seventh-wicket partnership, he and Clem Hill adding 165 on the Melbourne ground in the 1897–98 tour. He was a plucky batsman, with a powerful cover drive and a great defence.

Six feet 4 in (193 cm) in height and well built, Mr Trumble was a medium-pace, off break bowler who, because of his great height made the ball rise at least an inch higher than any other bowler of his type. He bowled an off-break and varied it with a ball that went away with his arm. A slow ball was used occasionally. It was so well flighted that even the best batsmen often were uncertain. He kept a remarkably good length and had the facility of quickly finding out the weak spots of the batsman. His brother Mr JW [John] Trumble, now a leading solicitor, was also a Test cricketer. Another brother, Mr. T Trumble, was secretary for defence, and afterward went to Australia House in London.

Mr JJ 'Jim' Kelly became New South Wales' first great wicketkeeper, having learnt his cricket in Port Melbourne where he'd first played with Railways United. After two seasons in senior club ranks with St Kilda he was lured north with the promise of recognition, consistently denied him in Melbourne through the enduring presence of Jack Blackham.

Tall for a wicketkeeper at 6 ft (183 cm), he stood up to all but the fastest of Australia's golden-age bowlers. He was to tour England four times and in the 1901–02 Ashes Test in Sydney, became the first Australian to claim eight catches in a match, a record which was to stand until after World War II.

From 1896 to 1905, he played 36 consecutive Tests, never being dropped, his off-field popularity matching his on-field acumen. *Australian Cricket: A Weekly Record of the Game* said this of Kelly in 1896: 'It is a treat to see a man in any department of life's activity combine intrepid valour, sedulous perseverance and manly modesty in his practical everyday character. All these good qualities centre in Jim Kelly.'

The old Borough boy retired after the '05 English tour on medical advice having been struck over the heart in the Manchester Test.

The Herald, writer unknown (Melbourne, 15 August 1938); additional Kelly research: *Down at the Junction There's a Cricket Ground: St Kilda Cricket Club, the First 150 Years,* Ken Piesse (St Kilda Cricket Club, Melbourne, 2005)

DAINTY, DECEPTIVE AND DANGEROUS
*The arrival of 42-year-old spin maestro Clarrie Grimmett
in England for the 1934 Ashes summer was greeted with acclaim.
Here was a true champion, at the height of his powers.*

He is an unobtrusive little man, with a face that says nothing to you at all; seldom is he heard by the crowd when he appeals for leg before. He walks about the field on dainty feet, which step with the soft fastidiousness of a cat treading a wet pavement. He is a master of surreptitious arts; he hides his skill, and sometimes, when he is on guard at cover, he seems to hide himself. He knows a trick of getting himself unobserved, as he darts forward to run a man out like somebody emerging from an ambush.

'Gamp is my name and gamp is my natur'.' That is a dark metaphysical saying; the meaning cannot be put into words, but nonetheless we can grasp it by the instinct for eternal substances. It is like that with Grimmett; the name penetrates to the quiddity, like 'curl', 'twist', 'slithery'; his name is onomatopoeic. I love to see him bowl a man out behind his back, so to say round the legs; the ball gently touches the stumps and removes perhaps only one bail.

The humorous cunning of it reminds me that the Artful Dodger used to walk stealthily behind his master and extract the handkerchief from the coat-tails without making a tinkle on the little bell. Compare Grimmett with the wonderful leg-spin bowler he succeeded in the Australian XI, Arthur Mailey. An Australian wit once said to me: 'Mailey bowled the googly stuff like a millionaire; Clarrie bowls it like a miser.' Mailey tossed up his spin with all the blandness in the world; his full-tosses were like a generous sort of fattening diet before the killing and the roasting! Mailey did his mischief by daylight. Grimmett goes to work with a dark lantern; his boots are rubbered. Mailey's wickets were like a practiced and jolly angler's 'catch'; Grimmett's wickets are definitely 'swag'. When he goes off the field after he has had seven for 57, I can see the bag he is carrying over his shoulder.

He is the greatest light-handed spin bowler of our period. The comparison with Mailey was employed not to stress resemblance, but difference; Grimmett is less a googly than a leg-break bowler. He uses the 'wrong-one' sparsely; he is content to thrive on the ball which breaks away and leaves the bat; that is the best of all balls. A straight ball, wickedly masked, is Grimmett's foil to the leg break. He makes a virtue of a low arm; his flight keeps so close to the earth that only a batsman quick of feet can jump to the pitch of it.

And then must he be aware of Oldfield, the most gentlemanly of wicketkeepers, who stumps you with courtesy; he does not make a noise to the umpire, but almost bows you from the wicket. Or he is like a perfect dentist who says when your heart is in your mouth: 'It's all over; I've already got it out; here it is.'

To play forward to Grimmett, to miss the spin and then to find yourself stumped by Oldfield – why, it is like an amputation done under an anesthetic!

The Guardian, 'the Cricketer' Neville Cardus (Manchester, July 1934)

THE PRINCE OF WICKETKEEPERS
*Jack Blackham was one of Australia's most
skilled and popular 19th-century cricketers.*

Mr JM Blackham, known as the 'prince of wicketkeepers' and a former Australian Test captain, died in a private hospital in Melbourne early today, after a long illness. He was 79. 'When Blackham was

A Formidable Quartet: Jack Blackham (sitting left) with Billy Murdoch, Harry Hyslop and Harry Boyle.

behind the wickets,' said Mr Hugh Trumble, secretary of the Melbourne Cricket Club today, 'he made the bowler 20 per cent better.'

Speaking for the Marylebone Cricket Club and the English Test team, Mr PF Warner, joint-manager of the team, said that cricketers all over the world would learn of Jack Blackham's death with deep regret. 'Blackham's name,' he said, 'will live in cricket. He was a superb wicketkeeper and he was one of the great Australians. He, [Frederick] Spofforth, Charles Bannerman and [Billy] Murdoch spread the fame of Australian cricket the world over and to the last he took the keenest interest in the game in which he was such a distinguished figure. The last of his eight visits to England was in 1893, but his feats as a wicketkeeper are still remembered and discussed.'

Mr Blackham is survived by a brother, Mr Fred Blackham of Bright, and two sisters (Mrs Hinricksen and Mrs Easdown).

FUNERAL ARRANGEMENTS: Members of the Victorian Cricket Association and past and present players are invited to attend a special service at St Paul's Cathedral at 11 am tomorrow. The service will be conducted by the president of the VCA [Canon ES Hughes]. Immediately afterward, the funeral procession will leave for the Melbourne Crematorium at Fawkner, arriving about noon. There will be a short service at the crematorium. Funeral arrangements are in the hands of Messrs AA Sleight Pty Ltd.

The Herald, writer unknown (Melbourne, 28 December 1932)

BLOSSOMING LATE

Ernie Baillie profiles 46-year-old 'late-bloomer' Don Blackie, one of Australia's few success stories in the one-sided 1928–29 Ashes summer.

Don Blackie has been successful against the Englishmen for the simple reason that he can spin the ball – and he knows how to vary his deliveries. All the Englishmen were in trouble when facing him.

His figures of six wickets for 94 in the first innings of the [Melbourne] Test this week were testimony to his skill.

It was a remarkably fine achievement for the St Kilda veteran and effectively silenced those critics who had freely [voiced] the opinion that Blackie was a bowler of the past.

Blackie's fine form against the Englishmen is the best reason why Australia should cultivate spin bowlers. In recent years swerve bowling has been an obsession with bowlers. Spin bowling has been neglected. The result has been on perfect wickets, batsmen have helped themselves to runs.

A spin bowler like Blackie, however, has always been closely watched. His success should be an inspiration to any young bowler in the Commonwealth.

There are wonderful opportunities ahead for young bowlers who are prepared to practise the art of spin bowling assiduously and can learn all they can about varying their pace.

The great pity of it is that Blackie is not younger. Unless Australia can produce some bowlers of class, prospects for the English tour in 1930 are not particularly bright. It has been a hard enough job to get the Englishmen out here, but on their own soil the task will be much more difficult, unless some good spin bowlers step up.

Blackie has lived a good, clean life. A trip to England [in 1930] would be a deserving reward for a great sportsman. On his form this season he is still at his best. There seems to be no fear that he will lose his bowling skill. True he will be a year older by the time the Australians go to England, but though a mature man in years, he has the heart and spirit of a boy and there seems little doubt that he will be able to keep going with the best of them.

First-class bowlers in Australia today are as rare as nuggets in the goldfields. Two stand out in Victoria – Blackie and [Bert] Ironmonger – [Ted] a'Beckett and [Hans] Ebeling also show great promise. South Australia provides one in Clarrie Grimmett, the most accurate slow bowler in the Commonwealth. New South Wales has provided some of the best bowlers in recent years in men such as [Jack] Gregory, [Arthur] Mailey, [Charlie] Kelleway and [Charlie] Macartney.

Blackie's wonderful success with the ball is all the more astounding when it is recalled that after 11 years' service to Prahran, he went out of cricket for five years. He hardly saw a bat or ball during that time and the cricket public had almost forgotten him. Don, however, staged a comeback with St Kilda and delighted everyone, except opposing batsmen, showing all his best form with [the] ball.

Beginning his career as a junior in a South Yarra competition, he bowled promisingly and showed form as a left-hand batsman. He joined Prahran later and soon revealed his talents. With Jim Cahill, Worrall, 'Dodger' O'Connor, Dave Smith and Billy Osborne as clubmates, it was not long before Blackie made rapid development. Worrall gave him expert coaching and he benefitted considerably. Blackie bowled at medium pace and with a good length and the faculty of varying his deliveries he soon had batsmen in trouble. Spinning the ball from the off, he gave much trouble and had many great hauls of wickets.

Though Blackie was on the verge of interstate selection with Prahran, he never figured in Sheffield Shield cricket. One comes to the conclusion that if Don was as good a bowler then as he is now, the Victorian bowling at that time must have been superlatively good. Blackie played once against Fiji and in several colts' matches. He also played in Edgar Mayne's XI against Warwick Armstrong's side. He made some good scores against other clubs. Once he scored 99 against Fitzroy. Business compelled him to give up cricket much to the regret of the Prahran officials. Blackie, however, had been playing baseball and he kept this sport up.

To all intents and purposes, Blackie's cricket career had terminated but, like a comet, he reappeared in the firmament in the 1922–23 season with St Kilda.

When he returned to the game he was somewhat sceptical of his ability to show his old form, but within a few games he was at his best again. Some of his muscles were rather stiff after five years but these were soon loosened up.

The coming of Ironmonger to St Kilda soon afterwards resulted in the formation of a bowling combination that has never been equalled in club cricket in Australia. One prominent district batsman put the position to me in this way: 'I thought I could bat a bit,' he said, 'but Blackie and Ironmonger have repeatedly convinced me that I am not much class.' The batsmen who have made 100 runs individually against St Kilda in recent years can be counted on the fingers of one hand. St Kilda was premiers for four seasons in succession [from 1923–24 onwards] and Blackie and Ironmonger had a lot to do with the success, because of the havoc they wrought with the ball.

Blackie's variation of pace with the ball in the air is most disconcerting. There is a ball which he tosses up slowly which hangs momentarily and then drops quickly. Often a batsman thinks that the ball is overpitched, steps out to crack it, misses and is stumped. Some of his deliveries make considerable pace off the wicket. His variation in pace is always troubling batsmen. To combat Blackie successfully, a knowledge of footwork is essential, as his length is also superb ...

One could not wish to meet a more genial and happy cricketer. Don delights in the game and is as keen as a young boy just starting the game. Behind Blackie's seemingly boyish temperament is the mastermind of a tactician. He is a close student of the game. His bowling is characterised by brainy work. He studies the weaknesses of the batsmen and plays up to them.

Aggressiveness has often been successful against Blackie but few batsmen have been game enough to hit him. Blackie, who is well over 6 feet and of angular build, takes a nice, easy loping run to the wicket. His arm delivery is smooth and he varies the height from which he lets the ball go. Bill Ponsford, his clubmate, considers that is where he is better than most bowlers because of his great variety. Every ball bowled by him appears to be different. His stock ball is the medium-pace off break of very accurate length. Now and again he whips in a fast one which can be observed by spectators more easily than the batsmen pitted against him. He often skittles batsmen with his fast ball. Occasionally, however, his fast ones go well over on the leg side.

Career-best Day: Super-veteran Don Blackie claimed six wickets to restrict England's lead to just 20 runs during the Christmas Test in Melbourne in 1928–29. Blackie's St Kilda teammate Ted a'Beckett also had a fine day with a wicket and two important catches.

After having been out of representative cricket for a long time, Blackie reappeared with Victoria in the 1924–25 season and has been a regular member of the side since then. In interstate cricket he has proved his value to Victoria. In the 1926–27 season, he claimed 33 wickets at 24.72. Last season he took 31 wickets at 22.22. Blackie went to New Zealand with the Australians and captured 35 wickets.

This season he was not chosen for the first Test match in Brisbane. He played in the second in Sydney, however, and bowled well without much success.

The Melbourne wicket has always suited him best and he proved that conclusively on Wednesday. At the end of England's first innings on Wednesday, he had taken 10 wickets for 242 runs in the Tests and in other first-class games this season he had captured nine wickets at a cost of 297 runs. He is what you call a 'late bloomer'.

The Sporting Globe, Ernie Baillie (Melbourne, January 1929)
Blackie played just one more Test, a month later, but continued as a St Kilda frontliner, playing in the firsts until he was 53. In all, he took 504 wickets and figured in six district cricket 'A'-grade premierships.

THE WORLD'S BEST UMPIRE

His unfailing care for accuracy and passion for the game was the hallmark of RW 'Bob' Crockett.

The passing of Bob Crockett meant the loss, not only of 'the world's best umpire' as PF Warner described him, but a man who brought a new dignity to a position which has not always been held in high regard.

Bob was only a ground bowler when he first acted in Test cricket, but in 38 years no bowler ever cavilled at any of his decisions. His integrity and ability were always taken as a matter of course. He was never flurried and 'bluff' appeals generally ended with a smile on the face of the bowler. A well-known English bowler, who was up to all the tricks of the trade, summed the great umpire up admirably when he said, 'You can't get more than you earn out of Bob.'

His strong Scottish character was shown when he came to the city from Daylesford in 1887 to take a position on the Melbourne Cricket Club ground staff. Daylesford was then a thriving mining town and he came to Melbourne with the fixed purpose of becoming a qualified assayer [an analyst who performs chemical tests on metals].

He achieved his object, but the call of cricket was so strong and his services were in such demand that mining lost a man who would assuredly have made his mark.

I once asked him if he felt the strain of umpiring. 'Not particularly,' he replied, 'but I shall never forget one day. I was standing in a public school match with the thermometer at 107 [around 41.5 degrees Celsius]. Play began at 10.30 am. Then I had to be at the Working Men's College at 1 pm and put in three hours in the furnace room.'

It was such grit which enabled him to put his daughter through a university course and give his son a public school education.

There probably has never been an umpire with such a strong personality. The laws of the game were a religion with him; but he was bigger than the laws and he did not hesitate to exercise his authority under Law 43, which states that the umpires are the sole judge of fair and unfair play.

In a match between Victoria and England in the 1907–08 season, the visitors were well behind but hoping to make a drawn game of it. [Arthur] Fielder, the last man, joined [Joe] Hardstaff [Sr] and Hardstaff drove the last ball of an over to run a single and keep the strike. The outfield kicked the ball to the fence to make Fielder face the bowler, but Crockett declined to signal a boundary. His courage received a glowing tribute in the English press.

It is significant that until [Andy] Barlow 'called' [Ron] Halcombe and [Eddie] Gilbert in recent years, Crockett set the standard in judging fair and unfair bowlers. Several of them had gone unquestioned till they came under his eye in pennant matches. Several of them were promptly called – and then other umpires followed suit.

Though he had a typical Scottish sense of humour, there was one joke against himself that he was never able to appreciate. When Jack Marsh, the great Aboriginal bowler, appeared against Victoria in Sydney, he was called by Crockett 17 times in an over. The sensation can be imagined and it was a relief to everyone when the over was at last completed. Marsh, of course, was taken off, but Syd Gregory, the New South Wales captain who was a great little wag, had something up his sleeve. He gave the ball to Tom Howard and there was a further simmer in the crowd. Bob called the first five of Howard's deliveries and the crowd roared with laughter for Howard was the most notorious 'chucker' in Sydney! I don't think Crockett ever quite forgave Syd.

It is an adage that it takes a big man to admit that he is in the wrong. In a match between Prahran and St Kilda in 1921, Crockett gave a St Kilda batsman out when the ball was driven back and broke the wicket at the bowler's end with the batsman out of his ground. The umpire was certain that the ball had been deflected into the wicket by the bowler's foot. Noticing the other batsman limping, Crockett found on inquiry that the ball had hit his (the non-striker's) foot. The umpire met the incoming batsman, sent him back and insisted on the man he had given out continuing his innings in spite of the opposition of fieldsmen and the other umpire. How many umpires would have had such courage?

He loved to recall instances of good sportsmanship. A favourite anecdote concerned Arthur Gilligan, captain of the 1924–25 English team. One of the balls provided had been in use only a few minutes when Gilligan took it to Crockett and pointed to a big scar on the leather. Bob pointed out that this was an advantage to the bowlers. 'That is why I am asking for a new one,' said Gilligan. 'I don't want anything that would give us the slightest advantage.'

The match which remained his most vivid memory was between New South Wales and Victoria in Sydney in 1895. It was the last appearance in first-class cricket of 'Jack' Blackham and Harry Moses. Charlie Turner also was soon to retire. For the first time Harry Trott led Victoria. Harry and Albert Trott had a share in dismissing all the batsmen and no other name of the fielding side would have appeared on the scoresheet had not Bob McLeod cornered a run-out with the last man in. Either of the Trotts could have also got it and the brothers did not fail to remind McLeod of the fact.

Bob had an almost reverential regard for Hugh Trumble and loved to relate how the great bowler ended the discussion with the remark: 'You did the right thing. When in doubt, leave it to a Scotchman.'

The Herald, 'RH' (Melbourne, 14 December 1935)

MATCHLESS GRACE AND GENIUS

Archie Jackson's early death robbed Australia of an emerging champion.

BRISBANE: 16 February [1933] – A batsman who was a great deal more than a run-getter was Archie Jackson, who died early today in hospital in Brisbane. Although Jackson was a highly successful scorer, the great charm of his batting lay in the way he made the runs – polished mastery of all the best strokes known to cricket.

It was this delightful style which led critics to liken Jackson to [Victor] Trumper – 'Victor, the Nonpareil' – whose batting in the first decade of the century is remembered more for the matchless grace, freedom and audacity of genius than for the pile of record feats he left. As with Trumper, who died when 37, Jackson was never robust because of the lung ailment which caused his death at 23.

Perhaps the main similarity between these stylists of different periods was the willowy ease of their every movement at the crease – the stance when awaiting the ball, the perfect balance during footwork movements and the rhythmic play of body, shoulders and wrists in the sweep of the bat.

Young Guns: Archie Jackson (with cap) and an equally young Don Bradman in 1928–29.

While Jackson never reached the heights of Trumper, his displays before his health began to fail stirred memories of the master batsman.

Jackson's style was not the result of study of Trumper's methods, as he was only five when the champion died. It is believed that the Trumper influence on the young cricketer's play was conveyed partly by seeing the batting of Alan Kippax. Kippax, as a boy, watched Trumper at every opportunity, with the result that he captured some of the elegance of the peerless Victor.

Taking Kippax as a model, knowingly or unknowingly, Jackson acquired some of the strokes of the old masters. But his play approached nearer to Trumper than Kippax, because of his freer use of punishing strokes in front of the wicket. In his mastery of strokes, it is difficult to say which was his best – his glorious driving, slashing cover-hits, gliding strokes to leg or crisp cutting.

[The] youngest of all batsmen to score a century in Tests between

England and Australia, Jackson was 19 when he hit up 164 in his first Test innings, in 1929.

Born in Scotland in 1909, he was brought to Australia as a child. His health was doubtful when he went to England for the 1930 Tests and he never again was completely fit. Jackson's appearance in Brisbane cricket early this summer, when he transferred from Sydney, was followed by his final breakdown.

In six Test innings he scored 350 against England (average 58) and in all first-class cricket 4493 runs (average 46), including 12 centuries.

The Herald, writer unknown (Melbourne, 16 February 1933)

FIRST OF THE GREATS

FR Spofforth, 'The Demon', was Australia's first truly great bowler.

Frederick Robert Spofforth, who has been described as the greatest bowler of all time, was born in 1855. His performances and his fierce manner in approaching the wicket when bowling was such that early in his career he was called 'The Demon Bowler', and the name never left him. He had many wonderful performances in Test cricket. In his book, *With Bat and Ball*, George Giffen, the famous Australian all-rounder, said: 'I question whether a bowler achieved more remarkable success throughout a season than Spofforth did in 1884. His average was almost to a decimal point the same as in 1882, but considering that there were more hard wickets and the calibre of our opponents was, on the whole, higher, there was no doubt that his 216 wickets for 12.2 runs each was an immeasurably better record than his 188 wickets at a cost of 12.1 runs each in 1882. As usual, some of [his] finest performances were against [the] strongest teams. The Demon has, I think, been absolutely the greatest bowler of my time. He has made a deep study of the art of bowling, had a wonderful control over his pitch and he seldom turned the ball unless [if] it was allowed to pass the bat, it would hit the wicket. What a sight it was to see Spofforth bowling when a game had to be pulled like a brand from the burning! He looked the Demon and I verily believe he has frightened more batsmen out than many bowlers have fairly and squarely beaten.'

Spofforth figures in many Test match records. Four times (twice in one game), he took seven wickets in a match and he was the only bowler to take 14 in a match; the feat being performed at the Oval in 1882. In the first innings he took seven for 46 in a total of 101; then seven for 44 in a total of 77. This was the famous match which Australia won by seven runs. Spofforth also took 13 wickets for 110 runs in Melbourne in 1878–79. In Sydney, in 1884–85, he took five for 30 in England's second innings of 77, he and [Joey] Palmer (four wickets for 32) bowling unchanged. In Melbourne in 1878–79, he performed the hat-trick. His complete figures in Test cricket are: bowling: 30 innings, 4185 balls, 416 maidens, 1731 runs, 94 wickets, 18.41 average; batting: 18 matches, 29 innings, six times not out, 217 runs, 50 highest score, 9.43 average.

Mr Spofforth went to live in England after the 1886 tour and sought to benefit by the experience he had gained in the National Bank, Melbourne. Eventually he negotiated with the Star Tea Company's supply stores and since 1898 had been in sole control of a very profitable business in which his two sons are also associated. Mr Spofforth, after an absence of many years, revisited Australia last year [1925] and witnessed several of the Test matches between England and Australia.

The death of Mr Spofforth reduces the list to just four surviving members of that famous team of Australian cricketers that blazed the trail in England in 1878. The only surviving members from that first team are C Bannerman, J McC Blackham, GH Bailey and TW Garrett.

The Argus, writer unknown (Melbourne, 5 June 1926)

'NO SADDER SHOCK HAS EVER BEEN EXPERIENCED'

*Outstanding batsman-wicketkeeper Billy Murdoch
died while watching a game at the MCG.*

MELBOURNE (Monday): The famous cricketer WL 'Billy' Murdoch died (aged 55) on Saturday afternoon at about five o'clock, in Dr W Moore's private hospital [11 February 1911]. When I entered the Melbourne Cricket Club pavilion shortly before noon, I greeted him while he was chatting pleasantly with Charlie McLeod and Harry Rush. In a few minutes I left to get round to my spot beneath the trees. Coming back in the afternoon, I had not been long seated in the balcony when the veteran scorer J Taylor brought the sad news that the famous cricketer had been suddenly stricken by apoplexy in the Melbourne Cricket Club committee room and that, in an unconscious condition, he had been taken to a private hospital. In the pavilion Dr Ramsay Mailer, Dr Dyring, Dr Leary and Dr Horne did what they could to restore him, but their efforts were of no avail. He had luncheon with the MCC committee and was sitting next to Major Morkham. Just after luncheon he put his hand to his forehead, and the Major said, 'What's the matter?'

'Neuralgia, I think; I have a pain here.'

These were the last words uttered by the grand old champion. He sank back unconscious and remained so until the end came. In the history of Australian cricket no sadder shock has ever been experienced than that we all felt when the sad news came back from the hospital that the great old warrior had gone to his account.

The Australasian, Tom 'Felix' Horan (Sydney, 25 February 1911)

LONG LIVE VICTOR TRUMPER

Some talk of Alexander,
And some of Hercules
Of Hector and Lysander,
And such great names as these;
Yea, all those heroes breezy
Will live beyond all time,
Because their names were easy
To jingle in a rhyme.

But there is one Australian
Whose praise few poets sing
Because his name is alien
To almost everything.
Unjust it is I know it,
But he must yield his claim –
The most perspiring poet
Can hardly rhyme his name.

Long life to Victor Trumper
That record-breaker fine;
I drink it in a bumper
Of clear Australian wine.
And verses would come thronging
Ev'n as I drink it down,
If only (foolish longing)
His name was Jones or Brown.

Long life to Victor Trumper!
That brave, hard-hitting soul,
That pounder, smasher, thumper
Of all that Rhodes can bowl.
Ground, press-box, and pavilion
Have seen what he can do
His worshippers are million,
Although his rhymes are few.

Ask no more rhymes for Trumper;
There is no English name,
From King to counter-jumper,
That knows a wider fame.
And in my verse I'd gather
His records till the morn,
If only Victor's father
Some other name had borne.

The Argus, Oriel (Melbourne, date unknown); reproduced from *Trumper: The Definitive Biography,* Peter Sharpham (Hodder & Stoughton, Sydney, 1985)

A LEFT-HANDER WITH SKILL AND SWERVE

Unable to make it in one state, WJ Whitty was a champion in another.

A newcomer to the East Torrens team in 1908–09 was WJ [Bill] Whitty, who proved to be a lethal wicket-taker in his seven seasons with the club. The story of how Whitty came to join East Torrens is curious. Born in Sydney, he was 21 years old and playing for a minor team, the Newtown Footballers Cricket Club, when New South Wales selector and schoolmaster George Barbour got word of his reputation as a bowler. Barbour invited Whitty to bowl to the first XI boys of

Sydney Grammar School. Big-boned and with boyish features, Whitty bowled whippy deliveries with a sweeping arc of his left arm. The action regularly produced wickedly swinging balls that tested even the best of batsmen. Barbour immediately recognised that Whitty had rare ability and successfully pressed for his inclusion in the New South Wales team for a match against Queensland, despite the fact that he had not yet appeared in NSW Cricket Association grade cricket. The selection must be seen in context, for Queensland were not then a competitor in the Sheffield Shield competition and were considered as a much inferior opponent to Victoria and South Australia. The matches between the northern states had for some years been used as trial matches for New South Wales' aspiring cricketers.

Another who was impressed by Whitty during 1907–08 was the South Australian captain Clem Hill, who faced the novice when the Australian team practised prior to the Test match in Sydney. South Australia conceded totals of 8-660, 699, 572 and 404 during 1907–08 and Hill was understandably determined to avoid a continuation of the drubbings in the future.

On his return to South Australia, Hill spoke to those who had influence in these matters and arrangements were made for Whitty to take up employment with G & R Wills and Co, agents and distributors. Whitty, a keen Australian Rules footballer in his younger days, had met Roy Hill and Len Chamberlain when the Norwood Football Club played in Sydney in 1907 and joined them in the East Torrens team in 1908–09.

Before his first season in South Australia had concluded, Whitty had won selection for the Australian team to tour England in 1909. He would remain one of Australia's leading bowlers until the First World War and contributed to many East Torrens triumphs during this period. It is not due to chance that Whitty's arrival coincided with the club's second 'A'-grade premiership as he claimed inexpensive wickets throughout the 1908–09 season.

Parade to Paradise: 101 Seasons of East Torrens Cricket and Cricketers 1897–98 to 2002–03, East Torrens CC, Peter Herbert & Geoff Sando (East Torrens Cricket Club, 2003)

Whitty was to play 14 Tests for Australia, taking 65 wickets with his swerving left-armers. In Sheffield Shield cricket, he claimed 154 wickets in 37 matches before finishing his career with lustre in Mt Gambier.

A FAMOUS HITTER

JC Davis remembers the great Percy McDonnell.

The famous hitter Percy McDonnell succumbed to consumption at Brisbane, on 24 September 1896 in his 36th year. The youngest of the trio of great hitters in the 1882 team, he is thus the first to pass away. HH Massie still wields the bat, with energy and success, in ordinary club engagements; [he] gets an occasional century – two in one week this year – but, of course, his form is not that of the early '80s. He still fields with a keenness that would put many an intercolonial aspirant of today to shame and he is also an enthusiastic disciple of the wheel. G [George] Bonnor is located at Orange, in the western districts of NSW.

The name of PS McDonnell as a dashing bat is imperishable, chiefly for the unique effort against the North of England, at Manchester, in 1888, when he made 84 out of 86 for the first wicket, on a very bad pitch. AC [Alick] Bannerman, who went to the wickets to open the innings with McDonnell, had made 4 not out, when the Australians, having made 101 runs for the loss of five wickets, won the match. Many other feats of fast and brilliant batting are associated with the name of Percy McDonnell, who will, for all time, be spoken of by followers of cricket as one of the brightest exponents of that hard-hitting school of Australians of whom JT Lyons alone remains.

Born at Kensington [London] on 13 November 1860, he came to Australia when but four years of age; his parents settling in Melbourne. His father, the Hon MA McDonnell, was at one time Attorney-General for Victoria. PS was educated at St Patrick's College, Melbourne. He was only 17 years and three months old when he first played for Victoria against New South Wales in 1878. The match took place in Sydney, and in it he failed to get a run – 0, b Evans and 0 not out. In his second match, however, he made top score for his colony, and thereafter success was his. He visited England with four Australian teams and captained that of 1888. He also represented Victoria, New South Wales, and Queensland in intercolonial matches. He played but once against South Australia, scoring four for Victoria.

The names of McDonnell and [Arthur] Shrewsbury are the only ones with three centuries standing opposite them in Test matches between England and Australia.

Australian Cricket Annual: A Complete Record of Australian Cricket in 1896–97, edited by JC Davis (George Robertson & Co, Melbourne, 1897)

THE 'ALBATROTT'

PJ Moss remembers the great Albert Trott,
the only man to hit a ball over the Lord's pavilion.

You think of [Albert] Trott as a bowler, and how would you describe him? You can hardly do it. Trott's fast one, particularly that fast yorker, was a holy terror. It might be followed by a slow off break or a leg break. He was unique in his variety and he never minded how much he was hit.

More than one youthful cricketer, too, has had to thank Trott for the full toss to leg to complete his first century in first-class cricket. The next ball might spread-eagle the stumps, but it was Trott's kindly spirit that prompted the easy one.

The 'Albatrott', as Rip [Roland Pretty Hill of the London *Evening News*], who loved to sketch Trott, always called him, was bitterly disappointed because the Australian authorities did not choose

The Albatrott: Albert Trott's formidable hitting was a feature of his play.
The Beldam Collection

him for their side to visit England in 1896. 'Very well,' he said, 'I will go on my own account,' and qualifying for Middlesex, he first played for the county in 1898.

His best year was in 1899. I remember one hot afternoon in July when Middlesex were batting, having a chat and a cooler with Trott and he told me he was going to break all cricket records that season by scoring 1000 runs and taking 200 wickets. It did not look possible, but he did it for the first time in the history of the game. In all, he made 1175 runs and took 289 wickets and the next year he repeated the feat by scoring 1337 runs and taking 211 wickets.

Few men could tell a good story better than Albert. In a match he was always the life and soul of the professionals' room and many a well-known cricketer will recall some quaint practical joke played on him by the humorous Australian.

How Do You Do?: Stockbroker-cricketer Jim Burke, flanked by Colin McDonald (obscured), Ken Mackay and Ron Archer meet Lord Alexander, the Marylebone Cricket Club president, April 1956.

Trott at slip was wonderful. I can see him now, legs wide apart, and perhaps the biggest pair of hands I ever saw, eager for the edged ball. If it came straight to him it was a catch certain, but he made many wonderful catches handling the ball on either side, when many fielders would have turned and looked towards third man and said, 'Yours.'

As a batsman Trott was impatient. He loved to use the long handle and for years had an ambition to break the clock face on the old racquet court and to hit a ball over the [Lord's] pavilion. I do not remember him accomplishing the former feat, but he did carry the pavilion and to this day holds the record. I forget the match, but I shall never forget the shout that went up from the crowd as the ball sailed over the building.

Trott's biggest score was his 164 for Middlesex against Yorkshire at Lord's in 1899. His greatest bowling feat was accomplished in 1907 in his benefit match, which was against Somerset – how like the man! He took four wickets with consecutive balls, and later on, in the same innings, he did the hat-trick. Trott also took all 10 wickets against Somerset in 1900 at Taunton.

Trott, at one time, wrote a weekly article for a periodical of which I was sporting editor, and his racy stories made it one of the best columns of the kind ever turned out by a professional cricketer.

Cricket: A Little Book for Lovers of the Game, edited by SJ Looker, story by PJ Moss (Simpkin, Marshall, Hamilton, Kent & Co, London, 1925)

OCCUPATIONS OF
AUSTRALIAN TEST CRICKETERS
From milkmen to posties, our cricketers have done it all.

G Alexander	abattoir owner
FE Allan	civil servant
TJE Andrews	stonemason
WW Armstrong	pavilion clerk, whisky industry employee
AC Bannerman	coach: NSW Cricket Association
C Bannerman	coach, umpire
W Bardsley	government clerk, company agent
SG Barnes	journalist, author, salesman
BA Barnett	pharmaceutical company representative
JE Barrett	doctor
JM Blackham	bank clerk
DD Blackie	electricity company worker, postal department employee
DG Bradman	journalist, commentator, author, stockbroker
HF Boyle	sports warehouse worker, collector
W Bruce	solicitor
JW Burke	stockbroker, commentator
W Carkeek	blacksmith
H Carter	undertaker, sports shop employee
PC Charlton	doctor
HL Collins	bookmaker
A Coningham	tobacconist, book salesman
G Coulthard	Melbourne Cricket Club groundstaff
J Darling	farmer, sports store employee, politician
H Donnan	Colonial Sugar Refinery worker
CJ Eady	solicitor
E Evans	inspector of horses
AG Fairfax	journalist
LE Favell	salesman, coaching co-ordinator, commentator
JJ Ferris	bank clerk
JHW Fingleton	journalist, author
L O'B Fleetwood-Smith	gardener

TW Garrett	solicitor
G Giffen	cricket coach, post office employee
WF Giffen	South Australian Gas Corporation employee
H Graham	coach: Dunedin High School
DW Gregory	accountant: Department of Treasury
EJ Gregory	curator: Sydney Cricket Ground
SE Gregory	post office employee, sports shop clerk, Water Board employee
CV Grimmett	painter, signwriter
RJ Hartigan	auctioneer
AEV Hartkopf	doctor
AL Hassett	sports shop proprietor
GR Hazlitt	schoolteacher
C Hill	writer, Racing Club steward
JC Hill	civil servant
JH Hodges	bootmaker
RM Hogg	milkman, greengrocer, after-dinner speaker, coach
T Horan Sr	journalist
HV Hordern	dentist
WP Howell	beekeeper
FA Iredale	journalist, author, secretary: NSW Cricket Association
H Ironmonger	gardener
A Jackson	sports shop employee
BN Jarman	sports shop proprietor
AH Jarvis	coachbuilder
TJ Jenner	sports shop proprietor, blinds salesman, coach, public speaker
CB Jennings	accountant, secretary: Adelaide Chamber of Commerce
IW Johnson	football and cricket commentator, television announcer, secretary: Melbourne Cricket Club
E Jones	customs officer
SP Jones	schoolmaster: Auckland Grammar School
T Kendall	newspaper employee, coach
AF Kippax	sports shop proprietor

F Laver	senior clerk: Law Department for the Colony of Victoria/ Laver Bros & Co [fruit and vegetable preserving business], writer, photographer
DK Lillee	coach, salesman, television advertising presenter
JJ Lyons	stockbroker
CG Macartney	clerk
AA Mailey	clothes presser, saddler's assistant, glassblower, Water Board employee, journalist, author, painter (oil), cartoonist, shopkeeper
HH Massie	banker
TJ Matthews	curator
SJ McCabe	sports shop employee
CL McCool	market gardener
CC McDonald	schoolteacher, councillor: City of Melbourne, tennis administrator
PS McDonnell	broker, banker
TR McKibbin	sheep-shearing machinery repairer
PG McShane	curator
RB Minnett	doctor
AR Morris	clerk: Prosecutions Office Sydney Town Hall, car salesman, tenpin bowling promoter, George Wimpey and Co [building and engineering company] employee, Wormalds [security firm] employee
S Morris	curator
H Moses	wine merchant
WH Moule	barrister, judge
WL Murdoch	lawyer
H Musgrove	manager: opera company
HC Nitschke	grazier, racehorse owner and breeder
MA Noble	dentist, manufacturing representative
OE Nothling	doctor
LP O'Brien	taxation clerk
WA Oldfield	tramways clerk, sports shop proprietor
WJ O'Reilly	schoolteacher, journalist, author
RL Park	doctor

CE Pellew	farmer, coach
RJ Pope	doctor
VS Ransford	shipping and custom agency work, secretary: Melbourne Cricket Club
JC Reedman	postman
AJ Richardson	coach
VY Richardson	commentator, salesman
RH Robinson	labourer, coach
J Ryder	boot factory employee
JV Saunders	railway clerk, coach
HJH Scott	doctor
FR Spofforth	bank clerk, tea company director (UK)
JM Taylor	dentist
GR Thoms	gynaecologist
JR Thomson	florist, coach
N Thomson	coach, umpire
GE Tribe	engineer, coach
AE Trott	umpire, Lord's groundstaff (UK)
GHS Trott	postman
H Trumble	bank clerk, secretary: Melbourne Cricket Club
JW Trumble	solicitor
VT Trumper	storeman, teacher, clerk, sports shop proprietor, shopkeeper, secretary: Australian Rugby Football League
CTB Turner	banker
FH Walters	hotelier
WJ Whitty	agent and distributor for G & R Wills & Co [ship-owning and merchant firm], grazier
WM Woodfull	schoolteacher, headmaster
SMJ Woods	secretary: Somerset County Cricket Club
J Worrall	journalist

The Cricket Statistician (Association of Cricket Statisticians & Historians, Nottingham, UK, Autumn 1990 & Spring 1991); research by Philip Thorn; extra research by Mark Browning, Stephen Gibbs, Alf James & Ian Woodward

Specialist: Dirk Nannes quit the first-class game to concentrate on more lucrative Twenty20 and limited-overs cricket.
Garry Sparke/Cricket Victoria

5
UP CLOSE AND PERSONAL

A LATE BLOOMER

On the eve of the 2010 Indian Premier League [IPL] tournament, Ken Piesse spoke with skier-turned-cricketer Dirk Nannes who just days earlier, in mid-season, had announced his retirement from Sheffield Shield cricket to concentrate on the shorter, more lucrative forms of the game.

KEN PIESSE: Few have had as tumultuous ride in the last 12 months as late-blooming paceman Dirk Nannes. From winning the Sheffield Shield to playing for two countries, the Netherlands and Australia, in the same calendar year, Nannes has been a headliner. He joins us today, in the middle of packing bags for more cricket, this time with the Delhi Daredevils in India. Welcome Dirk.
DIRK NANNES: Thanks for having me Ken. It's good to chat.

It's year three of the Indian Premier League. Dirk, you're heading into unsettled waters. Are the questions of security and wellbeing still an issue with you and your young family?
Of course. It has been a tricky ride for a lot of guys. The trouble has been, there are security plans in place, but no one has said, 'Yes we will abide by those security plans.' There has been a lot of conjecture. There are 10 days to go before the tournament. Hopefully it'll get signed off then.

What was the key element for you in deciding that you would go?

I have always felt pretty good in India. Security can be a bit of perception. If you feel safe, then you probably are safe, but the reality may be completely different. I wasn't comfortable in making that decision myself, but luckily the Australian Cricketers' Association, our union, did a lot of investigating and have been pushing to make it a lot safer for us. They haven't signed everything off but they believe over the next week as things keep progressing that everything will be fine.

Adam Gilchrist described IPL as like 40 days of the Olympic Games. It has been brilliantly marketed ...

It's like a circus when you go there, all the owners trying to outdo each other, flashing their money around. I can't wait to get to Kolkata and Eden Gardens where there will be 100,000 all screaming against us. It should be good fun. Indians are quite respectful of both teams. It makes for a fantastic experience and atmosphere. When I first was involved, I didn't expect it to run so well. But everything went like clockwork. It's fantastic to be involved.

The Indians worship their champions like [Sachin] Tendulkar, don't they ...

All they have to do is raise a finger and people go mental. You can't understand how crazy people go just for a cricketer. He's just like you or me and all he has done has made a few runs in his time and he's like God. It's a different world; but certainly very enjoyable.

Amidst all the hoopla, back home your Victorian teammates are limping towards this summer's Sheffield Shield final, their fourth in five years. Many of the boys feel had you made yourself available in recent weeks, the team would already have qualified and for a home final ...

The reason I have stopped playing first-class cricket is because my body can't handle it.

Even if I made myself available, there is no chance of my playing the last few games. I have a back issue at the moment. It's fine for playing shorter forms but tough for me to back up day after day, especially if I bowl say 17 or 18 overs.

There is a real brotherhood amongst the Victorian squad and right now the family is fracturing a little with yourself and Brad Hodge both retiring mid-season with an eye on the IPL ...

It's certainly not through any lack of desire to play. I sat back and made a decision based on my cricket going forward and it [Sheffield Shield] is just not for me. There is a good community and a great atmosphere with the Victorian guys. I have enjoyed my time and hopefully it goes on for a long time yet. It's tough from a feeling of letting your teammates down by not being able to play but it's not through lack of want in doing it. It's purely because my body is not able to do it.

Since coming into the squad there hasn't been a season where you haven't been injured.

The most I have played in an 11-match year is eight games of Shield cricket, last summer [2008–09]. The next best is five or six [in 2007–08]. People don't understand the rigours of what you are actually going through trying to bowl as fast and as flat out as you can every single ball. If you bowl 20 overs that's 120 balls and it's hard. It gets to you.

We're all still getting our heads around specialisation in cricket and I know many of your Bushranger teammates remain hurt at your nonavailability ... cutting to the chase, some consider you an out-and-out mercenary ... and I realise whatever monies you make for Victoria are likely to be multiplied three and four times in the IPL ...

There can be a case for people getting a bit upset but when they sit back and look at the facts I'm sure 99.9 per cent of them will say that I am doing the right thing. Sure I can slave away for years playing Shield cricket, but cricket is essentially my work, my business. You have to do what is best for business and what is best for family. Beating myself around playing Shield cricket and having only another two years on my career is certainly not going to be [as] smart business-wise as being available for the next five years of IPL cricket. It's a no-brainer. I'm comfortable that every single person in the squad understands my position. Some may disagree with it. [But] I'm incredibly comfortably with the decision I have made and haven't lost a wink of sleep [over it].

It has been a heady few months for you, especially playing your first Australian Twenty20 games including one here in your home town [of Melbourne] ...

It has been spectacular. I still shake my head a little and sit back when I think about representing my country. I've had a whirlwind career. To see [Shaun] Tait bowling 160 km/h on the first night at the MCG and here I am, the guy at the other end trying to supposedly match him and I could bowl 'only' at 153 km/h. It was exciting to be involved and I hope it can continue.

Few left-handers have bowled faster than you and Mitchell Johnson. And you remain one of the few, too, to open both the batting and the bowling for Victoria ...

Aren't I the only one? I actually bowled the first ball in that game [v Queensland in Brisbane in 2006–07] and took the first ball with the bat [in the second innings]. I was pretty good that day [making three], but I did bat until we were two or three down ...

Albeit as a nightwatchman!

Arr, come on ... I got stuck into the batters at stumps. But I was pretty restless that night. I was as nervous as I've ever been. I'd never had nerves like that as a bowler.

What are your most cherished moments, so far, in your career?

Definitely Victoria's Shield victory last summer [2008–09]. It was my first after playing in two losing finals. Also very special for me was my first Twenty20 final [against Western Australia in Perth, 2007–08], which we won, our third win in a row. I played well in that game [taking four for 23] which made it even more special. Outside that, winning the first game of the World Cup last year [2009] first up [for the Netherlands] at Lord's was unforgettable. It was the most remarkable game of cricket I have been involved in. And the other [in February] was playing for Australia in front of more than 60,000 here in Melbourne. That was really something.

It's a different career pathway, representing Australia via the Netherlands ...

It was a strange time. Australia named a squad of 30 for the World Cup. And I wasn't among them. Given that I was 33, rising 34, I thought 'that's it for me. My days of thinking that I could play for Australia are done.' I decided I'd go play for Holland [given his parentage] and play IPL and forge a career that way. I guess what I did for Holland at IPL level forced the selectors' hand and made them pick me. There was no domestic cricket back in Australia, nothing to change their minds.

Given that you didn't play at senior club level in Melbourne until you were 25 and for Victoria until you were 29, who were among the most responsible in your late development?

I never had a great deal of coaching. David Saker, Victoria's bowling coach, has been excellent since I have been in the system. But the most important person for me was Peter Roach, the ex-Victorian cricketer who now works at the ACA [Australian Cricketers' Association]. Without him I wouldn't actually be playing much cricket. At the time, 10 years ago, I was going away skiing [each Australian summer] and Peter said, 'If you hang around, you might play for Victoria.' I thought, 'No, he's kidding me. That possibly can't be.' But I started to think about it after that and I did hang around, and ended up getting a game for Victoria. Peter has been mentoring me now for a long time. I appreciate his friendship and support.

With the Shield final upcoming, there is no Brad Hodge, no yourself and one or two others are also missing. But I have no doubt that you will be supporting the Victorians 101 per cent, should that be possible ...

If you were in India, it would be 110 per cent [he said, breaking into Indian 'staccato']. That's what they say over there. I am rapt for the guys to get there. I hope they give a good account of themselves. If the past couple of seasons are an indication, they'll win the title. They certainly deserve it. They have a fantastic squad and more and more players are being recognised [for representative cricket]. We've been the best side for the last five years now. It would be fitting if we did win.

From Monday, you'll be a Delhi Daredevil. What happens after that?

That's going to be up to the selectors. Hopefully they'll pick me to go to the Twenty20 World Cup and that begins the day after the IPL final. So hopefully it'll be straight to the West Indies for me. Then I'm going to England to play at Notts. We have only a few weeks' rest before we're back here again [in Melbourne] preparing for the Champions League with Victoria again. There is little or no time to rest.

I can see lots of ice baths ahead Dirk ...

And lots of Voltaren as well!

Radio Sport 927, Ken Piesse (Melbourne, March 2010)
Victoria successfully defended its Sheffield Shield title, the Delhi Daredevils finished eighth in the 2010 IPL series and Nannes represented Australia in the Twenty20 World Cup in the West Indies.

BOBBY'S LIFELONG PASSION

Bobby Simpson's 50 years in cricket went like a flash.

Bobby Simpson says the passion for cricket in Australia never ceases to amaze him. In Brisbane for a three-day coaching camp before Christmas [2002], he was told many of the boys had come from the far north just for the opportunity to meet and work with him.

'I asked one young kid: "How long did it take you to get here?" . . . and he said two days!

'One of the kids had had his property flooded-in so his dad organised a helicopter for him to Townsville and he flew down from Townsville to Brisbane. When you see that sort of enthusiasm, it gives you a great incentive to want to help.'

Now 66, Simpson is at the World Cup as a commentator and the keenest of observers. The Holland team had wanted him to assist in a specialist coaching role leading into the tournament but he had to reluctantly decline as all his energies were spent in moving to a smaller house in Sydney and having things set up for wife, Meg, before his departure.

'I was in Jamaica in November for Jackie Hendriks and I work regularly in India too. There's enough work for me,' he says.

A former Test captain and national coach, Simpson says he has always enjoyed working with young people and in 1977–78 when recalled, aged 41, to captain Australia against Bishen Bedi's touring Indians, having had 10 years away from international cricket, he loved every moment.

'Coming back wasn't physically hard at all,' he says. 'To get back into the routine involved and get your focus back was the important thing. Quite frankly I was the youngest [at heart] in the side. There was no generation gap as some claimed there would be.'

He was remarkably successful, too, making centuries in Perth and Adelaide, the second ton, his 10th in Test cricket, coming at the age of 41 years and 360 days – the oldest ever in Australia.

He'd played at Sydney grade level regularly and says adapting to five days of Test cricket was never going to be a problem as he'd always revelled in the environment.

Originally from Tempe Intermediate High School, Simpson was equally adept at golf as he was at cricket in his teens and was off scratch at the age of 16 at Marrickville before he was chosen for NSW and immediately concentrated on cricket. 'Golf didn't have the profile as it does now,' he says, 'but I still love it.' He remains a single figures golfer, too, off nine at Concord Golf Club.

Asked if he remembers much of his debut Sheffield Shield match, in which he made 44 not out and 8 not out and took a wicket against Victoria at the Sydney Cricket Ground [in 1952–53], he says he hit a 6 from the bowling of Australian captain-to-be Ian Johnson – 'over cow corner' – and remembers

Bobby Simpson: Enjoys contests, not walk-overs.

the verbals from fellow spinner Jack Hill who considered him a lucky young so-and-so after finding the inside edge on a number of occasions. His teammates in that match were Ron Briggs, Sid Carroll, Jim Burke, Jimmy de Courcy, Ray Flockton, Alan Davidson, Alan Walker, Geoff Trueman, Tom Brooks and Reg Pearce. Ted Cotton was 12th man. He'd been selected at the eleventh hour after Sid Barnes declined an invitation to play.

Simpson retains a keen interest in state and international cricket and says the standard of bowlers, away from Australia, is not as strong as it was. 'I still enjoy the tight clashes. I like to see a struggle going on. I get bored if they're scoring at five an over in a Test match as that just shouldn't be possible. I don't care how good the team is. Test cricketers should be capable of keeping it down to at least four an over.'

He says young New South Welshmen Michael Clarke is technically very good and being a western suburbs boy [like Bobby] has had a head start on others! 'People haven't had a chance to really look at him and work him out. Technically though, he's the best of what is around [among Australia's next-tier players].'

The [2003] Sydney Test match, the one in which Steve Waugh made a memorable 100, was an ideal opportunity to catch up with old teammates, from ex-teammates like Davidson to the super veterans like Stan Sismey, who kept for Australia during the 'Victory' Tests of 1945. 'In many ways we played in the last age of innocence,' he said. 'It was a good era where the bond between players from all states was very much in evidence. You'd go up to Queensland for example and 'Slasher' [Ken Mackay] would have you out for a barbie or a game of tenpin bowling. That was the way it was done. It was a wonderful era.'

Cricket Week, Ken Piesse (International Publishing Group, Sydney, 5 March 2003) *Simpson made almost 5000 runs at an average of 46 in his 62 Tests for Australia. He also coached the Aussies to their first World Cup success, in India in 1987.*

THE RISE AND RISE OF 'BACCHUS' MARSH

Gary Stocks interviews Rodney Marsh on the eve of what became his final international season in 1983–84.

Many Australians still look back on World Series Cricket with a degree of scepticism, but had it not been for Kerry Packer and his 'circus' one of the game's finest would have retired prematurely. Record-breaking Test wicketkeeper Rod Marsh would have quit first-class cricket after the 1977 tour of England, had it not been for the emergence of World Series Cricket, or, more particularly, the chance to play the game professionally.

Homage for a Hero: Rodney Marsh leads the Australians from the Melbourne Cricket Ground after breaking Wally Grout's Australian record of 187 dismissals during the Centenary Test in March, 1977.

At that stage Marsh had a good career job with the Swan Brewery and he was looking to the future. He couldn't play cricket for a living, so he had to look to his job.

'It was a difficult decision to join World Series Cricket, just the same,' Marsh said. 'I was one of the last to sign and the only reason I did was that I knew I couldn't be satisfied playing at anything but the highest level. If I had continued to play established cricket I would have been in line for the captaincy because I was the only bloke left with any Test experience at all. I knew that all the other guys had signed and that I wouldn't be happy playing at a level lower than that which I was capable, so I joined up. What that meant was that I could play cricket longer than I had expected to. I enjoyed the job at the brewery and I think that had it not been for WSC, I would have retired after the 1977 tour of England. I have now seen another seven years of cricket and during that time some of the most significant changes made in the game have occurred. So I suppose I have been lucky in that regard. While WSC was in operation, Australia played 23 Test matches. Had I played in all of those matches I could now possibly have played in more Tests than any other man, but records are made to be broken anyway so it means nothing to me.'

Even by missing two seasons of Test cricket, Marsh still has a formidable record. He has represented his nation in 91 Tests and completed a record 334 dismissals (322 catches and 12 stumpings). He has also scored 3558 runs at an average of 26.75, including three Test centuries, the first ever made by an Australian wicketkeeper.

But Marsh is more than just a cricketer. He is a character. A great man, a loving husband and father, and cricket has made him one of the nation's most recognisable figures.

And the way he has started his 15th season, he will be a member of Australian Test teams for a while to come yet. 'One thing I have always said is that while my fitness is good, my form is good and the desire is still there, I will keep playing,' the athletic keeper says. 'I have no aims to play for one more year or five more years. As soon as any one of those things changes I will give the game away. And that change could come overnight. I am now 36 years of age.'

It's impossible to write about Marsh without referring to his magnificent understanding with another truly remarkable West Australian cricketer ... Dennis Keith Lillee. 'I don't know how many of Dennis' deliveries I have taken over the years,' says Marsh. 'But it all comes down to experience and if I don't know what he is doing by now, I am a slow learner. I guess I know him better than any other bowler. He will quite often come up to me and ask me if his action is right or whether he should have a rest ... because he knows I know. Obviously Dennis has to take most of the credit for our combination because he does most of the hard work. I think I have probably dropped less catches off Dennis than anyone else, but then again he gives me more opportunities. It's just something we have built up over the years and it has been terrific.'

If Marsh has one regret in his illustrious career it is the fact that he has not had as many opportunities to keep to slow bowling as he would have liked. 'Over the last two years we have used two spinners quite extensively and I kept to Bruce Yardley quite a bit,' he says. 'I love standing up to the spinners and that is probably the one regret I have. I think my keeping has improved to the spinners in the last couple of years, but it is obviously not as good as I would like. I would like it to be as good as Alan Knott, because he is the best wicketkeeper I have ever seen. I would love to say that I am nearly as good as Knott.'

Marsh's first recollection of wanting to play top-level cricket came as soon as he realised there was such a thing as an Australian team. That was about 1953, when he used to sit with his parents and listen to the radio broadcasts of Test matches from England. He was just six years old then, but immediately decided it was for him. The first major step towards achieving that goal came when he was chosen in the [Western Australian] state schoolboys side [or under-14s, as it was known then] in 1960 and 1961.

At the same time he had his first taste of interstate competition and his first trip away from home. In his initial year in the junior team he travelled to Sydney and in the second to Brisbane. Little did he know it then, but these trips would become a regular part of his life.

Marsh began his wicketkeeping career for Armadale, aged eight, for the club's under-16s. In those early days it was his brother Graham and father Ken, who also played for Armadale, who helped him along. Graham later hung up his bat and opted for a set of clubs to become one of the nation's leading golfers. After being chosen in the state schoolboys side, Rod went from Armadale to play under-16s for West Perth as a 12-year-old, so the potential to become a champion was there at an early age. 'I also played fourth grade that year,' he said. 'I used to play juniors in the morning and seniors in the afternoon. I'd catch a train from Armadale at about 7 am and get home at about 8 pm I used to spend hours and hours playing cricket in the backyard and on school holidays I played every day. When it was the wet season it was time to bring the footy out. As far as I was concerned it was cricket in the summer and footy in the winter.'

Young Marsh quickly rose through the ranks until eventually he played first-grade and Sheffield Shield cricket. His dream of representing Australia was just a matter of getting the right breaks at the right time. And when he was eventually chosen in 1968 it came 'as a hell of a shock'. He was a solid, ever-so-chunky wicketkeeper and a thumping middle-order batsman and in the 1970s he had the potential to be Australia's No. six batsman. 'I was just lucky I had raw talent as a batsman and made the most of it in those early days,' the modest champion says. 'Keeping was always the major part of my game though. As a batsman, opposition sides have approached me a lot differently in the last five or six years. They don't try to blast me out any more. They have become more professional and now they try to graft me out.'

Marsh had to come up to Test cricket the hard way. He made his state debut at a time when WA players believed they had to perform almost twice as well as players from the east to earn a Test berth. As one of the mightiest careers of all nears an end, he says that his next sport will be golf. He intends to play pennant golf and work his way down from his current six handicap to around the two or three mark, and undoubtedly he will achieve that goal because he is a professional in everything he does. He has been a credit to the game of cricket and when he plays golf, or any other sport for that matter, he will be a fine ambassador for that game.

Cricket West (WA's own cricket magazine, 1983–84 season), Gary Stocks (Sportscene, Leederville, WA, 1983)

'I KNEW IT WAS ALWAYS HOPELESS TO CHASE BRADMAN'

To the first 12 or 13 questions, Bill Ponsford answered either 'yes' or 'no'. The young reporter, me, was starting to panic, before the ever-so-modest champion relaxed and started to reminisce . . .

More than 50 years ago, Bill Ponsford, the champion who was colourblind, first graced the Test fields and earned the label of 'the Record-breaker'. Ponsford's insatiable appetite for runs became

Ponny: Characteristically in control, Bill Ponsford forces through cover point during his near-century at Old Trafford in 1930. George Duckworth is the wicketkeeper.

legendary in an age which produced some of Australian cricket's greatest batsmen: Don Bradman, Bill Woodfull, Stan McCabe and Alan Kippax.

The prolific opener, born and bred in Melbourne's inner suburbs, developed a single-mindedness to his batting, something akin to present-day Englishman Geoff Boycott. [Unlike Geoff, 'Ponny' married, his honeymoon coinciding with his Test debut in Sydney in 1924–25.]

Ponsford this month enters his 80th year and is almost the same sprightly, quick-thinking figure who plagued opposing attacks in the 1920s and early 1930s. He lives at Woodend, a Victorian farming hamlet several hours from the Big Smoke, with his second son Geoffrey and his grandchildren.

Since his wife, Vera, died several years ago, Ponsford admits to leading 'a lonely life'. He still goes to the Melbourne Cricket Ground for the big matches to see his mates and to reminisce. He enjoys his lawn bowls at the local bowling club, but fishing, one of his greatest joys, has been totally neglected for years.

All in a Day: On its way to a new world record of 1107 against New South Wales in Melbourne in late December, 1926, Victoria goes to stumps at 1-573. Four weeks later in Sydney, with its Test stars away, the Vics were to be bowled out for 35 in the return game!

Many said Ponsford would have been Australia's greatest batsman if Don Bradman hadn't come to the big city from the NSW southern highlands. Some tried to create a run-making feud between the two, but not Ponsford – 'I knew it was always hopeless to chase Bradman. He was ruthless,' he said.

'On a good wicket he was the best player I've seen. He had a wonderful eye, saw the ball early, quicker than most people ... that was the reason for his wonderful success. On a wicket that was doing a bit, however, the best bat was [England's] Jack Hobbs.'

Ponsford claimed Bradman 'had the second shot' at him. 'The records were there to break ... he did play some wonderful knocks especially in England.'

There's no jealousy here. Ponsford considers one of his greatest privileges was to share with The Don partnerships of 388 [at Leeds] and 451 [at the Oval] in the final two Tests of his career in 1934. Surprisingly, the two batted together only rarely.

Ponsford has generally shied away from publicity and interviews, despite five years as a full-time journalist with the Melbourne *Herald* after a retirement many considered premature, given that he'd made a double-century in his last Ashes Test match.

Perhaps his first-hand experiences with the press has coloured his judgment. As guest of the Queensland Cricket Association for its 50-year Test celebrations in Brisbane last summer [1978–79], Ponsford refused television and public appearances. 'I don't like publicity,' he says. 'I like keeping in the background. That's my nature ... I can't help it. I suppose I go out of my way to dodge it.'

For a man who didn't like the public eye, he did his best to stay foremost in the attentions of millions of fans around the world. Victorians and particularly those who run the Melbourne Cricket Club regard him as a favourite son [the club again naming its western stand in his honour at its re-opening in 2005].

In 13 years of first-class cricket, Ponsford amassed some amazing scores. For a man known as 'Puddin' he was ruthless against the faster bowlers and gave the slow bowlers no chance with feet which sparkled as much as his. A half sniff of anything over-pitched and he'd be in heaven, skipping yards up the wicket, eyes level, crashing it through mid-off or mid-on. Rarely did he hit anything in the air. Bert Ironmonger said he felt helpless bowling against Ponsford. He'd treat net practice like a Test match. He still remains the only Australian to twice score 400, his best [437 against Queensland in

1927–28] being a world-record score until Bradman broke it two years later.

Ponsford averaged 86 with Victoria, 48 with Australia and 65 in all first-class matches. Few have more formidable records and only Bradman rivalled his appetite for runs. He made 352 against NSW [in 1926–27], being bowled by the medium-paced Gordon Morgan after the ball hit his boot and trickled onto the stumps. Famously he said at the time: 'By cripes, I'm unlucky!'

Ponsford remembers the story – and the quote – with a smile. 'I *was* disgusted,' he said. 'I whacked my bat on my leg in annoyance. Alan Kippax [the NSW skipper] really got into me. "What are you going crook about. You've been in long enough."

'I was just starting to see them too! That was the match we broke our own world-record score [1059] by scoring 1107.' Two weeks later NSW dismissed Victoria [which was without its Test representatives including Ponsford and Woodfull] for just 35! Funny game, cricket …

Ponsford's most prolific season was in 1927–28 when he hit 1217 Shield runs at an average of 152.12 – a record run aggregate which still stands today for Victorian cricket [and wasn't surpassed until 1982–83 when Graham Yallop made 1418 runs in 12 matches. In 1927–28, Ponsford played six.]

Ponsford's scores were: 133, 437, 202, 38, 336, 6, 2 and 63. Not even Bradman could rival this sequence. Ponsford fondly remembers his run-making feats. 'You never know what's around the corner, so you make as many runs as you can. It's just as well to make every post a winner. My teammates didn't complain.' [Victoria won the Sheffield Shield.]

Ponsford's thirst for runs began at North Fitzroy state school in Alfred Crescent in 1910. 'I made quite a lot of runs at school. I made runs instead of doing my lessons! I was also playing for a Fitzroy metropolitan team in a batting competition. When my parents shifted to [Orrong Road] Elsternwick during the First World War, I joined St Kilda [under the residential rules of the time]. Fitzroy secretary Les Coady had recommended I go down. I was in knickerbockers and anyone with a pair of white trousers, short or long, got a game in those days. Ironically, my first game was against Fitzroy at the Junction Oval. I was just 14 and the other side included Ted McDonald, one of Australia's greatest fast bowlers, and WH [Bill] Cannon, a slow bowler who also played for Victoria. My contribution was 11 singles in an hour. It wasn't bad going. I couldn't hit the ball past the bowler then. I was pretty small.'

Ponsford's first state game was against Tasmania in Launceston in early 1922. Going in at No. 8, he made 162. Two years later he was in the Test side and in his first two matches made 110 and 128. A star was born.

'I remember my first Test particularly,' he said. 'Maurice Tate was playing. He was the hardest bowler I ever faced and had the ability to gain tremendous pace off the wicket. I was batting No. 3 and Tate beat me several times in the first over. Herbie Collins was captain and he came down and said: "I'll give you a chance to have a look at him."

'Collins took most of his bowling until I had a chance to settle down. It was a particularly exciting time. Vera and I had just been married. That [Sydney] Test was our honeymoon.'

Ponsford teamed with close mate Bill Woodfull in three double-century opening stands in 1926–27 with Victoria, including a partnership of 375 in the record score against New South Wales. Teammate Edgar Mayne nicknamed them 'Mutt and Jeff', but to this day Ponsford isn't sure who was who! The pair was soon to be opening for Australia, establishing themselves as one of the best new-ball batting combinations for many years. The two were to have a testimonial match at the MCG in November 1934 after the return of the Australian team from England. Woodfull made 111 and Ponsford 83 and 48 but rain on the Saturday interfered with the game. Ponsford remembers: 'We were unlucky as it was wet. In those days people worked on a Saturday morning. When it rained, people would go home instead of going to the cricket match. Our funds diminished somewhat.' Asked how much he had made, he quipped: 'I couldn't tell you that. The income tax people might be after me if I started making statements!' [The pair actually split 2084 pounds, more than 22,500 fans attending the Saturday play, despite the leaden skies.]

Ponsford's success wasn't confined only to first-class cricket. He helped St Kilda to four Victorian District cricket premierships in a row from 1923–24 to 1926–27 and having transferred to Melbourne played in another four consecutive premiership teams on his retirement from Test cricket from 1934–35 to 1937–38.

With war looming, he wanted to join the RAAF and went to a Collins Street optometrist for what he thought was purely a routine visit, only to be told he was colourblind. 'I couldn't tell between the greens and the reds,' he said. 'I started to guess at them. I told the specialist that I never worried about the colour of the cricket ball. The longer I batted the bigger it got!'

Bodyline and the infamous 1932–33 tour remains a bitter memory and hastened his retirement. He was struck six times in three Tests and missed the second Test with a broken finger. After a poor year against the South African speedsters 'Sandy' Bell and Neville Quinn the previous summer, the hostile leg theory of Harold Larwood and Bill Voce took its toll. Ponsford played courageously but without his usual machine-like consistency. His best effort was in the controversial Adelaide Test which saw wicketkeeper Bert Oldfield floored. Ponsford made 85 [equal top score in the match with Walter Hammond] after coming in at 3-34. He was bruised all over his body, adopting the tactics of turning his back on many of Larwood's bouncers and allowing himself to be hit rather than bunting a catch to one of the short-leg fieldsmen. Larwood was the quickest bowler he ever faced. 'I'm sorry you brought Bodyline up,' he said, after a long pause. 'It wasn't the game. Larwood and Voce were bowling to strict orders from Jardine and [Arthur] Carr [said to be "the Father" of Bodyline]. It wasn't very pleasant with six or seven chaps around your body. You had to take it, get smacked or get caught. Bradman tried to back-cut them; I used to take the knocks. There was no let-up. In addition to Larwood, they had Voce, [Gubby] Allen [who refused to bowl Bodyline] and [Bill] Bowes.

'There were certainly some fine fast bowlers around,' Ponsford said. 'Jack Gregory and Ted McDonald weren't that far behind Larwood [in pace]. There was very little in it. Gregory was all arms and legs. He'd bring it down from a big height. McDonald was the smoother bowler but just as fast. He had a beautiful rhythmic run-up. Others included Jack Scott, who first bowled leg theory to me and, of course, Eddie Gilbert. Scott was short and had to pitch the ball in short. I'll always remember my first meeting with Eddie. I'd never seen him bowl before. He had got Bradman for a blob the previous week. In those days we went up to Brisbane by train and we were chipped all the way up: 'Wait until Gilbert gets you.' Next morning, we won the toss and Woodfull and I went out to bat. They had the slips literally three-quarters of the way to the fence. We thought: 'Gee he must be fast.' But he didn't turn out to be that day. He had a pair of new boots which hurt him, so he took them off and bowled in bare feet! I can still remember those boots just lying at the back of the umpire until he had finished his over. Naturally he couldn't bowl as quickly. I made

96 that day. Leo O'Brien ran me out. That's another thing I won't forget.'

Ponsford was renowned for his extremely heavy bat. He called it 'Big Bertha'. Once, in Sydney, an umpire put a gauge to the bat and found it to be too wide – and thereby illegal. The constant striking of the ball in the 'middle' of the bat had flattened and squashed the willow.

After making 266 and 22 in the Oval Test of 1934, Ponsford retired, his last first-class match being the Woodfull–Ponsford testimonial. He was just 34.

He joined the Melbourne *Herald* for five years and then worked at the Melbourne Cricket Club as office manager until the late 1960s. He didn't lose his keen interest in the game and was a Victorian selector for several years in the 1950s.

Go-between: Leo O'Brien set up a rare interview with his mate Bill Ponsford on the eve of Ponny's 79th birthday.

'I'd go through the same life again,' he said. 'You meet some wonderful people, especially in England [he had three tours]. They couldn't do enough for you. [But] the money we'd make out of cricket wouldn't keep you in tram fares.'

When we met, Ponsford had just returned from his fifth trip to England where the old champion visited Sevenoaks, Kent and stood under the famous tree which still stands metres inside the boundary, where he used to field to Frank Woolley and Co. 'Whenever it was hot, everybody wanted to go down and field under the tree. It was very shady,' Ponsford said.

The Ponsford name re-emerged, briefly, after the war when Bill Jr, Ponsford's eldest son, made the firsts at Melbourne. Like his Dad, he was an opening bat, but was 'only a 20s and 30s man' according to his father. One of his grandsons, David, 16, attends Caulfield Grammar but shows more promise at basketball than cricket. David speaks glowingly of his grandfather ... it's little wonder. For his 'Pa' was indeed one of the best.

Cricketer, Ken Piesse (Melbourne, October 1979)

EDDIE'S PRIVATE WORLD

David Frith meets the renowned
Aboriginal fast bowler Eddie Gilbert.

The Queensland Aboriginal cricketer Eddie Gilbert, famed for his bursts of express bowling during the 1930s, had not been heard of for so long that I took it upon myself when in Brisbane to track him down. An old-timer in the suburb of Red Hill, where Eddie was last seen, thought he had died about five years before. We checked in the general store run by a cricket fan of some 60 summers: 'I'd just about swear to it. Old Eddie went right out of circulation and we never heard nothin' of him for ages. I reckon he must've died 10 years back at least. They had him in Goodna for a while.'

I drove out to the psychiatric hospital along the Ipswich Road in the hope of establishing the truth of the matter. The superintendent, barely concealing his surprise at my questions, led me through to the records office, where he produced Eddie Gilbert's hospital history card. 'Eddie was admitted on 8 December 1949. His age was shown as 37.' I thought he would have been slightly older than that; perhaps the paperwork was completed hastily that sad day.

'If you're writing about him,' the superintendent volunteered,

Eddie: Eddie Gilbert in Melbourne for a Sheffield Shield game in 1931–32. He was to be no-balled for throwing.

'I can tell you a few things. He took six wickets in his last game for Queensland. Terrific bowler – only ran half a dozen steps. He got the knack from boomerang throwing. Some reckoned he chucked, but I never thought so. It was just his funny wrist action. Wish we had somebody like him right now.'

Some weeks earlier Bill Hunt, the prewar New South Wales player, had been in no doubt about it: 'Eddie threw me out! By cripes, yeah! And later on I deliberately did the same to him. And do you know what he said?

I'll tell you. He put his arm around my shoulder and said: "Well bowled, Bill. That was a beauty!" So you see, the little fella couldn't tell a bowl from a chuck anyway! Nice chap, but.'

It was Hunt's contention that Stan McCabe, whose name will live for three classic Test innings, himself considered his best hand to have been a 229 not out against Queensland at Brisbane in 1931 after Eddie Gilbert had served Don Bradman with 'the luckiest duck I ever made'.

The lithe black man, that day bowling with horrifying hostility on an under-prepared pitch, had New South Wales in ribbons at 3-31, with Alan Kippax in hospital after a dreadful blow on the temple from a mis-hook off ['Pud'] Thurlow. At that point McCabe took command . . .

So long ago. Now here was I seeking to trace the conclusion of a life story. The superintendent glanced up from the history card. 'He was married at the time he came here. Nobody's visited him for ages. He used to be violent occasionally, but he's all right now – no trouble. But he's bottled right up within himself. You won't get him to talk. We've tried everything. He'll never change. Just as well perhaps. If he went out again he'd be back among the plonkies down at the Adelaide in no time.'

'You're telling me he's here . . . alive?'

He nodded. 'As I say, he's completely withdrawn. It's impossible to get through to him. He walks the grounds all day – he's content in his own private world. We've tried to interest him in some kind of recreation: his reflexes are still sharp. But when we put a cricket ball in his hand he just stared at it.'

It came as a shock. Eddie – still ticking after all! Even the locals had seemed so certain. I had fallen into line with them and quietly and briefly mourned their popular hero of long ago, the fast bowler to whom they had bellowed encouragement to 'give Jardine a taste of his own Bodyline medicine'.

In *That Barambah Mob*, David Forrest's amusing blend of fact and fantasy, Eddie has already been immortalised – on the top of Henry Stulpnagel's head was imprinted [in reverse] 'manufactured in Australia' . . . a living souvenir of a Gilbert bumper. 'When that ball hit the concrete,' he exclaimed, 'she'd smoke!' Mr Stulpnagel also knew why Eddie never became a Test cricketer: 'He made an ape of Bradman and he was black and he was born in Queensland and they didn't like the look of that whippy wrist of his.'

I made my reverent plea to the superintendent: 'I'd like to see Eddie.'

'It's no use. He won't talk.'

I pressed him. I had to see the historic cricketer.

He picked up the phone and asked the attendant at the appropriate wing to 'find Eddie'. We walked across the sunlit lawns, past slumbering patients, small talk lost in the insistent buzz of insects. The coolness in the outer block was a relief. Eddie was some time in coming. Sitting in the office, I scanned the grounds through the open window. Suddenly a male nurse was standing at the door and behind him, reluctant to advance, was a thin man in a maroon T-shirt and black shorts. His hair was white and close-cropped, his skin glistening ebony. It was unmistakably Gilbert.

He shuffled into the room, head to one side, eyes averted, impossible to meet. His physique would have been insignificant beside Tom Richardson, Keith Miller or Fred Trueman, yet he was not the midget legend has depicted. Five feet eight (173 cm), with long arms: the devastating catapult machine he must once have been was apparent.

'Shake hands, Eddie,' his attendant urged kindly.

The hand that had propelled the ball that had smashed so many stumps was raised slowly; it was limp as a dislodged bail. He was muttering huskily and incoherently, gently rocking his head side to side. 'Want a fag, Eddie?' the nurse asked softly. Eddie grunted, watched the cigarette begin to smoulder and puffed at it. His legs, typically of his race, were thin. He turned on them restlessly. He was an outdoor man; a room was a cage.

When I asked the nurse if Eddie could write his name for me, he coaxed him to pick up the ballpoint. At the end of an agonising minute Eddie backed away, leaving only a tortured 'E' on the paper. His squinting eyes, deep-set and bloodshot, flashed briefly across all of us.

I thought then of what Archie Jackson, Australia's batting genius, had written about Eddie Gilbert in 1933. 'The adulation he has received has not affected his mental equilibrium. Such a player is an ornament to the game; may he continue to prosper!'

Eddie walked off, still breathing his wheezy monotone; he wandered through the meal hall and the last I saw of him was as he drifted, a desolate individual, across the parched grass.

Australian Cricket, David Frith (Modern Magazines, Sydney, December 1972)

THE SQUIRE OF BURRANEER BAY

Few passports were as full, or as varied, as cartoonist-cricketer Arthur Mailey, one of the biggest names in Australian cricket spanning both world wars.

But for a supple wrist, dexterous fingers and an imagination, it's possible that Arthur Alfred Mailey today, at 60, would be an earnest worker with the NSW Water Board looking forward to approaching retirement. Instead he leads a life that office workers, gazing gloomily over their ledgers, dream about. So do a lot of other people, because Mailey spends most of his time following the sun and watching Test cricket in all parts of the world.

He has put some half a million sea and air miles behind him and has played cricket and watched cricket in at least 11 countries. He is on first-name terms with more dukes, lords and high-ranking politicians than most people even see photographs of. He has an international reputation as an after-dinner speaker, an English writer once classing him third to Sir James Barrie and Bernard Shaw in the art.

That's not a bad effort for a boy who left Waterloo [Sydney] Superior Public School rather prematurely at 13 to get five shillings a

All-rounder: With his painting, writing and illustrating, Arthur Mailey remained a high-profile personality in cricketing circles for years after his retirement from the game.

A 22-yarder: Bowling directly opposite the stumps, Arthur Mailey tosses one high into the air tempting Andy Sandham in the opening Ashes Test in Sydney, 1924–25. He dismissed Sandham twice for single digits on his way to seven wickets for the game, which lasted into a seventh day.

week from a 'scoundrel in Sussex Street' for pressing trousers and who lost the job when he sought an increase to seven and six.

It came about primarily because Mailey, spurred by the success of the famous English slow bowler [Bernard] Bosanquet, who fiddled out Australian batsmen with a ball that should have broken to the leg but broke back instead, spent hours in his backyard developing this new weapon. This led him finally to Test cricket as one of the greatest slow bowlers of all time. Then he found that big cricket, plus an ability to sketch with some humour and a later-developed ability to write amusingly about the game and its players, paid off in cash and travel opportunities.

Inspiration: The famed English googly bowler BJ 'Bosie' Bosanquet.

Mailey didn't play cricket at school ('they wouldn't give me a game') but started a few years later with Zetland juniors as a fast bowler, a phase that lasted only until Bosanquet fascinated him with his tricks of spin. In these years Mailey was in and out of several jobs very smartly. For a time he toiled in a saddler's shop at Redfern, making those neat lines on leather straps. Then he got a job at Zetland Glassworks and finally attained the position of glassblower – ink bottles were his specialty.

When out of work, he would

spend part of most days at the art gallery and would then stop off at the Domain where there was always plenty of opportunity for cricket practice. Word reached Redfern Cricket Club that there was a kid in the district who could bowl a wrong-un and Albert Vincent, now a state selector, invited him to play with the club. He was given a game in the thirds but wasn't game to try his wrong 'un for some time. 'I could bowl it all right but I had no idea where the ball might land,' he says. Mailey claims he first bowled the wrong 'un in a match against Callan Park Mental Asylum team. It's a good story, even if it mightn't be strictly accurate!

He was really keen at this time. After working in the glassworks throughout the day he would rush to Redfern Oval for cricket practice, back home to change and then into the JS Watkins school for art class. He was eased out of the class because of a penchant for caricaturing teachers and fellow pupils instead of working on the set subject.

Somewhere about 1909 or 1910 – Arthur is never good about dates – Mailey bowled against his idol Victor Trumper for the first time in a grade match at Redfern Oval. The somewhat nervous Mailey bowled three leg breaks, which Trumper knocked to the boundary and then produced his 'bosie' [wrong 'un]. It broke back viciously, leaving Trumper yards down the wicket. He was duly stumped. Trumper sought out Mailey after the innings, congratulated him and added, 'Don't take too much notice of the crowd, kid; they'll turn on you at times.' Mailey has something of a reverence for Trumper, both as a cricketer and a man. There are only two pictures of cricketers on show in the Mailey home – Trumper and Archie Jackson.

After another period out of work, Mailey got a labouring job with the Water Board about 1913 and almost immediately got his first big cricketing break. Victorian Edgar Mayne was organising a private team to play in Canada and the US and he invited Mailey, who at that time hadn't even played for NSW, to make the trip. He found Mailey 'messing around with a meter in Crown Street' and the newly appointed Water Board labourer didn't take long in accepting the invitation. Austin Diamond led that team, which included Warren Bardsley, Herbie Collins, Charles Macartney, Percy Arnott, Les Cody, Gordon Campbell, Sid Emery and Jack Crawford, the Englishman who had settled in Adelaide after coming here with an English team.

Mailey had a magnificent trip – the team even played a match in Bermuda – and collected a bonus of 100 pounds, which was real money to him in those days. He hadn't been back in Australia long before there was an invitation to tour New Zealand with a team organised by Frank Laver and which included Trumper, MA Noble and Vernon Ransford. Mailey, married at this time, moved to Drummoyne and played cricket with Balmain in the war years after being rejected by the army. Two [of his] brothers were killed in the war.

He later moved to Manly and from that club was selected in the 1921 Australian team to tour England, a famous combination led by the Falstaffian autocrat Warwick Armstrong. Before this, Mailey, who had started sketching almost before he could write, achieved some modest success with caricatures and cartoons in the *Arrow,* a sporting weekly. At this time he was too modest to put his name to them but signed them 'Bosey'. An English editor learned of his work and a flabbergasted Mailey found himself with a 1000-pound contract to draw for the *Graphic and Bystander* while on the tour.

Many will remember the delightful Mailey cartoons of that tour, in which he lampooned his own efforts and dealt amusingly with those of his teammates and opponents. A famous one was of little Charlie Macartney who, having made some 200 runs in rapid style, is shown saying, 'I think I'll take my heavy bat out after tea and have a go!'

The Water Board had no chance of getting Mailey back after this tour – not while money could be made in this pleasant fashion. He joined the Sydney *Sun* as sporting cartoonist and cricket writer, though he claims to have had a narrow escape later when someone got the idea of attaching him to the publishing department, 'probably because my cartoons were so bad'. He had a long association with the *Sun,* later transferred to the *Daily Telegraph* and then became a freelancer. He claims his most harrowing effort was during the last war when he was 'shanghaied' for general reporting. Mailey's story is that he had to cover a big funeral. 'I got the names of the mourners right – they all left cards at the church before ducking off to play golf – but I got that of the corpse wrong!' he says.

Mailey played Test cricket between 1921 and 1926, twice touring England. *Wisden* tells that he created a Test record by taking nine wickets in an innings against England on the Melbourne Cricket Ground in 1921. Mailey also drily adds that it was on the same ground that he was belted to the tune of four wickets for 362 by Victorian batsmen. It was after this latter performance that he made the crack that his bowling average would have been better 'but for a man in the trilby hat 20 rows back dropping Jack Ryder three times' [Ryder making 295 and Bill Ponsford 352 as part of a new world-record score of 1107].

But he was an outstanding bowler, a bowler with imagination who regarded each batsman opposing him as an enemy whose weaknesses were to be explored and exploited. He never minded conceding a few boundaries to a batsman if he could finally trick him out. In this he was the direct opposite to contemporary Clarrie Grimmett, every run off whom was like a shilling being taken from his pocket. Mailey's duels with English captain Johnny Douglas will always be remembered as one of the comic highlights of big cricket, though slow-footed Douglas, apparently mesmerised by spin, probably didn't view it in that light.

Mailey was also a wonderfully good slip fieldsman and, though a tailender who always ridiculed his batting, could make occasional valuable contributions. The record books will show you that he once made 46 not out in a Test against England [at Sydney, 1924–25] and also that he and Bert Oldfield once made 124 runs in 40 minutes in a match against an English county [Warwickshire at Birmingham, 1921]. He also once opened for Australia in a Test match and made the winning run.

Mailey left big cricket in 1927 when officials informed him they would not pick him again because of his newspaper articles in which he has always been likely to refer to officials or selectors as 'nitwits', his almost permanent term of disapproval. He found it rather ironic that his newspaper articles should have disqualified him because in 1919 the NSW Cricket Association got him to write an article in an attempt to publicise the game, then in the doldrums! He continued to play grade cricket until 1934 and had a brief moment of glory in the Ryder testimonial match at the MCG in 1930 when he clean bowled Bradman in the first innings [for 73] and caught and bowled him in the second [for 29]. Two years later, he took Don Bradman, then newly married, to America and Canada on a privately arranged tour that didn't please cricket officials, either. That team included Stan McCabe, Vic Richardson, 'Chuck' Fleetwood-Smith and Alan Kippax and the tour was a major success.

He left the team in the United States and went to England to travel to Australia with Douglas Jardine's MCC [Marylebone Cricket Club] tourists, the Bodyline team. Since then, with the exception of the war years, Mailey has rarely been far away from cricket grounds and cricketers. For instance, after touring England with the last New

Zealand team, he flew to South Africa and picked up the Australians touring that country, a double effort that kept him travelling for almost a year. The war years provided Mailey with a variety of interests. Some years earlier he had bought a mixed business at Burraneer Bay, near Caringbah, for his two elder boys, Walter and Norman. At this time Mailey achieved the reputation as a champion tomato grower. Some of these tomatoes were sold in the shop but a far greater number were carted away by Mailey's friends or distributed by the proud grower.

Walter and Norman Mailey enlisted early and Mailey found he had a shop on his hands. There was nothing else to do but run it. 'You've never seen such a friendly store,' he said. 'I used to get so far behind in the work that you'd often see the customers helping themselves while I scrubbed the floor. Or they'd be out the back picking the tomatoes which I hadn't got around to.' However, the system apparently worked satisfactorily as the family business is still flourishing and Mailey is now building a butcher's shop next to it to enable the residents of this superb section of Port Hacking to do all their shopping locally.

During the war, the late John Curtin, then prime minister, enlisted Mailey's services in a war-bond drive. The idea was for Mailey to address and organise sporting rallies. Mailey started with a bang – he made a strong attack on racing and racegoers for continuing their sport in peacetime fashion and on peacetime scale! A few days earlier a crowd of 74,000 had attended Randwick and Mailey claimed enough money had been gambled to have bought 50 planes. The attack brought a frenzied scream from the racing interests but, Mailey says, very little loan money into the booths that were erected on the courses for the purpose.

Since the war, Mailey's time has been divided between travelling with cricket teams all over the world and resting peacefully in a modest shack, built largely by himself, on a piece of land that runs down to the water at Burraneer Bay. It's an odd-shaped block that belongs to the Mailey family, the store standing on one comer of it. When domiciled at Burraneer Bay, as he is now, Mailey lives an extremely simple life with his two younger boys, Norman and Arthur. He is there most days, clad in old khaki pants, an exceedingly worn sports coat with a scarf tied round his neck. Even in this garb he looks most distinguished, almost like a diplomat, incognito, on holiday. He'll cook a chop or make a cup of tea for a visitor and serve it as naturally as he'd order a cocktail at the Savoy Hotel, London. A most unmethodical man, he is currently trying to tie himself down to a couple of hours writing each morning. He has three books on the skids but they've been in that state for a long time. Painting is his major hobby. He claims he is out of the amateur class because he has sold a painting. When in England last year he was invited to play in a picnic match at Norfolk – 'one of those champagne and strawberry affairs' – and during the day began to paint the peaceful scene. An enthusiast, 'who couldn't have known anything about painting', later approached Mailey and bought the effort for five pounds. Says the artist: 'He would have got it for two shillings if he had put that price on it.'

People, writer unknown (Sydney, 16 August 1950)
Mailey's classic autobiography Ten for 66 and All That, *a title inspired by his 10 wickets in an innings in a match at Cheltenham during the 1921 tour, was released in 1958. Mailey died four days short of his 81st birthday on New Year's Eve, 1967.*

GILLIGAN ON MAILEY

'If there is one mortal who bowls in his sleep, it is [Arthur] Mailey. He beats all records for his keenness on the game.' – Arthur Gilligan, England's 1924–25 touring captain

ALMOST INVINCIBLE
As left-arm chinaman bowlers go, George Tribe was as good as almost anyone and but for circumstance almost certainly would have been part of the most-celebrated touring party of all, Don Bradman's 1948 Australians to England.

My most successful match at the Melbourne Cricket Ground just happened to also be the last time I ever played for Victoria. I'd been dropped after the second Test [of 1946–47] and we were playing the MCC [Marylebone Cricket Club] in a return match. We were batting and were six down overnight. Dorothy and I had been married in 1946 and were living in Newport. I caught the train up to Flinders Street and for some reason this morning it stopped right on the viaduct at Banana Alley. We were there for ages and I was beginning to worry I'd

Debonair: George Tribe (front) with the 1946 Victorians.

be late to the ground so I jumped off the train, ran along the line to the street and got a taxi telling the driver that I was supposed to be at the ground and that I was in next! I get to the ground and a wicket fell while I was madly trying to change. Out I went and went bang, bang, bang, made 60 and then went out and got six wickets to help me get back in the Australian side for the final Test. Two of the wickets were back-to-back and Alec Bedser was on strike for the hat-trick ball. To the very first ball he knocked the cover off it through to our keeper Ernie Baker. Off I ran down the wicket with a big smile on my face only for the umpire Andy Barlow to give it not out.

'What happened, Andy?' I asked.

'You ran in front of me, George. I couldn't see!'

Alec was walking, too. I never was to take a hat-trick in first-class cricket and I was never to play another first-class game in Australia.

When I was picked to come back to Sydney [for the final Test], Don Bradman said to me: 'Don't forget to come back and try again in '48.'

I told him: 'I'll be back', but it just didn't work out.

Out of the blue I'd got a telegram from the Milnrow Cricket Club in the Central Lancashire League saying that I had been recommended by Alan Kippax. Syd Hird from NSW was supposed to be their professional. But he had prior commitments in South Africa. He and Kippax had played together at Balmain. I asked Dorothy what she thought and she said: 'Why don't we go with all expenses paid and then come back?' The problem was that she was pregnant and didn't want anyone to know, so off we went. I never realised that once I went to England I was ending my Test career. I did try and get us a passage back, but it was hard. Money was very tight. I was a bit shy and maybe a bit stupid. I could have probably called Bill Dowling [at the Victorian Cricket Association] for help.

We ended up staying the winter and six weeks before Dorothy was due to have the baby we were told she was having twins, the twins Janet and David being born in July 1947 in England. David was kept in hospital a month because there was gastroenteritis going through the hospital. Quite a few babies died. The photograph of the twins appeared on the front page of the Melbourne *Sun News-Pictorial*.

Sid Barnes was also over there at the time and he was going to fly back, but ran out of money and finished up going back by sea.

I'd had no correspondence from anyone in Australia asking what I was doing. I probably wasn't forceful enough. I was wintering in England and Australia was playing India back in Australia so it was difficult for me, but the circumstances of having the two babies changed everything. Blackouts and rationing was on and I had to go and seek baby milk as well. People were extremely good. I will never forget the help we got from people in England. When the 1948 boys came across, I caught up with them and explained to Don what had happened. Don said that the door was always open. He also said, 'Don't worry about me when the match is on because I am just as likely to walk straight past you.'

[Northants teammate and fellow Aussie] Jock Livingston was another one Bradman always made feel welcome. In fact all of the boys made us very welcome. I think if I had gone home I would have made the 1948 side. After all, I'd played three Test matches against England in 1946–47.

My parents hadn't seen the children and they were 14 months old, so Dorothy and I came home at the end of the season in 1948. I'd signed a two-year contract with Milnrow with an option for a third season during which they'd give me a benefit match. We landed in Melbourne on Prince Charles' birthday, 14 November, and I was determined to play. We were at Brunswick Street against Fitzroy and there would have been 3000 in. Neil Harvey made 50-odd and I finished with four for 70. I played through only until the Australia Day holiday round [31 January] as I didn't want to break my contract. One of my last games was down at the Lakeside Oval against South Melbourne and Lindsay Hassett made 150. I bowled 26 or 27 overs, virtually all of them to him. He wouldn't let me near the younger ones like Keith Kendall, who was just beginning then. I took three or four for 100-plus and bowled pretty well but I couldn't get anything past Lindsay. He just kept knocking them onto the off side. He was the best Australian player I ever bowled against. He had lovely touch and would just play the ball off the pitch ...

I only bowled once to Bradman ... in the nets in Brisbane on the morning of his comeback Test [in Brisbane in 1946]. I actually knocked him over first ball. I couldn't believe it. Keith Miller and I went out and Don, too, followed by all the photographers. Don walked into the nets and straightened the stumps up and first ball I bowled over they went. He just turned around, threw the ball back to me, straightened the stumps up and then looking at them, took his [new] guard right out on the off stump. He wanted to make certain if he missed it was going to hit his legs. He wasn't going to be bowled out again! I did learn something that day. If you are in trouble, always bat off stump.

I never did get to bowl at him again in the nets. Normally we would bowl only against our own [state] players. New South Wales bowlers wouldn't bowl to our blokes in the nets. It didn't matter that you were playing for Australia. If you were a Victorian we would only bowl against each other. Guys like Ray Lindwall [from NSW] wouldn't bowl to you. It just wasn't done.

Pavilion (Australian Cricket Society, Melbourne, 2010), George Tribe speaking with Ken Piesse in Rye, Victoria, 2002
George played three Tests for Australia, 13 games for Victoria and 233 games for Northants, taking more than 1100 first-class wickets. He died in April 2009, aged 88.

INTRODUCING THE 'TIGER'

Fresh from his 10 wickets in the second Bodyline Test of 1932–33,
Bill O'Reilly chats with WS 'Jumbo' Sharland.

William J 'Tiger' O'Reilly, of the Australian eleven, has nobody to thank for his bowling success against England in the second Test but himself and the able backing he received from other members of the team in the field. O'Reilly is a self-made bowler. He has not modelled himself on anybody's style. He has developed his own methods, adhered to his own grip when experts tried to make him change it and found experience the greatest teacher and practice the best way to improve.

A few years back he could not get a game in the Sydney Teachers' College XI. Now he is the greatest bowler in Australia – if not in the world – of his type.

A chat with the man who played the greatest part in Australia's

THE MATCH BETWEEN THE ALL-ENGLAND ELEVEN AND TWENTY-TWO OF THE NEW SOUTH WALES CRICKETERS, PLAYED IN THE DOMAIN AT SYDNEY.—SEE NEXT PAGE.

e All-England Eleven v Twenty-two of NSW, the Domain, Sydney, 1862. *Illustrated London News*

-rounder Sam Jones and opening bowler Fred 'the Demon' Spofforth were two of Australia's emost early players. Spofforth took 94 wickets in 18 matches.

Sailing on the steamer *Assam*, the Australians left from Sandridge on 16 March 1882 and arrived 48 days later in Plymouth on 3 May. Belatedly granted a Test match in August, they caused a stir by defeating the All-England team by seven runs at the Oval. From left: Sam Jones, Alick Bannerman, Fred Spofforth, George Bonnor, Jack Blackham, Billy Murdoch, Joey Palmer, George Giffen (the solitary South Australian), Harry Boyle, Tom Garrett, Hugh Massie, Percy McDonnell and Tom Horan ('Felix' of the *Australasian*). *Illustrated London News*

A view from the mounds of the 1894–95 'Heatwave' Test at the Adelaide Oval, won convincingly the Australians. Debutant Albert Trott made 110 runs without being dismissed and claimed eight second-innings wickets

n Kelly, Australia's long-term 'golden-age' cketkeeper after Jack Blackham, was the pride Port Melbourne. He shifted states to make an pression.

The arrival of the Australian eleven invariably triggered the publication of an array of publications, including this one, the lion v the kangaroo, from the makers of the *London Sportsman*. *John O'Sullivan Collection*

ilt in 1881, the famous Melbourne Cricket Club members' pavilion served members and their ale guests until 1926. This picture from the early 1900s shows the ground being prepared for the stral Wheel Race. *Melbourne Cricket Club*

Australia's 'WG' George Giffen was the outstanding colonial all-rounder in the 1880s and 1890s.

England's Ted Arnold, 1903.

Charlie Kelleway, 1926.

The great Prince Ranjitsinhji.

Australian glove Sammy Carter.

Long-time Australian captain Bill Woodfull built his game around a near impregnable defence.

The menu for a celebration dinner in honour of Arthur Gilligan and his men from Marylebone at Sydney's Hotel Wentworth, November 1924.

Vol. 5; No. 14. {Registered at General Post Office Melbourne, for transmission by post as a Newspaper.} Saturday, November 29, 1924 Price 3d.

FREE WITH THIS ISSUE

ART PHOTOGRAPH OF J. M. GREGORY

Published Weekly: For Australian Boys

ck 'Gelignite' Gregory, then at the height of his powers and popularity, is featured on the front ver of *Pals* newspaper, produced weekly in the 1920s 'for Australian boys'.

Debuting at 46, mature-age Ashes rookie Don Blackie had trouble remembering names, so called everyone 'Rock'.

Diminutive, popular and plucky Bert Oldfield was a fixture in Australian teams between the world wars.

Cricketing dentist, Queenslander Percy Hornibrook claimed seven wickets in the Ashes decider at the Oval in 1930 and would have been an even bigger force had he hailed from the more recognised cricketing cornerstone, Sydney. *The Referee*

This 1928–29 colour fixture notably makes no mention of the young Southern Highlander Don Bradman, who was to break into the Australian team from the first Test and score two centuries in his dazzling opening summer.

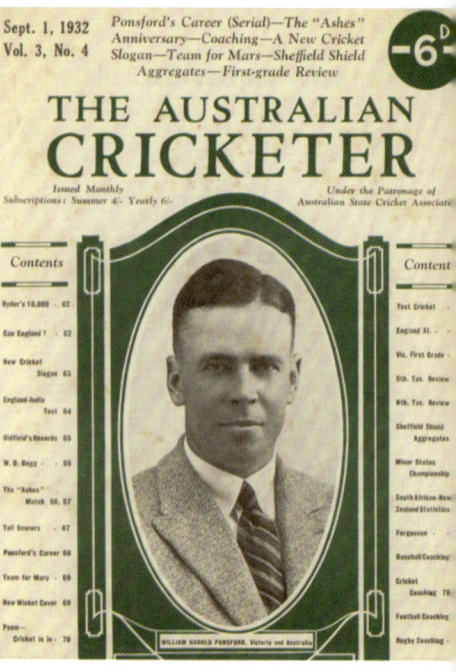

England's formidable fast bowler Harold Larwood, as pictured in 1932 on the front cover of the *Australian Cricketer*. He struck 34 batsmen in just 15 Anglo-Australian Tests, the majority in 1932–33.

Australian opening batsman Bill Ponsford was also featured on one of the *Australian Cricketer* covers in the lead-up to the 1932–33 Tests.

Vic Richardson returns some of the Larwood fury during the fourth Test match in Brisbane, 1932–33. He led off with 83, having replaced Jack Fingleton at the head of the order.

The Don with ex-Olympian EW 'Slip' Carr, the Australian Army's physical training superintendent, on arrival in Melbourne for what was to be an abbreviated stint in the Army in 1940–41.

stralia's favourite sporting son Don Bradman, depicted by renowned cartoonist Jim Russell his *Jim Russell Cricket Book*, released in 38.

blic idol No. 1, the Don as featured on the nt cover of *Today* magazine in 1934.

Best of enemies: Don Bradman with writer-author-cricketer and one of his harshest critics, Jack Fingleton.

The Field, and Land and Water, January 2, 1937

JANUARY 2, 1937

THE FIELD

THE COUNTRY NEWSPAPER

PRICE
ONE SHILLIING

30

UNDER THE AUSTRALIAN SUN

Verity, shown calling on the high heavens, nearly gets Fingleton caught by Leyland, who is seen gathering the ball on the bounce, during the first Test match at Brisbane. Hammond, too, has moved across in an attempt to make a catch, while R. W. V. Robins is seen behind "in the country." The England team's fielding in both Test matches has been in marked contrast to that of the earlier State matches, and if the high standard is maintained in the present Test match it is possible that we may have won the "rubber" by next Tuesday. In the Brisbane Test twelve Australians were caught and seven clean bowled. At Sydney, eight were caught and ten bowled (three l.b.w.). These figures p   to the fact that the English fieldsmen are backing up their bowlers in admirable fashion, so now that the team is well acclimatised they   l probably show better form in the State matches, and give Australian spectators a chance of seeing English cricket at its best

Jack Fingleton is all but caught by an advancing Maurice Leyland from the bowling of Hedley Verity during his fighting century in the New Year Test in Melbourne, 1936–37. More than 350,00 witnessed the match, a new world record. *'The Field', The Country Newspaper, 2 January 1937*

The 1936–37 MCC team was at its ambassadorial best, helping to erase the bitter memories of the Bodyline summer four years earlier. They won the first two rain-affected Tests before losing the last three. Back row, left to right: Arthur Fagg, Les Ames, Laurie Fishlock, Charles Barnett, Stan Worthington and George Duckworth. Centre: Captain R Howard (manager), Jack Sims, Hedley Verity, Bill Voce, Ken Farnes, Bill Copson and Joe Hardstaff (Sr). Seated: Wally Hammond, Walter Robins, 'Gubby' Allen (captain), Bob Wyatt and Maurice Leyland. *The Western Mail (Perth), December 1936*

The ultra-competitive wrist spinner Bill 'Tiger' O'Reilly was one of many cricket champions to be featured on blotters from the Vacuum Oil Company in 1939.

W. J. O'Reilly, the Sydney medium-pace bowler, who bowled magnificently in the second Test match.

"The Australasia"

Large-sized colour prints were a feature of the *Australasian* in the '30s. This one features Bill O'Reilly.

The Test WRITING PAD 1938

England—Australia.

writing pad from 1938 includes pictures of each of the Australian Ashes tourists to England.

Ashes heroes Keith Miller (left), Len Hutton and Ray Lindwall were three of the most popular players to have their images on Argus badges in the early '50s.

Melbourne children listening to a synthetic broadcast 'from London' in 1938.

Coles card portraits of Australia's first Test team, 1950–51; from left: Don Tallon, Ray Lindwall, Sam Loxton, Lindsay Hassett, Keith Miller, Neil Harvey, Arthur Morris, Jack Moroney, Ken Archer (12th man), Jack Iverson, Bill Johnston and Ian Johnson. On debut, shooting star Iverson didn't get a bowl in the first innings and took four for 43 in the second.

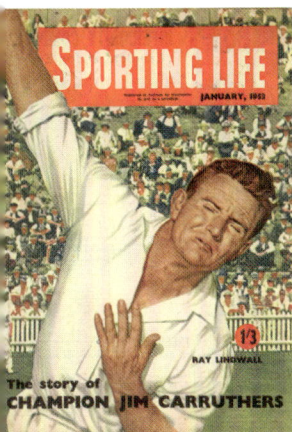

All-sportsman Ray Lindwall, cover hero of *Sporting Life* for January 1953.

Child prodigy Neil 'Ninna' Harvey was Australia's outstanding batsman of the 1950s. *Sports Novels (Sydney)*

A rare cricket front page from the *Bulletin* following the tragic death of David Hookes outside a Melbourne hotel in January 2004.

Justin Langer wanted to get physical with the selectors after being told he'd been dropped from Australia's opening Ashes at Edgbaston in 2001.
Nick Atley

A. MORRIS   J. MORONEY   K. ARCHER   J. IVERSON   W. JOHNSTON   I. JOHNSON

Champions of the world – centurion Ricky Ponting after Australia's World Cup final triumph against India at Johannesburg in 2003. Ponting made a brilliant 140 not out from just 121 balls in the final.

memorable win convinces me that O'Reilly is a cricketer above the average intellect. He is imaginative and a fighter. He says a thing and means it. A pleasant fellow and a fine stamp of Australian. Those are the chief impressions of O'Reilly.

He was pleased with his great performance and asked the *Globe* to thank the public for the wonderful ovation they accorded him. Of special delight were the messages of congratulation he received from his own people and folk at the place of his birth, Whitecliffs, on the north coast of New South Wales.

'What pleased me more than anything was the fact that I got the wickets against the Englishmen,' said O'Reilly. 'My success against the South Africans gratified me immensely, but I never got the same thrill out of it as I did when taking wickets against such fine cricketers as the Englishmen.'

While talking modestly about his own performances, he did not forget his fellow bowlers and fieldsmen. '[Tim] Wall deserves great praise for his sustained pace and persistency. [Bert] Ironmonger bowled like a hero when we needed him. A great word of praise is due to Clarrie Grimmett, who was so unlucky in the first innings. The fact that Clarrie morally had [Herbert] Sutcliffe's wicket twice on Saturday helped to shatter the English morale for the game, because Sutcliffe is such a certain batsman.'

O'Reilly's first association with cricket was at St Patrick's College, Goulburn. 'I was keen on the game, but not what you would call a howling success,' stated O'Reilly.

'In those days I bowled the leg break and tried to vary my pace as much as possible. I have never altered it, though I never had much of a length at school. I had no Test match aspirations then and I don't think even my schoolmates thought I was destined to become a success,' he added.

Leaving school, O'Reilly decided to study for the teaching profession and he went on to the Teachers' College. Keen on cricket, he played the game at every opportunity, but evidently did not make much of an impression at the college for he could not gain a place in their team. But junior match play in Moore Park, one of Sydney's great homes of the aspiring young player, found him repeatedly figuring in the role of wicket-wrecker. His command of length and spin of the ball had most junior batsmen in trouble.

He broke into grade cricket with North Sydney in 1926–27. It was at that time he was strongly advised to change his grip. He would not.

He has always worked up his spin in the same manner. That continual swinging of the arms as he runs up to the wicket for delivery all helps him. It is his natural style. Take that away from him and his bowling would be ruined.

O'Reilly is no stranger to 'hat-tricks'. He took four in junior cricket and one in grade cricket. Some day he may emulate the feats of FR Spofforth, Hughie Trumble and Jimmy Matthews and take a hat-trick in the Tests.

O'Reilly does not consider No. 13 unlucky. The North Sydneyite takes 13 strides of 13 yards to the wicket when delivering the ball. In Sydney there has been considerable discussion about the 13 strides, but it has not worried O'Reilly. Those 13 strides spelled disaster for the Englishmen.

O'Reilly's six seasons of grade cricket and three of first-class cricket have taught him that a man cannot neglect his practice. 'I practise two nights a week in Sydney, but in midsummer I don't bowl overmuch, because I have so much to do in the actual matches,' he said. He teaches at the Kogarah High School on the Illawarra [train] line. Naturally his friends are elated with his success and at the high school he will be accorded a great reception when he resumes duty.

O'Reilly is a great believer in targeting the stumps as much as possible. 'A bowler has to bowl for his field,' he said, 'and vary his deliveries considerably, but a good number of them should be aimed at the stumps,' he declared. 'I believe in making the batsman fight for every run. Loose bowling is no good in any grade of cricket. You must keep a length. I have found the leg break my best ball, but without variation in spin and length you would be nowhere. Variation is the secret of any bowler's success. Without it you can't hope to succeed in big company. I still have much to learn and experience to gain in big company and cannot expect always to be so successful as in this match,' he stated.

O'Reilly pays particular attention to the methods of each batsman. A certain ball will trick one batsman but not another, so he exploits various deliveries to obtain results.

O'Reilly smiled when I asked him if he would like to tender any special advice to young bowlers. 'To succeed means hard work, always,' he said. 'You must make sacrifices and look after yourself. Practise, practise, practise until you get length and spin combined and then learn everything you can by concentration.'

O'Reilly, who is 27, stands 6 ft 3 in (191 cm) and weighs 13 st 5 lb (85 kg). Asked if he ever felt tired after his bowling, he replied in the negative. He has not experienced any bodily weariness or strain, so that is a happy sign for Australia.

The Sporting Globe, WS 'Jumbo' Sharland (Melbourne, 7 January 1933)

THE KING OF OL' CARRINGBUSH

Few cricketers were as popular as Jack Ryder, the 'king' of Collingwood who in 1928–29 became Australia's new Test captain.

It has fallen to the lot of only five players – RE Foster and WR Hammond of England and WL Murdoch, SE Gregory and J Ryder of Australia, to score a double-century in a Test match, so it might easily be anticipated that Australia's present Test captain, Jack Ryder, would regard his double-century day at Adelaide in the 1924–25 season as his greatest day in cricket.

Ryder has played many fine innings and some of the best have been during this season's series between England and Australia, but the one that meant more to him than any other was that double-century effort in the exciting third Test at Adelaide four years ago. 'What made it all the more welcome to me,' says the tall Victorian, 'was that I had not played in the first and second Tests of that season.'

After his 201 and his second-innings score of 88, each innings being top score of the side, Ryder was in the team to stay and he played also in the fourth and fifth Tests of that season.

In his big innings he featured his driving, which has always been his greatest asset. That he missed scoring a century in the second innings by only 12 runs shows that he was then at the top of his form. 'Another day that will always stand out in my memory,' he told me, 'was the opening day of the first Test at Brisbane this season, for that was the first time I captained Australia in a Test match and naturally, I was very proud about that.'

Many bowlers have suffered at the hands of the hard-hitting Ryder. From the point of view of run-getting and the time in which his runs have been made, his greatest effort was that for Victoria against New South Wales at Melbourne in 1926. That was the occasion when Victoria ran up a total of 1107 and while Ryder was at the wickets, he rattled together 295 out of 449 runs – and he made his score in just over four hours! One who witnessed that innings told me that for sustained hitting it was the greatest innings he had ever seen. Ryder plied the long handle in amazing fashion. He hit six 6s and thirty-three 4s. It was the highest score Ryder ever made in first-class cricket and one that will never be forgotten, especially by the unfortunate New South Wales bowlers.

In 1921–22, Ryder made 242 against South Australia at Melbourne, including 96 runs in the final session on the opening day. His first century in big cricket was for Victoria against Western Australia in 1912–13.

The Australian captain, than whom there is no more popular cricketer in Victoria, tripped to England in 1921 and in 1926. His first Test was at Sydney in the 1920–21 season. With [Warwick] Armstrong's team in 1921 he scored 1032 runs at an average of 38. On the 1926 tour, when he played in four Tests, he scored 1193 runs at 36.

Ryder made four centuries on his last visit to the Old Country and he regards his 100 against Kent at Canterbury as the best century he made in England. He gave English spectators a taste of his spectacular hitting ability, scoring his runs at the rate of 163 in 100 minutes. He also played a very fine knock against the South of England at Bristol, on that occasion figuring in a fighting partnership with Tommy Andrews. The fixture was interrupted by rain, but before that Australia was 60 runs behind with six wickets down. Ryder and Andrews gave a brilliant display of forceful cricket, putting on 177 runs in two hours. Ryder scored 108 not out and Andrews 74 not out, Australia taking the lead.

This season [1928–29] the tall all-rounder has enjoyed a good batting series, his best efforts being innings of a fighting type. His second Test century was his 112 at Melbourne in the third Test, when Alan Kippax was his partner in a great stand.

Everybody knows that Ryder is the idol of the suburb of Collingwood. There is nothing remarkable in that, for Ryder has been associated with Collingwood for 23 years and for every year in which it has been engaged in senior [Melbourne district] cricket. For most of the time he has been captain. His popularity is remarkable – but not remarkable, perhaps, when one learns that this sturdy, clean-living Australian is regarded as one of the best club men in Australia. He has done wonderful things for the men from Carringbush, not only as a player, but also in the matter of assisting and encouraging young performers.

Ryder has proved himself a grand sportsman and when he enjoys a big success, everybody who lives or has lived in Collingwood is delighted. To illustrate the esteem in which he is held, it may be mentioned that a suggestion has been made that the new stand at Collingwood football and cricket ground [Victoria Park] should be named the Ryder Stand.

The Australasian, 'Wayfarer' (Sydney, March 1929)
The new stand at Victoria Park was named after Ryder, in 1929.

'I FELL IN LOVE WITH HIM AT ONCE'

CA Redgrave chats with Victor Trumper,
then at the peak of his powers.

In view of the approaching visit of the Australian eleven to New Zealand, I thought the readers of *The Young Man's Magazine* would appreciate a chat with one of their representative men. I therefore took advantage of my stay in Sydney to call upon Victor Trumper and solicit an interview on behalf of New Zealand's young men.

Trumper is without doubt the most popular cricketer in Australia today and is generally recognised to be the best batsman in the world. Twenty-six years of age, well proportioned, standing over 6 feet in his socks, with square shoulders, well-made limbs and a bright open face, he strikes one as being a fine type of the young colonial. I fell in love with him at once. The most striking thing about him, however, is his manner. Cordial, frank and absolutely unaffected, he charms you and commands your friendship at once. He put me at my ease straight away with his warm handshake and entire absence of side. 'Certainly,' he said, 'take a seat and I will only be too glad to give you any particulars in my power.'

'How old was I when I first played cricket? Well, that's more than I can remember. I know that it was when I was 13 playing for the second Carltons under the captaincy of Charles Bannerman [Test

Our Vic: The pride of the nation, Australia's ultimate golden-age hero, Victor Trumper.

cricket's first centurion] that I first attracted any notice and then it was as a bowler.'

In January 1895, being then 16, he was first picked for the NSW team and has represented his colony ever since.

Asked as to his best performance, Mr Trumper said his highest score was 300 not out, made against Sussex during the '99 tour.

Although holding a higher individual average than any other batsman in Australia, he had been passed over by the selectors and it was only after a great remonstrance by his supporters that he was finally included as an 'extra man' on a different footing from the others as to sharing the [tour] profits. After the Sussex game, however, the team met and decided to extend to him the full [financial] rights of original membership [the players rather than cricket administrators controlling the finances in those days].

'And what would you say has been your proudest moment of your cricketing career?' I enquired. 'Oh, I don't know,' he replied evasively. 'I know I have felt jolly wild very often when I have gone out for a duck when I should have made a score, but I don't remember ever feeling too pleased with myself.'

'Do you ever suffer from nervousness, Mr Trumper?' I asked.

'Yes,' he said, 'when starting an innings. It is a bit of an ordeal meeting the first ball or two and knowing that there are 20,000 pairs of eyes watching you. I never feel safe for the first half-dozen strokes and have often lost my wicket to a ball that I could have confidently got a 4er off when properly set. After the first couple of overs, however, one forgets all about stage fright and forgets almost that there is an audience. His only thought then is to make a score.

'As to training? It's largely a matter of practice, although of course there are some boys who never could become first-class cricketers – it's like schooling – whereas one fellow is always top for mathematics he may never be able to get placed for Latin or French. However, given a liking for cricket, consistent practice is what is needed to bring you to the fore and keep you there; practise if possible with better players than yourself. Dieting is quite unnecessary. As long as a man keeps straight he need not worry as to what he should or should not eat. Neither will smoking hurt, providing it is in moderation. Drinking, however, is sure to have a bad effect on a man's play. It is very unsteadying and the would-be "Rep" should give it a wide berth.'

Mr Trumper is both a nonsmoker and a teetotaler. Asked about the behaviour of the members of the team on tour, he replied that they are usually very steady. 'You see,' he remarked, 'the trip [to England] lasts from May to September, during the whole of which time we never miss a day (Sundays excepted) and have to travel from place to place at night. If any member shows an inclination to misbehave himself, the others object strongly as it not only means more work for them but may prejudice the chances of the whole team. Unlike your football teams we only have two banquets during the whole course of the tour. So our fellows are not similarly tempted.' The NSW XI boasts three abstainers.

Mr Trumper, in partnership with ['Sep'] Carter the NSW wicket-keeper, keeps a cricket and tennis outfitting shop in one of Sydney's busiest streets and our talk was subjected to many interruptions. It was Saturday morning and he continually had to break off our conversation to sell a bat or a ball. 'One of *Wisden*'s best, I can guarantee it,' he told one buyer.

'And why is it, Mr Trumper' I asked, 'that we cannot produce any really first-class cricketers in New Zealand? Is it the climate?'

'Perhaps I'd better wait until [we see how] they shape [up] before I answer that, or I may get myself into hot water,' he said. 'I will reply when I meet you in Wellington.'

After thanking him for his interview, I took my leave. We shook hands and as I looked into those clear blue eyes and heard his cheery voice bidding me farewell I felt that I had been conversing with a true man, one whom success had not spoiled and of whom Australia may well be proud.

The Young Man's Magazine, CA Redgrave (New Zealand, 1 February 1905)
The 1905 Australians played six matches in NZ on their way to England. Two were against combined NZ, the matches not being given Test status. The first at Christchurch was drawn and Australia won the second at Wellington by an innings, Trumper making 84 in the first match and 172 in the second.

OUR FIRST TEST TEAM BY RGtTTUS

Australia's Test team which met the Englishmen at Trent Bridge Oval, Nottingham, in the first Test of 1948 series.

6
TESTS OF NERVES

'I wanted to fight the decision, fight the moment, fight the world, fight the journalists and fight the selectors ...' – JUSTIN LANGER

THE GRANDFATHER OF ALL ASHES FINISHES

Few could thrive on taunts like Shane Warne, and there were many in 2005.

Warne-bashing was high on the agenda of English cricket fans throughout the Ashes summer, especially at Edgbaston where many in the crowd wore fancy dress and delivered stinging salvos and taunts at a rapidity matched only by their intake of pints.

After his most-public split from his wife and young family, Shane Warne was a prime target for a vociferous, out-of-control Barmy Army.

From apparently harmless ditties like 'You All Live in a Convict Colony' (sung to the tune of 'Yellow Submarine'), the Army slipped into the gutter with their particularly tasteless 'Where's your Missus Gone? – Far, Far, Away' (to 'Chirpy Chirpy Cheep Cheep').

No matter where you stand when it comes to Warne's *joie de vie*, he didn't deserve the abuse. And that's what it was. Maybe it was meant to be funny, but the delivery was venomous, uncouth and befitted a pack of hooligans, leaving a giant, most regrettable black mark on the greatest Ashes summer of all.

With Australia all but out of the game, Warne launched a stunning counterattack of his own, hitting the English where it counted most: on the scoreboard.

In taking six for 46 from 23.1 overs in England's second innings,

Go-to Man: Shane Warne during the 1993 Ashes series, his first in England.
Cricket Victoria

Warne stood taller than ever before, in his own unsinkable zone, thriving on the taunts. Far from being demoralised by the rowdies, he strutted and cavorted, spinning and ripping and enjoying the theatre, as bizarre as it was.

As he ripped through the English middle order one by one, he'd eye the crowd in the Hollies Stand leg and doff his hat. Even under the most intense personal fire, he was still cricket's magnetic man, the showman supreme.

I thought it Warne's finest-ever moment, especially given his roller-coasting emotions and Australia's dire predicament entering the weekend. It was remarkable how he could separate a world falling apart off the field and be so dominant on it.

As a Coodabeen Champion, he'd wanted to take the wicket which turned the game. At Edgbaston he took 10, and backed up with a gallant cameo the following morning which all but led Australia home from nowhere in the closest Ashes Test of them all.

Few have imposed their will on a game or a series as successfully as Warne did throughout 2005.

While he had some mates – most notably Glenn McGrath at Lord's, Brett Lee at Edgbaston and Ricky Ponting at Old Trafford – no one since Steve Waugh in the Windies in '95 had been so crucial to Australia's bottom line.

Single-handedly, he lifted Australia out of the mire, forcing the grandfather of all Ashes finishes at Edgbaston, stunning England at Trent Bridge and giving Test cricket a rare run in even the tabloids.

With McGrath struggling to stand up, Warne was Australia's 'go-to' man and while the English occasionally got to him, their success was only temporary.

In matching his fabulous figures from his dreamy debut tour in 1993, Warne substituted science for spin and in a series of stirring solos turned back the clock with his batting to be Australia's outstanding player.

It was an extraordinary effort from one of the game's all-time greats and ensured he would remain ahead of his Sri Lankan mate Muthiah Muralidaran in the Test wickets race for at least a few more months.

Australian Cricket Tourguide, Ken Piesse (Universal Magazines, Sydney, 2006)

HEROES ALL

The top 11 Ashes batsmen of them all, position by position.

So just who would you want to bat for your life? And in what slot? You have the choice of the best players from any era, the only proviso being that only Ashes battles count.

Other than Don Bradman at No. 3 and Steve Waugh somewhere in the middle order, few picked themselves.

The early champions like Victor Trumper were disadvantaged, given the uncovered wickets of their era.

It was tough, too, to truly rate the overall contribution of the modern-day heroes, like Matthew Hayden for example when his runs were being scored on shortened boundaries with bats as wide as wood splitters and seemingly as lethal.

Ricky Ponting, Australia's modern-day Bradman, may be averaging more than 100 for the Test calendar year, but overall his average from No. 3 is not quite 60, well below The Don's 93.

The most prolific Ashes openers are:

Player	Country	Runs	Average
Jack Hobbs	England	3483	53
Geoff Boycott	England	2945	47
Herbert Sutcliffe	England	2708	67
Mark Taylor	Australia	2496	41
Len Hutton	England	2306	56

Others with 1000-plus runs included tough-as-teak John Edrich (1692 at 48) and pioneering pair Archie MacLaren (1717 at 37) and Dr WG Grace (1089 at 32).

Among Australian openers, Trumper averaged 28 in an era of low scores and sporting wickets, Bill Lawry 48 and Arthur Morris 50.

Champion: The great Yorkshire Len Hutton averaged 56 opening up against Australia.

After The Don at No. 3, those with the highest average were Englishmen Walter Hammond (70) and David Gower (60).

Hammond's high rating was built around his extraordinary 1928–29 summer when he amassed 905 runs, an incredibly prolific summer featuring two double-centuries, in Sydney in mid-December and in Melbourne in the New Year. In Adelaide, too, he notched twin 100s on his way to 1553 first-class runs, a record by a visiting player and one likely to go unsurpassed with abridged modern-day tour schedules.

Ironically, 1928–29 was the season in which a young Don Bradman made a century in his second Test and showed signs of what was to come with 340 not out against Victoria. Amazingly, as he was applauded from the Sydney Cricket Ground, he looked fresh and ready for more, despite batting for eight hours and tweaking a groin in the process!

The debate over the best Ashes all-rounder is always spirited, Keith Miller having his normal host of admirers, as does Ian Botham. Many feel Adam Gilchrist simply has to be the best No. 7 of them all, but former Test captain Warwick Armstrong has the most imposing average of all: 50 runs per innings.

Coming to the best No. 11s, the most prolific five have been:

Player	Country	Runs	Average
Bob Willis	England	186	10
Brian Statham	England	152	25
Arthur Mailey	Australia	151	13
Tom Richardson	England	149	10
Jeff Thomson	Australia	146	16

The best Ashes bats of all time: position by position

AUSTRALIA

Position	Player	Innings	Runs	Average
1 & 2	Sid Barnes	11	771	77
1 & 2	Bobby Simpson	22	1244	62
3	Don Bradman	41	3349	93
4	Allan Border	32	1542	59
5	Steve Waugh	32	1559	62
6	Steve Waugh	33	1389	60
7	Warwick Armstrong	15	601	50
8	Alan Davidson	14	364	30
9	Bert Oldfield	11	311	51
10	Dennis Lillee	13	210	30
11	Jeff Thomson	17	146	16

ENGLAND

Position	Player	Innings	Runs	Average
1 & 2	Herbert Sutcliffe	45	2708	67
1 & 2	Michael Vaughan	10	663	63
3	Walter Hammond	26	1695	70
4	Ken Barrington	14	872	67
5	Denis Compton	11	608	76
6	Tony Greig	25	948	39
7	Ian Botham	16	653	46
8	John Emburey	12	389	43
9	Maurice Tate	10	276	30
10	Alec Bedser	14	136	17
11	Brian Statham	17	152	25

Pavilion, Ken Piesse (Australian Cricket Society, Melbourne, 2007); statistics by Charles Davis

ON FORFEITING THE ASHES

*Ricky Ponting joins a shortlist of postwar
Australian captains to lose the Ashes in England.*

We have lost the Ashes. I hoped I would never have to write that, but it is a reality after a day that summed up the series for us.

We had our chances but failed to take them, and England were good enough to not just claw their way to safety but to reach it in some comfort, thanks to an amazing performance from Kevin Pietersen.

He hammered seven 6s, the most in Test history in a single innings against Australia, and together with Ashley Giles shut the door on our hopes of getting out of jail at the eleventh hour.

Pietersen is such a powerful player that he even managed to hit mistimed shots for 4 or 6 and as he scored at an incredible rate, he took the game away from us, despite another Herculean effort from Shane Warne and brave ones from Glenn McGrath and Brett Lee.

The fact that Warne is on the losing side in this series is a travesty, as there have been large chunks of this series where he has carried the side almost single-handedly. He took another six wickets in this innings, for a match haul of 12 and his overall figures for the series – 40 wickets and 249 runs – are both career-best marks.

Warne is the only player from our squad who can look at himself in the mirror and know he has played to his full potential; the rest of us have just hinted at the form we are capable of and that has cost us the series.

The hardest thing about our defeat is that we know what went wrong: we failed with the bat, lacked penetration and control with the ball (Warne and McGrath excepted), dropped catches, bowled far too many no-balls and lost Glenn McGrath to injury for the vital Edgbaston Test.

But that was what went wrong; the reasons why we failed remain a mystery. England played well, putting us under pressure with bat and ball and that was definitely a factor in the series loss. However, despite their excellence, we should still have been able to compete far more effectively than we did.

Even now, with the series loss confirmed, I still believe we prepared as well as we could. Our meetings were constructive, our plans were sound and our practice was intense, but despite all those positives, we could not put it all together on the field on a regular basis.

The reasons for those collective failures may be hard to establish, but one thing is certain: there will be some tough questions about our performances in the days, weeks and months ahead. I discovered that this evening, just minutes after the match ended.

As soon as I sat down in my post-match media conference, a reporter I have never seen before got to his feet, announced that he was from *ABC Radio* and asked me: 'Would Australia have won the series with a more positive and aggressive captain?'

With a question like that, the reporter obviously knew what he was talking about, so my reply was short and sweet: 'You tell me, mate. You must be the expert.'

If the ABC reporter was suggesting that by stacking the slip cordon with fielders we would have won the series, that clearly is rubbish. Our bowlers regularly failed to bowl to the fields we originally agreed on and that inconsistency forced us onto the defensive. Although we had attacking plans for every England player, our inability to execute those plans forced them to be torn up.

That sort of question suggests that by the time I get back to Australia on Wednesday, the media will be asking other, serious questions about my future as captain. On that same agenda, I am sure, will be John Buchanan's future as coach – his current contract ends in the next few weeks – and the positions of several players in our squad.

If those questions are asked of me, I will respond in the same way to each of them. The fact is that when we arrived in the United Kingdom we were regarded as an outstanding outfit; three months down the line we have lost two Tests and suddenly the captain is useless, the coach is hopeless and the players are either not good enough, too old or both.

I do not accept that. We have had a blip and although the margin of this series loss probably flatters us, we have not gone from world-beaters to deadbeats in one series.

We underperformed massively, but the core of players in this squad knows that, and I remain convinced that we have the right men to put the record straight. I expect us to do that over the months that will follow – and I hope we do it with me as captain.

If the powers that be – the selectors and CA's [Cricket Australia's]

Board of Directors – decide that a change of captain is required, that's their decision. [But] I have no plans to walk away from the leadership.

Ashes Diary 2005, from Victory in India to the Most Dramatic Test Series of the Century, Ricky Ponting (Harper Sports, Sydney, 2005)

SORRY MATE, YOU'RE OUT
Justin Langer on the agony of omission.

Throughout my cricket career I have had my fair share of droughts when I have felt like I was living in the wilderness of Australian cricket. After every one of these droughts has come an oasis in the form of a triumph and I have become a stronger person. As easy as that is to say now, each disappointment has felt like the end of the world. At the time I have felt like one of those weaker saplings, withering away and perishing in the desert sun.

On Monday, 2 June 2001, I was forced to stare one of these potentially disastrous droughts straight in the eyes. There was a knock on the door of my hotel room at about 9.30 am. With the first Test of the 2001 Ashes series getting underway the following day [at

Happier Days: Justin Langer in 1999 at Barbados.
Chris Nevins

Edgbaston], I was in an upbeat frame of mind. Bouncing to the door, my world turned blue in an instant, as the expression on my skipper Steve Waugh's face said it all. Without saying a word I knew I hadn't been selected. I had been dropped from the Australian cricket side for the first Test of the Ashes tour. The moment was over quite quickly, and yet it was utterly unbearable.

My rise in Australian cricket can be attributed in some ways to the faith the captain has had in me as a player and as a person. Guys like Matthew Hayden and myself have benefited from the confidence the captain has had in us since he took over the reins. He has a way of getting the best out of his men, like a respected general gets his men to fight to the death if necessary. Steve Waugh is the type of bloke you would stand in the trenches of war with and to me this is the highest compliment I can pay a person.

Stephen has supported me when others may have doubted me and lifted me up with his words and actions in times when I may have doubted myself.

Beach Cricket: Some impromptu practice for Justin Langer during the '95 tour of the Windies.
Patrick Eagar

With this in mind, you may understand why the moment of my sacking was so unbearable.

Standing in front of me, with a steely look in his eyes, the captain, who was a tour selector and a very good mate, told me: 'The selectors have decided to go another way for the first Test. Sorry mate, but 'Marto' [Damien Martyn] is in and you are out. He is in such great form and our gut feeling is that this is the way to go. This may seem like the end of the world, but there is no reason why you can't fight your way back. You have before and you can again if you work hard and keep backing yourself.'

There was nothing much more for him to say. I wanted to scream and shout and abuse him for taking away my position. I wanted to tell him that I always came up with the goods when the team most needed it. I wanted to shout out that I would put my life on the line for the baggy green cap and my teammates. I wanted to read out all of my statistics from the previous three years while batting at No. 3 for Australia. I wanted to cry out for more of his support and ask him why he had turned his back on me on this occasion. I wanted to tell him that the decision wasn't fair, that I always seemed to be the easy option to be dropped. I wanted to abuse the other selectors and tell them exactly what I thought of them at that moment. I wanted to ask Steve how I was going to tell my family and friends on the other side of the globe. I wanted to plead with him to change his mind, even though I knew he couldn't and wouldn't.

I wanted to ask Steve how I was going to look my teammates in the eye at training later that morning. I wanted to fight the decision, fight the moment, fight the world, fight the journalists and fight the selectors.

But then, what would that have achieved? We were standing arm's distance from each other and for a second I can't remember if I saw 'Tugga' as a punching bag or a big brother who I wanted to hug and use as a shoulder to cry on.'

The Power of Passion, Justin Langer (Swan Publishing, Sydney, 2002)

DREAMS AND NIGHTMARES
Sir Donald Bradman on the dilemma
of an Ashes tour selection.

The high watermark of any young Australian cricketer's ambition must surely be a tour of England. The thought of playing at Lord's, the Oval, Trent Bridge, Old Trafford and elsewhere against Australia's oldest and traditional cricket rival is an irresistible lure. Once more we are indebted to the ABC for bringing out a booklet, this time associated with the 1968 tour, and I am happy to accede to their request for some random thoughts, even though readers will appreciate the limitations on views I may express by virtue of my being a selector.

But this very fact greatly heightens my personal interest and responsibility. Australia's unofficial selectors can have great fun choosing their fancy, secure in the freedom from responsibility, whereas I and my official colleagues will have months to meditate on the contradictory advice we shall receive during the season from 'experts', and the abuse we shall almost certainly suffer when the job is done. Perhaps we shall even reflect upon the more subtle approach as typified by this description of an English sporting parson's opening prayer: 'Oh Lord – as thou wilt doubtless have seen in this morning's paper' – linking it with the exclusion of Bloggs from the best team – 'in thy great mercy open the eyes of the selectors.'

According to my rough calculations, the selectors between them will spend in the summer of 1967–68 upwards of 1000 hours watching first-class cricket. They will debate on many occasions the merits of possible candidates with particular emphasis on the type of player likely to be successful under English conditions, the combination from which their ideal XI can be chosen and having regard to reserves in case of illness or injury.

I have often been asked whether 17 men are too many for an English tour. My answer is yes – provided they all remain fit and well and in form. But lack of form, coupled with illness or injury – and the number is too few. In 1938, through such misfortunes, I found myself more than once reduced to nine fit men.

The tour is a great physical strain for the leading and successful players. Nevertheless cricketers on tour want to play as much as possible. The unhappiest man is the spare part, such as a second wicketkeeper, who is unlucky enough not to be chosen in even one Test.

Above all, a heavy responsibility falls on the captain.

Clearly he is expected to possess great cricket ability coupled with the power of leadership, but more and more the modern world also demands diplomacy and an aptitude for public speaking. To a young Australian without any special background or training, the ordeal of speaking before a distinguished audience at say the Royal Empire Society lunch – perhaps broadcast and televised as well – is much worse than having to bat in a Test match.

Some may ask why can't the manager attend to the speech-making? He is normally an older man of wider experience who does not have 'on field' responsibilities. The answer simply is that audiences want to hear the captain. His doings, not those of the manager, receive daily publicity. Moreover, he is expected to produce something worthwhile.

Unless he is a born orator – rare among champion cricketers – this will involve considerable preparation, as indeed it should if the captain is properly to acknowledge the importance of the occasion. Twice a week the captain must confer with selection committee colleagues to pick teams and this aspect needs a great deal of thought and judgment.

Combinations must be tried out in county games to sort out the best Test side – the right opening bowlers, opening batsmen, etc. How many people reading this article will believe me when I say that with 17 men, there is a choice of 12,376 different elevens? Moreover, in teams of 11, selected from the 17 players, the captain has the choice of 494,010,316,800 different batting orders. But it is true, audited and found correct by a qualified actuary friend of mine.

There is scarcely time to experiment to this extent in a tour of some 30 matches.

Cricket lovers have a natural tendency to compare players and teams of different eras. Whilst this is fascinating, how valid is the comparison? Take for instance the 1938 and 1948 sides to England, which I had the honour of leading. The 1948 tour was dominated by an experimental law enabling a new ball to be taken after 55 overs. This had a profound influence on the type of bowler employed, team selection and so on. The new-ball rule in 1948 was fervently embraced by those superb fast bowlers [Ray] Lindwall, [Keith] Miller and Bill Johnston, supported in no small measure by medium pacers [Ernie] Toshack and [Sam] Loxton. But what did it do to the slow leg spinners [Colin] McCool and [Doug] Ring? Both were splendid exponents of the art but they were virtually unemployed. Contrast this situation with 1938, when the Australian touring side had only one fast bowler, [Ernie] McCormick, supported by two medium pacers, [Merv] Waite and [Stan] McCabe. In 1938, under the rules then applying, the spin bowlers held sway. To illustrate graphically the difference, let me quote the figures. In 1948, the fast bowlers Lindwall, Miller and Johnston between them took 67 wickets in the Tests. The leg spinner Ring took one. In 1938, the faster bowlers McCormick, Waite and McCabe between them took 13 wickets. The spinners [Bill] O'Reilly and [Chuck] Fleetwood-Smith took 36.

It is essential to bear in mind such information in making any sensible appraisal of comparative skills. Moreover, it greatly affects captaincy and tactics.

Bill O'Reilly was a captain's dream. You could design and place an attacking field secure in the knowledge that he would contain the best of them. All English batsmen feared him with maybe one exception – Maurice Leyland. Being a left-hander, Maurice presented a different target and with typical Yorkshire relish and confidence said: 'I can handle O'Reilly ... and what is more he knows I can.' And he mostly did, his 187 run-out in the fifth Test at the Oval being substantial evidence. Fleetwood-Smith was a different proposition – a captain's nightmare. One minute a superb, unplayable ball; then two full tosses and one which bounced twice. His field had to be designed to give protective cover; otherwise an aggressive batsman could tear him apart.

I have barely touched the fringe of the problems confronting a captain. There is the constant need to maintain harmony amongst

Different Days: Don Bradman's 1938 touring Australians included just two faster bowlers, Ernie McCormick and Merv Waite, and four specialist spinners, Bill O'Reilly, Frank Ward, Chuck Fleetwood-Smith and Ted White, who filled the first four places in the first-class bowling averages.

different temperaments – to weigh the scales of justice evenly between players' opportunities and, above all, to preserve cricket's future by developing and even enhancing its finer characteristics.

The game of cricket seems to be perpetually on trial, and how often have I said that its future lies so much in the hands of the players whose interpretation of its character is of paramount importance. I started to play cricket as a young boy because I loved it. My youthful joy turned to more serious issues in due course and it was well nigh impossible to play Test cricket before 80,000 people with quite the same abandon as when defending a kerosene tin wicket in Pickard's paddock.

Responsibility alone alters the sense of values. But even under great stress and strain, I still hope and believe I played cricket as enjoyment and that my enjoyment of it was visible to the spectators. I don't believe it necessary to look as though you are performing an onerous duty in order to give of your best.

ABC Cricket Book, Don Bradman (Australian Broadcasting Commission, Sydney, 1968)

MIDSUMMER MADNESS

Len Hutton's decision to insert Australia in the opening Ashes Test of 1954–55 in Brisbane saw England humbled by an innings.

What was Len Hutton thinking? The 38-year-old builder's son from Fulneck, near Pudsey in Yorkshire, was the first professional cricketer to lead an MCC side in Australia and, on an unusually cool morning at the Woolloongabba Ground in Brisbane, he won the toss and asked the Australians to bat.

Almost half a century later, Geoffrey Howard – the tour manager – looks back with bewilderment. 'It's amazing that he worked it all out and put them in. I wonder how often, as a Yorkshire cricketer, he'd seen his captain win the toss and put the other side in; with uncertain bowling, too. He only had four bowlers and he must have had doubts about Alec Bedser's fitness.'

EW 'Jim' Swanton was the cricket correspondent of the *Daily Telegraph* and he was a traditionalist. He did not approve of Hutton as captain, did not approve of playing just four bowlers, not one of them a spinner. He certainly did not approve of asking Australia to bat. 'It was a sort of midsummer madness,' he thundered.

By the time the manager arrived by tram from Lennon's Hotel, the innings had started, and he took his seat to see Alec Bedser running in to bowl to the left-handed Arthur Morris. The England wicketkeeper was Keith Andrew, making his Test debut in place of a feverish Godfrey Evans. He stood up to the stumps, as Bedser always demanded, keeping to him for only the second time in his life and in Bedser's third over the ball caught the inside edge of Morris's bat and deflected sharply to Andrew's right. It was at best a quarter-chance, but it was not held. A day of misfortunes had begun.

Bunbury Beginnings: Len Hutton (with cap) and Bill Edrich open the MCC batting in the first tour game of the 1954–55 Ashes campaign.

Within the hour Denis Compton was chasing a ball to the boundary. He grabbed at the white picket fencing, lost his footing and slipped, his left hand becoming impaled on one of the rungs. With a broken finger, he was effectively out of the match, [and] out of the next Test as well.

The day became scaldingly hot. Other catches were dropped, run-out chances were missed and at close of play Australia was 2-208. 'Upon Hutton will fall the odium of an unsuccessful gamble,' Swanton wrote.

'At close of play on the first day,' Geoffrey Howard remembers, 'Len couldn't speak. He was so depressed. Alec Bedser happened to go by. "What's the matter with you, Len?" he said. "There's no bloody bombs dropping, you know."'

At the Heart of English Cricket: The Life and Memories of Geoffrey Howard, Stephen Chalke (Fairfield Books, Bath, UK, 2001)

'THEY MIGHT BE TRAPPIN' THAT'

In a rare interview with the BBC, 'Chuck' Fleetwood-Smith speaks of Len Hutton's epic 364 at the Oval in 1938.

FLEETWOOD-SMITH: It was a marvellous exhibition of concentration, durability and stubbornness and proved the fact that he was so fit that he was still running short, sharp singles when he was over 300.

BBC INTERVIEWER: Was it without blemish?

FLEETWOOD-SMITH: Without blemish, except one occasion when he was in his 40s and getting towards 50 and I happened to spin one ... I think the only one for the whole match and Hutton thought he was bowled and [Ben] Barnett thought it had bowled him and he forgot to stump him and Len went back and he said: 'I'm not coming out again today,' and he didn't. I remember I said to him, 'Len, we'll break the monotony. I'll give you a couple of full tosses on the leg side and you hit 'em for 4, liven it up, give us something to do like.' 'No,' he said, 'they might be trappin' that.' So he didn't do anything.

Cricket on the Air: A Selection from Fifty Years of Radio Broadcasts, David Rayvern-Allen (BBC, London, 1985)

THE BEST 32 OF HIS LIFE

Having pasted rising wrist spinner 'Chuck' Fleetwood-Smith four years earlier, effectively delaying his Ashes debut, Walter Hammond came face-to-face with Fleetwood, on a Melbourne 'sticky' in 1936–37 ...

Fleetwood-Smith came seeking his revenge on me. The Australians had won the toss and in the first innings I slipped and hurt myself and had to go inside for a time. They got 9-200 and then rain came, producing the dreaded Melbourne gluepot and Bradman promptly declared. This was perhaps the worst wicket on which I have ever played.

When I was padding up, 'Gubby' Allen came to me and said: 'We're in a hole. You've got to stick it [hang in there].'

Fleetwood-Smith has a most expressive face and if ever an expression said: 'I'm going to pay you back for what you did to me four years ago!' ... it was visible then.

I got down over my bat. Maurice Leyland, so many times England's saviour, was at the other end and I could think of no one I would rather have had there. For over after over Fleetwood-Smith tossed down those horrible off breaks, whisking away [from the left-handed Leyland] into the slips like firecrackers.

The presentation at 3LO Melbourne, on 15th March, 1929, of a Silver Tea and Coffee Service, from Australian Wireless Listeners to Mr. W. R. Hammond, the famous English Cricketer, as a wedding present and in recognition of his feat in scoring two double centuries in successive innings in Test Matches.

In this photograph (from left to right) are Messrs. R. H. Campbell, "Patsy" Hendren, Eric Welch, the Hon. Donald MacKinnon, (President Victorian Cricket Association,) Senator J. D. Millen, Mr. W. R. Hammond, Major W. T. Conder, (General Manager 3LO) and Mr. E. J. Lewis, (Studio Manager 3LO)

Wedding Present: Walter Hammond's run-scoring feats and his impending nuptials saw him recognised with a special presentation at the ABC offices in Lonsdale Street, Melbourne in March, 1929.

Hitting was impossible and whenever it could be done, the ball had to be left alone, though it had to be followed until it left the pitch, as no one could say where it might go.

The Australian fieldsmen drew nearer and nearer. I would have given a good deal to be able to stand up and send the ball hissing at them to drive them further out. Fleetwood-Smith trundled down plenty of innocent-looking ones to tempt me to do it.

When Leyland had got 17, he was tempted by just such a ball. He jumped out and sent a crashing hook towards the square-leg boundary and young Len Darling, his body almost parallel with the ground, clung to it with the fingers of his left hand. Leyland went out, while 65,000 spectators made the ground rock with their applause. I knew that I should have to try to hit out, for it was no use saving my wicket while batsmen at the other end formed a procession indoors: no one else was likely to stay as Leyland had done.

A few minutes later, a ball whisked from the pitch that looked like an easy 4. I cracked it away to leg ... and once more young Darling made an almost incredible catch. The crowd got up bodily, clapped and yelled without pause for five minutes and as the din was dying down, someone called for three cheers [for Darling]. You should have heard them!

My total was 32, out of England's 9-76 declared. We lost the Test and Fleetwood-Smith claimed his place among the greatest bowlers. In the next Test he took 10 wickets.

I shall never forget Don Bradman's generous tribute: 'No other present-day batsmen could have equalled Hammond's and Leyland's performance. In such conditions, I don't believe Australia could have made 50.'

Source unknown, Walter Hammond (22 September 1946)

A BODYLINE UMPIRE'S VIEW

Rather than outlawing the bouncer, Bodyline-series umpire George Hele says fast bowlers should be encouraged to bowl short ... within limits.

If cricket is to remain a man's game and youth are not to be discouraged from taking up the hard cricketing life of a fast bowler, it is time we started thinking clearly and unemotionally about the place of the bumper in cricket.

I have stood behind a long line of bowlers in first-class cricket who have sent down scores of bumpers, and I have never heard of the slightest grumble from any batsman against the legitimate bumper.

I agree heartily with the Victorian Cricket Association, which is not in favour of the alteration of Law 43 as proposed by New South Wales Cricket Association and our own [Australian] Board of Control. A lot of nonsense has been talked and written about the intimidating aspect of the flying ball, or bouncer, as such a ball is called in England. What is intimidating about a bumper bowled to an orthodox field against a batsman who has learned to play the hook shot?

When I say legitimate bumper, I exclude the Bodyline attack of Harold Larwood and Bill Voce in 1933. I am strongly opposed to short-pitched bowling directed at the batsman's body while he is completely frustrated by a packed leg field.

I do not desire to rake over the embers of that Bodyline controversy beyond saying that only two Test umpires in the world saw that attack at close quarters. They were George Borwick and myself. We were out there in the middle from the time Larwood bowled his first ball to the last and we were able to appreciate exactly how intimidating that form of attack was.

When round-arm bowling supplanted underarm lobs, John Nyren, in his book *The Cricketers of My Time* in 1833, said, 'It looks as if the scientific game of cricket will degenerate into an exhibition of rough and coarse play.' I wonder what Nyren would have written 100 years later when Douglas Jardine devised the Bodyline attack and Larwood became its spearhead?

I have often been amused to hear cricketers and even umpires who never saw Larwood bowl to a packed leg field, lay down dogmatically what they would have done if they had been in the position of Borwick, or myself. I would like to know what rule they could have invoked at that time to make Larwood open up his tight leg field and give batsmen the chance to play the hook shot without committing suicide? It is absurd to compare the occasional bumpers of the late A 'Tibby' Cotter, Jack Gregory, Jack Scott, Ernie McCormick, Tim Wall, Ray Lindwall and Keith Miller with the concentrated fury of the Bodyline of Larwood and Voce. When a batsman ducks under a flier from Lindwall or Miller, the only cricket fans who yell 'Bodyline' never saw the real Bodyline.

From a lot of the talk I have heard, one would imagine that Lindwall and Miller were the first fast bowlers to drop a few balls short and make them fly. You would think that these two very competent pace bowlers had discovered some fearsome secret weapon! How absurd this is!

Then you hear the equally uninformed argument that Lindwall and Miller are in some way culpable in this matter, that they are doing something not quite fair, while English pace bowlers, with the exception of Larwood, have clean hands. Such an argument is just as ridiculous.

When England had fast bowlers who could make the ball really fly, every one of them used the occasional bumper. Tom Richardson bowled them and so did that superb left-arm pace bowler Frank Foster. Bill Hitch let fly his odd bumper and so did Harry Howell and Kenneth Farnes. No Australian batsman objected. On the contrary some of our stars of the past welcomed the bumper as a picking to slam to the fence.

When the first West Indian side came to Australia in 1930–31, it pinned its faith to a pace attack with relays of fast bowlers. [Learie] Constantine, [George] Francis and [Herman] Griffith all sent down the occasional bumper. And how were those bumpers punished by swift-moving batsmen like Bradman, Ponsford, Stan McCabe and Alan Kippax!

With the South Africans in the following season, fast bowler 'Sandy' Bell used to bumper from time to time. Bradman, then at his peak, played havoc with him and all the others. I can safely say that all the Australian, English, West Indian and South African fast bowlers I have mentioned bowled bumpers by the score.

And batsmen like Jack Hobbs, Frank Woolley, Herbert Sutcliffe, 'Patsy' Hendren, Walter Hammond, Ponsford, Bradman, McCabe, Charlie Macartney, Kippax, Archie Jackson, Johnnie Taylor and 'Nip' Pellew, who were all able to get into position quickly for the hook, dealt with them without mercy.

When Tests were resumed after the war, Australia, in Lindwall and Miller, had two of the finest fast bowlers in the world. Our batting line-up was sufficient to retain the Ashes, but England did not have a fast bowler of quality and this is always a great handicap for a touring side. In addition, in Bradman, we had one of the greatest Test captains Australia has produced. During this period Lindwall and Miller provided a shock attack for Australia. They bowled many bumpers, but to censure those bumpers is really to censure the two postwar Australian captains Bradman and Lindsay Hassett. If there is anything really wrong, unfair or intimidatory about an occasional bumper, those who criticise them are in effect criticising Bradman and Hassett and implying that they were wrong in allowing bumpers to be bowled.

Those critics also in an oblique way are casting a reflection on the postwar Test cricket umpires. If bumpers were really intimidatory, why didn't those umpires act? They had the power to act, which we did not have in 1932–33. They could have invoked the law adopted in 1934 which was designed to eliminate Bodyline. That law covers any type of bowling, which, in the opinion of the umpires, might be regarded as intimidatory.

Postwar umpires, of course, took no action against bumpers. Why? Because they did not regard such balls as being intimidatory. Rather, I think, they looked on them being gifts to the batsman who has learned how to play the hook shot properly. I am convinced that if Lindwall and Miller had bowled more bumpers, there would have been more boundary shots in the scorebooks.

Sporting Life, George Hele (Sydney, April 1953)

THE BODYLINE HITS

There were 32 instances of Australians being struck during the Bodyline summer, 23 of them by the Nottinghamshire express Harold Larwood.

FIRST TEST – December 1932, at Sydney:

WH Ponsford [first innings], when eight, was struck by a fast ball from Larwood on the hip. He rubbed his hip with vigour and walked about until the pain ceased.

JH Fingleton was hit also on the hip by Larwood.

AF Kippax received a sharp rap on the knuckles from [Bill] Voce, causing play to be suspended for a moment.

VY Richardson began with a painful blow on the inside of the right knee, which caused him to writhe in pain. This was followed by a knock on the left thigh which made him squirm, and when 10 he took a third blow from Larwood, this time on the thumb of his right hand, which split the top and caused him to drop his bat in pain.

Ponsford [second innings] tore off his glove and wrung his hand in pain when Voce struck him on the finger.

SJ McCabe was struck high up on the thigh by a ball sharply rising from Voce.

SECOND TEST – December 1932, Melbourne:
Fingleton [first innings], when 25, took a ball from Larwood on the knee, and winced in pain; at 27 was hit on the hand by a lifting ball from [Bill] Bowes and, in the same over, another ball got him on the hip. When 67, he was hit on the thigh by a ball from Larwood and he took some time to recover from the pain. At 68, a ball from Larwood hit him on the thumb.
McCabe, when 20, was hit on the left arm by Voce.
WM Woodfull [second innings], when three, stepped across to a fast ball from Allen and it struck him a nasty blow on the chest, but he soon recovered.

THIRD TEST – January 1933, Adelaide:
A ball from Larwood rose sharply and Woodfull [first innings], when five, stepping in front of his wicket, was facing square on to the ball when it beat his bat and struck him a severe blow over the heart. He dropped his bat and reeled away from the wicket. Supported by members of the English team, he recovered after a few minutes and resumed.
Ponsford, when three, was hit on the shoulder by a bumping ball from Voce. When 15, he was hit on the back by Larwood.
Ponsford [second innings] was hit twice on the body in the first two overs from Larwood.
WA Oldfield had made 33 when a fast ball from Larwood bruised him severely on the thigh. At 41, he tried to pull a rising ball from Larwood to leg, but missed, and the ball struck him on the forehead. He staggered from the pitch and fell. Woodfull went on to the ground and took Oldfield to the pavilion. He took no further part in the game. A medical examination disclosed that he had suffered a linear fracture of the frontal bone of the forehead.
McCabe, when eight, took a fast ball from Larwood on the hip.

FOURTH TEST – February 1933, Brisbane:
Woodfull [first innings] was hit on the thigh by the last ball of Larwood's opening over; when 24, he ducked to a rising ball from Larwood, which struck him on the back.

Richardson, when 46, was struck on the thumb by a ball from Allen and wrung his hand in pain.

McCabe, before scoring, was hit on the biceps by Larwood and there was a short spell.

EH Bromley, when two, was hit on the thigh by a kicking ball from Larwood and the next ball, but one struck him on the hand.

FIFTH TEST – February 1933, Sydney:

McCabe [first innings], when one, was hit on the shoulder by one of Larwood's 'fliers' and play was held up for a few moments.

DG Bradman, when one, was hit high up on the thigh by Larwood. At 27, he was smacked hard on the left shoulder by a rising ball from Larwood. He dropped his bat and walked about for a moment to recover from the blow.

Woodfull [second innings], when nine, ducked to a ball from Larwood and received a heavy blow between the shoulders. He evidently felt the pain of it and play was suspended for a few moments. At 11, he was again hit by Larwood, this time on the thigh and he rubbed the spot vigorously. When 24, he was struck near the shoulder again when he ducked his head to a rising ball from Voce.

Some Statistics Concerning Cricket Casualties (Showing Batsmen Struck By Bowlers in Test Matches Between England and Australia), RH Campbell (ABC, Sydney, 1933) *Many consider this the very first* ABC Cricket Book.

Australian batsmen struck in Ashes tests from 1876–77 to 1932–33

No. of times hit	Players
11	WM Woodfull
7	WH Ponsford
6	JH Fingleton
5	C Hill, A Jackson, SJ McCabe
4	DG Bradman, G Giffen, VY Richardson
3	WW Armstrong, J McC Blackham, J Darling, HV Hordern, SP Jones, CE McLeod, RB Minnett, MA Noble
2	TJE Andrews, GJ Bonnor, EH Bromley, HL Collins, H Graham, AJ Hopkins, FA Iredale, C Kelleway, AF Kippax, WA Oldfield, VS Ransford, GHS Trott

No. of times hit	Players
1	C Bannerman, WW Bardsley, BB Cooper, TW Garrett, DW Gregory, SE Gregory, CV Grimmett, HL Hendry, PM Hornibrook, JJ Lyons, CG Macartney, GE Palmer, JC Reedman, J Ryder, FR Spofforth, N Thomson, AE Trott, H Trumble, CTB Turner

Match summary

No. of matches in which players were hit	Period	Australians hit
7	1877–84	11
7	1885–87	7
7	1893–96	11
7	1897–1902	9
7	1902–05	6
7	1905–11	4
7	1911–21	14
7	1921–25	2
7	1926–30	14
6	1930–33	40

Total Australian injuries: 118

Total Englishmen injuries: 85

'WE ARE MERELY PLAYING THE ENGLISH BATSMEN IN . . .'

*Sidelined star Bill Ponsford steps on the toes
of some, including St Kilda teammate Ted a'Beckett,
in calling for a rookie paceman to be promoted
for the fifth Ashes Test of 1928–29.*

One thing noticeably lacking in the fourth Test from an Australian standpoint was an opening bowler with some fire. It will be necessary to include one in the team to meet England in the concluding match of the series.

It is rather a difficult matter to change the side which put up such a great fight at Adelaide, because the honours of the game were just as much with the losers as with the winners. However, I feel sure the Australian attack would be considerably strengthened by the inclusion of a new opening bowler, preferably a man with pace.

The English attack has in [Harold] Larwood and [Maurice] Tate two outstanding bowlers, who take full advantage of the new ball. They attack the batsman by bowling at the wicket right from the jump off and therein lies their success.

[Ted] a'Beckett and [HSTL 'Stork'] Hendry, our opening bowlers, cannot be said to be in the same class as the English pair and probably this is just about the difference in the teams.

A'Beckett has not had any outstanding success, principally because he has relied more on bowling outside the off stump. This was noticeable in the game at Melbourne; also in the first innings at Adelaide. However, I noticed in the second innings that he concentrated on the wicket and he met with better results. Hendry cannot be regarded as a bowler at all, yet we find him opening the attack for Australia. The position is all the more remarkable because Hendry bowls only on rare occasions for his club Melbourne. Opening with such bowlers simply means that we are merely playing the English batsmen in, instead of enhancing our chances of getting them out while the new ball is dangerous.

The selectors should certainly make a change for the fifth Test and give a young opening bowler a trial. Should I be asked to name a man, my vote would be for [Tim] Wall, the 23-year-old South Australian.

'Gelignite Jack': Jack Gregory in action during his last Test in Brisbane at the Exhibition Ground in 1928–29. He was to break down shortly afterwards, forcing his premature exit from international cricket.

He is not a real express, but he is fairly fast and has considerably improved lately.

We must discover someone to take the place of Jack Gregory – and while speaking of Jack, I am of the opinion that his injury was the severest blow Australia has suffered for years.

Wall's last performance this season was against New South Wales at Adelaide when he secured six wickets for 170 in the match. Seeing that the Adelaide wicket does not suit a fast bowler, which was emphasised by Larwood's failure during the last Test, Wall's performance was a good one.

Wall should bowl better in Melbourne, too, because he would be able to make the ball fly much more than in Adelaide. Wall's selection would be a popular one with the public.

The Herald, Bill Ponsford (Melbourne, February 1929)
The Australians duly selected two new-ball bowlers in Melbourne, Tim Wall taking eight wickets for the game, and fellow debutant, Queenslander Percy Hornibrook, who took four, a'Beckett and Hendry among those dropped. Australia won its only match of the summer.

BOWLING TO WIN
Former MCC captain AO Jones on a
great Australian advantage.

The Australian is far ahead of us in bowling. Why is it? Because on the perfect wickets out there it would be impossible for him to get any batsman out unless he made the ball do something. Watch an Australian bowler: he is always doing something to the ball with his fingers and never bowls a ball down unless he has some object in view. I think perhaps the best instance of an Australian bowler, and our Englishmen know him best and that is why I take him as an example, is Albert Trott. He holds the ball in the most extraordinary way; in fact, sometimes you would think it would be impossible for him to get rid of it. Another great thing in his favour is that he is always willing to 'speculate'.

Cricket: A Little Book for Lovers of the Game, edited by SJ Looker (Simpkin, Marshall, Hamilton, Kent & Co, London, 1925)

FAST BOWLERS I REMEMBER

'The Prince' of Australia's umpires RM 'Bob' Crockett
on the finest pacemen of his time.

What is all this fuss about fast bowling? It has so captured the public mind that one might be forgiven for thinking that [Douglas] Jardine and his men had introduced something new into the glorious game of cricket. It is highly amusing to have an awe-stricken Australian steal to my side (I usually sit under the canopy in the members' reserve at the MCG) and ask with oh so serious an expression: 'What do you think of this fast bowling attack? Is it playing the game?' Of course it is. There have been fast bowlers in the past who, by comparison, would have made [Harold] Larwood [look like] a medium-paced bowler. Batsmen were hit in those days, but nobody complained!

I recall that on one occasion W Barnes [not Syd the bowler] was hit by an Australian bowler who offered his apologies. Barnes, however, brushed them aside with 'Serve me dom well right; 'aven't I got a bat in ma hand?' And that was the philosophy of the great batsmen of other days.

Today our batsmen go out to bat covered with armour almost like a knight-at-arms. There is the thigh padding, the chest protector and a covering for the forearm. Perhaps they have caught the spirit of ancient days and believe that they, too, must slay a dragon. To me, this extra protection suggests a lack of courage, a dearth of enterprise and no confidence – summed up . . . an inferiority complex.

Although I have seen fewer than a dozen international fast bowlers, I believe I have seen the best the game has produced. To name the men I have been associated with, there were Tom Richardson, Bill Lockwood and Arthur Fielder for England; and Ernie Jones, Albert Cotter, Jack Gregory and Ted McDonald for Australia. Here was talent that might have overawed any batting list, but the contemporary batsmen accepted fast bowling as part of the game. Batsmen were hit very often, but there was no outcry and many a sound pasting the bowlers received!

I recall a game in South Australia where Victoria was the visitors. Ernie Jones was rolling them in at his top pace, but was meeting with little success. Jim Giller was piling up runs at the expense of 'Jonah'. Ernie had been hit to every part of the field, and after such an over he could contain himself no longer. 'Bob, this chap is making me look like a schoolboy. What am I to do?' he asked. Now Jones was the fastest bowler of all time and a good bowler at that. He was yards faster than Larwood, yet the batsmen of his day played him with confidence and more often than not hit him about. Jonah hit many batsmen but he scorned the suggestion that it was deliberate. Nor would any batsman of that day have believed that Jones was bowling at his body. Both accepted the knocks as part of the game.

On one occasion in England, Jones hit Jackson, the English captain. While Jackson was writhing in pain Harry Graham went across to Jones and asked, 'Where did you hit Mr Jackson?' He laid a slight emphasis on the 'Mr'. That was Jonah's cue. 'In the stomach, of course. Where did you think I would hit the Honorable MISTER Jackson?'

The Englishman Lockwood was a devil-may-care fellow. On one occasion, to win a wager, he jumped off a boat into the Sydney Harbour and tried to swim ashore.

Tom Richardson had plenty of pace, but here is a secret. I always held a suspicion that he threw his fastest ball. I was never sufficiently sure to no-ball him, but I never ceased watching his delivery. To illustrate what I mean by the initiative of old-time batsmen, Graham and Albert Trott were forced to face Richardson on a damaged wicket in Sydney one day. It was dangerous work and many a resounding clout both batsmen received. 'The Little Dasher', as Graham was called, made light of the bowling and knocked up a sound hundred. Albert Trott was not out for 76. The Englishmen were very disappointed at not having captured Trott's wicket and [Billy] Brockwell remarked: 'We have never been able to get Trott out in a Test match.'

The tactics of the fast bowlers of the past varied according to their natural swing; however, they wasted little time in bowling outside the stumps. They attacked the batsman's defence all the time. Fielder, whom I consider to be the best fast bowler I have seen, would pitch on the stumps, but his out-swerve would carry the ball away outside the off stump. Fielder lacked concentration, but for this I blame his captains. They allowed him to maintain a too general plan of attack. Often the field was not set for a surprise move by Fielder and his figures suffered. Had his captain made him concentrate as ['Monty'] Noble or [Warwick] Armstrong would have done, the field and the bowler would have worked in harmony and with great success. Fielder was a right-hander with a high delivery. He ran a fairish way and the delivery of the ball was full of body swing.

His ability to make the ball swerve and nip made him dangerous.

Ernie Jones was the fastest bowler I have seen. He took a long run and threw his whole weight into the delivery. Jones, although bowling with such pace, was able to turn the ball back from the off. He was a great comedian – a man with whom it was a pleasure to play. Nevertheless, he played the game hard, and would never apologise if he hit a batsman. He just smiled and made ready for the next delivery. Jones believed that it was the batsman's fault if he was hit. It was a view the batsmen hurried to accept themselves. We could do with a little of that spirit today.

Albert ['Tibby'] Cotter, in some respects, resembled Jones, but his delivery was lower. The manner in which he made the ball kick up at the last moment always puzzled me. Cotter kicked higher than Jones and on one occasion RE ['Tip'] Foster and Johnny Tyldesley were having a hot time. Foster said to Tyldesley in my hearing, 'It's not worth it while trying to play this fellow, Johnny. Look after yourself.' I mentioned the conversation to several of his teammates and they were disgusted with Foster's attitude. 'Haven't we had to play Tom Richardson on worse wickets than this?' asked one. Anything savouring of a squeal was discountenanced by the prewar batsmen.

The greatest fast bowling attack either country has sent into the field was that supplied by Gregory and McDonald. They were great bowlers here, but in England were almost unplayable. The manner in which Gregory made the ball kick and the immaculate length of McDonald made the combination ideal for unsettling opening batsmen. Yet I have never thought for a moment that either bowled at the man. Both hit batsmen and hurt them, but it was all part of a Test match. Neither man, however, placed a leg field.

Great as Larwood and [Bill] Voce might be, Australian batsmen have met even greater without flinching. The only left-hand bowler comparable with Voce was FR [Frank] Foster. Foster was a really dangerous bowler and in Adelaide pitched outside the off stump and repeatedly hit Trumper on the legs. For a moment Trumper was annoyed and accused Foster of bowling at his body. When I pointed out that Foster was pitching outside the stumps and that it was his swing that was doing the damage, Trumper was satisfied and apologised. Foster swung the ball so much that I never gave an lbw decision in his favour.

Source unknown, RM 'Bob' Crockett (1932–33)

THE WICKETS RAN EAST AND WEST

Ernie Baillie on the first 50 years of the Melbourne Cricket Ground.

Were any of the members of James Lillywhite's English team of 1876–77, which played in the first Test match against Australia on the Melbourne ground, alive today and visited the ground, doubtless they would be amazed at the transformation, not only in the appointments, but in the actual playing area itself. It was a very fine ground, as grounds went in those days, but it is a very different ground now and ranks as one of the greatest in the world.

In those days there certainly were stands and other accommodation for the public, but they were crude compared with the palatial buildings that have come into being since.

The members' stand was a small, almost insignificant thing; it was replaced two or three years later by what was regarded as almost the last word on the subject in the stand that was pulled down four or five years ago to make room for the present palatial members' stand.

The passing of that stand was regretted by old members, for it had hallowed associations for them. Across its floors had trod, during a period of nearly 50 years, most of the great cricketers of both sides of the world; through its doors the champions of England and Australia had passed onto the green field to perform deeds that were to live in the memory for all time.

But to the old-timers it had an even greater sentimental value, for it was there that they foregathered on the occasion of every big match and fought these battles over again. There they had thrilled to their own triumphs with bat or ball, or both, and from there they had watched the triumphs of later generations. And in their reminiscences of the past and in their fighting over their battles again, they renewed their days of their youth in the sun when the plaudit of the crowds was as music in their ears.

To them the place does not seem the same. The new members' stand is a very fine structure, but there is not the atmosphere that there was about the old stand. No doubt, in time, there will grow up traditions connected with the new stand but they are not yet [present]. Progress demanded new members' accommodation, therefore the old stand had to go; time alone will bring to the new one the hallowed memories of the building that has vanished.

Yet to the players of the day there may not be the same appeal in the new stand that there was in the old one, for to a great extent they do not come closely into touch with it. In the old stand the players had their dressing-rooms and from it they passed onto the field. Under the new order, the players are housed in the Grey Smith stand alongside it and some of them venture into this new members' pavilion only occasionally.

In the members' reserve, however, there was no Grey Smith stand in Lillywhite's day, nor was there for many years afterwards. This fine stand, for so many years one of the features of the ground, was erected in comparatively recent times and was named in honour of Mr Frank Grey Smith, at one time president of the club and a great worker in its interests. While the members' stand is jealously guarded against the intrusion of women, they have the free run of the Grey Smith stand and of that portion of the big general grandstand that is in the members' reserve. That stand, too, would cause amazement to the giants of 55 years ago. [Women were not to be admitted into the pavilion, even as guests, until 1983. The first woman member was admitted in 1984.]

In the 'outer' in those days, practically the only shelter from the sun was provided by the elms planted by members of the first English team 15 years earlier and other trees which grew there. These trees disappeared years ago. There was, in those early days, no Harrison stand, no Wardill stand, nor any other stand that was worthy of the name.

The concrete stand alongside the Grey Smith stand is, of course, a recent addition to the structures on the ground. Near where it now is, in the old days [was] the wooden press box, which was about on a par with some of the makeshift press boxes now seen on suburban

Mecca: Melbourne has traditionally attracted the biggest crowds to international cricket, including more than 200,000 for the memorable four-day Test over Christmas–New Year in 1932–33, the only one during the Bodyline series the Australians were to win.
Melbourne Cricket Club

grounds. We did not, in those days, have an army of pressmen from all quarters of the world to describe the Test or other matches.

Nor would our visitors of 1876–77 have seen anything approaching the present-day elaborate scoring boards that are of such value to cricket patrons in following the game. In those days, the primitive method of posting the runs on an inadequate board in tens or at the fall of a wicket, was the custom. In the first Test, this board was hung to one of the corners of the then members' stand.

The present elaborate system of scoring was devised many years afterwards and is now used on all the Australian grounds where big cricket is played. In this respect we lead the world, for in England they still cling to the old, primitive method and people who wish to keep in touch with things have every few minutes to buy cards of the scores which are produced in a continual stream from printing presses on the ground. Until a few years ago there were two of our modern scoring boards on the Melbourne ground, but it was felt that more than one was unnecessary and the second one was pulled down to make room for the concrete stand.

But it would not be only the wonderful change in the accommodation for onlookers that would impress our Englishmen of 1876–77; the actual playing conditions are different. Good wickets were made on the ground in those days, but the fielding area was nothing like what it is today.

One of the things that would strike the visitors of those days would be the change in the direction of the wickets. In the early days, the wickets, instead of being north and south, as they now are, ran east and west, and it was on an east-west wicket that the first Test match – and a number of subsequent ones – was played. Complaints were

made, however, that with the wickets in this direction, the sun late in the afternoon was in the batsmen's eyes and in the early '80s a change was decided upon.

Ever since then the wickets have run north and south and doubtless they always will do so.

Changes in the next 50 years may not be so great as they have been in the last 50, yet the visiting Englishmen half a century hence undoubtedly will see things that the present-day player will know nothing of. There is talk of big changes in the near future, but what they will amount to no one can say at the moment.

The Sporting Globe, Ernie Baillie (Melbourne, December 1932)
Within five years the Southern Stand was built, flanking the entire outer side of the MCG, adding comfort and shade for tens of thousands. In 1936–37 with it yet uncompleted, a world-record 350,000 fans attended the six days of the holiday Test.

AN ORDEAL TO REMEMBER

Bill Ponsford on the relentlessness of cricket at the highest level.

To a young fellow taking part in his first Test match the atmosphere is most trying. I shall never forget my first Test match, particularly on that account. It was the first match against [Arthur] Gilligan's team on the Sydney Cricket Ground four years ago (1924–25) ... almost 35,000 pairs of eyes were on a young fellow walking out to combat Maurice Tate, who was bowling like a demon, and a tenseness that could be felt, was sufficient to try the strongest nerves!

I had taken part in a few keenly fought interstate games, but never had I played in an atmosphere such as this. The feeling of tenseness lasted throughout that match and has been equally pronounced in most of the other Test matches in which I've played.

An old campaigner probably would not be affected by this tenseness to the same extent as his less experienced colleague and probably would revel in the grimness of the fight.

The ambition of every young cricketer is to play for Australia, but how few realise the ordeal that is in front of them!

I certainly was overjoyed when I found that I had been chosen as one of Australia's representatives, but it was not until I got into the game that I realised the grimness and the relentlessness of Test cricket.

Things that I have learnt about Test cricket are that to do himself justice a man must be in perfect physical condition; that he must endeavour to keep his nerves under complete control and that while the anxiety to do well is natural, the player should endeavour to avoid overanxiety as much as possible. It is overanxiety that causes a very large percentage of the failures among new men in these keenly fought games. One does not imagine that the keenness of the players will be any less marked in the coming games than it has been in those of the past. Both sides are so keyed up that nothing will be given away; each will be out to do his utmost to swing the pendulum in favour of his own side. Both sides will be in deadly earnest from the call of 'Play' until the last ball is bowled.

The Sporting Globe Cricket Book 1928–29: Records of the Tests, International and Interstate Games and Players, edited by EHM Baillie, story by Bill Ponsford (Herald & Weekly Times Ltd, Melbourne, 1928)

MEMORIES THAT NEVER FADE

*Some favourite stories from one of the great
early Australian captains, MA 'Monty' Noble.*

After the strain of an arduous cricket career, one leaves the active sphere with the comfortable assurance of deeds performed, however imperfectly, at least to the best of one's ability and with a pleasant feeling of anticipated physical rest, combined with contented reflection.

When the mind goes back over the years of action, memories, mostly gems of rare lustre, compensate, in a more or less degree, for the loss of personal associations and active participation in the great classical contests.

As time goes on, many of these memories grow dim in the constant battle of life and are only revived by some chance reference to the details or circumstance of their birth. But some, at least, are never forgotten, chiefly because of the effect they had on a particular game; sometimes the extraordinary ability and versatility shown or the magnetic personality of the player with whom the deed is forever associated.

Memories of this kind are very precious and when one has for so long a period left the arena of international cricket, it's difficult to realise that once one walked boldly and fearlessly in that exclusive atmosphere where now it would only be done in fear and trepidation.

As I once read, 'the power and daring have left me, but thank Heaven the wish remains'. These lines are penned as a prelude to a few notable incidents which occurred when I was playing in Test matches.

꙳

An event which left an indelible impression on my mind and a lasting belief, concerns Jack Hobbs, who, playing for England in the third Test match at Leeds in 1909, played a ball between short leg and mid-on, and in doing so knocked a bail off the stumps. Believing it was done in the act of playing the ball, we appealed for hit wicket, but the umpire gave him not out on the ground that he had completed the stroke *before* his foot touched the stumps. Two or three balls afterwards Hobbs made what appeared to be a weak attempt to play a straight one and was clean bowled. My impression of the incident at the time was, and still is, that, believing himself to be legally out, he deliberately allowed himself to be bowled. It is a most difficult thing to allow yourself to be bowled without betraying the fact to the bowler or someone fielding near the wicket. It was a match of small scores and the loss of a player of Hobbs's ability probably had a determining influence on the success of Australia.

꙳

There is a good story of Jim Kelly, our wicketkeeper, whom we affectionately called 'Mother'. Some of our supporters, to celebrate the win by three runs in the fourth Test of 1902, had some champagne brought to our dressing-room. After many congratulations, and one or two glasses of wine, Jim said: 'I'm going to pack my bag.' So he walked round the room, incidentally refreshing himself as he went, and asking 'Has anyone seen my gloves?'

Nobody took any notice of him. 'Has anyone seen my gloves?' he shouted.

Clem Hill looked at him. 'Ha! Ha!' he laughed. 'Look at old Mother, having a drink with his gloves on!'

꙳

Clem Hill's run-out in the first Test match at Sydney against [PF] Warner's team in 1903 caused quite a stir at the time and must have had a big influence on the result of the game. Australia was 270 runs behind in the first innings and the score was 3-191 when [Victor] Trumper joined Hill, who was 37. They carried the score by superb batting to 3-253, Hill being 51 and Trumper 44. What possibilities with two such batsmen well set, for Trumper finished with 185 not out.

In stealing a short run, Clem ran well past the wicket. The ball was returned from the off side, was misfielded, and went away past mid-on, who chased it. Another run was attempted, Hill having to run about 30 yards. Mid-on [Albert Relf] gathered the ball, and, taking deliberate aim, threw it straight to [Dick] Lilley, who made no mistake and Hill was run out. In the endeavour to beat the ball he sprinted fast, and, believing he was safe, ran on and did not hear the verdict. He turned round to walk back to the crease, only to find he was out. Then the crowd took a hand, and made no effort to conceal their disapproval of the decision. Speaking to the umpire [Bob Crockett] afterwards, he was quite emphatic that Hill was run out by a yard. [In an interview two generations later, Wilfred Rhodes told historian David Frith that Hill was clearly out.] I may here say that I was of the same opinion, though my position was not so favourable for a proper view of the incident as many of the public who stood in line with the stumps and were equally emphatic that he should not have been given out. Yet none of us was so well placed as the umpire who gave the decision and in whom the players of both teams had, and still have, the greatest regard and utmost confidence.

In England's second innings of the second Test match at Lord's in 1909 Warwick Armstrong was responsible for perhaps the finest piece of bowling on a good wicket I have seen. It was a memorable match and proved the turning point of the tour. In the preceding two weeks we had lost to Surrey by three runs, to MCC by three wickets and [to England in] the first Test match by 10 wickets. Our reputation suffered accordingly and we were subjected to a deluge of criticism. Some critics considered that the tour was doomed to failure, others advised us by letter and telegram to fade away and go home, but we did not share their opinion. We knew the narrow margin of two of those defeats, and they only served to reveal our weakness, if we could profit by it. When the names of the English XI were published, Armstrong and I agreed that if we could not, with equal luck, beat them we had better go home. Of course, everyone knows we won by nine wickets, after which we were unbeaten for three months, until Lord Londesborough's team beat us at Scarborough, the Waterloo of many Australian teams. This was our fourth and last defeat. This surely shows that, rather than having a depressing effect upon the team, those early defeats acted as a tonic and brought out that fighting spirit which is surely inherent in every Australian and of which 'WWA' is so notable an example!

England made 269, Australia 350; England's second innings realised only 121 and Australia lost one wicket for 41. It was in England's second innings that Warwick bowled so magnificently. There is quite a slope across the wicket at Lord's, which suited his leg breaks. He at times got the off spin with the leg break action and turned the ball uphill. He bowled both [John] King and [George] Hirst with two beautiful balls, both being 'wrong 'uns'. These two breaks, in conjunction with his overspin, which is called the straight break and makes pace off the pitch, together with his marvellous accuracy, had all the batsmen guessing and wondering what was coming next. At one stage he had five wickets for eight runs and finished with the wonderful analysis of six for 35 off 24 overs and five balls with 10 maidens. There is no doubt his great bowling gave us the victory, and was a wonderful stimulant to our morale, the effect of which was apparent in the play of the team individually and collectively during the remainder of the tour.

The Sporting Globe Cricket Annual 1924–25: Records of the Tests, Interstate Games and the Players, edited by EHM Baillie, story by MA 'Monty' Noble (Herald & Weekly Times Ltd, Melbourne, 1924)

THE FATE OF NATIONS HANGING IN THE BALANCE

A smile at a miss-shot was met with a stony glare,
says Ashes debutant HV 'Ranji' Hordern.

There is an atmosphere about an All-England v Australia Test match that can almost be felt. The game itself is played right up to the hilt, with no let-up on either side; so much so, that on the completion of a match you are apt to feel not only physically but mentally weary. Notwithstanding all that, it is really splendid to find yourself in opposition to the very best in the world; it is a fight certainly, but a nice, clean, honest one.

Perhaps I would have been a little less than human had I not felt a rather nice 'prickly feeling' run up and down my spine on filing out through the little gate at the Sydney Cricket Ground with the Australian eleven, in my first Test match against England [in 1911–12]. Surely a dream come true; for here was I apparently on an equal footing with Victor Trumper, Clem Hill, Warwick Armstrong, A 'Tibby' Cotter and all the other Australian cricketing giants; and then, in opposition, the cream of England. I could not indulge in the 'nice prickly feeling' for long, as a Test match against England is a rather serious matter and I was soon in the thick of it.

'Ranji': Leg-spinning dentist HV Hordern was dubbed 'Ranji' because of his tanned complexion.

Perhaps it was my temperament, or the amount of 'nice, friendly cricket' I'd played so much of, but it took me some little time to understand the utmost dourness and unrelenting seriousness with which these matches are played. Everybody flat out, no little asides with your opponents, only a grim and determined effort all the time.

An unnoticed incident in this first Test will show you what I mean. I was batting to [left-armer] FR 'Frank' Foster and after playing two inswingers from him, I endeavoured to leg-glance his third ball. Well, it did not 'inswing' this time. I mistimed it badly and instead of a leg-glance, it went off the back of my bat through the slips for 4. The shot was so palpably a shocking one that I instinctively turned with a grin to Foster, only to be met with a most stony stare. Foster was quite right. I had forgotten for the moment that I was playing in a Test match and that the fate of nations hung in the balance. But I don't mind telling you, dear Unknown, in confidence, that after that little lesson, if by any kind of a miracle I had been able to drive Foster for 4 off the handle of my bat, I should not have offered up even a faint smile in explanation.

Googlies: Coals from a Test Cricketer's Fireplace, Dr HV Hordern (Angus & Robertson Ltd, Sydney, 1932)

Extraordinary: Few champions experienced as great a slump in form as Greg Chappell in the summer of 1981–82. But once back in form, he made up for lost ground...
Cricketer

7
THE EXTRAORDINARY

'Everyone got turkey for Christmas; our Greg got four ducks ...'

RUNS 291, AVERAGE 291

Up Wangaratta way, Brian Hargraves has always had a reputation for being hard to dismiss. In 2009–10 he won the Wangaratta and District Cricket Association 'C'-grade batting averages with 291 runs at 291 for his club team Whorouly-Gapsted. He estimates he has carried his bat 15 times over his 40-year club career, including two or three times in 2009–10.

DUCK FEVER
Even the champion players can have their moments ...

Duck fever is universal and hits you when you least expect it. Greg Chappell had a massive dose of it in 1981–82 when he scored seven ducks in 15 internationals, including four ducks in a row.

It was all quite inexplicable because the Australian captain had started the season confidently with a dazzling 162 (with two 6s and twenty 4s) in the opening match for Queensland against Pakistan and in the same month a brilliant 201 in the Brisbane Test [also off Imran Khan and Sarfraz Nawaz].

It was run-scoring business as usual for one of the most consistent postwar batsmen. Or so it seemed. But soon there was a hiccup. And then another. And another. Before long he was into a massive freefall.

Extraordinary: Few champions experienced as great a slump in form as Greg Chappell in the summer of 1981–82. But once back in form, he made up for lost ground...
Cricketer

Here is how Chappell struggled in international cricket from 15 December 1981 to 26 January 1982:

Greg Chappell's scores, 1981–82			
Date	**Opponent**	**Match**	**Score**
15 December 1981	Pakistan	Melbourne Test, second innings	0
17 December 1981	Pakistan	Sydney, One-day international	0
20 December 1981	West Indies	Perth, One-day international	0*
26 December 1981	West Indies	Melbourne Test, first innings	0*
28 December 1981	West Indies	Melbourne Test, second innings	6
3 January 1982	West Indies	Sydney Test, first innings	12
6 January 1982	West Indies	Sydney Test, second innings	0*
9 January 1982	Pakistan	Melbourne, One-day international	35
10 January 1982	West Indies	Melbourne, One-day international	59
14 January 1982	Pakistan	Sydney, Limited One-day international	36
17 January 1982	West Indies	Brisbane, One-day international	61
19 January 1982	West Indies	Sydney, One-day international	0
23 January 1982	West Indies	Melbourne, One-day international	4

24 January 1982	West Indies	Melbourne, One-day international	1
26 January 1982	West Indies	Sydney, One-day international	0
* denotes first ball			

Thus, in 15 consecutive innings [including five innings in three Tests] Chappell made just 214 runs at an unChappell-like 14.26 with two 50s [a highest score of 61] and seven ducks. He was out first ball three times, twice in Test matches.

In five successive Test innings within 23 days [from 15 December 1981 to 6 January 1982] he made 0, 0, 6, 12 and 0. In all, 18 runs at 3.60. To extend the sequence a little further, Australia had also played the final Test against India at the MCG the previous season. In the second innings, on 10 February 1981, Chappell was out first ball. Thus, in one calendar year, 1981, he had scored three ducks in three Melbourne Tests: 76 and 0 v India; 22 and 0 v Pakistan; and 0 and 6 v West Indies.

Cartoonists had a field day depicting Chappell's plight, and a poster on the first day of the Sydney Test in January 1982 read: 'Everyone got turkey for Christmas, our Greg got four ducks.'

Chappell recovered his form sufficiently in New Zealand with a masterly 176 in the Christchurch Test two months later [and he was 'away' again] ...

Out for a Duck, Kersi Meher-Homji (Kangaroo Press, Sydney, 1993)

ONE THOUSAND RUNS AGAINST TOURISTS
It is a feat unlikely to again be reached.

Ian Chappell has added his name to the shortlist of those that have scored 1000 runs in a first-class season against tourists. That list includes Bradman twice, Compton and Sobers once and one begins to see why Jack Fingleton recently spoke of Chappell as the finest Australian batsman for 40 years – and to wonder whether he meant to rate him better than Bradman or not!

The details of the previous four such successes are in that astonishing quarry by BJ Wakley entitled *Bradman the Great* – we have merely filled them out in respect of [Denis] Compton and [Garry] Sobers. They are as follows:

Date	Name	Opponent	Matches	Innings	Not out	Highest score	Total	Average	100s
1931–32	DG Bradman	v South Africa	7	8	1	299*	1190	171.00	6
1947	DCS Compton	v South Africa	8	14	0	208	1187	84.78	6
1947–48	DG Bradman	v India	7	10	2	201	1081	135.12	6
1957–58	GS Sobers	v Pakistan	6	10	3	365*	1007	143.86	4
1968–69	IM Chappell	v West Indies	8	12	1	188	1062	96.55	5

* denotes not out

Cricket Quarterly, edited by Rowland Bowen (Eastbourne, UK, Summer 1969)
Statistician Ken Williams says Chappell is the last Australian to make 1000 runs against a touring team in a season 'Down Under'.

CRICKET BALL DRIVEN 300 YARDS

Waratah footballer Geoff Storey is not in the [national rugby] team to visit South Africa next season, but his friends assert that he is in line for an even more attractive trip – to England with an Australian cricket team. They argue that no man in the present Australian team can hit a ball as far as Storey did for the I Zingari eleven the other week and estimate the distance at 300 yards.

Playing at Cranbrook College, Storey hit one over the fence. Several fieldsmen went over after it without success. Then a passer-by volunteered that he had seen the ball rolling merrily down the slope towards Rose Bay. He was right. The fieldsmen found the ball in the gutter past Rose Bay pier.

'Dressing Room Echoes', *The Referee,* writer unknown (Sydney, 15 February 1933)

A DROP KICK FOR 4

Against Fitzroy in January 1928, [South Melbourne's] Bob Lawson was bowling to [Bert] Lansdowne. After the batsman failed to connect with several balls bowled outside the off stump, the batsman deliberately walked across to the next ball and made a beautiful left-foot drop kick to the fence, for which four leg byes were registered.

Our Proud Heritage: A History of the South Melbourne Cricket Club from 1862, Robert Grogan (South Melbourne Cricket Club, 2003)

FORGOTTEN MAN

*Cricketing doctor HO Rock is one of only three players
to average 100-plus in the Sheffield Shield.*

If a player ends his Sheffield Shield career with a batting average in excess of 100 and scores a century on debut against three other states, one would expect that player to be a household name. Instead, Dr Harry Owen Rock remains one of those extraordinary players whose career is remembered only by cricketing aficionados. What makes his career even more extraordinary is that he was dropped from matches because better-quality batsmen were available!

Harry Owen Rock was born in Scone, New South Wales on 18 October 1896. His father, Claude William Rock, had been a Cambridge Blue, played for Warwickshire and then played three matches for Tasmania between 1888–89 and 1892–93. He then moved to New South Wales in 1894.

Rock moved to Sydney for his education and boarded at the King's School, Parramatta. Here he received coaching from the former Australian Test player G 'Gerry' Hazlitt and EF 'Mick' Waddy, who was the Australian 12th man against England at Sydney in the fifth Test of the 1907–08 series.

Rock enlisted with the First AIF [Australian Imperial Forces] during World War I. He was severely wounded in France, which forced him to adopt a very upright batting stance. The war also left him with chronically weak knees, which also affected his cricket. On return, Rock attended Sydney University where he commenced studies for a doctor's degree. He played for Sydney University in the Sydney grade competition from the 1919–20 season onwards. Between 1920–21 and 1923–24, Rock scored more than 500 runs in each grade season but was never chosen to play for NSW. The closest he got was to be 12th man against South Australia at Adelaide in the opening match of the 1921–22 Sheffield Shield season. His sole contribution was to catch LV Pellew off the bowling of OP Asher in the South Australian first innings.

Rock's chance finally came with the New South Wales v South Australia match at the Sydney Cricket Ground in November–December 1924; HL Collins, W Bardsley, C Kelleway and CG Macartney were unavailable and later JM Taylor dropped out of the team. Rock was brought into the team as an opening batsman to replace Collins.

He did not waste the chance, scoring 127 and 27 not out. His century took just 140 minutes. Journalists writing in the Sydney newspapers were very impressed by the right-handed opening batsman's rather belated first-class debut at the age of 27. They commented on his upright, stiff stance, powerful driving and cutting and his ability to place the ball and keep the scoreboard ticking over.

Rock declined an invitation to travel to Adelaide to play in the return match against South Australia. His next match was against Victoria at the Sydney Cricket Ground in late January 1925. The late finish of the third Test between Australia and England at Adelaide meant that a brace of regulars could not play. Rock opened again in New South Wales' first innings and scored a career high of 235, made in 387 minutes with fifteen 4s and three chances. His partnership of 268 for the third wicket with AF Kippax [212] is still the New South Wales record for the third wicket against Victoria. Despite his solid 51 in the second innings, New South Wales lost the match. Rock also kept wicket after tea on the last day; NSW wicketkeeper AT Ratcliffe fielded after taking a couple of blows.

Rock missed the return Sheffield Shield match against Victoria in Melbourne, as it commenced the day after the Sydney game. The match had been postponed from earlier in the season due to Test commitments and rain. He also missed the second NSW v MCC match at Sydney in February 1925 due to university exams. He ended the 1924–25 season with a first-class aggregate of 440 runs at 146.66. He also topped the Sydney grade competition with 656 runs at 54.68.

The 1925–26 season was an important summer, with an Ashes tour to England looming. Rock started the season as he had left off in 1924–25, scoring 151 against Western Australia at Sydney in November 1925. The West Australians were making their first tour of the eastern states. Rock played his usual quick scoring style; his innings was scored in 125 minutes with nineteen 4s.

In December 1925, a match was played at Sydney between an Australian XI and The Rest as a trial to aid selection for the 1926 tour of England. This match was crucial to Rock's representative ambitions but it was the only time that he failed, with scores of 12 and 35. According to newspaper sources, Rock was unlucky in the first innings. He had established himself when he was bowled by an unplayable outswinger from JM Gregory.

Rock travelled to Adelaide for the match against South Australia in December 1925 but was made 12th man on the morning of the game. In Sydney there was widespread criticism of his omission. The expert JC Davis in the *Referee* claimed Rock's demotion to be 'the most extraordinary case of the omission of a player from the New South Wales team for over 30 years. On the fast, true wickets of Australia, I consider no NSW batsman is superior to Rock. Rock is easily the finest cover driver in Australian cricket today.'

Luckily for Rock, fast bowler SC Everett strained his side in the match and could not be considered for the next Shield game against Victoria in Melbourne, also in December 1925. Batting at No. 7, [as] Collins and Bardsley had returned, he contributed 81 to the huge NSW total of 705. He was considered unlucky, being given out lbw off an inside edge.

Rock missed the next game in the Shield against South Australia at Sydney due to a critical university exam. His final first-class appearance was against Victoria in Sydney in January 1926. Once again, batting at No. 7, he scored a run-a-minute 39 as NSW amassed another huge 700-plus total.

After the end of the 1925–26 season, Rock had passed his medical examinations at Sydney University and was now a qualified doctor. When he was not chosen in the 1926 touring team to England, he retired from all cricket and set up practice as a doctor in Newcastle, 160 kilometres from Sydney. He may have retired just one season too early. In 1926–27, New South Wales was without Collins, Bardsley, Gregory and Kelleway, so a player with his obvious talent should have been an automatic choice in any first XI.

Three to average 100-plus in the Sheffield Shield

Average	Batsman	Matches	Innings	Not out	Highest score	Runs	100s
112.00	Harry Rock (NSW, 1924–25 to 1925–26)	4	6	1	235	560	2
110.19	Don Bradman (NSW & SA, 1927–28 to 1947–48)	62	96	15	452*	8926	36
104.09	Barry Richards (SA, 1970–71)	8	13	2	356	1145	4

* denotes not out

The Cricket Statistician, Graham Clayton (Association of Cricket Statisticians and Historians, Nottingham, UK, Winter 1997)

A MEAN UNDERARMER

Teddy Lockwood took 10 wickets in a match five times in the Geelong Cricket Association at the turn of the century, including 37 wickets in 1900–01 and 1901–02 – all bowling underarm! Teddy and his twin brother George were also champion footballers of the day, playing in back-to-back premierships with Collingwood in 1902–03.

HIS EYE WAS IN

One of Lockwood's contemporaries was Geelong's Ernest 'Bung' Newling, who played 150 games of VFL [Victorian Football League] football. He also was a prolific run-maker in local cricket and in one match for Geelong 'B' he made 148 at first XI standard, his feats all the more extraordinary because he had the sight only from one eye.

ALL-AUSTRALIAN BOYS

The Melbourne *Age* says: 'The cabled particulars of the first day's play against the MCC disclose a remarkable incident at one stage of it, which would be hardly likely to pass unnoticed in the pavilion at the time. It was when Albert Trott joined Sam Woods at the wickets. Every man at that particular time taking an active part in the game – batsmen, bowlers, and fieldsmen, all included – was an Australian native!'

Cricket: A Weekly Record of the Game, edited by CW Alcock (London, 10 August 1899)

GREAT BOWLING

A bowler named A Nixon, in a small match at Adelaide, took nine wickets for eight runs, and twice did the hat-trick during the innings. All the runs were made before he had taken his second wicket. Seven of the wickets fell to him in nine balls.

Cricket: A Weekly Record of the Game, edited by CW Alcock (London, 8 January 1897)

AMAZING BUT TRUE

George Giffen, a young member of the 1884 side to the 'Motherland', lost not one, but two diamond rings over the side of the ship while eating an orange and throwing some peel over the side into the Mediterranean.

With Bat and Ball, George Giffen (Ward Lock & Co, London, 1898)

ALMOST 10 FOR NONE!

For a junior XV against a mixed XII from Port Melbourne, in a match played on 9 January, a young bowler named Parkinson at the fall of the 10th man had clean bowled nine wickets for no runs. When the last man went in the record was 14 and Parkinson then had a bit of bad luck, his second ball to the newcomer being put up in the slips and badly missed. Four runs were got off him after this, and his average altogether was 10 wickets for four runs against the team including six of the best Port Melbourne batsmen. The *Australasian,* from which these particulars are taken, is right in calling this a very fine bowling performance.

Cricket: A Weekly Record of the Game, edited by CW Alcock (London, 25 February 1886)

First Test Century: Neil Harvey after making a century in hometown Melbourne in only his second Test, against India, in 1948.

8
BOYS WILL BE BOYS

❝"Tell me, Neil," he said. "Your eyes aren't that brilliant.
Who leads you out to bat?"❞

CONVICTS ALWAYS

Commentator extraordinaire Henry Blofeld
had an answer for everything.

On arriving in Australia for the first time and being asked by Customs and Immigration: 'Do you have a criminal record?', Henry Blofeld of 'My Dear Old Thing' fame said in his ever-so-English voice: 'Is it still compulsory?'

THERE WAS ONLY ONE MERV

It was a particularly critical stage in a Sheffield Shield match in Melbourne and Victoria's captain Simon O'Donnell stood at the dressing-room as tailender Merv Hughes gathered his gear. 'Merv,' said O'Donnell, 'No big hits today ... I'll tell you when you can go for it.'

Tim May was floating up his offies and to the first the big fellow faced; the temptation was too much for Merv and, attempting to be the first man to swipe a ball into the old Jolimont railyards, he top-edged an easy catch.

O'Donnell was almost purple with rage and just as he was preparing to give Merv the biggest spray imaginable as he trudged back into the rooms, Merv looked at him and said: 'What? ... Haven't you ever got a good one early?'

MAVERICK UMPIRE

The maverick Australian Cec Pepper, among the best players *never* to play a Test, was umpiring the Lancs–Northants match at Blackpool in 1968. Jack Simmons, later to captain Tasmania, was making his first-class debut. Like Pepper, 'Flat Jack' was a product of the Lancashire League. Pepper took an immediate liking to the kid and kept encouraging and advising the off spinner where and when to bowl. He made sure none of his comments were heard by the batsmen. Finally, after going around the wicket, Simmons took his first wicket for Lancashire when Pepper gave left-hander Hylton Ackerman out lbw, adding as he raised his finger, 'I told you I was right.'

Pavilion 2011, Mark Browning (Australian Cricket Society, Melbourne, 2010–11)

YES, COME ON, GO GO GO

Scarborough Park's match in the St George district lower grades had finished early. The boys walked back to their cars, watching an adjoining game between two of the top teams in the same grade.

They were intrigued by the mid-off fieldsman decked out in a white shirt with 'F**K OFF' in large letters emblazoned on the front. The fielder had a cigarette in his mouth and was holding a transistor to his ear. Apparently the feature race from Rosehill Gardens was just about on.

The batsman on strike nicely leg-glanced a delivery to fine leg, ran through for a run and was contemplating a second when he heard 'YES ... COME ON ... GO GO GO'. Turning blind he made a mad dash to the other end only to join his stationary partner at the other end and was run out.

'It wasn't me saying GO GO GO,' said his partner. 'It was the bloke with the trannie at mid-off.'

The umpire's decision stood and back to his mates went the unfortunate batsman. Eyewitness Graham Goulder says in the commotion it went unrecorded if the punter had won the money.

FAVOURITES FROM FAVELLI AND CO

No one sledged as hard and often as Les Favell, South Australia's 'Mr Cricket' throughout the '50s and '60s.

Long-time South Australian teammate Barry Jarman said Favell would abuse the bowlers while he was batting, some being so taken aback they'd complain to the umpire!

'It was hilarious and he was good at it,' Jarman said. 'He used to tell them that they couldn't bowl and then proceed to hook and cut them all over Adelaide Oval.

'Terry Jenner was bowling against us one day for Western Australia and Les kept charging down the wicket to him saying "Happy Birthday!"

'Ian Chappell was at the other end and went to call Les through for a single. "You don't think you're getting down this end son do you!" said Les.'

Having hooked New Zealander Bob Blair into a grandstand at Christchurch [in 1957], Favell sauntered down the other end and said: 'I hope they don't take you off!'

Neil Harvey made 21 Test centuries for Australia, without once being able to see the scoreboard, his long-range eyesight not being good enough to allow him to read anything at distance!

The Australians were staying at the Victoria Hotel in Johannesburg and a cricket-mad optometrist, who had his practice next door, offered a free eye check for all members of the team. 'We had an hour to kill and in I went,' said Harvey. 'He put the chart up there and I gave him some funny answers which obviously weren't right. He said: "Listen, come back tomorrow and have another go."

'I sat in the same chair, looked at the card and gave him the same set of wrong answers. "Tell me, Neil," he said. "Your eyes aren't that brilliant. Who leads you out to bat?"'

At a team reception at a country town one day, fun-loving Lindsay Hassett began his speech with, 'Never in my whole life have I seen such a gathering of so many ugly men!' and amidst the gasps, he said, 'and never before have I seen so many gorgeous women.'

Colin Miller couldn't believe it. Here he was in faraway Antigua and four Australian supporters sporting FUNKY MILLER FAN CLUB T-shirts were waving and cheering outside the ground at St Johns. Not only did Miller ask the bus driver to stop, he hopped out, shared a beer and had his picture taken with his fans while his Australian teammates from the Waughs to Warnie enjoyed the moment.

All Out for One and Other Australian Cricket Anecdotes, Ken Piesse (Viking, Melbourne, 2005)

THERE WAS ONLY ONE FREDDIE

Freddie Trueman loved Australia and Australians loved him.

On being shown the Sydney Bridge for the first time and being told what a marvel of engineering it was and so on, Freddie Trueman said: 'Aye, it should be, it were mostly constructed in Middlesbrough, Yorkshire [by Dorman Long] and you buggers haven't finished paying for it yet ... '

LATE NIGHTS WITH RICKETTY-KATE

Late-night parties sitting around the lounge-room radiogram or crystal set listening to the Ashes broadcasts 'from England' were all the rage in the '30s.

Ricketty-Kate! Ricketty-Kate! A wicket had fallen and thousands of cricket-hungry Australians would sit forward eagerly in their armchairs to hear the latest score from England.

This was cricket mania 1930s-style. The era of the 'synthetic' Test cricket broadcasts. The days when it was commonplace not to go to bed until 3.30 am after the final ball of the day.

The ghost broadcasts from Melbourne and Sydney created enormous interest. Bleary-eyed enthusiasts would drag themselves to work the next morning, but it was all worth it, especially if 'The Don', 'Ponny' or everyone's favourite Stan McCabe were among the runs.

Many would dream about Ricketty-Kate, the novel doll which belonged to the innovator of the broadcasts, Melbourne radio station 3DB. Her eyes would light up and the 3DB sports-team led by the whimsical Charlie Vaude would go through their paces, singing songs and generally entertaining their appreciative audiences.

Four 'synthetic' Test series – the 1930, 1934 and 1938 Australian tours of England and the 1935–36 tour of South Africa – were broadcast to all parts of Australia. The Wimbledon tennis finals and the Australian rugby union Tests in South Africa were also broadcast 'synthetically' to the sports-minded Aussies.

The 'ball-by-ball' descriptions of the cricket action in England were formulated from regular cables which were transmitted to stations and media throughout Australia. 3DB and its Sydney affiliates and the Australian Broadcasting Commission were mainly responsible for Test-match fever sweeping the continent.

Teams of broadcasters used to interpret the English cables and provide the commentary for listeners. Although they were 13,000 miles away, the commentaries became so expert that many people thought they were broadcasting direct from England.

Cricket fever was established as Bradman rampaged the English attack of 1930, scoring a record 974 runs for the series, as Woodfull's Australia defeated 'archenemy' England 2–1 in the five Tests.

As Bradman scored centuries, seemingly at will, the sales of crystal sets ballooned. Nearly 200,000 wirelesses were sold during the 1930 tour, creating an unusually heavy demand on electric light plants around the country.

In the first broadcast, many whimsical appeals to cease broadcasting

Hear the Cricket IN ENGLAND!

WITH A RADIO EQUIPPED WITH

EVEREADY

RADIO BATTERIES

See inside for 1953 TEST ITINERARY

were received from women whose husbands refused to come to bed. During the third Test many calls came from men whose wives were insisting on staying up! A tremendous impetus was given to feminine interest in cricket – and 3DB [Jack Ryder], 2UE Sydney ['Monty' Noble] and the Australian Broadcasting Commission had to explain almost nightly what the 'gully' and 'slips' meant.

Cricket gave commercial radio its greatest lift. At 1 am on the second day of the first Test match of 1930, the manager of 3DB leaned over the shoulder of commentator Frank Russell, and speaking into the microphone said; 'We would appreciate it if listeners would let us know if they desire us to continue the Test broadcasts into the small hours. Are you staying up? Would you like us to keep going? Our phone number is F2118.'

Within minutes, 50 trunk line calls for 3DB were lodged in Victoria, four in Queensland, 16 in New South Wales and 10 in South Australia.

The trunk line operators were asked to take messages, for local calls which swamped all suburban exchanges completely blocked 3DB's switchboard. The telephoning continued until the station closed, many messages coming from parties of up to 50 people.

The 3DB staff, which included Ryder, a former Australian Test captain, Russell, Charlie Vaude, Renn Millar and Eric Welch, were staggered. Then the telegrams and letters began to arrive. All day, telegraph messengers panted up 3DB's stairs, the daily average by the last Test being 200 telegrams between nine and five. Altogether, more than 2000 telegrams and thousands of letters arrived.

Presents for the 3DB crew came every day from appreciative listeners from all over Australia – oranges from Mildura, boxes of cigars from the Riverina, crayfish from Port Pirie, cases of wine from South Australia, even cases of beer all the way from Launceston and Hobart.

Jack Ryder, now 87, can still vividly remember the 3DB broadcasts. He retired as Australia's captain after the 1928–29 series against England in Australia and was immediately 'signed up' for the radio commentaries.

'The broadcasts were tremendously popular,' Mr Ryder said. 'We'd start about 8 and go through to about 3.30 in the morning ... then go to work! It was pretty hectic. The first night we had an open-air type broadcast [outside the Athenaeum Theatre] in Collins Street. We were all up on a platform and people came and watched. However, it was an unsuccessful night as the cable service from England broke down and after that we moved back to the studio at the 3DB-Herald offices. I will always remember that first night. Thousands of people were around. There was a huge crowd outside the *Age* office in Collins Street, cheering each wicket as they were posted on the makeshift scoreboard. When the cables did break down, Charlie Vaude would get up and entertain the crowd, telling jokes or singing songs. It would certainly ease the tension in the studio, too. When a message was overdue, Charlie would say, "The latest cable is just coming around Spring Street by cable-car. We'll soon have a score for you," even though Charlie was in a little room, nowhere near Spring Street!', Mr Ryder said. 'We made our broadcasts pretty professional, with dubbed sounds which added atmosphere. I think we fooled a few of the people into thinking the broadcasts were coming live ...'

Centenary Test, Melbourne, March 12–17, 1977 (official souvenir publication of the Australian Cricket Board), Ken Piesse (Sportsplan Marketing, Melbourne, 1977)

HEAD DOWN, PLAY STRAIGHT
There was only one Ernie McCormick ...

In the old days of club cricket in Melbourne there were few greater characters than Les Keating, who for quite some time was captain of the Richmond Cricket Club's first team. Ernie McCormick, a tall, lean and taciturn fast bowler who played 12 Tests for Australia in the 1930s, tells a story about his young days at Richmond under the captaincy of Keating. He recalls a game at the Punt Road Ground, bordering the MCG, when he was last man in with just 10 runs required for victory.

Ernie tells it this way: 'I admit I wasn't much of a bat in those days.

On the Attack: Australian bowlers of the 1930s, as depicted on Allen's confectionary cards of the mid-'30s.

My teammates were well aware of this, too, so before I went in I got plenty of advice from them about keeping my head down, playing straight and leaving the run-scoring to the bloke at the other end. As it turned out, Les Keating was the fellow at the other end when I went in, he buttonholed me on the way out and told me to keep my head down, to play straight and leave the scoring to him. Well and truly fortified by all of this advice, I took guard and faced up. The first ball was well up and without thinking I took a wild swipe at it and away the thing went over square leg, out onto Punt Road. Les and I met in the middle of the wicket and the old fellow put his arm on my shoulder and said, "That's the way son, head down and play straight ... the shots can come later."'

The Wit of Cricket, Ian Brayshaw (The Currawong Press, Milson's Point, Sydney, 1981)

199 NOT OUT

It was a formidable harem ...

In the old days a new ball could be taken after 200 runs had been scored. An Australian team was on its way to England in the '30s and had stopped off at Bombay where the tourists were being introduced rather ceremoniously to a very wealthy and influential Maharajah.

As the players stood in two neat lines awaiting the great moment of introduction, they were addressed by the team manager: 'I would like very much to introduce you to the Maharajah of So-and-so ... not only is he the richest man in the world ... he also has 199 wives.'

From the depths of the back row came the quip: 'One more and he'd need a new ball!'

The Wit of Cricket, Ian Brayshaw (The Currawong Press, Milson's Point, Sydney, 1981)

JARDINE THE DIPLOMAT

There was another side to England's ultra-competitive
Bodyline tour captain Douglas Jardine.

Together with the Englishmen, we journeyed 50 miles to York [Western Australia] to a country race meeting. From memory, it was the only time on that tour that Australians and Englishmen fraternised socially; portents of the squabbles ahead were possibly seen at the racecourse when two small boys simultaneously arrived to sell Jardine a race book.

Jardine was in a quandary [as to] which one to patronise, when suddenly gloves were produced and the boys set to with a will. It was a spirited bout, but Jardine stopped it by buying a book from each. It was the only known diplomatic move he made in Australia.

Cricket Crisis, Jack Fingleton (Cassell & Company, London, 1946)

KING CRICKET

Oriel on the things that really matter.

Will Germany heed Britain's plea,
    And with her peers in peace-talk share?
It matters not a jot to me;
    I do not know and do not care.
One theme alone holds me in thrall –
Should bowlers bounce head-high the ball?

What now will De Valera bold
    Propound? What new preposterous claim?
The Irish question leaves me cold,
    Whatever be his little game.
Far weightier things my thought demand,
For Jardine's men have reached our land.

The pact at Ottawa late made
    Will it be spurned by Britain? – us?
A sterner game is to be played.
    O'er trivial matters shall we fuss?
One questions on the lips of men –
Shall Bradman wield the bat or pen?

A poser for the USA –
    To keep her tariff or her trade?
Thus experts talk, the cables say;
    But what is this affair when weighed
Against the tidings great and grim,
    That Voce's ankle's troubling him?

What will the Country Party do
    When voting on the Mortgage Bill?
That duty on bananas, too –
    Will Page's men work any ill?
Forget it, man! But hear aghast
That hefty Bowes is bowling fast.

The Nawab of Pataudi bats.
    With wristy strokes to off and on.
His feet are quicker than a cat's.
    The Ashes are as good as gone!
Bowed with my weight of cricket cares,
How can I think of world affairs?

The Argus, Oriel (Melbourne, 22 October 1932)

OF BARRACKERS AND BARRACKING

*Approaching the deciding Test in 1930, cricket
fever was at a zenith, home and away.*

Fellows will be all agog for the start of the final Test match at the Oval, London, this Saturday, and so will find this pen-picture of one side of Australian cricket very interesting. 'Down Under' spectators keep up a running fire of comments on the play and players. 'Barracking', they call it, and our cricket expert has some lively tales to tell of their comments.

Just before the Australian cricket team commenced their series of matches in England, a gentleman from New South Wales called upon Mr Kelly, the manager, and announced: 'I have come all the way from Sydney to see your boys play. In fact, I have travelled many thousands of miles to barrack for you.'

He didn't know that there is no such thing as 'barracking' in England, nor that if he gave voice to his feelings here in the same manner as followers of cricket in Sydney sometimes do he would be promptly squashed by those who sat or stood in the vicinity.

For the most serious form of barracking in England is sarcastic clapping by the crowd when batsmen score too slowly.

But unkind barracking is not merely confined to spectators in Australia. Players themselves have been known to indulge in it, although they take care not to allow their remarks to be heard at any great distance.

I have been to Australia with an MCC side and I know that barracking has simply grown out of sheer enthusiasm for cricket. I remember seeing about 25,000 spectators on the Sydney ground before a ball was bowled. There was no shelter from the scorching sun, yet those people were content to go through torture in order to witness the game they loved.

Immediately he arrives on the ground, the spectator removes his coat, waistcoat and collar and settles down to enjoy the game – to get all he can out of it, and to while away the hours with good-natured banter – barracking at the least provocation.

Sometimes, however, the 'hooligan' section of an Australian crowd makes itself heard in [a] very forceful manner, two instances being connected with one of our best-tempered professional cricketers EA 'Patsy' Hendren.

Now, Patsy is not renowned for his good looks, but there was no need for a barracker at Sydney to bawl out: 'Hey, Patsy, you wasn't chosen for yer looks!'

Hendren ignored the remark and the man became more offensive. At last the Middlesex man, who was fielding on the boundary line, turned to his tormentor. 'If you don't keep your mouth shut,' remarked Patsy, 'you'll get something that will hurt!'

'Oh, and what'll that be?' asked the man.

Patsy looked him over very calmly and said: 'Well ... judging by the size of your mouth you will get your insides sunburnt!'

There was a roar of delight from the crowd and the cricketer was not worried again that afternoon!

On another occasion, at Sydney, some similar remarks about Hendren's looks were shouted from the crowd and at the end of an over he asked his captain if he could change places with [Andy] Sandham. So 'Sandy' was sent to the boundary line.

The Surrey man does not always wear a cheerful expression and the English eleven were convulsed with laughter when, at the end of the over, the same barracker shouted: 'Hey, for the love of Mike ... let's have old Patsy back here again!'

But the barrackers of Australia do not vent their remarks solely on the visitors. In one Test match at Melbourne the score stood at 320 for no wicket, [Jack] Hobbs and [Wilfred] Rhodes being able to do as they liked, when an advertising balloon passed over the ground and a dummy figure, which was attached, dropped onto the field.

'Hey, Clem,' shouted a dozen voices [Clem Hill being Australia's captain], 'here's another bowler for you!'

Yet there are some very kind barrackers. For instance, in one Test match in Sydney three members of the English team got 'duck's eggs' [no score]. On the following morning a carrier called at the hotel and delivered three fine York hams addressed to the three failures, with covering letters explaining that the hams were sent to be eaten with the 'eggs' scored on the previous day!

Another instance of kindness comes also to mind. When we were leaving Australia for home, a huge packing case was delivered on the ship. It contained enough cigarettes for the whole party for about three months and a letter explained that it was a present from a party of barrackers. 'We've had a great time at your expense. Now have these smokes at ours,' ran the missive. 'Come again and we'll give you more barracking than you will be able to bear.'

The Modern Boy, 'An Old County Cricketer' (London, 16 August 1930)

BEN BOWYANG'S TEST
Few luvved their crikit an drinkin like Ben Bowyang who not only was an ossie cartoon hero, but a keen criket observa.

Melbin Crikit Groun
7 am Fridy

Deer sir

i arriv in melbin lars nite as per contrack in good elth an spirits an fare stranin at the leesh to git to me jurnalistic jootys of reportin this test match in my own fathful an original stile.

as akordin to our agreement I am doin this job on time wurk an not peace work or per article I was down at the criket groun brite an early this morning

but you are orful late risers here in melbin

me on mundy

(drawed by mr wells)

One of a Kind: The irreverent CJ Dennis creation, Ben Bowyang.

you mitent beleeve it but altho the sun was well up there wasent a sole abowt

owever I am countin it in as time on jooty as it wernt my falt ther was nuthink doin

so I went back to the pub an ad a bit of brekfus then I cum back an as there was still no wun abowt I clum over the fence so as to be sure of a seet

8.20 am

you mitent bleeve it but i been chuked out an ime ritin this agen a tree in the moter park an i rekin im ernin me muney

9.50 am

i ave clum over the fence agen an tore wun [1] pare of pants for wich i will charge on my akount.

this jurnalistick life as its ups an downs asnt it

the gaits is now open an to [2] men ave cum in but thay aint startid playin yet

11.20 am

i been avin a bit of a nap avin slep poorly lars nite

there is a orful lot of peepil ere but you is terrlbul slow startin yure matches in melbin

11 45 am

england as won the toss

sumow I dont think this is goin to be mutch of a match

12 miday
thay is cumin out

12.30 pm
ime orful sorry but I bin too ixcited to rite any think for the last arf
our
the skore now is jardeen 12 obbs 5 ex tees 3 totil 10
ime orful ixcited
gosht that wun neerly got im
why dont they chuk in quicker
jardeens cot out
no he aint
wat sort of umpirin do thay cal that
the man sittin nex me will git wot es b lookin for if he dont stop chipin
the orstralians
orray obbs is stumped
no e aint
the umpirins rotten
the skores is
neerly cot neerly cot ows that umpire
the skores
this is the slowest battin i ever see

12.50 pm
If its all the saim to you mister editer ile leeve the rest of my ritin til
i git back to the pub tonite an git a bit of peese
Ime that ixcited now i dunno wether ime on me ed or me eels
hoppln you are the saim
yures truly
Ben Bowyang
p s 1.46 pm jardeen is run out
p s no. no. 2 1.50 pm the umpire sez e aint ... this is orful

The Herald, CJ Dennis as Ben Bowyang (Melbourne, 8 March 1929 – day one of
the Test)

ONLY WONDERS NEED APPLY
Notable bush poet and author CJ Dennis invariably
enlivened a cricket match with his unique humour.

Without wishing in any way to lower the dignity of the game or to detract from the traditional seriousness of cricket, may one be allowed to point out that in the matter of keeping a complete list of the records, much is yet to be desired?

Indeed, so far from the flippant is my intention and so earnest my enthusiasm for preserving faithfully all details of the history of this great game that I would suggest the appointment at once of another official. The duty of this official – preferably a shorthand writer – would be to sit beside the scorer and set down rapidly all the records as fast as they are established.

As matters are at present, despite the earnestness and enthusiasm of our amateur and unofficial record detectors, many interesting records, some of them world records, go unrecorded and are lost forever in the rush and flurry of the game.

For example, despite the vigilance of enthusiast it has never yet been even mentioned, as far as I know, that Duckworth, in the match now in progress, established a record unique and unsurpassed in cricketing annals.

[George] Duckworth is the first man in the world, in a Test or any other first-class match, at Adelaide, to secure a catch behind the wicket while wearing a piece of steak in his glove! Incidentally, [Bill] Woodfull is the first man to be caught behind the wicket at Adelaide by a man wearing a piece of steak ... Woodfull thus establishes yet another record all his own.

Think how England will thrill when this fact, now recorded for the first time, is broadcast to the ends of the Empire. There is only one other instance, so far as I am aware, of steak in cricket. This was during the famous match between Gunn's Gully and Yabbie Creek back in 1912 when Bill Smith, fielding at silly point, wore a piece of steak, but not in the glove. He wore it on the eye, which had stopped a fast one earlier in the match. I could, if I wished, give a long and exciting list of similar records established during the present match, but one or two will suffice.

Is it generally known, for instance, that Maurice Tate is the first bowler to bowl the first batsman in the first Australian innings for one run while he [the bowler] had his left bootlace untied? Think of it. Never, since the earliest days of cricket, has this been done before in a Test match!

Also, [Archie] Jackson is the first man to strain a particular thigh muscle during his first day's fielding in his first Test match; and [12th-man Tommy] Andrews, who is the first man to field as substitute for the first man who first strained a thigh muscle in his first Test match, thus establishes a unique record without even being a member of the first XI.

I could go on like this for hours; but could England's nerves endure it? It's very doubtful.

Yet, for the sake of posterity, I would urge that an official recorder of records be appointed at once – a fine, alert, quick-thinking, painstaking man who would let no opportunity slip and no detail escape his notice.

Where shall we find such a wonder?

The Herald, CJ Dennis (Melbourne, 5 February 1929)

THREE DUCKS . . . IN THE SAME GAME!
HV 'Ranji' Hordern on a world record . . . of sorts.

You have been very patient, dear Unknown and I am going to try your patience just a little further. I want to be boastful this time and tell you how I created a world's record. You didn't think I was a world-beater? Well, I am. I did something which no one had ever done before and no one will ever do again. If that is not a world's record I don't know what is; and I did it as a batsman – no Victor Trumper, Jack Hobbs, Charlie Macartney – none of them did what I did or, I might add, ever wanted to.

It happened this way: there was a 'bye' in both the first and second elevens of the North Sydney Club and as we were all frightfully keen, a match was arranged combining the two elevens; and the players were selected to make a more or less even balance.

As we were all clubmates, naturally there was a fair amount of chaff beforehand as to what we were going to do to one another. I know I was very prominent in the 'going-to-do' line.

Our side lost the toss on a beautiful wicket. My effort with the ball was something like three or four wickets for 100; anyway, nothing to write home to one's people about. And now comes the record-breaking performance.

We also batted on a perfect wicket. When my turn came I had to face AJ 'Bert' Hopkins and a particularly fine bowler he was. His second ball I edged into the slips and was caught – for zero. Towards the end of our innings it came on to rain, soaked the wicket a bit, and then a hot sun – the result, a sticky devil! We followed on and in my second effort I was clean bowled by Syd Redgrave for another round figure. Two innings, two duck eggs.

Now, I admit getting two ducks in a match is not unique; but listen! The wicket improved, the rot stopped and a good stand was made; so good and substantial did it appear that the last two batsmen, lulled into a feeling of security, drifted off to a nearby hotel for 'a quencher'. Then, as so often happens in our glorious game, a few more wickets fell rapidly and as the beer-drinkers were still AWL [absent without leave], there was no one to go in to bat. After waiting awhile, one of the fielding side suggested that I should come in again. Nothing daunted I did and promptly collected my third egg! And that's how I won the battle of Waterloo – and created my unbeatable record. I don't mind telling you . . . that I travelled for the next week by an early train, as I just couldn't face the music!

Googlies: Coals from a Test Cricketer's Fireplace, Dr HV Hordern (Angus & Robertson Ltd, Sydney, 1932)

THE GREAT AUSTRALIAN PEST

Broken Hill's most famous turn-of-the-century sporting son was Ernie Jones, the 'Broken Hill Catapult' who worked in the mines Monday to Friday and on weekends bowled faster than any Australian before him.

Before venturing to the Big Smoke and being part of South Australia's inaugural Sheffield Shield team in 1892–93, Ernie 'Jonah' Jones's feats with the Souths club in Broken Hill, 'the Silver City', were legend, the locals reckoning he broke just as many bones as he took wickets.

Jonah was the Merv Hughes of his day, a giant Australian pest! He'd think nothing of wrestling teammates in the dressing-rooms, clothes on or off. Once when he sent a short ball through WG Grace's beard, he was claimed to have said: 'Sorry Doc, she slipped.'

On enquiry from the Prince of Wales as to whether he'd attended St Peter's College, one of Adelaide's most prominent private schools, Jonah said yes, he did, every day, carting the night soil!

Bradmans of the Bush: The Legends & Larrikins of Australian Bush Cricket, Ken Piesse (Penguin Australia, Melbourne, 2002)

WHISKERS V NO WHISKERS

Pick-up games were commonplace in the colonies in the early days.

Antecedent to the Victorian gold discoveries, towards the close of 1851, a bearded man was as much a *rara avis* in Melbourne as a bearded woman is in 1884.

Whiskers of the patterns known in slangology as the 'mutton chop', or the 'Newgate fringe', were hirsute luxuries tolerated by the usages of city and suburban society and though the bare faces were largely in the majority, whiskerandoes were to be frequently encountered. The Melbourne Cricket Club included amongst its members individuals who wore whiskers and those who did not; and this is how it came about that a match was made between elevens of the Whiskered and Whiskerless. It was played on 26 April [1888] when there was a prime day's fun on the Trans-Yarra Cricket Ground.

There was a very large attendance, the day was fine and the work commenced at 10 o'clock. The result was that the 'hairy side' won by seven wickets to spare, and here is the scoring total:

NO WHISKERS first innings: 87
WHISKERS first innings: 144
NO WHISKERS second innings: 90
WHISKERS second innings: 36 for 3 wickets

As an amusing reminiscence I append the names of the players of this remarkable occasion. WHISKERS: Messrs JC Brodie, TF Hamilton, W Philpott, Geo Cavanagh, - Were, - Sims, E Bell, WH Hull, EP Sturt, WH Campbell, T Thorpe. NO WHISKERS: Messrs - Lister, - Hervey, - Hart, DS Campbell, H Creswick, Robt Russell, M a'Beckett, - Locke, E a'Beckett, V Stephen, Fitz Stephen.

The wonderful progress in cricket for the last 30 years has been well and often described in book and newspaper, and, perhaps, there is no incident in the strange eventful history of Victoria more calculated to exemplify the extraordinary development of the colony, than a comparison of the first cricket match on Batman's Hill in 1838 and the cricketing feats recently witnessed in Melbourne. The astonishment evolved cannot fail to be amplified when it is borne in mind that Russell, one of the founders of the MCC, and Halfpenny, of the Union, still live and move amongst us and

Always Time for Cricket: Few loved cricket like long-time Australian Prime Minister Sir Robert Menzies, whose affairs often took him to England around Lord's Test match time. *Melbourne Cricket Club*

though not as lively as of yore, like two old crickets chirping about the city, and beholding, with just feelings of self-exultation, the results of a movement of which they were the originators, though, in the cricketing world of today their names, if not unknown, are probably never mentioned.

The Chronicles of Early Melbourne, 1835 to 1852, Centennial Edition, Vol II, 'Garryowen' (Fergusson & Mitchell, Melbourne, 1888)

THE LAST WORD

At a dinner given by the Australian Cricket Society to a group of Englishmen and women from the Cricket Society, London, broadcaster-critic Jim Swanton referred to a 'love-hate relationship' between England and Australia. 'We can't do without each other,' he said.

Sir Robert Menzies told the gathering: 'Next to seeing good cricket, the next best thing is talking about good cricket. When old cricketers get together they say, "Do you remember that great innings?" or "Do you remember that marvellous bowling?" or "Don't you remember that wonderful fielding?" They always say they do, whether they did or not.'

Australian Cricket, Eric Beecher (Modern Magazines, Sydney, March, 1971)

MCG Epic: Kim Hughes's gallant century against the West Indies in the 1981–82 Melbourne Test remains one of the greatest of all time. *Cricketer*

9
MATCHES AND MATCHWINNERS

A WHIRLWIND START

Free-flowing Michael Slater takes 17 runs from the opening over from Darren Gough in Australia's opening 2001 Test campaign at Edgbaston.

I took block from the umpire and looked down the pitch to see England's star bowler Darren Gough way back at the top of his run-up, rearing to go. The crowd was roaring, their faith in England restored by [Alec] Stewart and [Andy] Caddick's heroics. But I couldn't hear the noise: I rarely did when I was batting. I settled over my bat and looked towards 'Goughie' and saw a familiar, yet blurred, sight. I couldn't focus on him at all. All I knew was that he was on his way, charging in at me with a new ball in his big paw. My Ashes series was about to start and I felt like I was in some kind of parallel universe. The struggle to end England's innings had allowed me way too much time to think about how big this tour was for me and my cricketing future. I knew my bat needed to do all the talking on this tour, given the doubts that were creeping in from the people around me. And now with the willow in my hand I knew what I had to do.

Goughie's first ball landed short of a length, well outside off stump. It was the perfect ball to let go and give myself time to get it together – but it was also the ideal ball to square cut. Instinct took over. I smashed it through point for 4 and ended up tearing 17 off that first over. By stumps I was 76 not out off only 78 balls. I'd been quite shaky until I hit a straight on-drive back past Caddick. That's a hard shot to play at any time, so when you get one right you know you're playing well. I hit that ball for 4 and thought, 'Okay, this could be a good day.'

I hadn't planned to bat so aggressively, yet it worked incredibly well. But I got out early the next day when I should have settled in to score a big hundred, which would have been the perfect start to the series. Instead of giving myself time, I blasted away and was dismissed. Still, we had already knocked the stuffing out of the Poms by the end of the first day. For a while, especially during that Stewart and Caddick stand, England thought they could match it with us, but by stumps we were totally in control. And the fact that I had attacked so hard emphasised that. At a press conference at the end of the series, Steve Waugh said that my innings had been one of the most significant factors of the whole series. But by the time he said that, I was already out of the team.

Slats: The Michael Slater Story, Michael Slater (Random House Australia, Sydney, 2005)
Slater finished with 77 as Australia made 576 to win by an innings, its first of four wins for the Test summer.

A SPECIAL DAY

Ian Healy hits a 6 to win a Test . . . and a series, at Port Elizabeth in 1997.

By day four, the wicket had flattened out a bit, but it was still tricky. Fortunately for us, Mark Waugh, in at 2-30, picked this moment to play his greatest innings in Test cricket, and he took us to the brink of a famous victory. As I'd predicted, the partnerships were the key – 83 for the third wicket with Matty Elliott on day three, then 54 with his brother, 25 with 'Blewie' [Greg Blewett] and 66 with 'Bevo' [Michael Bevan]. However, just 12 runs from our target, Junior [Waugh] was bowled by [Jacques] Kallis. I was in. Straightaway, without another run being added, Bevo fell to ['Hansie'] Cronje. Still 12 to get, with only three wickets in hand.

I don't mind admitting I was very, very nervous. Second ball, Warnie slogged Cronje over mid-off's head and when we took off for the first run, my legs felt like jelly. Still, we managed three. My mind was racing and I found myself preoccupied with the noise of a large contingent of schoolchildren, and a motley brass band

whose members had brought
their instruments to the game. I
started singing a song to myself
between balls, to prevent my mind
being distracted, and the song –
'Have You Ever Really Loved a
Woman?' by Bryan Adams, which
proved I was mellowing – lodged
there. It worked, too, as I swung
Cronje away over square leg to
the boundary. Five to win. At the
end of the over, Warnie and I had
a conference, mid-pitch, where
we decided to keep it simple,
win each moment, and let the

Six for Victory: Ian Healy's 6 at Port Elizabeth finished a memorable Test.

result look after itself. We also chipped the umpires about the South
Africans' tactic of dropping the backward square-leg fieldsman back
as Cronje was running into bowl. Later, South African coach Bob
Woolmer claimed it was legal, but we weren't so sure. First ball of
Kallis' new over, Warnie was lbw. Now Jason Gillespie was in, just
Glenn McGrath to come, and I was stuck at the bowler's end with
five balls still to come. Fortunately, Dizzy was calmness personified,
the complete antithesis of Warnie and me. If blocking out the rest
of the over is what you want, Heals, then that's what I'll do. Kallis
was bang on line, but Dizzy kept him out comfortably. Now it was
Cronje's turn. And mine.

Before the first ball of the new over, the South African captain took
out his second slip and moved him to deep on the leg side, in front
of square. There was no way I was going to hit one out there, maybe
behind square, but not there. The new field placing suggested he was
going to bowl a middle-to-leg stump line, the intention, I assumed,
being to limit me to a single so they could have another go at Dizzy. If
Cronje had known how anxious I was, he might not have been quite
so conservative. I looked down at the vacant third-man boundary, and
thought, 'If he pitches outside off stump, I'll be aiming down there.'
Bob Simpson had always bagged me for trying to late-cut the first ball
I faced in an innings; here was my chance to demonstrate the true
value of that shot.

'Just watch the ball,' I told myself as Cronje moved in, 'and play
the moment.' First ball, I defended; same with the second. The band

played on, the schoolkids kept singing, and then, third ball, Cronje drifted into my pads ...

I didn't mean to hit it for 6. When I saw the ball pitching short of a length on leg stump I reacted instinctively: 'I'll go with that.' The ball came off the bat sweetly and I looked up and thought, 'Gee, that's gone.'

The moments straight after remain a blur. Arms raised, I turned to the Aussie dressing-room, where I could see that pandemonium had broken out. Dizzy ran up for an exuberant mid-pitch embrace that almost broke my back. The South Africans were disconsolate, then some fans were on the pitch and we were running for our lives to join the dressing-room party. I've never had a feeling like it. I was exhilarated, numb, wobbly, all at the same time. Steve Waugh grabbed me and shouted, 'Karachi's gone, mate!' I was glad it was over and so proud, satisfied and vindicated that I'd come through the way I did. Back at our hotel, I interrupted the celebrations to ring Helen and Mum and Dad, before heading back to revel in the victory some more. It was a special day.

Hands and Heals: The Autobiography, Ian Healy (Harper Sports, Sydney, 2000)

'WELL PLAYED, MAN ... WELL PLAYED'

It remains one of the greatest centuries ever at the Melbourne Cricket Ground, the day Kim Hughes stood up against one of the most fearsome attacks of all, in the 1981 Christmas Test against the West Indies.

'Concentrate,' he [Hughes] roared between deliveries. He roared it even as the bowlers stormed in. At slip, Viv Richards clapped Kim's half-century. Still Kim beseeched himself: 'Concentrate.' He put on 56 with [Rod] Marsh and 34 with [Bruce] Yardley. He hooked [Andy] Roberts once and attempted an encore – only to realise, the seam shaving his skull, that the first bouncer was the slow sucker one. 'Roberts gave me a look that said: "don't get too clever."' [Dennis] Lillee spanked a skier to cover, looking for once like he'd rather be any place than the MCG. [Michael] Holding yorked [Geoff] Lawson. Prospects of a heroic hundred vanished. On 71, Kim was joined by a man in a doormat-sized thigh pad. Kim wished No. 11 Terry Alderman luck. 'You'll need it,' he thought to himself.

Alderman was a scrapper with a trapdoor back-lift who took nine first-class matches to break his duck and had a Test average of six. Better treat this like a one-dayer, Kim decided. He jumped down the wicket at [Joel] Garner. The ball was short and ribcage-bound. Kim pulled it away off the front foot: textbook-perfect, but for the maniacal dash. Next ball was short again. Kim leapt back and across, square cutting with gusto. Ian Chappell disliked Kim's habit of pre-empting bowlers' deliveries. On this occasion, Chappell sensed, he was reading their minds impeccably. 'In fact, Hughes seemed to have the bowlers in tune with his thought processes,' Chappell hypothesised decades later. 'The more he hooked, pulled and cut, the shorter they pitched. The harder he hammered the ball, the harder they ran in.'

Alderman was sticking. Smacked on the helmet and elbow, he straight drove [Colin] Croft for 4. He had once chaperoned Ian Brayshaw from 39 to 100 in a last-wicket rearguard for Western Australia. Now Kim crashed into the 90s. [Thoughts of] Rix [his wife's father, the seriously ill Rix Davidson] re-entered his head. He knew Rix would be watching. Bowlers and fielders tried every trick to keep Kim off strike. But in 56 minutes Alderman faced only 26 balls. Two scampered runs to an empty midwicket – which Larry Gomes was supposed to keep to one – took Kim to 96 ...

[The] scrambled two meant he was still on strike to Garner. He wound back his bat: a rainmaking back-lift. He jabbed down. The force of the stroke made him topple backwards. The ball screeched past point. Uncharacteristically, he punched the air, twice. His tears were for his father-in-law. One hundred not out in a total of 198. Nobody else passed 21. Even now, Ian Chappell considers it the greatest postwar Australian knock. In Chappell's imaginings, only [Stan] McCabe's 187 and [Don] Bradman's 334 could possibly be finer.

Striding off, Kim noticed Croft whirling towards him. Fear was Kim's first instinct. 'He's been trying to get me all day. Maybe now he's going to thump me.'

But for once, Croft spoke. 'Well played, man ... well played.'

Golden Boy: Kim Hughes and the Bad Old Days of Australian Cricket, Christian Ryan
(Allen & Unwin, Sydney, 2009)

BOUNCING BOYCS

A bumper blitz on England's master batsman Geoff Boycott
fast-tracked Geoff Lawson into the Australian team.

[Geoff] Boycott took strike [with England needing just four runs to defeat NSW, in a 1978–79 tour game]. I raced in for the first delivery and pitched it up outside off stump to which Geoffrey replied with the trademark no-shot. That was the attempt to get him out – now it was time to try out the bounce in the middle of the wicket. My second ball was not quite at the halfway mark but climbed to shoulder height and Boycott went underneath with a degree of haste. The third ball of the over pitched in the same spot as the second, after which umpire Tom Brooks stepped out from behind the stumps as I began to walk back up the wicket after a slightly exaggerated follow-through; I sensed there was something on his mind. He told me quietly that 'two was enough'. The next ball was identical to the previous two, but Boycott, expecting something pitched up, was on the front foot early and was caught with his weight going forward. This time he only just got under the rising ball. The slips cordon looked as if they were enjoying the proceedings.

This time Tommy Brooks was not amused. He rushed out from his spot and met me several yards in front of the bowling crease: 'That's your first warning ... don't do anything silly,' he reprimanded. I continued busily on my way back to the mark and didn't catch the reactions from our players or the batsmen, but I sensed genuine discomfort, if not fear, from Boycott and I wasn't going to let him escape by getting onto the front foot to the next ball. It didn't matter now if I got a second or third warning anyway. The fourth short one was the pick of the bunch. This time Boycott was totally convinced he was getting a delivery well in his half of the pitch. He managed to get his glove in front of his nose just in time to save it from permanent re-alignment and the ball flew over Graeme Hughes's hand at third slip by inches and down to the boundary for the winning runs.

Tom Brooks now wasn't disguising his emotions. 'Apoplectic' seems a reasonable word. Meanwhile, I was cursing because the ball hadn't gone to hand – which would have been the perfect result. Umpire Brooks wouldn't give my sweater back until he had delivered a stern lecture. I reminded him that the game was now over and it didn't matter how many warnings he wanted to give out, there was no more play.

Henry: The Geoff Lawson Story, Geoff Lawson (Ironbark Press, Sydney, 1993)

A TITANIC FINISH

*Noted umpire Dickie Bird on the chaotic finish
to the 1975 World Cup final.*

So it was that Dennis Lillee came to the crease as the last man, with the score on 9-233 and the Aussies still needing 59 for victory. He took guard, winked at me, and said, 'Don't worry, Dickie, we'll get these.' I looked at him, smiled, and thought to myself, 'Dream on, Dennis, my old mate, you've no chance.' I couldn't see Australia doing it, not in a million years. But slowly the runs started to accumulate and the crowd became more and more excited as the gap closed. I began to wonder if miracles did, indeed, happen. Could Dennis the menace be right after all?

It was obvious that the West Indians were having doubts as well. They had decided to allow the last pair a diet of singles in order to save the boundaries which Australia needed if they were to reach their target, but both Lillee and Thomson played very sensibly, taking the occasional risk of a big swing, and making it pay.

But then Thomson took one chance too many, failed to connect cleanly with one almighty heave and saw the ball describe a graceful arc before falling into the safe and grateful hands of Roy Fredericks. The crowd immediately went wild. They thought it was all over – and we were soon engulfed in mid-pitch. I felt my white cap snatched from my head, along with three sweaters that had been draped round my waist and a spare ball from my pocket.

For a moment or two I felt dizzy, but recovered my senses when I saw that Thomson and Lillee were still running between the wickets. You see, what they and the rest of us on the field had heard, but the crowd obviously had not, was Tommy Spencer's shout of 'no-ball'.

'Keep going, keep going,' panted Lillee. 'We'll soon have it won at this rate.'

'How many is that you've run?' I asked him.

'You should be keeping count,' he grumbled. 'But I make it 17!'

When order was eventually restored thanks to some friendly police persuasion and it finally dawned on the crowd that it was not all over after all, I had to disappoint Lillee by telling him that I was giving him only four out of 17 for his gallant running exploits. Fredericks, after catching the ball, had hurled it at the stumps in a bid to pull off yet another run-out off the no-ball. It missed and disappeared into the middle of the onrushing tidal wave of spectators. According to the laws we had, therefore, to award four runs and call the ball 'dead' due to 'interference with the ball' – much to Lillee's breathless disgust.

Inevitably, though, it was a fifth run-out which ended the brave Australian last-wicket resistance, Thomson being the last victim and that left the West Indians victors by 17 runs. It was a close-run thing.

For the second time that day the ground was invaded. There was simply no stopping the fans who were keen to pick up a memento from that unforgettable game. Thomson lost his bat, his pads were ripped off him, and they even had poor old Keith Boyce on the floor as they took the boots from his feet. The stumps disappeared, but what the people who took them did not realise was that we had removed the good set at tea and replaced them with some old ones, anticipating such an eventuality. Those scenes were some of the most amazing I have ever experienced. It was sheer bedlam.

Dickie Bird: My Autobiography, Dickie Bird (Hodder & Stoughton, London, 1997)

THE 'COMPUTER TEST'

A double-century from The Don and another Australian
win at Lord's . . . in cricket's controversial 'Computer Test'.

It was the most controversial non-event of the season, when England met Australia at Lord's late in September on an NCR computer. Twenty-two all-time greats from different eras 'met' in a titanic struggle of integrated circuits.

The press and public did not know how to cope with it. Some newspapers carried long accounts, especially the *Australian,* while of the vanquished, the *Times* looked upon the event with a remarkable degree of scepticism. One Sydney paper, after great details for two days, decided the whole thing was ridiculous and said so.

Sir Donald Bradman selected his team from the stars of the last

50 years – the players he'd seen – as: Bill Ponsford, Arthur Morris, himself as captain, his boyhood hero Charlie Macartney, Neil Harvey, Bob Simpson, Keith Miller, Richie Benaud, Ray Lindwall, Don Tallon and Bill O'Reilly. A few eyebrows were raised over several omissions, particularly Stan McCabe, Clarrie Grimmett and Bill Woodfull. Still, it was a useful enough unit!

President of the MCC, GOB 'Gubby' Allen picked the English team: Sir Jack Hobbs, Sir Leonard Hutton, Walter Hammond, Denis Compton, Maurice Leyland, Peter May (captain), Godfrey Evans, Harold Larwood, Maurice Tate, Jim Laker and Hedley Verity. The big surprises were the omission of Hubert Sutcliffe, the failure of Ken Barrington to make the shortlist and Godfrey Evans being preferred ahead of Les Ames.

Australia won the toss and batted on a true Lord's pitch, unlike the 1961 one where after Australia had beaten England by five wickets, the pitch was found to have a ridge in it. The weather was fine, there was a slight breeze blowing from the nursery end and the pitch spun on the last two days. The absence of rain was attacked by the cynics, but in fact only two Lord's Tests between England and Australia have been ruined by rain in the 50 years [1964 and 1968].

Morris and Ponsford started off with a confident opening stand of 83 and all was going well when Laker had Morris leg before. In came 'The Don' and at 1-116 at lunch, Australia seemed set for a mammoth score.

But the computer spent the break digesting its digits, as it had been fed all the scores and analyses of every England v Australia Test since 1921. The scene was set for a huge Bradman score, as his average against England was a boundary or two under 90.

Alas, just after lunch The Don played forward to Verity's quicker ball and according to the computer was caught and bowled for 22. The cynics swung into full operation, comparing Bradman's record to his 22 measly runs and denounced the match as a fraud, and the computer (English-made) as biased.

However, the computer had eaten the scores, and proceeded to make the 'knockers' sit back and have a rethink. Bradman had played in two Tests at Lord's against Verity, who had dismissed him for 36, 13 and 18 … 67 runs at an average of … yes … 22!

Australia recovered slightly with Ponsford making 81 and Macartney 31 (apparently the computer hadn't been told about his 99 at Lord's in 1912) and finished the day at 8-289.

The next morning Keith Miller went on to score 75 which was not surprising as he always did well at Lord's. Tate took three wickets, which was unusual in as much as his best figures were in Australia, while Verity claimed four for 31. This maintained his success, as in 1934 he took 15-104 and in 1938, 6-132.

England started off badly, losing Hobbs for 8, Hammond for 10 (the machine forgetting or choosing to ignore his 240 in 1938). Compton also fell cheaply before Hutton and Leyland then put on a brisk 159. As Hutton holds the record in England v Australia matches of 364 [at the Oval in 1938] and Leyland scored seven centuries against Australia their big scoring was anticipated.

Opening bowlers Lindwall and Miller ran through England's tail on the third morning and England trailed by 55 runs on the first innings.

Bill Ponsford was out early in Australia's second innings, but The Don silenced all critics with a massive 222, before falling, once again, to old foe Verity. At the other end the still-polished Arthur Morris compiled 142 and they added 265 for the second wicket, which reminded everyone of their massive stand of 301 at Leeds in Australia's second innings in 1948.

Once they were out, there was a collapse, the last seven wickets adding only 80 runs against Laker and Verity. Surprise greeted the double failures of both Neil Harvey and Bob Simpson, but Harvey's average at Lord's was just over 20 runs per innings and of the 31 Test innings he played in England, 16 were under 20. Simpson also made a double failure, his figures as a down-the-list batsman far inferior to his figures when going in first.

Harold Larwood returned the disappointing figures of none for 75 and none for 78. In 1930, when playing against Woodfull's 1930 tourists when Bradman was so dominant, Larwood took just four wickets in the series for just under 300 runs. He'd played just twice in 1926 and wasn't selected in 1934.

Verity's seven wickets for the game were justified by his 15-104 in 1934, while Laker's second-innings success was probably triggered by his 1956 series when he claimed 46 wickets in five matches, including his incredible nine for 37 and 10 for 53 at Old Trafford.

England was set nearly 500 runs to win, a far greater target than they have ever achieved against Australia, but Hobbs, Hammond, Leyland and captain May all reached half-centuries. Denis Compton was the failure, but despite his average of 42 against Australia, as his form was often erratic (in four Tests in 1950–51, for example, he made only 53 runs at 7.57) his scores of 5 and 25 were understandable.

In the end, England was all out for 327, 165 runs behind. Even this was anticipated, as in the 11 Tests at Lord's since the First World War, Australia have won five, five have been drawn, and England's only victory, in 1934, was achieved on a rain-damaged wicket.

For Australia, Richie Benaud revived memories of the fourth Test in 1961 when he wrecked England's second innings batting single-handed, the machine giving him figures of four for 66. Among the other bowlers, Bill O'Reilly returned shock match figures of 1-158. His 102 wickets against England were taken at 25 apiece – maybe the computer developed a mid-match glitch!

Australian Cricket, writer unknown (Sydney, November 1971)

ENGLAND v AUSTRALIA, Lord's (NCR), 21–25 September 1971
AUSTRALIA: first innings

AR Morris	lbw Laker	39
WH Ponsford	b Verity	81
DG Bradman	c & b Verity	22
CG Macartney	b Verity	31
RN Harvey	b Hammond	4
RB Simpson	c Hobbs, b Verity	18
KR Miller	lbw Tate	75
R Benaud	c Compton, b Tate	22
RR Lindwall	c Evans, b Laker	15
D Tallon	not out	6
WJ O'Reilly	b Tate	0
Extras		8
Total		321

Fall: 83, 128, 157, 166, 195, 202, 253, 284, 321, 321
Bowling: Tate 33.3-9-84-3, Larwood 26-4-75-0, Hammond 25-4-76-1, Laker 24-5-47-2, Verity 20-9-31-4

ENGLAND: first innings

JB Hobbs	b Lindwall	8
L Hutton	c Tallon, b Miller	86
WR Hammond	b Miller	10
DCS Compton	b Miller	5
M Leyland	b Benaud	80
PBH May	not out	38
TG Evans	lbw Miller	1
H Larwood	c Lindwall, b Miller	7
JC Laker	b Lindwall	17
M Tate	b Lindwall	0

H Verity	b O'Reilly	8
Extras		6
Total		266

Fall: 8, 25, 31, 190, 196, 201,213, 214, 241, 266
Bowling: Lindwall 29-7-57-3, Miller 27-10-46-5, O'Reilly 29-5-61-1, Benaud 25-5-70-1, Macartney 10-1-26-0

AUSTRALIA: second innings

AR Morris	b Tate	142
WH Ponsford	b Laker	14
DG Bradman	c Hutton, b Verity	222
CG Macartney	c Evans, b Tate	1
RN Harvey	lbw Laker	12
RB Simpson	b Laker	13
KR Miller	c Larwood, b Laker	0
R Benaud	c Evans, b Verity	5
RR Lindwall	c Tate, b Hammond	15
D Tallon	c & b Verity	0
WJ O'Reilly	not out	7
Extras		6
Total		437

Fall: 40, 305, 317, 357, 407, 408, 411, 415, 425, 437
Bowling: Tate 34-16-73-2, Larwood 25-6-78-0, Hammond 36.3-7-101-1, Laker 41-8-105-4, Verity 33-9-74-3

ENGLAND: second innings

JB Hobbs	c Tallon, b Miller	60
L Hutton	b Lindwall	21
WR Hammond	c & b Benaud	58
DCS Compton	c Miller, b Benaud	25
M Leyland	run out	60
PBH May	c Tallon, b Miller	54
TG Evans	b O'Reilly	30
H Larwood	c O'Reilly, b Miller	8
JC Laker	c Simpson, b Benaud	1
M Tate	b Benaud	2
H Verity	not out	0
Extras		6
Total		437

Fall: 45, 131, 151, 197, 267, 299, 309, 311, 317, 327
Bowling: Lindwall 29-3-91-1, Miller 29-7-65-3, O'Reilly 31-9-97-1, Benaud 27-7-66-4
Australia won by 165 runs.

CRICKET ON THE SABBATH

Sheffield Shield cricket was scheduled for the first time on a Sunday on 22 November 1964, at Brisbane's Woolloongabba.

BRISBANE, Sunday – A crowd of 4108 watched today's play in the Queensland–Western Australia Sheffield Shield match. It was the first time in Australia in a first-class match that play had continued on a Sunday. Officials said early morning rain and a threatening sky probably prevented the attendance going over 6000.

Attendances for the first three days of the match are up by more than 4500 on the figure for the four days of last year's match. The attendance last year was 6299 (receipts 763 pounds and 17 shillings) compared to 10,769 (receipts 1434 pounds and 9 shillings) for three days this year. On the second day last year, a Saturday, 2475 people attended for receipts of 315 pounds. Yesterday, the second day of the 1964 game, the attendance figure was 4412 with receipts of 563 pounds and 15 shillings. On the first day, last Friday, 2249 people paid 288 pounds.

Queensland's already strong first-innings position was further strengthened when Western Australia ended the day with six for 257. Western Australia was chasing Queensland's first-innings total of 503.

The Courier Mail, writer unknown (Brisbane, 23 November 1964)

QUEENSLAND v WESTERN AUSTRALIA, Woolloongabba, Brisbane, 22 November 1964
QUEENSLAND: first innings
Total: 503

WESTERN AUSTRALIA: first innings

P Wishart	lbw Allan	0
K Slater	lbw Duncan	12
J Inverarity	not out	115
B Shepherd	c Burge, b Allan	44
D Chadwick	c & b Duncan	69
D Hoare	c Lihou, b Duncan	3
J Parker	c Grout, b Allan	2
G McKenzie	not out	4
Extras		8
Total		6-257

Fall: 1, 18, 113, 236, 246, 249
Bowling: Allan 22-4-60-3, Duncan 17-6-49-3, Mackay 13-3-46-0, Veivers 17-6-32-0, Lihou 15-0-62-0

The match was eventually drawn, WA making 290 (John Inverarity 129 not out, Peter Allan five for 76, Ross Duncan five for 63) and 5-218 (Barry Shepherd 97). Queensland batted just once, Bill Buckle making a career-best 207 and WA's Des Hoare capturing five for 98.

MAGIC, SHEER MAGIC

*Australia's first-time Ashes tourist, captain-to-be
Brian Booth on the finest ball he ever saw.*

It remains the stellar playing moment for Richie Benaud. At 1-150 needing 256 [at Old Trafford, 1961], England was careering to an emphatic victory. Having won at Leeds, the Englishmen were eyeing a 2–1 Ashes lead with one Test to play. Ted Dexter had just struck Benaud for a magnificent straight 6 and England was all but 'home'.

Eyewitness Brian Booth was playing his first Test and was fascinated by the duelling. 'We were in trouble, that's for sure,' he said. 'Richie conferred with our vice-captain, Neil Harvey, and immediately went around the wicket, looking to bowl into some of the rough mainly caused by Fred Trueman. His first deliveries were beauties. The last

ball of the over was a topspinner. Dexter's bat flashed but the ball took the outside edge and Wally Grout did the rest.

'In comes Peter May, England's captain and champion batsman. He had scored a magnificent 95 in the first innings. Richie continued to bowl from around the wicket. His second delivery to May was perfectly pitched. May played forward as if to let the ball go or allow it to hit him on the pads, but unfortunately for him it had so much spin on it that it drifted late in the air, pitched outside his pads and spun sharply to bowl him around his legs. It was a classic leg break that utilised the conditions to perfection. England was suddenly 3-150 and we'd gone from being the hunted to the hunters. They were huge psychological blows that turned the game. In that spell Richie took five for 11 or 12. It was magnificent bowling, and that drifting, big-spinning delivery, given the significance of the game and May's standing as one of the world's very best players, remains the finest ball I ever saw in my time playing first-class and Test cricket. It was magic, sheer magic.'

The Extraordinary Book of Australian Cricket, Ken Piesse (Penguin Books, Melbourne, 2009)

THE MOST FAMOUS DRAW OF ALL
Ken 'Slasher' Mackay on the Adelaide epic of 1960–61.

At two minutes to six [Frank] Worrell took the ball to bowl to [Lindsay] Kline.

'Good, the last over. Spinner can handle him all right.'

Worrell breezed through his over so quickly that after he had bowled six balls I knew there would be another over to face. I had to stop that somehow. I had noticed during the last 10 minutes that some of the crowd was over the fence and on the field. If only I could get umpire Col Egar to shift them before Worrell finished his over, time would be up.

I called out: 'Hey Col, look at that crowd over the fence. Better shift 'em back. They're on the field.'

Col took a quick look at the crowd, a more searching one at me and said: 'They've been there for some time. They're not bothering anyone. Play on.'

Worrell's over ended at 15 seconds to six and he threw the ball to Hall.

Slash: Ken 'Slasher' Mackay was one of the most popular Australian cricketers of the late '50s and early '60s.
Sporting Life

'All right, Wes,' he said. 'You bowl the last one.'

As at Brisbane, Wes was to make the grandstand finish.

In Australia, when Hall takes the ball there is always a spontaneous crowd reaction. Aussies love him. He's menacing, colourful and entirely unpredictable. The homage of the Adelaide crowd was as eloquent as it was silent. There wasn't a murmur. Strangely I was relieved. Wes was not the man for this last over; [Garry] Sobers, [Alf] Valentine or [Lance] Gibbs, but not Hall. There were footmarks at my end made by Hall, Frank Misson and Des Hoare. They were on a spinner's length but too far up and too wide for Wes to exploit.

What an over. It took 10 minutes, more than five times as long as the previous one by Worrell.

I'm used to these situations now but nothing before or since has matched that period for mental torture. Thoughts crowded in, blotting out everything in the ground except the sight of Hall pounding into the wicket. He looked a mile away when he started to run. Now he was looming closer, ebony arms pumping in perfect harmony with long, driving legs.

Now Slash, if ever you've had a job to do, this is it. This is war and that big bloke pelting in is not going to beat you. The first ball was a beauty and I jammed down on it at the last instant. *Boy that was quick and into the wind too. There shouldn't be any bouncers on this wicket, but one might stay low; better get your nose down lower.*

Hall's next two balls flashed past the off stump. I knew I could safely let them go. *Five more of those, Wes, and I'll be happy.*

The fourth had to be played. I cracked it firmly past point and could have had two runs. But what was the use? *No one bawling from the stands: 'Run yer mug.' That's good. They are with me.*

The fifth I watched go by the off stump. *What's the matter, Wes, you are wasting them. Hello, there's something cooking. Worrell's having a yarn to him. So he's going to bowl around the wicket. Trying a new angle, perhaps hoping for an lbw or to find something on the pitch. Well, it won't do you any good.*

Balls six and seven were screamers and dead straight. *Crikey they were good ones. One ball to go, Wes. This is your last chance. All right, let's get it over. I've been here nearly four hours, you are not going to shift me with your last ball.*

In came Hall, round the wicket. But he didn't bowl. He lost his step, raced over the bowling crease then bounced the ball on the wicket in front of him in disgust. I don't know if that legally constituted a delivery but I was not game to ask. It was a no-ball anyhow. Back went Hall, and in again, this time over the wicket.

'No-ball,' called umpire Col Hoy.

But the crowd didn't hear him.

A wave of cheering schoolboys swept onto the oval, racing towards the wicket. The police, aware that something was amiss, leapt into action. In different circumstances, the sight of policemen lumbering in pursuit of small boys, agile as monkeys, would have looked riotous. But my nerves were stretched to the limit. All I could say was: 'Get 'em off, get 'em off.'

It was as well this did not happen in India. The match would never have ended.

When the boys were herded back to the boundary, Wes made his third attempt to bowl the last ball. He trudged back to his bowling mark. On to the field toddled a small boy, autograph book in hand.

The crowd roared. This was too much. I'd soon have to appeal against the light.

I know Wes loves kids, but the look he gave that little bloke should scare him off a cricket field for life. Police again cleared the area and Wes steamed to the wicket for the 10th time in this over. Again, every ounce of concentration was needed. *Come on, let's get this game over. What are you going to dish up, Wes? If it's not on the stumps there's no way in the world I'm going to touch it. It'll be a short one for sure. Here it comes. It's short! Let it hit you. Ouch, that hurt! Watch it doesn't roll on to the wicket. Good! We made it.* I felt I had a knife in my ribs and staggered to the side of the wicket fighting to stop myself from going down. They had not got me out and they were not going to knock me out. The match was over and we had drawn it ... 'Spinner' [Kline] and I were half-pushed, half-dragged to the dressing-room, where we learnt that the tension was tighter there than in the middle. We heard how Wally Grout, after being dismissed, had showered and packed his gear intending to down a quick beer before the match ended. Wally cracked later and spent the last 20 minutes in hysterical giggles. Richie Benaud had smoked 16 cigarettes in the last-wicket stand.

The West Indians crowded into our dressing-room, a happy bunch of real sportsmen.

It was an hour before I could get to the shower and learn that my bruise was no worse than half a dozen Col McDonald had taken through the series. When I came from the showers only Benaud and a few others were in the dressing-room. Richie who had said nothing to me since I came in from the field walked over then and said one word – 'Thanks.'

Slasher Opens Up, Ken Mackay (Pelham Books, London, 1964)

A CENTURY TO SAVOUR

It was the century of Neil Harvey's life, a matchwinning knock on a wicked Durban turner, one of the highlights in Australia's unprecedented five-year run without defeat.

Patsy Hendren compared him to Clem Hill, Sir Neville Cardus to Mozart, while the most grudging observer would have to place him among the greatest left-handers of all time. But perhaps the most apposite tribute to Neil Harvey came from the *Times* which simply stated that he was 'a player who never grew old'. Whether dancing down the track to hit against the spin or darting in from cover to save a single, the dapper Victorian exuded the jauntiness of youth . . .

Having established himself on the tour of England, Harvey cemented his reputation on the Veld, becoming the first in a distinguished but unfortunate line to be dubbed 'the new Bradman' and with a Test average of 132 at the end of his first South African series, he perhaps came closer to emulating the great man than any subsequent pretender. A teetotaler, nonsmoker and just 5 ft 8 in [173 cm] and 10 st 7 lb [67 kg], Harvey would hurry to the wicket with short, business-like strides, always capless, his dark, wavy hair neatly

1949–50 Tourists: Neil Harvey (back row, extreme left) won the 1949–50 Durban Test for Australia with an extraordinary innings on a dusty wicket.

combed and an eager look on his face. With a complete range of strokes and sparkling footwork, he was indeed 'impossible' to bowl at in his early years.

After winning the first Test in Johannesburg by an innings, Australia took hold of the series with an eight-wicket win in Cape Town, where Harvey made a swashbuckling 178. In spite of the mauling South Africa were getting, a big crowd turned up in subtropical Durban on the first day of the third Test – and they could not have asked for more. Not only did Dudley Nourse and Eric Rowan lay a solid foundation by reaching stumps at 2-240, overnight rain convinced many that it was already a matchwinning total. 'After that,' recalls Harvey, 'it was a real battle of tactics.'

In [Lindsay] Hassett, Australia had the ideal skipper for the occasion. Even when he had to bow to umpires who insisted upon a resumption that was too soon for his tastes on a rain-sodden pitch, he was always in command. 'Our tactics were to keep them in as long as possible and not do anything with the ball,' says Harvey, still barely able to suppress a chuckle some 44 years later. Rowan went on to make 143 and South Africa, oblivious to the bluff until it was too late, were all out for 311. It should still have been enough but skipper Nourse knew that valuable time had been wasted.

In a further effort to keep the South Africans guessing and shield his top batsmen from the wiles of [Hugh] Tayfield and 'Tufty' Mann, Hassett promoted tailenders [Bill] Johnston and [Ron] Saggers to open the innings. But when Australia lurched to 9-63 at the end of the second day, it looked as if Hassett's deception had been in vain. However, when the last wicket fell at 75 on the third morning, Nourse did not enforce the follow-on and lunched contentedly with his side at 3-85 in the second innings. With the pitch still a minefield, Johnston and [Ian] Johnson wrapped up the remaining seven wickets for just 14 runs in an hour and not even Hassett could put the brakes on, South Africa crashing to 99 all out. But the visiting skipper was smiling through clenched teeth: the target was 336 and there was still a day and a half to go.

The wicket now looked as if a herd of wildebeest had spent the night on it. 'It was full of divots, ball-marks and was a real turner,' remembers Harvey, 'and it wasn't just because it was unplayable that we were concerned, it was because they had as good a pair of spinners as any in the game.'

The strip's behaviour was not unlike that of the cobbled lane in

Fitzroy and when Harvey joined [Arthur] Morris at 3-59, he was soon springing lightly down to the pitch of the ball, smothering the spin and frustrating 'Toey' and Tufty as he once had his elder brothers. Australia reached 3-80 at the close, still requiring 251 and very much at the mercy of the weather. Harvey admits: 'One or two of the boys thought it was a lost cause but I remember Sam Loxton saying: "We'll win this match."'

As for Harvey? 'I always believed in playing my natural game and when we resumed on the final morning, we neither played for a draw nor a win. We just treated each ball on its merits.' The trouble was, each ball demanded the utmost respect and Morris spent two and half hours making 44. Harvey, too, was uncharacteristically subdued but 'time', he reminds you, 'was the least of our worries and I did not forget to hit the bad ball'.

As understatements go, that takes some beating, for Harvey was playing one of the game's great knocks. Once joined by his pal Loxton, the super-optimist, Harvey upped the tempo and at last runs began to come. With the bowlers blunted, the wicket losing its venom and Loxton determined to confound the sceptics in his own team, Australian hopes rose. A catch went down, too, at fine leg and South African heads dropped. Nourse looked worried. The Victorian pair won a moral victory when Nourse, now at his wit's end for a wicket, took the new ball. But still the breakthrough did not come. In three hours, 135 runs had been added to shift the psychological balance. Loxton eventually fell to Mann but Harvey, whose 100 had taken almost four hours, was in total command. And besides batting in a way that Cardus claimed 'defied statistical assessment', he had another worthy partner. Colin McCool knew a thing or two about spin and carried on where Loxton had left off. At tea, the score was 5-269 with 67 still wanted in two hours. It could hardly have been more tantalisingly poised and Harvey recalls: 'A few fingernails were bitten in our dressing-room.'

Harvey's were not among them as he and McCool confidently reached the target with 25 minutes to spare, the left-hander a magnificent 151 not out. He had not given a chance and had defied two of cricket's most lethal spinners for five and a half hours on a pitch that had been made for them. 'Yes, I think it was probably as good an innings as I've played,' he acknowledges. 'It was very satisfying but I had some good allies.'

That night in a Hollywood-style tribute, a tree was planted in

Harvey's honour. Sadly, it has now made way for redevelopment of the Kingsmead ground but the memory of that masterly innings will last forever.

Fifty Cricket Stars Describe My Greatest Game, edited by Bob Holmes & Vic Marks (Mainstream Publishing, London, 1995)

CLEM HILL'S COMEBACK, AT 62
*The oldies-but-goodies donned the flannels again for a
Saturday of celebration in Melbourne to aid the war effort.*

Feelings of comradeship were uppermost at the match on the Melbourne [Cricket] Ground on Saturday between the AIF [Australian Imperial Forces] team and contemporary Test players, but there was an air of sadness, because it will be the last appearance as a team who made history 20 years ago.

The attendance was 7000 and the [gate] takings 240 pounds. In addition, 24 pounds came from the collection boxes at the members' entrance and many tickets were sold. As the expenses of the Adelaide and Sydney players have to be met, the outlay will be nearly 300 pounds but there will be a surplus, which will be devoted to the fund to erect homes for war veterans.

There was an impressive scene after lunch when the Lieutenant-Governor Sir Frederick Mann was met by a guard of honour and band provided by the Royal Melbourne Regiment. He inspected them and met the players of both sides, who were lined up on the ground. The president of the Melbourne Cricket Club, Sir Edward Mitchell; the secretary, Mr Vernon Ransford; the state president of the Returned Soldiers' League, Mr George Holland; and the chairman of the match committee, Mr HJ Martin were also presented to

Sir Frederick. A flight by members of the Royal Victorian Aero Club, the sounding of the 'Last Post' and the playing of the 'Reveille' added to the solemnity of the proceedings.

Among a crowd of officials, Clem Hill and Herbie Collins walked out to the arena to toss. Collins threw the coin into the air, Hill called 'tails' and was wrong and again one heard the cry, 'Lucky Collins'.

With [Dave] Elder [the former Test umpire] and [Allie] Lampard [an AIF and state player] as umpires, Hill led his team onto the field with the remark: 'Come on; don't be frightened!' Roy Park, Jack Ryder, Bill Woodfull, [Vernon] Ransford and Jimmy Matthews [ex-Test players] were relief umpires. [Andy] Barlow and J Moore, regular umpires, also took a share.

[Charles] Kelleway, wearing spectacles and his usual air of determination, opened the innings with 'Nip' Pellew to the bowling of the St Kilda and Test combination [Don] Blackie and [Bert] Ironmonger and each opened his account quickly. Ironmonger bowled his left-handers below his old pace. Blackie seemed to be bowling much in his old style. Kelleway stepped back to a shorter ball and pulled it cleanly for 4. Off the next ball Blackie made his old apologetic appeal for lbw.

After Kelleway had made 14 in only 15 minutes, he skied Blackie behind square leg and [Charlie] Macartney – now much wider and thicker than his Test days – got well under the ball and held it.

[Johnnie] Taylor, with a few grey hairs, the only difference one could discern, was the next batsman and his great run of scores in one Test series in Australia, in particular, was recalled when he began with a characteristic push to leg.

When [Arthur] Mailey and [Clarrie] Grimmett, two of the finest slow bowlers since the war, took up the attack they found Pellew becoming entrenched and several more 4s saw him bring up the first carefree 50 in just half an hour. Taylor rushed out to hit the left-handed Macartney, missed and [Jack] Ellis cleverly whipped off the bails with his left hand.

'Hammy' Love, who had one Test match when he took the place of [Bert] Oldfield [hurt in the Bodyline year] in Sydney and who also played for Carlton and St Kilda and Victoria, as well as New South Wales, came next. He was again the deputy for Oldfield [injured finger] and was snapped up by the wicketkeeper.

With his same cheery smile, but carrying much more weight than previously, Jack Gregory was warmly welcomed on a ground where he has had many successes. His brilliant 100 followed by eight wickets in his first Test match on the ground in 1921 was one of several good performances talked about by spectators.

[Bill] Ponsford brilliantly misfielded the ball to give Gregory his first run. Then Grimmett tangled him considerably, but the old Gregory was seen in a powerful off-drive for 4 before he skied Blackie and was out.

Pellew reached a good 50 in 82 minutes and after lunch he began to hit furiously. He lifted Ironmonger beautifully for 6 and just missed a 6 with the next shot and mis-hit the next to be caught. Obviously he felt he'd batted long enough. In only 103 minutes, he made a splendid 77 and hit five 4s and one 6. [Bill] Trenerry was caught off the next ball by Hill, and the players flocked around the veteran to applaud him on a magnificent achievement. When Collins, the captain, came in, he was heartily applauded. His dogged batting and his many remarkable deeds as captain of both the AIF and Australian elevens were still remembered. Batting in unperturbed style he went onto make 18 not out. [Bill] Stirling and [Eric] Bull each hit one 4 and the innings ended for 191, made in the smart time of 143 minutes.

Gregory, without pace and long, fast run, but still with his kangaroo hop at the finish, opened the bowling for [the] soldiers against [Vic] Richardson and Ponsford. Kelleway, at the other end, seemed to have lost little of his skill or pace off the wicket. The score raced to 50 in only 29 minutes. Richardson was missed twice as the batsman began to go for anything. Richardson at last missed and was neatly stumped for a good 47 made in 45 minutes with four 4s.

Ponsford scored several runs off his hip in his old style. A splendid pick-up by Taylor off one of these shots was heartily applauded, the spectators realising that he had not lost his prowess in the outfield.

Ponsford swung [John] Murray's first ball for 6 to bring up the 100 in 49 minutes. After trying vainly to hit a catch, Ponsford walked in front, to be lbw for an artistic 44, made in 53 minutes with three 4s and one 6.

[Alan] Kippax was missed by Taylor at leg off the first ball. He showed much of his former skill and artistry until magnificently caught left-handed at mid-on by [Cliff] Winning and the crowd roared its applause at the catch.

Using his feet neatly, Macartney hit hard and loftily and found the vacant spots. At last one went to Pellew, who caught it confidently.

Hill, whose last Test appearance on the ground was in 1912, was given a flattering reception and the players stood in a group to receive him. He was the oldest player, being aged 62 years. More applause followed as he patted a full toss for a single.

When Hill's straight drive was helped on by Macartney – the batsman at the other end – Hill scored two more and the batsmen shook hands as they passed. An attempted leg glance failed, however, and Hill was bowled. In mock anger he disputed the decision before going out.

With time fleeting by, Grimmett and Carney retired, Mailey came and went and Blackie made the winning shot and was caught. Ironmonger, gallantly helped by Murray, who threw wide of the wicket, made a single. Then Ellis was stumped, and the innings ended for 95 runs – four ahead – made in 123 minutes.

Players of both teams attended a smoke night at the Victoria [Club] in the evening ... the state president of the RSL, Mr Holland, paid a tribute to the players who had come from the other states. They had seen in the match a combination of the 'digger' spirit and the spirit of Australian cricket and the result was something different.

In his response, the AIF captain Collins said that he had never played in a more enjoyable match and he was thrilled to see such players as Hill and Macartney in the field. Hill, Oldfield and Pellew supported him, Pellew saying how much pleasure the players had gained to run around such a great sporting field and to take two through the slips for intended drives to the on. Two silver cups were presented to Collins and Hill, the respective captains.

The Argus, Percy Taylor (Melbourne, 17 April 1939)

Scores

AIF

CE Pellew	c Blackie, b Ironmonger	77
C Kelleway	c Macartney, b Blackie	14
JM Taylor	stmp Ellis, b Macartney	15
JT Murray	c Macartney, b Grimmett	5
HSB Love	c Ellis, b Ironmonger	5
JM Gregory	c Ponsford, b Blackie	6
WL Trenerry	c Hill, b Ironmonger	21
HL Collins (c)	not out	18
WS Stirling	c & b Grimmett	9
EA Bull	b Grimmett	1
SC Winning	stmp Ellis, b Mailey	6
Sundries		14
Total		191

Fall: 26, 72, 79, 90, 103, 154, 154, 170, 178, 191
Bowling: Ironmonger 3-51, Blackie 2-32, Grimmett 3-28, Mailey 1-50,
Macartney 1-16

OLD INTERNATIONALS

VY Richardson	stmp Love, b Winning	47
WH Ponsford	lbw b Winning	4
CG Macartney	c Pellew, b Murray	5
AF Kippax	c Winning, b Stirling	15
C Hill (c)	b Murray	3
CV Grimmett	retired	18
P Carney	retired	9
AA Mailey	stmp Love, b Bull	3
DD Blackie	c Stirling, b Collins	4
JL Ellis	c Love, b Collins	6
H Ironmonger	not out	1
Sundries		10
Total		195

Fall: 92, 103, 137, 146, 157, 179, 179, 184, 193, 195
Bowling: Gregory 0-22, Kelleway 0-18, Murray 2-30, Trenerry 0-27,
Winning 2-37, Collins 2-6, Stirling 1-26, Bull 1-19
Old Internationals won by 4 runs.

THE FIRST BALL OF THE CENTURY

*He may have been eccentric and occasionally bizarre, but
'Chuck' Fleetwood-Smith could seriously bowl and one memorable
day in Adelaide won Australia an Ashes Test match.*

The [1936–37 Adelaide Test] match hinged on England's master
batsman Walter Hammond, whose defence was impenetrable and
who was playing with so much poise that the Ashes appeared to be
headed back to England. Hammond was at the height of his career
and was taking special delight in proving to be infallible when up
against the Australians.

On the last day England needed 244 runs with plenty of wickets
left and Hammond still at the crease. It was now the ultimate duel:
the master, Hammond, and the man whose career was nearly ruined
because of the savage treatment Hammond had handed to him
over the years. Fleetwood-Smith had bided his time in gaining his
revenge on Hammond, who had effectively kept him out of Test
cricket for three years after slaughtering him at the MCG before the

Bodyline series. Chuck had never forgotten that merciless hammering. Hammond was also prepared for the confrontation, later writing that Chuck was at that time 'panting to get his revenge on me for the delay I had caused to his Test career'.

On the eve of the final day, Fleetwood-Smith had convinced himself into believing that Hammond was his. His anger was rising, but he decided there was no need to get all riled up and spent the night well away from straying women or the drink. This may have had something to do with his wife Mollie accompanying him for the first time on a cricket tour. He had to be on his best behaviour.

Instead Chuck, his wife and Mr and Mrs Len Darling went out to see a play at the Regent Theatre, then returned to the Australian team hotel for a light supper. The happy conversation was broken by a drunk near the bar, who yelled at the table: 'Go to bed Fleetwood-Smith, you have to bowl England out tomorrow.' Fleetwood-Smith, Darling and their wives duly departed. Chuck also appeared to get the message, as the next morning he satisfied his taunter's requirements.

A Young Chuck: Leslie O'Brien 'Chuck' Fleetwood-Smith is pictured in the back row, fourth from the left, on this private tour of the USA and Canada in 1932. The team included a young Don Bradman and was managed by Test great Arthur Mailey.

Chuck had taken the first two English wickets, when [Don] Bradman remembered a remark made by wicketkeeper 'Sammy' Carter during Arthur Mailey's 1932 tour of America. Carter had said to Bradman: 'I'd love to be young enough to play one Test with Fleetwood-Smith. He could win a match for Australia some day.'

Bradman walked over to Fleetwood-Smith and, trying to inspire him, said in a cool voice: 'Chuck, if ever we wanted you to bowl that unplayable ball, now is the time.'

Fleetwood-Smith responded to the challenge, bowling probably the best, and certainly the most significant, delivery of his career. In the air the heavily spun ball swerved tantalisingly away from Hammond's bat and pitched on a worn spot outside the off stump. Hammond was drawn defensively forward, but was then caught in no-man's land when the ball viciously spun back between bat and pad, accelerating from the pace it made from the pitch, to conclusively bowl him. Fleetwood-Smith, who slumped to his knees in jubilation, turned to Bradman and shouted: 'Was that what you wanted?'

A Wayward Genius: The Fleetwood-Smith Story, Greg Growden (ABC Books, Sydney, 1991)

AUSTRALIA V CEYLON

The 1934 Australians stopped off in Colombo and played a lighthearted one-day match – without their major drawcard Don Bradman.

COLOMBO, 4 April: Half an hour in the tropic sun was the limit of endurance of most Australian batsmen in the cricket match between the Australians and a Ceylon XI today, but [Ernie] Bromley and [Bill] Brown resisted the temptation of iced drinks and the pavilion's shade. Bromley's 80 runs were a record by an Australian in Ceylon. Brown batted patiently until he had reached 50. [Bill] Ponsford was in fine form. He and Bromley each drove a 6 into the palms outside the ground. [Stan] McCabe, [Alan] Kippax and [Arthur] Chipperfield drove and pulled strongly. Most of the players managed to balance their topees, but Bromley took his off and carried it during a sharp run for a single.

The natives barracked lightheartedly. Each fall of a wicket brought calls for Bradman, who was not playing.

The wicket was easy. [Hans] Ebeling bowled best and chances were missed off him. Jayawickrema, who was bruised by the English fast bowler [EW 'Nobby'] Clark in the game against England, batted brightly, but he was nervous facing short deliveries.

By the Special Representative of the Australian Press Association travelling with the Australian team (April 1934)

AUSTRALIA v CEYLON, Colombo, 4 April 1934
AUSTRALIA: first innings

SJ McCabe	c Waldock, b Kretser	34
WH Ponsford	c & b Kelaart	41
WA Brown	b Porritt	56
AF Kippax	c Pulle, b Kelaart	37
EH Bromley	not out	80
AG Chipperfield	c Pulle, b Kretser	25
BA Barnett	b Kretser	6
Extras		5
Total	six wickets (closed) for 284	
(63 overs)		

CEYLON: first innings

WT Brindley	c Bromley, b Ebeling	7
E Kelaart	c Bromley, b Ebeling	2
Cloverbrown	lbw Fleetwood-Smith	18
SS Jayawickrema	c Woodfull, b Ebeling	56
Pulle	stmp Barnett, b Chipperfield	4
Waldock	not out	28
Fairweather	not out	5
Extras		5
Total		5-125

Did not bat: CH Gunasekera (captain), Kretser, Porritt,
Bowling: Ebeling 3-24, Bromley 0-27, Fleetwood-Smith 1-41,
Grimmett 0-8, Chipperfield 1-16, Kippax 0-4
Australia won.

507 RUNS IN A DAY

There was all-round laughter when The Don set a Bodyline field ...

SYDNEY: Tuesday – Cricket giants of former years tried conclusions with present-day players at the Sydney Cricket Ground today, when a match was played with the object of raising money for the Archie Jackson memorial fund. There was an excellent attendance and the fund will benefit to the extent of 182 pounds. The state players won the match, a feature of which was the rapidity of the run-making. One century occupied only 26 minutes and in 247 minutes, 507 runs were scored.

The onlookers were delighted with the bright cricket, which was a relief to all after the serious encounters in the Test matches. The team, comprising for the most part internationals of other days, made 218 in 138 minutes, and the state players scored 289 in 100 minutes. Players on both sides entered into the spirit of the game with great abandon, DG Bradman causing amusement by packing a 'Bodyline' field for GL Garnsey toward the close of the veterans' innings.

The Sydney Morning Herald, writer unknown (Sydney, 22 March 1933)

FORMER INTERNATIONALS v NEW SOUTH WALES,
Sydney Cricket Ground, 1933
FORMER INTERNATIONALS

HL Collins	c Marks, b O'Reilly	27
H Carter	c Hill, b O'Reilly	25
CG Macartney	c Bradman, b Marks	64
JM Taylor	b Hill	3
TJE Andrews	b Bradman	77
JM Gregory	c Marks, b Adrian	1
MA Noble (c)	stmp Easton, b Rowe	4
GC Horsfield	stmp Easton, b Bradman	7
SC Everett	c Easton, b Bradman	3
AA Mailey	b Brown	4
GL Garnsey	not out	0
Extras		3
Total		228

Bowling: Stewart 0-40, O'Reilly 2-36, Hill 1-15, Adrian 1-41, Marks 1-25, Bradman 3-37, Rowe 0-19, Solomon 0-2, Brown 1-0

NEW SOUTH WALES

WA Brown	c Andrews, b Garnsey	71
RC Rowe	c Macartney, b Everett	30
DG Bradman	c Macartney, b Mailey	98
CM Solomon	stmp Carter, b Mailey	44
AE Marks	not out	10
AF Kippax (c)	c Horsfield, b Noble	25
Extras		11
Total		5-289

Did not bat: GL Stewart, WJ O'Reilly, CJ Hill, FA Easton, BS Adrian

Bowling: Gregory 0-14, Mailey 2-55, Everett 1-43, Macartney 0-84,
Garnsey 1-57, Noble 1-11, Collins 0-14
Umpires AC Jones, ER Kent
New South Wales won.

USE YOUR BAT LIKE A WEAPON

How to bat like Charlie Macartney ... the NSW dasher tells.

Batting is best described as the 'sweets' of cricket. A good and successful bowler is always welcome, and badly needed, but a well-compiled century, or even a 50, receives greater recognition and undoubtedly gives far more satisfaction to the player.

Great batsmen are not necessarily made by coaching. They are born with natural gifts and no amount of instruction or explanation can make good the lack of such gifts. Fine batsmen reach their pinnacle of fame by keen observation, enthusiastic practice, experiment and experience. At the same time there are plenty of eager cricketers not so fortunately gifted who aspire each year to higher honours than they have yet reached. A little enlightenment on some vital points, which must be kept in view at the opening of a boy's career, may help him on his way to overcome more quickly the difficulties which so often depress young players.

First of all, there is the matter of choosing a bat. The most important point about a bat is its weight balance. Don't be too fanciful about white wood and pretty handles. The best bat is the one that hits the ball for 4 or 6 with the greatest ease and lasts well – that is, for a reasonable time. If you cannot satisfy yourself when selecting your bat, ask a reliable man who knows.

Next come pads and gloves. Choose the quality that affords most protection to knees and fingers respectively. See

Charley Mac: Ashes legend Charles Macartney, pictured in 1909.

that your pad straps are securely tucked away; or, better still, cut them back to the required length, thus combining neatness with efficiency.

Then as to boots. See that these are properly spiked. A fully spiked pair of boots will never let a batsman down, whereas many a player, through neglect in this direction, has lost his wicket by half a yard, and perhaps has lost 50 runs for his side. You are now prepared for the batting crease.

When there, every young player should bat in his natural style. By all means watch closely a first-class batsman at every opportunity; memorise the method of stroke, but play it in your own way. Never slavishly copy another batsman. That is fatal, for you cannot be anybody but yourself. But youth has wonderful powers of imitation and adaptation, and a boy, by watching a fine batsman, may become an equally fine player, making the same strokes, yet in a style of his own.

Hold the bat with both hands as close together as possible, the idea being to make the two hands work as one. Whether you grip the bat full length or halfway down the handle, or close to the shoulder is for yourself to determine, but grip the handle lightly until the bowler is about to deliver the ball, then take a firm grip in readiness for the stroke. Gripping the handle rigidly all the time is tiring to the muscles of the forearm. Don't keep patting the crease while waiting for the bowler to deliver – that is a waste of energy.

A straight bat is essential for defence, but not altogether for stroke play. It is obvious that a straight bat gives you more wood to play with than does a cross bat, but many strokes, such as the square cut, back cut, hook or pull and some of the drives, cannot be made powerfully with a straight bat. A little thought will make this clear.

It is impossible to overestimate the part that footwork plays in batting. In cricket today, good footwork is conspicuous by its absence and this is the main reason for the slow bowler's rise to importance. Slow bowling is rarely attacked as it should be, for to be treated judiciously, in the proper manner, quick and correct footwork is imperative. Even the purely defensive batsman requires balance of the body in playing his strokes and this can only be brought about by the correct placing and use of the feet. From what I have seen of the average schoolboy cricketer, he is very ignorant of the necessity for using his feet when batting. It is not often that a boy is seen moving into his wicket with his legs to protect it when playing a defensive stroke. Again, when playing forward to drive, the left foot does not point the way for the bat coming through later as it should, but usually this foot is placed straight out for deliveries of all directions, a habit which is entirely wrong. The wicket is left unguarded and in many cases a cross bat stroke is employed. This brings about the inevitable result. Immediately the ball does the slightest thing out of the ordinary, the wicket is hit or a weak, faulty stroke is made.

It should always be remembered that the bat is a weapon of offence and not defence altogether, and to use it effectively, correct balance brought about by footwork must be observed. A boy who overcomes these faults of his own accord, even in defensive strokes, is a player above the average. The schoolboy who jumps in to drive a slow bowler, or brings his right leg across to hook a short ball, is a very rare one. The great majority of strokes appear to be played from the one position. This is not only true of school cricket but can be seen in almost any class of cricket today.

A batsman's job is to make runs and make them from every ball, if possible. There are times, of course, when a batsman is scoring fast, that he requires a rest, and there are certain deliveries from the bowler of such good length and of such a wily culture, that they can only be countered by defensive strokes. It is a bad bowler indeed who does not bowl a good one occasionally. No bowler is so very accommodating that he will bowl half-volleys or long hops to suit a batsman; consequently, the batsman must make the ball to suit himself if he wishes to make any runs. This can only be achieved by footwork. On our hard Australian wickets, when the ball variably comes straight through after the swing has disappeared, a player with a good eye can defend most deliveries with the bat alone; but unless the feet and legs are trained to move correctly on these good wickets, it is impossible to expect them to be ready to do their job when a wicket becomes difficult either through rain or wear and tear.

There is such a thing as 'allowing' a bowler to bowl well, and this can only be remedied by attacking him. If a batsman jumps in to one ball and dispatches it to the boundary, invariably the bowler will drop the next one a little shorter. Provided it is short enough, should the batsman go right back and hook or pull it again to the boundary, it will be necessary for the bowler to think out other tactics and in doing so he is speculating.

Batting is not merely a matter of making contact between bat and ball. It will be found by analysis that the art of attractive batting is a combination of eyes, wrists and arms, after the feet and legs have made the correct position for the necessary stroke, all of which things make for timing, the secret of successful stroke play. But if the feet do not get the body into the proper position and balance, the combination of eyes, wrists and arms is almost valueless.

Another phase of batting which is not by any means treated with sufficient seriousness is running between the wickets. To run well and confidently between wickets one must follow an unwritten law. The striker must call for all runs from strokes played in front of the wicket, and the non-striker for those behind the wicket. The non-striker must back up for possible runs immediately the ball has left the bowler's hand. Obedience to calls is imperative, qualified, of course, with the necessary discretion. A bad runner between wickets can be a distinct menace to his own side. Much can be learned about running between wickets by observing first-class players in action. A fast runner is not necessarily a good runner. He must possess judgment apart from any consideration of speed.

Don't worry about success or failure in batting. Be modest about the one and learn from the other. It is by our failures that we learn most if the right stuff is in us.

The Sporting Globe Cricket Book, 1946–47, edited by EHM Baillie, story by Charlie Macartney (Herald & Weekly Times, Melbourne, 1946)

DOUBLING IT UP

Warwick Armstrong's 438 was the highest score ever made in senior cricket in Victoria.

The last days of the cricket season were signalised on Saturday by two remarkable records, which were a topic amongst all cricketers on Saturday night.

Armstrong, playing for Melbourne against the University, made 438, the highest individual score that any batsman has ever achieved in Victoria. On two occasions in pennant cricket a batsman had got over 400, the best on record on this side of the Straits until Saturday being 417 not out, by J Worrall, also against the University in February 1898. Later on, T Warne, another member of the Carlton club, of which Worrall was then captain, got within 15 of the record, his score against Richmond being 402.

Armstrong's fine innings is the more meritorious in that he made his runs on the short autumn afternoons, scoring at about an even rate all the way through, for he made 222 on the first afternoon and added 216 on Saturday, when he lost his wicket.

Although a first-class performance in every respect, it will not so rank in the records of Australasian cricket. The pride of place [is] still held by CJ Eady of Tasmania, who at Hobart in 1902 made 566 for Break O'Day against Wellington.

This is really the record score of the world, for an innings of 628 by a schoolboy named Collins in Clifton, England, was played on a small schoolground in a scratch match and should not be counted.

Eady is also the only Australian batsman who has twice scored a hundred in each innings of a match.

Armstrong's score stands out distinctively as the cricketing event of the season.

In making 222 on the first day, the only chance he made was to Clive Miller at mid-on when he was on 210. He tried to sweep a full toss to the on, got a big squirm on the ball and the fieldsman, misjudging it at first, made a fine effort afterwards to recover the catch.

On Saturday, Armstrong gave his second and only other chance when his score was 411. Myers, in the outfield, tried for a difficult catch and missed it.

That neither chance was easy is shown in the fact that both fieldsmen threw themselves down in their efforts to reach the ball.

Apart from these two defects, the innings was a fine exhibition of free driving – mostly past the bowler or a bit to the off and the pace at which the ball disappeared occasionally over the embankment towards Queen's College gave one the impression that it was bound for North Carlton. Armstrong only got one five and part of that was for an overthrow, but his innings contained forty-six 4s. His runs were made in six hours and 35 minutes, so that he went just a little faster than a run a minute all through.

In this respect it was a singularly even performance, his first hundred last Saturday being made in just over 80 minutes, and 200 in about three hours.

He had no 'indulgence' from the other side, the University bowlers being 'triers' all through. Among those who bowled against him was Bailey, a left-hander and a son of Mr George Bailey, the Tasmanian, who was a member of the first Australian XI to England.

Armstrong went in first and was out when the total was 668 so that he scored his 438 while the several other batsmen in with him made 230. He lost his wicket in trying to pull a short length ball, which beat him with unexpected pace from the pitch.

This innings is satisfactory for more reasons than one. In the early part of the season when he lost his place in the Australian XI, Armstrong was undoubtedly out of sorts.

He admitted on many occasions a listless feeling which made exertion difficult, without quite realising what was wrong with him. For the time he had undoubtedly lost tone, but each innings he has played towards the end of the season has been marked by quite his former vigour and style.

It is a good thing for Australian cricket that Armstrong has given this signal proof of his old efficiency. These periods of depression come to the best cricketers occasionally and this may be Armstrong's first and last experience of it.

In the second record of note, Monfries, the Melbourne wicketkeeper, shared with Armstrong the honours of achievement. Monfries went in when four Melbourne wickets had fallen for 235 runs. Before another wicket fell the score was 668, so that they added 433 for the fifth wicket.

It stands as a fifth-wicket record anywhere, but is the best partnership as yet recorded in Australia for any match.

The Argus, 'Observer' (Melbourne, 1903–04)
Eleven years later, Melbourne Grammar schoolboy James Sharpe was to surpass Armstrong's quadruple century when he amassed 506 not out against Geelong College in 1914–15.

MELBOURNE v THE UNIVERSITY, 1903–04
MELBOURNE: first innings

W Bruce	c Baird, b James	8
WW Armstrong	b Bailey	438
VS Ransford	run out	42
Fry	c James, b Rainey	20
Down	c Graham, b James	14
JE Monfries	c L Miller, b Rainey	123
Irwin	b James	11
Johnston	not out	16
Bowden	run out	0
Murray	not out	3
Extras		24
Total		8-699

Bowling: Bailey 1-145, James 3-155, Rainey 2-129, Le Couteur 0-133, Miller 0-29, Graham 0-16, Langley 0-34
Match drawn.

ENGLAND V THE KIDS

It may not have made the pages of Wisden *or* Cricket: A Weekly Record of the Game, *but 18 Melbourne juniors had a thrill-of-a-lifetime when they played against PF 'Plum' Warner's touring MCC team over two late-December days in 1903.*

Only once has a Victorian junior team competed against an English XI.

When the English team, led by 'Plum' Warner, arrived in Victoria during the 1903–04 tour, Jimmy Cantwell, official in cricket and football circles for 46 years, spoke to the then secretary of the Melbourne Cricket Club, Major Ben Wardill, and on behalf of the juniors asked for a match with the visiting eleven. Instead of getting the rebuff he expected, Major Wardill communicated with the Sydney office, who then controlled the visiting team's movements, and two hours later a match on the MCG against a team of 18 juniors was arranged.

On the day of the contest [on the eve of the second Test], the 34 selected players, who two days before had been thrilled with the idea of meeting Plum Warner's team, took the field riddled with nerves and could do little right. Youths who in club and inter-association games had excellent records, were all suffering from an inferiority complex. Even when given easy opportunities, they fumbled the ball.

The English team made 416 in the first innings and had no need to bat again. The best bowlers for the juniors were P O'Loughlin three for 85, and Chris Dwyer three for 77. In their first innings the juniors made 124, and in their second 193. Mick Grace 54 and Fred Delves 52 were top scorers.

The juniors' hopes were wrecked by [Bernard] Bosanquet, six for 27 and [Arthur] Fielder, four for 37 in the first innings and by [Len] Braund, eight for 43 and [Albert] Relf, four for 40 in the second. After the match Warner expressed the opinion that it was a mistake, 'from the lads' point of view', to pit them against such experienced players. He referred to the match in his book published after the tour, and said that it was a most enjoyable contest, watched by about 4000 people.

A team selected from the same squad of Melbourne juniors visited

South Australia that year and, as if to prove their ability, gave an excellent exhibition against Adelaide and suburbs and won by four wickets.

Bob Myers, vice-president of the Victorian Junior Cricket Union and one of the best-known officials of the game, still has the cuttings referring to the contest. The juniors who took part included: W McSperrin, afterwards treasurer of the Fitzroy Football Club; J Howe, who later took his medical degree; Chris Dwyer, well known later with Fitzroy – he visited England and after returning joined the South Melbourne footballers team; L Smith; P O'Loughlin, who played later with Brunswick; J Williams; A Sharpe; Frank Manallack, an excellent wicketkeeper, who also joined Brunswick; F Delves, later with Carlton and also an interstate representative; the late AV Moon; J Howell, also with Brunswick; the late Chris Kiernan, another interstate player and Fitzroy player; L Cogle; the late Mick Grace, a well known Carlton footballer; J Hexter; D Lanigan, who is still playing in junior ranks; J Cattanach; and T Lewis.

The Sporting Globe, writer unknown (Melbourne, January 1933)

ENGLAND v MELBOURNE JUNIORS, Melbourne Cricket Ground, 1903
ENGLAND: first innings

T Hayward	c Delves, b Smith	37
PF Warner	b Sharpe	76
AE Knight	b O'Loughlin	50
AE Relf	c Smith, b Lewis	30
LC Braund	c Lanigan, b Dwyer	33
GH Hirst	b O'Loughlin	87
BJT Bosanquet	c Cogle, b Dwyer	10
AA Lilley	b Dwyer	10
WR Rhodes	not out	42
A Fielder	b O'Loughlin	9
H Strudwick	b Lanigan	16
Extras		16
Total		416

Bowling: O'Loughlin 26-1-85-3, Howe 4-0-16-0, Sharpe 25-3-59-1, Lewis 7-0-18-1 (2 w), Smith 14-1-49-1 (1 nb), Cogle 3-0-8-0, Horgan 6-0-16-0, William 4-0-19-0, Lanigan 7-0-30-1, McSperrin 6-1-23-0, Dwyer 19-0-77-3

JUNIORS: first innings

F Delves	c Relf, b Fielder	3
AV Moon	c & b Relf	2
T Howe	run out	11
C Kiernan	stmp Strudwick, b Rhodes	14

L Cogle	b Braund	1
M Grace	c Bosanquet, b Fielder	10
J Hexter	run out	1
D Lanigan	stmp Strudwick, b Braund	0
J Cattanach	c Relf, b Fielder	6
T Lewis	c Bosanquet, b Fielder	8
W McSperrin	stmp Strudwick, b Bosanquet	24
J Horgan	b Bosanquet	3
M Dwyer	run out	18
L Smith	b Bosanquet	1
P O'Loughlin	c & b Bosanquet	4
J Williams	not out	8
A Sharpe	c Fielder, b Bosanquet	1
F Manallack	b Bosanquet	0
Extras		9
Total		124

Bowling: Relf 15-7-17-1 (2 nb), Rhodes 5-1-8-1, Fielder 19-7-37-4 (3 nb), Bosanquet 14-5-4-27-6, Braund 14-5-26-2

JUNIORS: second innings

F Delves	run out	52
AV Moon	c Hirst, b Braund	13
T Howe	b Relf	0
C Kiernan	c Braund, b Bosanquet	16
L Cogle	c sub (Whitfeld), b Braund	8
M Grace	stmp Strudwick, b Braund	54
J Hexter	b Rhodes	0
D Lanigan	b Braund	2
J Cattanach	b Relf	3
T Lewis	c Hirst, b Braund	1
W McSperrin	c & b Bosanquet	9
J Horgan	c Bosanquet, b Braund	12
M Dwyer	b Relf	9
L Smith	c sub (Whitfeld), b Braund	0
P O'Loughlin	not out	6
J Williams	b Rhodes	1
A Sharpe	c Strudwick, b Relf	0
F Manallack	b Braund	0
Extras		7
Total		193

Bowling: Relf 24-8-40-4, Rhodes 10-7-14-2, Bosanquet 11-2-53-2, Braund 19.5-4-48-8, Fielder 12-2-26-0, Hirst 1-0-5-0

How We Recovered the Ashes, PF Warner (Chapman & Hall Ltd, London, 1904)

PYROTECHNICS AT THEIR VERY BEST

There was only one Victor ... and when he played at his
consummate best, the whole cricket world celebrated.

The greatest innings ever played by Victor Trumper? Sydneysiders and
Victorians who watched his bewildering knock on the Sydney Cricket
Ground on Anniversary Day, 1906 [26 January] will acknowledge no
other feat as superior to that century made in an hour. 'Trumper is
done,' the fickle crowd had said. A new star – James Rainey Munro
'Sunny Jim' Mackay – had arisen to take at least part of the place in
the affection of the cricket public that Victor had held.

Mackay, the lad from Uralla, had compiled scores of 203, 90, 194,
105 and 102 not out (these two in the same match against South
Australia), 4 and 136, an aggregate of 834 before this contest, whilst
Victor's figures were but modest. The very variable Sydneyites might
have been pardoned for crying: 'The King is dead; long live the new
King!'

Came the time-honoured Anniversary Day match of 1906 and a
doubtful wicket which the very astute Alf Noble thought would be
quite all right. 'We will bat,' he remarked to Frank Laver when the
toss favoured the Paddington man; but the game had hardly started
when Noble realised that he had erred.

Victoria's bowling pair Jack Saunders and Fred Collins were the old
NSW two, Ferris and Turner, over again. The left-hander made the
ball do all sorts of fantastic tricks, spinning them from leg, baffling
Mackay and [Austin] Diamond with the extent of the break and the
excellent control he had over it. Sometimes it was that big that bat and
wicket were beaten; at others it just whizzed past the stumps. At the
other end Collins was playing the role of CTB Turner, the 'Terror' of
years before. What Saunders was doing from the leg side, Fred was
performing in the opposite direction.

With but 40 up, Sunny Jim Mackay tried to turn one of Saunders'
most hostile ones to the on, but the ball spun across to slips – an
easy catch and the New Englander was out for 18. Noble, lover of
situations that called for grit, came next, but there was little time
between his coming and going. He was caught at point without
scoring.

Enter Trumper, who was 'through' according to some. The first ball from Saunders took a coat of paint from his off stump. Getting down to the other end, he remarked to Saunders (to use the statement of JVS to Tommy Horan when the Victorians returned to Melbourne), 'This is no good, Jack. I'm going to have a slog.'

He did. From that moment onward, Trumper was a real wizard. Nothing worried him. The leg breaks bowled, with the greatest accuracy and in the most guileful manner by Saunders, were treated as if he was on a flint-like wicket which took all the hostility out of the most dangerous of bowlers.

Collins wondered what he had struck. From one of his overs came 20 runs, Victor getting 19 and the stolid Diamond a single. No stroke palled. He showed infinite variety. He pulled good-length balls to the boundary, making the most hair-raising shots. To others they would have been debited as flukes, but Victor repeated them with the carefree method peculiarly his own and all knew he meant them. They were the products of his remarkable batting genius. When Diamond was 27, he was caught on the off by Tommy Warne, off Saunders and immediately Reg Duff should have been out, but Matt Ellis, suffering from a blow on the foot, sustained at practice, could not get to a ball at square leg. The wicket was still lots of unorthodox things, but whilst Duff, whom few bowlers could steady, was a wee bit at sea, there was no curbing of Trumper.

Collins had retired before the terrific onslaught, giving way to Laver – not the easiest of bowlers on a wicket performing tricks – but good-length balls from the Victorian captain were whipped to the fence with charming sangfroid and in the same nonchalant way he stepped into one from Laver and lifted the ball onto the roof of the Northern Stand, a terrific, yet effortless, hit that would probably have sent the ball almost into the No. 2 area had the summit of the roof not intervened. By this time 78 runs had been added while Vic was at the wickets. Of these he had scored 64 in 31 minutes.

Arthur Christian was not a bad left-hand understudy to Saunders. He came next, but Trumper moved along with his pyrotechnics. At lunch, with NSW 3-130, he had scored 73 and his usual merry companion, Duff, was only 9.

Afterwards Saunders bowled Duff. The Rev EF Waddy joined the devastating Trumper, who soon afterwards reached the century, having batted just an hour. With the addition of a single he chopped Saunders onto the off stump, his 101 having been gathered in just 60 minutes at the wicket.

Things went well afterwards, some of those who failed in the first innings rehabilitating themselves, but *the* classic of [the] Sydney Cricket Ground had gone to the credit of Trumper. Saunders finished with seven for 122.

Scorer JG Jackschon supplied some very interesting figures – though mathematics seem to be rather too sordid to introduce into the atmosphere that Trumper provided that day, or, rather, that one crowded hour of glorious life. Victor received 67 balls, playing 61 and missing six. He scored from 34 thus: one 6, eighteen 4s, two 3s, four 2s and nine 1s. He made 51 off 23 balls from Saunders, 19 off six from Collins, 16 off 12 from Laver, nine off 15 from Christian and six off six from Warne. Ask Matt Ellis, Tommy Warne, Peter McAlister, Vernon Ransford, Tom Horan, Arthur Christian, now in the West, EV Carroll and EC Jones, survivors of the Victorian eleven who fielded during that hour, what they think of the innings! Not one would but laud it.

The Sporting Globe, 'Rambler' (Melbourne, December 1931)

SMOKERS V NONSMOKERS
A unique challenge match at the old East Melbourne
ground triggered the world's record score.

So fierce became the argument between those who smoked and those who didn't that a challenge was thrown out and a cricket match arranged between the 'Smokers' and the 'Nonsmokers' to prove which was right. Was smoking really injurious to one's health? An English team – the last, by the way, organised by the famous firm which did so much for international cricket, first as Shaw & Lillywhite and later as Shaw & Shrewsbury – was in Australia. No Test match had been arranged in Melbourne [in 1886–87], and there was a keen desire to see the Englishmen in the field.

Alfred Shaw and Arthur Shrewsbury were great cricketers and they were shrewd businessmen as well. They saw an opportunity of turning the tobacco argument to their own good financial effect, and from the Victorian and English teams they chose two elevens and arranged the match. The players entered wholeheartedly into the game, and a most interesting contest ensued, which, by the by, brought many hundreds of pounds to the coffers of the enterprising promoters.

[According to historian Ray Webster, Boyle led the Smokers onto the field 'each blowing a cloud from a cigar of colonial manufacture, but immediately the business of the day commenced, "butts" were thrown away'.]

The match, arranged as an exhibition, became a real battle, and resulted in the Nonsmokers making the world's record score of 803. The previous world's record in a first-class match was 775 by New South Wales against Victoria in Sydney, in the match in which WL Murdoch, the Australian champion, made 321, the record individual score in the world, surpassing WG Grace's record of 318 not out for Gloucestershire against Yorkshire at Cheltenham in 1876.

Although 51 years have passed since that match, the score of 803 has been exceeded only 11 times.

Of the individual performances, the scores of Shrewsbury (236), William Gunn (150), Billy Bruce (131) and 'Joey' Palmer (113) stood out in batting, and the record of Billy Bates, six wickets for 73, stood alone in bowling. The most remarkable individual effort, however, was that of Percy Lewis, the East Melbourne wicketkeeper, who in the score of 803 allowed only three byes, off the only ball he failed to stop.

The only survivor of those who took part in the game is WH Cooper, who was born on 11 September 1849 and was afterwards one of the best-known bowlers in Victoria, winning many championships.

The match, which was drawn much in favour of the 'Nons', ended sensationally, for when the last ball was bowled, and before the umpire [Jim Phillips] had called 'over', Will Scotton, anxious to retain the ball as a memento, picked it up and was promptly given out [for] 'handling ball', a most unusual way of getting out in any class of cricket. It was an evidence of the keenness with which the game was played.

The match attracted large crowds and produced some magnificent cricket, as well as some pertinent and impertinent barracking. I was at school at the time and many of us played truant so that we could watch the play. There we met boys from other schools, who, like ourselves, had paid their sixpence and sat out in the open, in the burning sun. The result was hailed as a victory for the opponents of the tobacco habit and thus was really a 'Test match'.

The Argus weekend magazine, RWE 'Old Boy' Wilmot (Melbourne, 27 August 1938); extra research: *First Class Cricket in Australia, Vol 1, 1850–51 to 1941–42*, Ray Webster (self-published, Melbourne, 1991)

SMOKERS v NONSMOKERS, East Melbourne, 1886–87
NONSMOKERS: first innings

A Shrewsbury (E)	c Duffy, b Briggs	236
W Bruce (A)	lbw Palmer	131
W Bates (E)	b Palmer	4
W Gunn (E)	b Boyle	150
RG Barlow (E)	b Palmer	29
R Houston (A)	c & b Briggs	57
H Musgrove (A)	stmp Lewis, b Briggs	62
J Worrall (A)	b Read	78
WH Cooper (A)	c & b Briggs	46
M Sherwin (E)	not out	5
W Barnes (E)	absent	0
Byes: 3, leg bye 1, wide 1		
Total		803

Fall: 196, 204, 514, 524, 515, 656, 686, 788, 803
Bowling: Briggs 4-141, Palmer 3-189, Boyle 1-60, Lohmann 0-113,
Flowers 0-93, Scotton 0-82, Duffy 0-52, Read 1-43, Walters 0-23

SMOKERS: first innings

JM Read (E)	stmp Sherwin, b Cooper	30
GE Palmer (A)	c Worrall, b Bruce	113
J Briggs (E)	c Shrewsbury, b Bates	86
W Flowers (E)	run out	69
G Lohmann (E)	c sub (Briggs), b Bates	19
W Scotton (E)	c Bruce, b Bates	11
HF Boyle (A)	b Bruce	7
G Browning (A)	b Bates	1
F Walters (A)	stmp Sherwin, b Bates 0	
P Lewis (A)	c Houston, b Bates	2
W Duffy (A)	not out	0
Byes 12, leg byes 2, no-balls 2, wides 2		
Total		356

Fall: 44, 204, 267, rest unknown
Bowling: Bates 6-73, Cooper 1-85, Bond 2-92, Worrall 0-30,
Gunn 0-27, Houston 0-31

SMOKERS: second innings

GE Palmer	c Houston, b Worrall	24
J Briggs	stmp Sherwin, b Bates	54
W Flowers	b Houston	25
W Scotton	handled ball	18
G Lohmann	lbw Gunn	2
HF Boyle	not out	0
Byes 9, leg byes 2, no-ball 1		

Total: Five wickets for 135
Fall unknown
Bowling: Bates 1-40, Barnes 0-14, Bruce 0-15, Worrall 1-22, Cooper 0-18, Gunn 1-1, Houston 1-13, Shrewsbury 0-0

TOO QUICK EVEN FOR JACK

In the cricket match between the Australian Xl and the Ballaarat eighteen today, [Jack] Blackham, the wicketkeeper, got a very hard blow from one of Spofforth's fast balls. He rolled on the ground and appeared to be very much hurt. A few minutes' rest, however, enabled him to resume his dangerous position behind the wickets.

Later, when a batsman was trying to play 'The Demon' [Spofforth], Blackham got another and more dangerous blow on the temple, and he reeled and was only prevented from falling to the ground by [Billy] Murdoch.

After a lapse of a few minutes, play was continued, Blackham standing back from the wickets, as far as play would permit. Ballaraat suffered a complete collapse at the hands of Spofforth, who was unplayable, and who took 11 of the 17 wickets.

The Herald, writer unknown (Melbourne, 13 January 1883)

A REMARKABLE SPECTACLE
*Australia's first match at Lord's began a tradition
of success at the game's spiritual home.*

Over 4000 persons visited Lord's ground yesterday to witness one of the most remarkable spectacles that has occurred at this place for a long time past.

The Australians were not thought very highly of in their recent contest with Notts, but they showed themselves in a very different light yesterday, for better fielding has rarely occurred.

Mr Ridley won the toss, and decided upon sending Messrs WG Grace and Hornby to the wickets. Mr Allan started bowling from the nursery end, followed by Mr Boyle from the pavilion. Mr Grace hit the former for 4, but from the next ball he was caught at short leg.

Mr Booth's off stump was struck before he scored a run. Mr Ridley then joined Mr Hornby and the score advanced to 25. At this stage Mr Spofforth, a renowned bowler, very soon disposed of the latter. In the next six overs, seven of the Marylebone wickets fell for six runs. Mr Allan bowled nine overs for 14 runs and took one wicket; Mr Boyle, 14 overs, 14 runs, three wickets; Mr Spofforth five overs and three balls, four runs, six wickets. He took three wickets with three successive balls in his fourth over.

C Bannerman and Midwinter began the Australian batting at 1.30, and within two hours, including luncheon, the whole eleven were got out for 41 runs – only one double figure. Marylebone resumed batting with Messrs Grace and Webbe, and great indeed was the disappointment caused by Mr Grace's quick retirement, without a run. It signified little who went in, for Messrs Spofforth and Boyle were determined upon their speedy dismissal. Four wickets fell for one run. Flowers and Wild held together long enough to bring the score up to 16. At 4.50 the innings closed for 19. The Australians required but 12 runs to win. This number cost them one wicket, so that the Colonials beat the greatest and most powerful club in the world by nine wickets. They were loudly cheered by the assembled multitude for their achievement.

The Times, writer unknown (London, 28 May 1878)

MCC & GROUND v THE AUSTRALIANS, Monday 27 May 1878
MCC 33 (Hornby 19, Boyle three for 14, Spofforth six for 4) & 19 (Boyle five for 3, Spofforth five for 16) lost to Australians 41 (Shaw five for 10, Morley five for 31) & 1-12, by nine wickets.

Searing Phone Call: Kepler Wessels'
early morning cross-continents
phone call to Kerry Packer prompted
a furious exchange.

10
TALL TALES AND TRUE

'Too many friends, too many parties,
too many social drinks ...'

❧

SCONED IN DURBAN

Andrew Symonds on an occupational hazard.

Seeing your own blood pooling on the ground in front of you is one of the most alarming experiences imaginable. On this particular occasion, I'd just been hit in the face by a cricket ball travelling at more than 130 km/h, but the funny thing was, there was no real pain. At

least at the time. We were playing the Proteas in the second Test in Durban in South Africa in April 2006, it was late on the opening day and the crowd had been baying for my blood. When Makhaya Ntini got a short one to jag back towards me, I guess they got what they wanted.

Over the years I'd copped the odd ball on the scone – it's an occupational hazard we all have to deal with – but I didn't wear a helmet until my second season with Queensland in 1995–96, preferring to bat in a floppy hat (à la Richie Richardson), or nothing at all. I'd been lucky, but I put a lot of it down to the rigorous coaching Dad gave me as a kid, even though I probably didn't

Symmo: Andrew Symonds was always 'in' the game, whether he was batting, bowling or fielding.

appreciate it at the time. He used to terrorise me on occasion and I'd wake up thinking, 'Oh no, he's going to do the short pitch stuff again this morning. He'll hit me in the head for sure!'

But he really was a great teacher and would break things down, ensuring you mastered them one at a time before moving on to the next. When it came to short-pitched balls – bumpers and bouncers – we spent a long time on the dos and don'ts. Thankfully, I learned pretty quickly, although when he'd say we were going to work on pulls and cut shots, I prayed I wouldn't mix them up.

The one that got me in Durban was a pretty fair nut. I'd scored a couple of runs but was intent on surviving the last few overs in what were less-than-ideal batting conditions. The light was bad – it was gloomy even though the floodlights were on – the ball was hard to see and as Ntini's action can angle it back at you from time to time, you've got to be vigilant. He'd hit Justin Langer during the first Test with an unreadable ball and the one that got me certainly seamed off the track. On the replay you can see that I dropped my hands to let it go, but it came back at me and caught me right between my lips and my nose, pushing my helmet grill back into my face.

I've no real beef with Ntini as it was partly my fault: my grill had been getting gradually closer and closer to my face due to the length and bulk of my hair and 'Pup' [Michael Clarke] had even noticed and told me I should adjust it. Of course I didn't. More's the pity.

It turned out my teeth had gone through my lip, my nose was bleeding, my front teeth were loose and a bottom tooth was chipped. I thought for a second he'd knocked some of them out: I couldn't feel them which was why I was a bit panicky.

Roy Going For Broke, Andrew Symonds with Stephen Gray (Hardie Grant Books, Melbourne, 2006)

MARK TAYLOR'S RESURRECTION

Prelude to a previously out-of-form Mark Taylor's record-equaling 334 at Peshawar at the start of his last international summer was a tortuous 16-week dawn fitness circuit, orchestrated by Sydney fitness guru Kevin Chevell.

Mark knew what he was in for this winter. He knew he had to be willing to work harder than he'd ever worked in his life. He knew he had to face me just about every day, and what I would dish out to him. He wanted to keep it to himself, though. He wanted to keep it private, the bone-wearing and backbreaking work we completed day after day.

Mark did not want to draw any attention to himself throughout those 16 weeks of his rebuilding process. He preferred to quietly get the required work done with me, then work on his batting and fielding skills with the New South Wales squad, for preseason training. It would then be left up to his performances with the bat in Pakistan and beyond to speak for themselves ...

During our months together, Mark and I would try to outsmart each other all the time. Mark would try to calculate my next instruction, so he could keep something in reserve during the exercise sessions. What a typical captain ploy! I'd catch him watching me calculate the daily routine in my mind. From his view, he was just trying to estimate what we were going to be doing that particular session, so he could pace himself to last it out.

So, when I had assessed in my mind the schedule for the day, I'd look across and ask him, 'Okay smartarse, what am I thinking?' Then he would rattle off a sequence of exercises in a particular order and how we were going to perform them.

The truth is most times he would get it right. In fact, he rarely would get it wrong. Then I would reply to him, 'There's no use in trying to guess, because I'm going to make sure you don't get through it anyway!'

He would call me names all the time. Not one day went by without him calling me a bastard, or something a little more descriptive. He would accuse me of having mental problems and that I must be mad or something because of the tortuous physical challenges I set for him.

I'd quite often catch Mark and [training partner] Glenn [McGrath] pulling faces and nodding their heads when I was turned away. I would look them both directly in the eye and just reply, 'Okay, you may hate me now, but you can thank me later. Come on and get up, let's keep going!'

The only thanks I wanted was to enjoy watching Mark and Glenn succeed out on the field scoring runs and taking wickets and enjoying their cricket for all it's worth ...

Mark and Glenn would tell me how nervous they would get driving out to Penrith every morning, especially when they knew it was scheduled for legs training, or we were due for a triathlon

Chevell-style. They would joke with one another about having sweaty palms and 'butterflies' in the stomach because they knew they'd be in for all-out exercise.

I noted the expression on Mark's face when setting up the equipment for exercising the leg muscles. I would wheel an electronic computerised cycle over to the squat rack, then set up the barbell with 40 kg to warm up.

Mark would do squats for 40 seconds, then immediately ride the bike for 60 seconds at level 12. Recovery time was only allowed while Glenn was performing a similar set. For the next set, I would load an extra 20 kg to the bar, for Mark to complete a repeat. With each succeeding set, there was an increase in weight of 10 kg up to a maximum load of 110 kg, always followed by a 60-second ride at the highest resistance level on the bike.

Monitoring his heart rate continuously throughout showed it was pumping at between 165 and 175 beats per minute with almost no rest. A session like this would last about 40 minutes, because that's how long he would last before total exhaustion. We didn't count the number of sets performed, or the number of repetitions. It's not that important. Each session was a challenge to see how much he could handle and how long he could last.

There they were at the end of the leg strengthening session. The Australian captain and his No. 1 fast bowler, Glenn McGrath, lying sprawled across the gym floor drenched from head to toe in a lather of perspiration. Both feeling sorry for themselves, breathing laboured, just waiting for their hearts to stop pumping out their chests.

Sometimes when they were together, I would introduce a challenge to the finish between Mark and Glenn while performing a standing shoulder press routine. We would select a light-medium weight of 25 kg.

I pegged one against the other to see who would give in first. The opening batsman versus the opening bowler; just the perfect combination for a real confrontation. And didn't they give it to one another!

Mark would start and perform 15 repetitions then pass the bar to Glenn for him to do the same. Then the bar would be passed back to Mark for another 15 repetitions. To and fro, set for set, this continued for nearly 10 minutes. Their shoulders and arms were screaming for relief, but neither was prepared to give in to the other. They were both hoping the other would surrender, or that I would call it off.

Their heart rates were both around 185 beats per minute. I knew they were waiting for me to make a call. So I did! I said just three more sets, to give them some signal that an end was near. But when they were starting the last of those three final sets, I said: 'Okay, I'm happy. It's now up to you both to call it off. You can stop now or you can keep going, whatever suits you.' Mark then glared at me and called me something I won't repeat here.

They both knew whoever gave in first would lose. Both were determined not to give in [so they continued] . . .

As the days and weeks passed, Mark began to reshape and take on a new appearance. He shed around 10 kg of body fat during those 16 weeks, plus he gained 2–3 kg of muscle tissue from all the exercise. None of his suits or casual wear would fit anymore. He had to pull out clothing he hadn't worn in years.

His 'tummy' was almost flat before the Pakistan tour and he was looking very sharp and athletic in the face. There was an air of confidence around him by then. He had been away from all the pressures of international cricket, out of the press and media spotlight. And he had spent valuable time with his family, plus working on other new projects in his life.

When he recommenced preseason training with the NSW squad, I asked him regularly how he was batting. The answer every time was that he was very happy. He felt that he was seeing the ball much earlier, and that his footwork felt better than at any time in his career, during any pre-season training period. My instinct right then was that everything we had done during winter was working perfectly for him and we had set the stage for a really successful summer of cricket, or at least he had given himself every chance possible to resurrect his status as opening batsman for Australia. I got all the right signals, that his hard work was already taking its effect.

Rebuilding Your Body, Your Mind and Your Life: the Chevell Program to a Better Life,
Kevin Chevell (Information Australia, Melbourne, 1998)
While batting for two days in the second Test in Pakistan in October 1998, Taylor
several times felt he was losing the mental battle through sheer exhaustion. 'When I
was just about to give it away, I'd think to myself: "Hang on. I don't feel as tired as
I did when I was in the gym with Kev. I'm going to keep going."' He made 112 on the
first day and 222 on the second to finish at 334 not out, equal to the highest ever Test
score by Sir Donald Bradman, amassed two generations earlier.

THANK GOODNESS FOR MOBILES . . .

*Test cricket on the ABC has been part of Australian
summers for 80 years, yet the first broadcast from
the subcontinent didn't occur until 1998.*

It's almost game time in Rawalpindi and the dreaded phrase 'equipment failure' has circulated through the ABC Radio team perched high in the grandstand. While Jim Maxwell hurriedly tests and tweaks the fickle equipment, colleague Tim Lane switches to 'Plan B' as Australian openers Michael Slater and Mark Taylor walk out. Without losing stride, he goes live from Pakistan to the masses back in Australia by mobile phone for 40 minutes. This is the cutting edge of cricket broadcasting and life in general on the subcontinent. You don't ever get very far without a Plan B while playing dodgems in a taxi or when the headsets are on. The ABC has been a groundbreaker for cricket listeners almost from the moment of the first ball-by-ball commentary of cricket in the 1920s.

In 1998, that meant bringing the sounds and almost the smells of cricket in India and Pakistan to Australians for the first time.

The reaction, judged by calls through ABC switchboards around the country, was 'phenomenal', according to ABC Radio sports editor Peter Longman. 'It was amazing. We got more feedback from these tours than for the more traditional destinations like England,' Longman says. 'A lot of the comments went beyond the cricket to the more exotic cultures of India and Pakistan that people were getting an insight to. This intrigued listeners, plus the fact there were so many good stories.'

Taylor's remarkable innings at Peshawar unfolded over two days for a big afternoon drive-time audience back home. 'What started as a big innings turned into something monumental,' Maxwell explains. 'Doing a running commentary on something like that, you just don't realise how significant it is becoming.'

Lane adds: 'Radio listeners missed a tied Test in Madras [in 1986–87] altogether and, at the last minute, picked up a BBC coverage of the 1987 World Cup final from Calcutta.

'Thankfully, we didn't miss Taylor's Bradman-equalling performance. We've now bridged an important gap going to the subcontinent.'

The 'Tim and Jim Show' also went beyond the boundaries that were marked so classically by the late Alan McGilvray. Maxwell interviewed taxi drivers in Lahore and helped turn the ABC's scorers, 'Mr Subramanya' and 'Mr Shakeel', into minor cult figures. During the Peshawar Test, Lane conducted a revealing interview with an Australian woman working with the Australian Volunteers Abroad program. She told of being stoned by local men for something as provocative as a short-sleeved shirt and risking more of the same just going to the cricket. Lane did a good imitation of a homesick Aussie, too, when he described listening to the AFL [Australian Football League] grand final on his short-wave radio in Karachi. 'We hoped people listening could almost taste the flavour of a Pakistani curry,' Maxwell quips.

The flavour is of a different sort this [1998–99] summer, with Maxwell, Lane and the BBC's Jonathan Agnew filling the ball-by-ball roles now that stalwart Neville Oliver has left the ABC. The recently retired Dean Jones is a bright and opinionated addition to the supporting 'experts'. He joins Keith Stackpole, Bob Massie, Terry Jenner, Terry Alderman, Geoff Lawson and Peter Roebuck.

Quest for the Ashes: Ansett Australia Test Series, Official Test Program, Jim Tucker (ACP Publishing, Sydney, 1998)

FANCY A SPOT OF ACTING?

Former Australian leg spinner Peter Philpott had a frontline role in the making of the Bodyline *television series.*

The Kennedy–Miller miniseries *Bodyline* [which premiered in 1984] was my most unusual coaching assignment. It was also one of the most enjoyable and informative.

Initially, I was contracted to coach cricket to the actors and I must admit that when I agreed to do this I had little idea what lay ahead. We worked and practised several afternoons a week at various schools over a period of several months before shooting began.

All the actors had one thing in common – they were very enthusiastic. But the variety of ability and experience was another matter altogether. For instance, Gary Sweet, who was lined up for the key role of Don Bradman, was quite a good player and only needed practice and a little tidying up. John Sherrin, who was to play Bill

'65 Tourists: Peter 'Percy' Philpott and Barry Jarman enjoy some time off in the Caribbean in 1965.

Ponsford, was also an experienced all-round ball player.

When it came to Jim Holt (to play Harold Larwood) and Hugo Weaving (to play Douglas Jardine) – both vital roles – the situation was quite different. Jim had not played cricket before, and, on his first attempt at a fast-bowling approach, he simply fell over. Somehow Jim had to be developed into an acceptable-looking fast bowler and we had about eight weeks to do it.

Much the same was true of Hugo. His cricket background was limited, his ball skills meagre, yet the viability of the entire film hinged greatly on Hugo's acceptability as a Douglas Jardine, both on and off the field.

The entire cast was similarly varied in cricket ability, ranging from good, to fair, to non-existent. Admittedly, the on-screen exposure of some of these players was quite limited but others appeared in cricket action scenes regularly, and it was essential that they appeared as authentic as possible. Everyone entered into the race towards reasonable authenticity with great energy, enthusiasm and high spirits. It was good fun, but there was much to be done.

At first, it was hoped that each actor might model himself on the cricketer he was playing. With that in mind, I was handed videotape which contained most of the existing film of the Bodyline days and the players who participated in the matches.

The tapes were fascinating and I absorbed them all hungrily, both for pointers to help with the series and for personal reasons. But several things soon became clear to me. Firstly, there was relatively so little film evidence that no one could obtain lasting impressions of any player's style from what existed. Secondly, those who had viewed the Bodyline series in person were few and far between and probably not particularly reliable witnesses anyhow, after so long.

Thus, I gave my opinion to the directors that any attempt to imitate individual style was hardly worth the effort and we should spend our time and energy simply trying to look like acceptable cricketers. And this we tried to do.

George Miller had decided that three men would direct the various episodes independently. Two, George Ogilvie and Karl Schultz, were very experienced dramatic directors, but had almost no knowledge or understanding of cricket before the series began. The third, Lex Marinos – who had also been involved in the writing with Terry Hayes – was knowledgeable both in theatre and cricket. It was a thrill to work closely with such men. As shooting time drew nearer, it became necessary to assess the individuals in the cast with the directors. Exactly what cricket action was required from each actor? Could he handle it?

My major concern was 'Larwood'. Jim had worked hard, was developing a reasonably rhythmical approach, but was still having problems with an acceptable delivery and follow-through. As for what happened after he released the ball – well, frankly, it was anyone's guess where it might go. It seemed that the directors were expecting to follow Jim's approach and delivery all the way on camera, then show the ball digging in short, careering over the batsman's head and thudding into the keeper's gloves. They asked how long it would take to reach this stage, and they began to understand the problems involved when I replied, 'About 15 years!'

I suggested a compromise. A few shots of the complete action but mainly cut-aways from feet, to face, to body, to batsman and so on. As for what happened after the ball was delivered – we would have to think again. It was fascinating work.

There were still parts to be filled, and as I came to know the production staff better they brought me more and more into their confidence. When the role of Clarrie Grimmett was discussed I half-jokingly nominated myself, and was immediately accepted. So now I had a part in the film too, and before long I had become a consultant on all things cricket. My involvement in the production was becoming ever closer, which suited me just fine.

The next step was a week-long workshop conducted at the Sydney Cricket Ground. All actors assembled each day for lectures, discussion, rehearsal and training. Already the group had become a fairly tight-knit one because of the practices and the drinks and yarns that so often followed. I enjoyed the camaraderie.

Dressing-room scenes were frequent, and I was asked to lecture to the assembled cast on the cricket dressing-room and its importance in cricket. Only then did I realise myself how integral a role the dressing-room plays in a cricket life. It is there that men share tension over very long periods of time, and share the fear, the laughter, the exhaustion, the exuberance, the joy and the wretched despair – all of which mould very special relationships among cricketers. I feared that my talk might sound contrived and over-dramatic to those who had not experienced the realities of a first-class career, but there was, in fact, no need to fear at all. For, as George Ogilvie at once pointed out, there was a peculiar similarity of emotion and atmosphere within the theatre dressing-rooms, and this realisation among the actors brought a certain relief in mutual understanding.

That afternoon at the Sydney Cricket Ground, rehearsals of the Australian dressing-room scenes took place where they belonged – in the Australian dressing-rooms. It was magical. The players were relaxed and at home. I really felt as if I were in a NSW or Australian dressing-room with a match in progress.

The next day, rehearsals of the English dressing-room scenes took place where they belonged, too. My reaction was quite different. It all felt wrong for me. The relaxation was not there, the normal comradeship and interaction was simply not there. Why?

Later, when all the actors went across Moore Park to the Bat & Ball for a drink, I began to understand what was happening. Actors playing the Australians unthinkingly gathered together noisily, beers in hand, on one side of the bar. The 'Englishmen' sat around tables on the other side of the room and in the company of 'Douglas Jardine' and 'Gubby Allen' were far more reserved and far less relaxed.

It seemed they were beginning to be their roles. Of course, 'O'Reilly', 'Kippax', 'Richardson', 'Fingleton', 'Ponsford' and Co created a dressing-room atmosphere that I could relate to. They were Australians and behaving like them. On the other hand 'Jardine' and 'Allen' were not relaxed with 'Larwood', 'Bowes', 'Paynter' and Co and the atmosphere in both hotel bar and dressing-room was strained, uncomfortable and decidedly un-Australian. For this was an English dressing-room in an age firmly enforcing class division between the amateur and the pro.

Now I do not believe this was being done deliberately. It was the product of the sensitivity of professional actors who were becoming fully involved in their parts. It was just happening.

I was now well and truly hooked on the whole business. When schoolboy scenes were required, Kings' schoolboys did it. When cricket extras were required, cricket enthusiasts from friends and family were signed up. Do you remember the umpire who caught the young Bradman so that everyone could get down to the pub before six o'clock closing? That was Graham Reed – an old friend, and, today, a Sheffield Shield umpire.

Unfortunately, I still had a full-time job to do at the Kings School, but in every spare moment I was off to a *Bodyline* location. And there were plenty of these.

First, there were the ship and dock scenes. These were carried out at the old Pyrmont piers and here I got my first view of the innovative professionalism of set and camera crews. I soon learnt that nothing is impossible for these people. Most on-ship scenes were taken during a two-day cruise south to Jervis Bay.

Second, there were the indoor scenes. Most of these were taken in a series of sets constructed in the Kennedy-Miller studios – the old Metro theatre in Kings Cross. 'Bradman's house' was a semipermanent indoor structure there: several 'cricket dressing-rooms' stood nearby; and upstairs were the restaurants, bars and offices that appeared throughout the film.

Third, there were the cricket-crowd scenes. All of these were taken over several days at the Sydney Cricket Ground – later they became Adelaide Oval, Melbourne, Sydney and Brisbane. Four or five hundred extras arrived around 6 am, dressing in their nondescript Depression attire, ate their breakfasts and lunches on-site, did their clapping, cheering and booing, managed to retain the anonymity that is preferable for professional extras, then, at sunset, went on their way.

Lastly, there was Rawson Park in Mosman. By chance this was a ground I had played on a great deal as a youngster and it was chosen as the location for *Bodyline* because it was quietly situated away from rail or car traffic noise. Noise interferes with filmmaking, so isolation is an advantage. At Rawson, only the occasional naval helicopter en route to Balmoral was likely to halt the camera's action.

Eventually, the state of wickets, the presence of gum leaves and a few other incongruities caused by the character of Rawson Park led to later criticism of sections in *Bodyline*. But there are always likely to be time and money constraints in any film and to shoot entirely on one of Australia's first-class venues was simply not possible. It would be churlish to emphasise this shortcoming when the management had taken so much time and trouble in every other area.

A day of shooting began around sunrise at Rawson. A few hours' work before a hearty breakfast produced by the catering crew was followed by a long day's work till sunset. The only scheduled interruption to this was the buffet lunch, which usually proved to be innovative and tasty. Everything was done with flair by Kennedy-Miller.

The work could often be exciting, amusing and very interesting. But inevitably, with constant repetition, minute attention to detail, unforeseen hold-ups for such a variety of reasons, time could drag. I am assured that this is the norm in any filmmaking.

Every on-field cricket action shot in *Bodyline* was filmed at Rawson Park. Every catch, every shot, every wicket that fell, every ball bowled, the setting of *Bodyline* fields, the joy, the dramatic 'sconing' of Bert Oldfield (so well played by Les Dayman) – it was all created here. Behind the efforts of talented enthusiastic actors were intelligent, empathetic directors, confident, highly skilled camera staff, and a multitude of additional staff who carry out that unseen mass of behind-the-scene activities involved in every film. The teamwork required of a film crew in action is greater than that of any sporting team. A major problem in the early stages was the leather cricket ball. Valuable camera equipment and protective cameramen did not appreciate the fast-moving 5-ounce missiles. Nor do actors enjoy taking full-blooded smacks in the ribs from a cricket ball when there are likely to be five retakes.

The first answer was foam rubber balls. They were certainly safer for cameras and crew, but as they floated around in the constant breezes of Middle Head, were blown away before contact by the swish of the bat and flopped all over the field, few could suppress laughter. And the cameramen, reluctantly, bowed to the inevitable.

The final compromise was a good one. A leather cricket ball was opened up, the centre removed, and the ball restitched. Now the disemboweled ball retained realistic trajectory, came off the bat, created a healthy crack as it struck the body, hurt a little, but not so much as to disable actors, and was reasonably acceptable to still-dubious cameramen.

Every bouncer that screeched past a reeling batsman, or struck some batsman a sickening blow, was such an empty ball thrown with an underarm flick from a range of about 8 yards. For every one shown on screen, another 50 or more were thrown in rehearsal or retake. Most of these were thrown by me, or by Doug Middleton, an 'old' cricketing/school friend, who was playing Wally Hammond. It was hard-going for an old dilapidated throwing arm – and I don't mean Doug's!

A day of shooting, particularly out in the sun on a hot summer day, is a hard day's work, but the aftermath was seldom questioned. Wherever the action was, the cast and crew would flock back to the studios in Kings Cross to view 'the rushes'.

Mostly still in costume, the whole team, often around 100, would gather on the staircase with cold drinks at hand and see the filmed product of the day. Often these days were 12 hours and often the actual shooting was more than half of that, but seldom did the completed film for the day exceed 10 minutes. Filmmaking is long, drawn out and highly skilled work involving large numbers of people, which begins to explain why it's so expensive.

I loved those months of *Bodyline*. I worked hard, learnt a great deal, met many people and made wonderful new acquaintances and friends. Happily, many actors gained a new interest. Many took up playing cricket, and continue to play. John Sherrin even joined my social team on a tour of England in 1984.

A Spinner's Yarn, Peter Philpott (ABC Books, Sydney, 1990)

'YOU'LL FIND OUT WHO YOUR FOOKING FRIENDS ARE NOW, JENNER . . .'

Terry Jenner is not only one of just over 400 to play Test cricket for Australia. He was the first to go to jail, a gambling addiction the centre of his freefall.

It was one of those nights that you didn't want to go to sleep. I didn't want to wake up and say goodbye. I cuddled up to little Trudianne not knowing if Jacky was ever going to let me see her again.

As much as I tried to ignore what was going to happen in the next 24 hours, I couldn't. In my own mind, I'd already been sentenced. I was on death row, thinking when I awoke, I'd die.

Twenty-second September, 1988 was my day of reckoning. I sat in court while Michael David QC pleaded for me. He was outstanding. As a batsman in Adelaide club cricket he'd been cautious, slow, laborious and hard-to-dismiss, prompting me in one of our games to cheekily call out to our team that if Michael stayed in, we'd win. Nobody on our side was allowed to get him out! It was just a heat-of-the-battle thing and nothing personal. But I reminded Michael before

A Young TJ: Terry Jenner in South Australian colours in the early '70s.

he started his plea that today wouldn't be a good day in which to get even!

Others spoke on my behalf. Then it was Judge Greaves's turn. He said some terrible things, calling me a parasite and a pathological gambler who had offended again and again. A Good Samaritan had come to my door, generously given me a job and I'd let even him down. He was right there.

Including the suspended sentence from 1986, he sentenced me to a total of six-and-a-half years, with three years' nonparole and no restitution. He added, in my case, he could see only a small hope of rehabilitation.

Before being led away, I looked around, saw Jacky and she couldn't look at me.

My mind was racing. What am I going to do? How am I going to survive this? What's on the other side of the door? They hadn't even let me say goodbye to her.

I was put in a small holding cell before being taken downstairs where they took my belt off me and detailed my possessions. Having had five days on remand in the Adelaide jail previously, at least I knew a little bit of the routine. I knew to make sure I had at least some money. I had $20 in my wallet. I was fingerprinted and handcuffed.

A prison officer, a former cricketer I'd played against, offered to arrange some protection if I wanted it. I thanked him and said, 'No, I'll be right.' It was the right answer, even if I didn't know it at the time. Later, I found out if you go into protective custody it gives the connotation that you could be a child sex offender. They are the lowest of lows in the prison system.

I was steered into a paddy wagon and one of the prison officers started to send me up. 'Gee, look what we've got here. Twenty bucks.' I was so low it didn't matter what they said, but I took it all in. I thought to myself when it was all over and I was out, they'd still be living that life. It was a short drive from the holding cell to the Adelaide Remand Centre. One of the blokes I was with was on charges of smuggling explosives into the Centre to blow it up and escape. He was to get nine years, with seven nonparole. He looked mean.

By now it was almost lunchtime. I went in and stood on a line in front of the counter until told to step forward. I was given a cheese-and-pickle and a cheese-and-tomato sandwich and a Granny Smith apple. They then took some details and gave me some prison clothes to get changed into. Blue everything; plus singlets, underpants, toothbrush and other incidentals. I was asked if I smoked and before I could answer, a packet of 20 Viscount cigarettes had been thrust my way.

The prison officers watched while I was getting changed. I was to get used to impersonal things like that. I handed in what I'd been wearing and as I was being led away to the cells, a big prison officer with an English accent, 'Yorky' Smith said, 'You'll find out who your fooking friends are now, Jenner.' I'd never felt lower.

TJ Over The Top, Terry Jenner (Information Australia, Melbourne, 1999)
Jenner was to be released within 18 months and became a cricket commentator and acclaimed coach, particularly known for his mentoring of Shane Warne.

REVERSE-CHARGE CALL FOR YOU, MR PACKER . . .

Kepler Wessels never took a backward step in his life, even when Australia's richest man was bellowing at him down a phone line across several continents.

The switchboard operator at the Clarendon Hotel in Bognor Regis, Sussex, was having to deal with an unusual request. She had been all set for tea on a quiet Wednesday afternoon when the gentleman in room eight asked to make a collect call to Sydney, Australia and she wasn't sure of the code. She searched, found it and spoke the numbers aloud as she dialled. Soon, it was ringing.

'Hello, hello. This is Bognor. Is that Australia?' she asked.

'Yes . . . this is Australia,' a voice yawned. 'Do you know what time it is, lady? It's nearly three in the morning.'

'Oh, I am sorry. I have a Mr Wessels on the line wanting to speak to a Mr Packer. Will you accept the charges?'

'Err . . . yes, all right . . .'

'Thank you. You may talk now.' With that, she replaced the receiver and settled back with her tea and shortbread.

There followed a shouting match across the oceans. At one end, paying for the call which had roused him, was Kerry Packer, one of the richest men in Australia; at the other end was Kepler Wessels, a professional cricketer not completely aware of the time difference between Bognor and Sydney.

The issue was simple. After the disbandment of World Series Cricket, Wessels had been told by the WSC office that he was a free agent, at liberty to play for whichever state he wanted in official domestic cricket. He dispatched letters to Rod Marsh in Western Australia, Ian Chappell in South Australia and to Greg Chappell in Queensland. When the replies came in, Queensland seemed the most keen. A contract was drawn up and Wessels' signature crawled along the dotted line. He was delighted to join Greg Chappell.

As a matter of courtesy, Wessels informed the WSC office of his decision. Thank you, Kepler. The following day, the storm broke.

Packer executives were suddenly adamant that he should play for New South Wales, warning Wessels that if he refused he would forfeit the balance of his $30,000 contract. The player was not bad at being adamant either. He said he was sorry but he was not going to tear up his agreement with Queensland. The row rumbled back and forth until, one quiet afternoon in Bognor, Wessels grew so exasperated he decided he would speak directly to Packer to explain his situation. Greg Chappell had told him to 'get on the front foot' with the boss. So he did, there and then; and he reckoned Packer could afford the call, as well.

'Wessels, you better understand that I own you and you will play for New South Wales. Have you got that?'

'No, you don't own me and no, I will not play for New South Wales. I just want you to see it from ... hello ... hello?'

Packer, angered by such impertinence, had hung up. Wessels, sitting with his wife in room eight, wondered if he'd gone too far but he was determined to play for Queensland. Firstly, he was attracted by Chappell; secondly, he was told it would be harder to get into the New South Wales side. Sally gamely accepted Brisbane would benefit his cricket, even if her own friends and family lived in Sydney. Fifteen minutes later, the telephone in room eight was ringing again.

'Hello,' Wessels answered.

'Hello Kepler, it's Tony Greig speaking. You've really upset Kerry now. What's the matter with you?'

Once again the intercontinental telephone lines turned blue as the conversation deteriorated from explanation to abuse, but Greig was no more successful than Packer had been. The more anyone threatened Wessels, the more resolved he became. That was it. He would play for Queensland. That evening the Wessels family counted the cost of their decision. The agreement had been that WSC would pay contracted players the difference between what they earned from their state side during the 1979–80 season and the $30,000 that would have been paid for another WSC season.

In Wessels' case, Queensland had offered him $25,000 for the season. His resistance had cost $5000. It was worth it. He would not be bullied. His sense of honour was notably laudable because it was likely that the repercussions would extend far beyond a mere financial loss. To upset Kerry Packer on a reverse-charge call was not the finest career move an Australian cricketer could make in the late '70s. Even after the disbanding of his series, Packer remained a highly influential figure within Australian cricket and an unforgiving adversary.

Kepler: The Biography, Edward Griffiths (Pelham Books, London, 1994)
Wessels was to represent Queensland in 62 Sheffield Shield matches from 1979–80 to 1985–86, scoring more than 5000 runs at an average of 52. The highest of his 18 centuries was 249.

SCOOP OF THE CENTURY

Colleagues Peter McFarline and Alan Shiell shared the 'exclusive' of their lives in 1977 when they announced World Series Cricket.

The planning of the Packer troupe and the series of so-called 'Supertests' in Australia during the summer of 1977–78 was undoubtedly the best-kept secret in sporting history. From the time of its birth, in mid-1976, until May 1977 the general public, and indeed those not involved, including players and administrators, suspected nothing.

I first learnt about it, in general terms, in September 1976 and on 2 October, wrote an article in the *Age* outlining Channel Nine's attempt to run a series of televised games, involving some of the world's best players. The story was quickly, and effectively, denied by Channel Nine's Melbourne office. Attempts to learn more about the operation met a wall of silence for some months afterwards. Another Australian cricket writer, Alan Shiell, was also aware of the plan, but neither of us quite realised its extent, even by the time we came to break the story from Hove on 7 May 1977, in time for the morning papers in Australia on 9 May. Shiell, a former South Australian Sheffield Shield batsman, who scored an unbeaten double-century against the MCC tourists of 1965–66 and who has many close friends among the players, covered the England tour for the Rupert Murdoch group of newspapers, including the *Adelaide News,* [the] Sydney *Daily Telegraph* and the *Australian*. We talked about the Packer plan many times during the summer and the early part of the England tour. We agreed to pool our resources and by 7 May had pieced together the broad outline. We also knew that two London papers, the *Daily Mail* and the *Sun,* were close to printing the story.

With play washed out after only an hour and 23 minutes on Saturday at Hove, Shiell and I decided to approach [Australia's captain] Greg Chappell for a comment about the Supertests. In a corridor outside the Australian dressing-room, while the rest of the team watched the Rugby League Cup final on television, Chappell listened politely while we told him what we knew. Then, 'You can say this: "It sounds an interesting proposition – I'd like to know more about it."' And there was only a hint of a smile on his face. Chappell, had, in fact, signed his Packer contract two months earlier.

The stories, for the *Age* and the *Australian,* were filed that night from Hove in secret. Later, I returned to the home of former England fast bowler and Packer-signatory John Snow and told him what I had written. With my permission, he then telephoned his friend and England captain Tony Greig to tell him the secret was out. Greig that night hosted a party at his magnificent home in Hove for both the Australian and English cricketers, and there was obviously more on his mind than partying. Early on the Sunday, the South African–born England captain took the extraordinary step of issuing a four-line statement through his agent, Reg Hayter, admitting that he had signed with Mr Packer. This had the effect of alerting every English newspaper to the story, which caused great chagrin to the *Daily Mail's* outstanding sports columnist Ian Wooldridge. Late the previous week, Wooldridge had obtained more detail on the Packer plan than any other journalist. He had taken his information to his great friend, former Australian captain and well-known commentator and journalist Richie Benaud and had it denied. But Wooldridge remained confident that he had a world exclusive, until the Greig statement and the feedback from the Australian morning papers. Nevertheless, when the Fleet Street editions hit the pavements, it was the *Daily Mail* who had more detail than anyone else.

Benaud, who was to act as tour principal during the Supertest series, had repeatedly denied any knowledge of the Packer deal prior to 5 April. It was then, he claims, that Packer approached his company, DE Benaud and Associates, to become consultants to the program.

The sum total of the stories was that 35 of the world's top cricketers had been contracted to Mr Packer to play a series of six Supertests – planned then to be between Australia and the Rest of the World – and a series of one-day matches in Australia in the summer. The matches would be telecast exclusively by the Channel Nine network in Australia, of which Mr Packer is managing director. The players were being paid between $16,500 and $35,000 a year and most had contracts which extended over three summers. The contracts were binding and did not allow the players to play in other games which clashed with Packer fixtures.

The 35 players who had signed included 18 Australians, 13 of whom were touring England. The others were captain Ian Chappell, batsmen Ian Redpath and Ross Edwards, all of whom had retired from representative cricket; Dennis Lillee, who had been unavailable for the tour because of medical and family reasons; and all-rounder Gary Gilmour, a surprise omission from the original touring party. The 17 players who would make up the Rest of the World sides came from England (4), South Africa (5), Pakistan (4) and the West Indies (4).

The full-list was: AUSTRALIA: Ian Chappell, Greg Chappell, Rod Marsh, Doug Walters, Ray Bright, Ian Davis, David Hookes, Rick McCosker, Jeff Thomson, Len Pascoe, Kerry O'Keeffe, Richie Robinson, Max Walker, Mick Malone, Ian Redpath, Dennis Lillee, Ross Edwards, Gary Gilmour. ENGLAND: Tony Greig, Derek Underwood, Alan Knott, John Snow. SOUTH AFRICA: Barry Richards, Mike Procter, Graeme Pollock, Eddie Barlow, Denys Hobson. PAKISTAN: Mushtaq Mohammad, Asif Iqbal, Majid Khan, Imran Khan. WEST INDIES: Andy Roberts, Clive Lloyd, Vivian Richards, Michael Holding.

The only player at that time sought by Mr Packer who had not signed was the controversial Yorkshireman Geoff Boycott (and that's another story) . . .

A Game Divided, Peter McFarline (Hutchinson of Australia, Melbourne, 1977)
Peter McFarline could be gruff, especially to the cadets experiencing the Age *sports desk for the first time. But he was also a teacher, a mentor, a mate and a very fine writer whose early death touched us all.*

TOO MANY PARTIES, TOO MANY SOCIAL DRINKS

Ray Robinson's poignant account of
'Chuck' Fleetwood-Smith's battles late in life.

A former Test bowler, close to death in hospital last year [1970], is back on his feet after one of the most extraordinary recoveries in Australian medical history, coupled with an inspiring comeback from the precincts of Skid Row.

Doctors at St Vincent's Hospital, Melbourne, call Leslie O'Brien Fleetwood-Smith the 'miracle man'. The left-hander with a corkscrew wrist that perplexed hundreds of batsmen was in hospital for a prostate operation when Hong Kong flu struck hard, bronchitis, pneumonia and septicemia supervened; more than enough to kill the average man. Five days they packed him in ice, trying to abate a burning temperature. Heart and kidney machines were used to keep

His Own Worst Enemy: 'Chuck' Fleetwood-Smith.

a last spark of life in existence. For a week Fleetwood-Smith was too weak to utter a word. (His plight was worse because of after-effects of malnutrition a year earlier, when, after his second marriage broke up, the cricket world was shocked to read of a court appearance giving the impression that he had become a park-bench no-hoper. On a charge of having insufficient means of support, a $20 good-behaviour bond was granted by a magistrate who could see beyond the shabby surface.)

For 18 days Fleetwood-Smith lay in St Vincent's intensive-care ward. Several times he was not expected to last until next morning. Somehow he pulled through the crisis but his wife, Bea, a former dancer, had to cook special dishes to tempt him to eat. At last he could take a few unsteady steps, seemingly doomed to finish life as an invalid. He frankly acknowledges that the court appearance spurred him to pull himself together and make a fresh start in the late '50s.

After the heady heights of bowling for Australia against England's batting idols, before packed crowds, he had failed to settle to regular employment as a salesman calling on hotelkeepers for orders for cordials. 'Too many friends, too many parties, too many social drinks,' he recalls with a twisted smile.

Everywhere I travelled during the Test tour of Australia this [1970–71 Ashes] season, people anxiously asked how 'Chuck' Fleetwood-Smith was faring. The man who shuffled out of hospital last August after losing 42 lb during his ordeal, had regained eight to 12 stone when I called recently to chat about fun shared touring before the war.

His brown eyes hold their old laughing expression as he recalls our camel race near the pyramids outside Cairo and the time he and I collected the team's autographs in response to a sick Welsh boy's letter and went to find the lad's cottage at Swansea and got soaked by a storm.

The neatly parted black hair that glistened in the sun as he loaded spin on the ball and the moustache that girl fans admired are inevitably streaked with grey.

'Besides the doctors and nurses, friends like Leo O'Brien [Test left-hand batsman] have been very good to me, better than I deserve,' he says gratefully of those who have helped him rehabilitate himself with a near-miracle of willpower to set beside the marvel of his physical recovery.

He has not tasted an alcoholic drink for two years and has put aside cigarettes, but puffs lightly at a pipe.

A husky throat is one of the after-effects of illness still requiring attention but the man nobody expected to be fit to work again has taken a job. To be gardener-caretaker of a block of 12 flats is hardly the summit of an Old Xaverian's ambitions but doctors recommended an outdoor occupation to help clear his bronchial tubes. Reunited, he and his wife live in one of the flats. The hand that cut back batsmen's averages now prunes hydrangeas and shrubs. He handles a garden fork more expertly than he ever did a bat, an implement he never tried to master. His garden is among the best-kept in one of Melbourne's choicest suburbs.

'I'd like to get to the ground more often; they always send us tickets,' he says, 'but most of the cricket I see is on television. [Garry] Sobers fascinates me. Makes me wish I could have a go at him, remembering some luck I had against left-handers who were a problem for our right-handers.

'Changes have occurred in the game, especially in the outlook. Nobody seems willing to buy wickets like I used to. Some say I paid far too much.' (Yet Fleetwood-Smith's 597 wickets in 123 first-class matches cost fewer than 23 runs each, a run less than Richie Benaud's and only half a run more than Clarrie Grimmett's. Chuck's striking rate was exceptionally quick, a wicket for every 41 balls.)

'Batting is different, too,' he muses. 'I don't see anybody batting like "Ponny" [Bill Ponsford] and "Napper" [Stan McCabe] used to. I don't bring Bradman into it, because he was something apart from all others.

'In Britain an English bowler asked me: "How do you bowl to this man?"

'I told him: "Now, what have you got to complain about? You only come up against him every fourth year. We have him all the time, every summer."

'The Englishman said: "Yes, but how do you bowl to him?" Over my shoulder as I walked away I said: "Sorry, old chap, but that's not my worry ... not just now, anyway!"

'I once told Ernie McCormick that unless he got more wickets he wouldn't hold his place in the Test side. It was naughty of me but Ernie bowled so fast in his next Sheffield Shield game in 1936 that Bradman was among those scared and Ernie's place was assured.'

Asking me to remember him to Alan Kippax, he says of the former New South Wales captain: 'In one of my early games against NSW at 23, I bowled "Kip". He passed near the bowler's end to tell me: "Well bowled, son. You'll play for Australia."'

Kippax's prophecy took two years and 36 more games to be fulfilled, because Australia already had a matchwinning pair of spinners, [Bill] O'Reilly and Grimmett. Yet Chuck reached 100 wickets in his first 16 first-class games, only one match more than Grimmett, five fewer than Jack Iverson and four games fewer than paceman Alan 'Froggie' Thomson in his sensational start for Victoria.

Sipping a glass of lemonade, Fleetwood-Smith reflects: 'A batsman

I can never forget was that great Englishman [Walter] Hammond. In a double-century against Victoria in 1932 he blazed 32 off a couple of overs from me. As he intended, that cooked my chance of Test selection then, but I managed to get on the 1934 tour of England with Bill Woodfull [as] skipper.

'I came up against Hammond as third-change bowler at Bristol and got a wrong 'un past to bowl him. As he walked by me, Wally said: "A good one, too early." Next meeting at Folkestone I bowled a succession of top-spinners to Hammond and [Bert] Oldfield stumped him off the last one, which he expected to turn from the off. Wally told me: "I didn't think you'd give me another one." So we finished all square.

'When Oldfield first had to take me, I was the only left-hand googly bowler around. So he took a pair of gloves out into the park. People walking through into the ground didn't suspect that two men in street clothes tossing a ball to and fro were Australia's wicketkeeper and new bowler.'

He hit the stumps of almost one-third of the 42 wickets he captured in 10 Tests.

I told Fleetwood-Smith that in South Africa I had come across a sidelight about an injury to his bowling hand, treated at Bloemfontein Hospital, which later kept him out of three Tests against England in 1936. A young doctor, having his first day on duty at the hospital, said to a nurse, softly; 'Now I'd like you to bandage this hand. I'll just stand by and watch.' But the nurse faltered: 'I'm sorry, doctor, but it's my first day on duty.'

When Fleetwood-Smith did reappear in the Australian XI in 1937, a civic reception followed in his hometown, Stawell, after he clinched the Adelaide Test by taking 10 wickets and kept the series alive for Don Bradman.

He was then 26, a gifted bowler of whistling spinners, who himself often whistled a tune in a tense match and was the only Test bowler I have known to clap a boundary hit off his own bowling.

Turning 60 this March, Fleetwood-Smith is bringing off a comeback which nobody prophesied. But we should have known it was not beyond a man who, in the Oval Test wherein Len Hutton made the Anglo-Australian record of 364, could bowl 87 overs in England's mammoth innings.

Australian Cricket, Ray Robinson (Modern Magazines, Sydney, March 1971)
Fleetwood died in 1971, aged 62.

MIGHTY HITS BY BATSMEN AT THE SCG

Alan Davidson's grandstand 6 at the Sydney Cricket Ground on the eve of the 1954–55 Ashes Tests triggered a raft of reminiscences and memories from readers of the Sydney Morning Herald.

SIR – I was interested to read Tom Goodman's breezy account (*Sydney Morning Herald,* 17 November) of Alan Davidson's big hit onto the roof of the SCG main grandstand in the closing stage of the MCC match against NSW.

This recalls an even bigger hit by a famous left-hander of other days. About 1897, as a schoolboy, I saw Joe Darling, the Australian captain, hit [Tom] Richardson, the famous 'Surrey Express', bowling from the Randwick end, clean out of the ground, over the top of the same stand.

The 1897 hit was a greater achievement as it was made against the fastest bowler of the time, bowling at top speed in the early stages of a Test match. Also the wicket, as in all Tests, was pitched in the dead centre of the ground. I forget who won the match, which matters not, but still remember this innings of Darling's as one of the most delightful I have ever seen, here or abroad. The faster Richardson bowled, the harder Darling drove and pulled him.
– GILBERT NEILL, Neutral Bay (*SMH,* 19 November 1954)

SIR – I enjoyed reading Tom Goodman's account of Alan Davidson's big hit onto the main grandstand in the closing stage of the MCC match against New South Wales.

In my younger days I saw a match at the Sydney Cricket Ground in which the famous wicketkeeper Jackie Blackham, who was batting at the Randwick end of the ground, hit a ball to leg right over the main grandstand into Moore Park. That was before the stand was altered to its existing height.
– WJ STEWART, Merrylands (*SMH,* 22 November 1954)

SIR – In my young days, I saw Bill Howell, a left-hand batsman, hit [Colin] Blythe, a slow left-hand bowler – member of an English team – over the grandstand and somewhere out onto the tramline. Howell was a mighty hitter.
– PL VEECH, Randwick (*SMH,* 24 November 1954)

SIR – I, too, am interested in mighty hits by cricketers. I remember well a game, New South Wales v England on the Sydney Cricket Ground in 1897–98. Bill Howell was playing for NSW. I was new to Sydney but had the good fortune to meet four or five old pals from the coast down Broughton Creek way. We were nicely settled on the Hill when 'Old Bill' came in at the Paddington end, took block and the first ball he 'tapped' to square leg. A great roar came from the crowd as the umpire signalled a 6er.

Huge Hitter: Bill Howell made 93 in an hour one day at the SCG.

Bill gave a splendid display in his score of 95 (in an hour with four 5s and fourteen 4s). We could not see where one 6er he hit landed, but suddenly there was a bloodcurdling roar and one of our group remarked: 'By cripes, Old Bill has hit a lion in the zoo.' [The zoo was then at Moore Park.]
– ANOTHER 'OLD BILL', Ashfield (*SMH*, 27 November 1954)

SIR – I think the mightiest hit ever made at the Sydney Cricket Ground was one I witnessed as a boy sometime in the '90s in the Sheffield Shield match between NSW and Victoria on 26 January. Warwick Armstrong, standing at the Randwick end, skied a ball bowled by MA Noble sheer over the clocktower of the members' stand.
– RH CLARKE, Willoughby (*SMH*, 27 November 1954)

SIR – I have read with great interest the recalling of mighty hits on the Sydney Cricket Ground. I would like to tell of the mightiest of all hitters. Back in the '20s, I was one of a capacity crowd on the Hill at the Sydney Cricket Ground, enjoying a hurricane innings by Jack Gregory. If I remember rightly, Frank Woolley had just relieved 'Johnny Won't Hit Today' Douglas at the bowling crease and I had called to Gregory: 'Lift him out of the ground, Jack!' It then happened. It landed on the point of my chin, exactly where I was scoring. It was quite dark at the time. The hit must have been very much higher than the clock in the grandstand. It was a big one all right.
– EB BALMAIN (*SMH*, 1 December 1954)

'ACKA . . . LET ME EXPLAIN MY ACTIONS'

Softly spoken champion-in-the-making Archie Jackson was a hero
for thousands, including his old teammates, says Neil Marks.

In the late 1920s, the press and public were clamouring for a policy of youth in the selection of the New South Wales cricket team. The 'Blues' had won the Sheffield Shield only once in five years. This was just not good enough for the cricket fans of the Waratah state, who were conditioned to winning. The great era, which had begun in the postwar years, was drawing to a close and legends such as [Arthur] Mailey, [Jack] Gregory and [Tommy] Andrews were no longer the dominant force they'd once been. So onto the greensward of the Sydney Cricket Ground, determined to make it their own, strode players like Archie Jackson, Don Bradman and my father Alec 'Acka' Marks – mere teenagers who had barely begun to shave.

The attitude taken towards these kids by the older players, now in the death throes of their careers, was polite but curt. For old bulls resent young bulls moving onto their turf, as they themselves were once resented. So the young players stuck together and became mates.

The New South Wales Cricket Association has never been renowned for its bountiful generosity. However, compared with those at the helm of cricket in 1928, the present-day hierarchy is positively philanthropic. In the old days players were even required to bring their own towels to all Shield games at the SCG.

One particular day, in his rush to get to the ground, my father grabbed the family's best guest towel and threw it into his kit. At the end of a long hot day Dad came in from the field, stripped and headed for the showers. After standing under the healing waters for some minutes, he felt a little refreshed and walked back to his locker to dress. As he did so, he noticed Archie Jackson, rummaging around in his bag. 'It looks as though I've left my towel out of my kit,' said Jackson.

'Here, have mine, if you don't mind it being a bit damp,' said Dad, throwing his friend the used towel. Jackson took the towel and Dad forgot all about it until he returned home.

'Alec, did you take my best guest towel to cricket this morning?' asked his mother in a tone which promised trouble.

'Yes I did, Mum.'

'Well don't do it again. It's the only good one we have.' [Like so many people in that era, the Marks family battled to make ends meet.]

'Now give it to me and I'll wash it.'

'Sorry, Mum,' he answered. 'I forgot to bring it home. Archie borrowed it from me after the game.'

The next day, Dad approached Jackson, explained his mother's wrath and asked for the towel. Jackson's face turned red. He walked to his bag and pulled out a towel which, obviously, had been recently purchased, as it was still in its wrapping. Clearly, it was not Ma Marks's best guest towel.

'The other towel has gone,' said Jackson, walking away without any further comment.

When Dad returned home that night he gave the new towel to his mother. She exploded. 'What's this supposed to be? It's cheap and nothing like my best towel. I couldn't give this to visitors. I can't understand Archie's behaviour – he always seemed like such a nice boy.'

Dad shrugged his shoulders and made a mental note that in the morning he would buy his mother a classy towel. This he did, and the incident was soon forgotten.

Archie Jackson became one of the greatest batsmen in the history of cricket. He was a player of grace and beauty, a classicist in the mould of Victor Trumper. In 1930, at 20 years of age, he was chosen in the Australian team to tour England. Life should have stretched before him excitingly, but it didn't. Archie Jackson was stricken with tuberculosis. The leading physicians of the day had advised Jackson not to tour, fearing that six months in the unpredictable climate of the United Kingdom would exacerbate his condition. Jackson ignored the advice of the doctors and toured with Bill Woodfull's great team, which returned home triumphant, with the Ashes regained. Archie Jackson conquered the British bowlers, but he could not overcome the cold damp days he spent on the playing fields of England. His chest became weaker and he was never the same again. Shortly afterwards he died.

Not long before Archie's death, my father visited his friend. They only spoke for a short while, because Archie was pale, drawn and very tired. Just as Dad was about to leave, Archie spoke softly, 'Acka, do you remember the towel you gave me that day at the

Cricket Ground? It was your Mum's best guest towel and I didn't return it.'

'Oh, that's okay, Archie,' said my embarrassed father. 'Well, I'd just like to explain my actions,' said Jackson. 'You see, I'd known for a few years that I had TB, so I made a point of never lending or borrowing any clothing from anyone. But that particular day, when you threw me your towel I dried myself without thinking. I didn't realise what I'd done until I returned home. That's why I bought you a new one. The man behind the counter said it was the best towel in the shop. I hope your Mum liked it.'

My father choked a little. 'Archie, Mum said it was the best towel she ever owned.'

That night, when he came home my father walked to his mother's linen closet and took out the towel Archie had bought. Then he walked into his bedroom, sat down on his bed, put his head into it and cried.

Tales from the Sports Field: The Best of Neil Marks, Neil Marks (ABC Books, Sydney, 2005)

'I FELT LIKE AN UNWANTED CUR'

*Sid Barnes's comeback onto the Test scene was squashed
for reasons other than cricket, says Rick Smith.*

When the selectors [Don] Bradman, [EA 'Chappie'] Dwyer and [Jack] Ryder sat down to choose the team for the third Test against the West Indies [in 1951–52], most thought that Sid [Barnes] would be returned to the side for the Adelaide game. When the list was announced, however, his name was missing. Immediately, there was much consternation and criticism. Australia had been struggling, particularly in the opening position and here was a proven batsman with an impeccable Test match record. Why on earth wasn't he in the team?

In most cases, such a decision would be put down as an aberration on the part of the selectors, something along the lines of leaving out Clarrie Grimmett from the 1938 touring team. These things had happened before and they would happen again. On this occasion, however, things were different. Almost as soon as the team was announced, rumours began to circulate that this was not the side chosen by the selectors. On the day the names of those selected were

Sid Struck: Sid Barnes reels away from the wicket having been struck by English tailender Dick Pollard while fielding close-on on the leg side at Old Trafford during the '48 tour.

released to the press, the [Sydney] *Mirror* reported that the Board had disapproved of one of those selected and sent the team list back for further consideration.

The situation that existed in Australian cricket then – and it still does today – is that each team chosen by the selectors has to be referred to the Board for approval. This is generally something of a rubber-stamp process, almost an act of courtesy, but the Board does have the power to veto a player, and if it does so the selectors have to find someone else. The ruling used was 'for reasons other than cricketing ability'. This option came out of the aftermath of the disastrous 1912 tour of England. A dispute over the appointment of the manager led to six of the country's best players – captain Clem Hill, Victor Trumper, Warwick Armstrong, Vernon Ransford, A 'Tibby' Cotter and Sammy Carter – refusing to tour. The selectors were forced to choose what was very much a second-string team, picking a number of players who, under other circumstances, would never have represented Australia. The ensuing tour was unsuccessful from a playing point of view, which was to be expected with so many top players staying at home, but as a social exercise it was a disaster. Some players behaved so badly that an inquiry at the end of the tour decided that certain individuals would never be selected again. To support this decision, the Board passed a resolution allowing a player's selection to be revoked 'on grounds other than cricketing ability'.

In the nearly 40 years since the resolution had been passed, it was not known on how many occasions, if any, the power of veto had been used. Certainly, it would have been rare. Now, apparently, it was reported to have been used on a player and it seemed that player was Sid Barnes. What was known was that Board chairman Aubrey Oxlade had sent a telephone message saying that the team chosen had been disapproved of by the Board and that the selectors had been asked to reconsider. As Sid was not in the side when it was announced, the inevitable conclusion was that he was the player. He first became alerted to what was happening when he read an article in a Sydney paper discussing the situation. In his autobiography *It's Not Cricket,* Sid wrote that he could accept not being chosen by the selectors, but 'to be tossed aside by the Board was the supreme insult'. He said he felt like an unwanted cur.

As the controversy gathered momentum, Sid was once again given the NSW captaincy for the return match against Queensland in Sydney. This game was played after the Adelaide Test where Australia's batting had been singularly unsuccessful and the team had lost by six wickets. Once again the opening partnership, this time between [Arthur] Morris and Jim Burke, had failed to give the side a decent start. Burke had been replaced for the fourth Test by another New South Welshman, Jack Moroney, and as this game was to be played at the same time as the Shield game, Sid once again inherited the captaincy from Morris.

Under increasing personal strain from the events in Adelaide, Sid won the toss and opened the batting with Burke. What followed put even greater pressure on the Board's decision. The two batsmen were in immediate control, Sid taking on the role of aggressor while his partner anchored the innings. In 190 minutes, they scored 213 for the first wicket with Sid being the first dismissed, for 128. The *Sunday Herald* called it 'a dazzling exhibition of stroke play'. To many, it recalled Sid's play of the prewar years when he concentrated on attack rather than defence. It would be difficult to contemplate a better reply to the Board than this one. Let them consider now whether he should be in the team or not. He hit thirteen 4s and his only chance came just three runs before he was dismissed. Taking into account the circumstances, this might be the finest innings he ever played. When asked the question, Sid would always nominate his Test century at Lord's, but for sheer performance under pressure this was an extraordinary innings.

The partnership with Burke helped set up the final total of 477, more than enough for Queensland, who were dismissed for 102 and 176. Playing concurrently, the Australians struggled to a one-wicket victory in the fourth Test with Moroney (26 and 5) and Morris (6 and 12) failing at the top of the order. Captaining the state side to a huge victory and top scoring in the match provided some satisfaction for Sid as he faced the media storm over his non-selection for the third Test.

Immediately the papers were on the side of the player. The *Mirror* pointed out that apart from Sir Donald Bradman, the Board members had little cricket ability and that they had usurped the role of the selectors whom they had appointed. The Board's action was an insult to its own selectors and also to the NSW Cricket Association which had enough faith in Sid to allow him to captain the state. When questioned, Sid for once said little, apart from stressing that he knew of nothing in his cricket career that could be used against him. His friend and former teammate Stan McCabe was more forthright, calling the situation 'scandalous'. Another old teammate Bill O'Reilly waded into the debate, deploring the actions of the Board in overriding the wishes of its own selectors. Arthur Mailey said the selectors should resign because the Board refused to accept their judgment.

Strangely enough, the Board's behaviour did not come as a surprise to everyone. Hec de Lacy, writing in the *Sporting Globe,* said after Sid's century in Melbourne:

> If Barnes doesn't make the third or fourth Test teams, don't blame lack of ability or the selectors. If the selectors were unanimous in wanting Barnes I doubt whether their wishes would be granted. When the selectors choose the side they must send it to the Board. That might be Barnes' biggest hurdle. Usually, approval is automatic. But I know for certain that if Barnes were named by the selectors, opposition by Board members would be strong enough to keep him out … They [the Board] feel that Barnes should be disciplined and intend to make every effort to keep him on the outer.

George Thatcher wrote a long article in the *Daily Telegraph* listing instances where players had clashed with the Board. He also mentioned Sid's misdemeanors, such as jumping the turnstile and parking in the

This Test Series COULD KILL Cricket

The deadly effect of slow scoring and time wasting fast bowling could well sound the death knell of cricket.

By SID BARNES

Always Provocative: Sid Barnes's writings were invariably straight to the point and regularly caused angst amongst administrators.

wrong car park at the Sydney Cricket Ground, countering them by describing his conduct on the 1948 tour as 'exemplary'.

Support came from all sources. Gordon's secretary Paul Harrison called the Board's action 'petty' and wanted them to name the player excluded. The Churches Cricket Union, where Sid had started his serious cricket with St Augustine's, also offered their support, citing a denial of natural justice in the Board's refusal to give reasons for their actions ... Even politicians became involved. Leader of the Federal Opposition, cricket lover and a member of the NSW Cricket Association, HV 'Doc' Evatt also came out publicly on the side of the player ... The *Sydney Morning Herald* thought the Board should have the courage to name the player and show reason rather than let rumour take over. The NSW Cricket Association had given Sid the captaincy, so their next meeting was expected to raise the issue. Although some discussion must have taken place, no public comment was made. In all the words written about the situation at this time, and there were plenty, perhaps the most perceptive came from Tom Goodman in the *Sunday Herald:*

> A vital difference was that Bradman held his tongue, Barnes didn't. Bradman went about his quest for fame and fortune systematically and kept his counsel (at the same time he helped Australia win Test matches). But Sid Barnes became ostentatious about his own gains. He was wont to declare his contempt for men who were content to 'play cricket for peanuts'. His criticism extended to officialdom. Some of his remarks about cricket officials made at film nights after the 1948 tour of England were sarcastic and indiscreet. And they were heard by some leading administrators who were shocked and hurt. This, as

far as I can see, is his 'crime' … that in the past he has thumbed his nose at cricket leaders and held them up to contempt. For this, some of the indignant 'old boys' have banded together and tossed him out of Test cricket.

Cricket's Enigma: The Sid Barnes Story, Rick Smith (ABC Books, Sydney, 1999)
Having stood out of cricket for three years, Sid Barnes launched a comeback for the start of the 1951–52 season and was recalled to the Test team only for his selection to be vetoed by the austere Board of Control, unhappy at Barnes's maverick behavior and controversial writings. He played his last big match in January 1953, for New South Wales against the visiting South Africans. He was the first of Don Bradman's 1948 tourists, The Invincibles, to die, in 1973, aged 57.

JOE DARLING ON 6-HITTING

One of Australia's foremost golden-age champions Joe Darling was notable for his 6-hitting, anywhere but in England.

I can remember when it was next to impossible to score a 6 on many of the grounds in England.

All a batsman in my time got for over the fence was 4, the same as if it went only to the boundary. I was really responsible for the authorities in England and Australia giving 6 for 'over the fence'. It used to be only 5 over the fence in Australia and to get 6 in England and Australia the ball had to be hit right out of the ground and on many grounds this was absolutely impossible.

I can well recall the first ball that I ever received from WG Grace. I hit it right over the fence, and got only 4. Again, I remember hitting a ball from [Charles] Townsend right over the pavilion at Crystal Palace and the umpire turned to Grace and said, 'Well, doctor, I suppose that's 6.'

The old man replied, 'No, only 4. The ball has to go right out of the ground for 6.'

I asked Grace how much further I had to hit the ball for 6 and he said: 'About a quarter of a mile.' These two hits would have gone right out of the Melbourne Cricket Ground and I got only 4 for each of them.

The Weekly Courier, Joe Darling (Launceston, 3 June 1926); reproduced in *Test Match Sixes,* Ross Smith (self-published, Invermay, Tasmania, 1998)

BONNOR'S THROW
A letter to WG Grace.

'I thought you might be glad to hear of an incident that happened at Plymouth on Wednesday, 3 May 1882, when a team of Australians landed here.

'They drove up to my business house and explained that a bet had been made on board the vessel that Mr GJ Bonnor, who was one of the team, would not throw a cricket ball 110 yards. The conditions were to be, first throw on landing and no other attempt to be made previous. I took them to our cricket ground, as both parties concerned asked me to act as judge.

'On arriving at the cricket ground, Mr Bonnor objected to the grass and said he would prefer a hard road or parade ground. We then drove to the Raglan Barracks, where there is plenty of space. And he said that would suit very well. The distance was marked off by newspapers and he took his stand, toeing a line. The ball, which he had previously purchased from me, was an ordinary match ball. This I handed to him and I had placed in my hand the two cheques for 100 pounds apiece.

'He threw the ball from where he stood to the line and did not run. It was a grand throw; it seemed as if the ball would never stop rising; and it pitched on a spot which was measured after to be 119 yards 5 inches from where he stood. As there was no objection made, I handed over the two cheques to Mr Bonnor, who then said, "I will back myself for 200 pounds to throw the ball 125 yards the next throw."' – William Hearder

The Cricketer's Weekend Book, Eric Parker (T & A Constable Limited, Edinburgh, 1952)

THE MAN WHO MADE
THE SHEFFIELD SHIELD
Melbourne jeweller Phillip Blashki designed the Sheffield Shield.

In 1894, Phillip [Blashki] won the tender to design and manufacture a shield to be donated by Lord Sheffield as a perpetual trophy for an annual interstate cricket competition. [His son] Aaron noted: 'Lord Sheffield limited the cost of the shield to 150 pounds, but my father was determined that the shield should be a very handsome trophy, which has generally been recognised to be the case. There was little or no direct profit from the transaction, but the name of Blashki is stamped on the shield and that's something.'

The minutes of the Australasian Cricket Council show that Lord Sheffield gave the money as a 'thank you' for the good time that was given to the WG Grace team when they visited Australia in the summer of 1892–93 and that the Council elected to have a shield made for competitions.

Originally Phillip Blashki showed a 'model' which had a facsimile portrait of Lord Sheffield at the top. But as he was a rather portly gentleman whose face was not his most memorable attribute, or perhaps because of his personal modesty, it was decided to substitute a woman's figure to represent Victory. So, fanciful Victorian symbolism won the day over the interesting, if plain face of a very generous and personable donor.

This was not the first shield made by Blashki. In 1893, the Hordern Shield was donated by Samuel Hordern Esq for intersuburban cricket in Sydney. This large and handsome trophy now hangs in the lounge of the NSW Cricketers Association. It is inscribed 'Manufactured by P Blashki & Sons, Melbourne and Sydney'. As P Blashki and Sons did not operate in Sydney till they acquired the regalia firm of Harvey C Smith Pty Limited in 1978, it can be fairly assumed that it was Aaron, living in Sydney and with his abiding interest in cricket, who arranged the project.

In 1893, the economic depression hit Phillip very hard. The banks and building societies in which he had carefully invested his savings all collapsed. As well as his business, his health was affected. [Sons] Aaron, Henry and Lou decided that it was time for Phillip to retire and Henry took over the firm of P Blashki & Sons. Then Phillip had time for all the voluntary charitable activities which had already begun to occupy him and were to absorb him for the rest of his life ...

Phillip Blashki, a Victorian Patriarch, Gael R Hammer (Blashki & Sons, Melbourne, 1986)

Skull: Kerry O'Keeffe bowled darting top-spinners which occasionally turned. He also was a keen and above-average batsman who once opened for Australia.

11
WHAT HAPPENS
ON TOUR . . .

'Ardent women wanted us to write risqué rhymes in their autograph books. They reminded me of bees around honey: no time nor inclination for philandering here ...'

'HAVING ONE WITH US TONIGHT, SKULL?'
1970s Australian leg spinner Kerry 'Skull' O'Keeffe
on the perils of abstinence.

We had arrived in Christchurch for the first of two Tests against New Zealand in February and March 1977. I was rooming with Doug Walters and quite enjoying the experience. As luck would have it, Kiwis are notoriously poor players of wrist spin and going into that initial Test, I was the leading wicket-taker on tour and still having time to share numerous brews with my roommate. Still, Tests are about discipline and focus and I'm not about to compromise my performance by over-imbibing of an evening. Nonetheless, I concur with the team ethos that a man is not a camel and that there would be a time and place for plenty of elbow-bending before the series was out. But not at Test time for this little brown duck!

Lancaster Park has a history of favouring the pace bowlers, so the selectors leave out Ray Bright and I am chosen as the spin backup to Dennis Lillee, Max Walker and Gary Gilmour. New Zealand looks reasonably strong on paper, with Glenn Turner heading the batting and Richard Hadlee to take the new ball. Turner wins the toss and sends us into bat. There is a little sideways movement for the quicker bowlers and, though a number of our early order get starts, nobody manages a half-century until my roommate Doug enters the fray at No. 6. Rod Marsh falls cheaply at 7 and with the scoreline reading 6-208 it could well be the Kiwis' day. At No. 8 is the burly left-hander Gary Gilmour from Newcastle. Now 'Gus' is an amiable fellow with a casual attitude to his cricket and the potential to be the next Alan Davidson – this may be an opportunity for him to really nail down the all-rounder's spot in the Test team. As next man in, I put the pads on and sit in the players' area hoping that these two can see out the first day. They do more than that – the pair launch a blistering counterattack. Dealing primarily in boundaries, Doug and Gus assault the Kiwis with a succession of drives and heaves. At stumps, we are 6-345 with Walters unbeaten on 129 and Gilmour 65.

What a great opening day for us, I reflect as I quickly unpad and head for the showers. As I dress and head for a taxi I notice that the not out batsmen are still in shirts and jock straps and seem to be settling in for a few more beers – and was that a scotch bottle I saw next to Gus? Good heavens! Will the day of full professionalism ever arrive? I'm back at the Avon Motor Lodge where I eat alone – a pasta main course, cheese and biscuits, a nice cup of coffee. Civil and responsible. It's 9.30 pm and I decide not to join what I can hear are familiar voices drifting loudly out of the bar area. After all, I'm next man in and there will be a new ball available to the New Zealanders early on the second morning.

I'm in bed and feeling good, I lapse into a beneficial sleep. I'm dreaming of a chanceless half-century when suddenly I'm woken by chortling and the sound of a key trying to find its way into a lock. The door opens, two figures appear. It's Walters and Gilmour. And they're both as full as a state school. I glance at the bedside table where the clock shows 12.50 am. Within seconds, lights are flicked on and half a dozen bottles of local beer are

Masterly: Doug Walters… few played as well, yet practised less!

hurried into the room fridge. They're sitting on my bed – and both are up for some fun. 'Skull, we'd like you to have a beer with us,' Doug suggests. 'Yes, come on, Skull, let's have a drink on Dougie's century,' Gus says, prising a top off yet another beverage. I sit up and decline. 'Thank you, but I have a job to do this morning and I intend to give myself every chance of doing it . . . unlike you poor misguided fools!' They're not to be denied and they drink on, all the while asking me to join them in a tipple. I knock back every invitation. 'Oh, don't be like that, Skull, one beer isn't going to hurt,' they chorus. I'm not happy at this stage – it's now 2 am and they're still drinking – and I'm on the front foot. 'This is ridiculous, you two have let yourselves down, you've let your teammates down, your job is only half done, you'll both be out in the first over of the morning and I'll be in there on nought facing Hadlee with a new rock. Thanks a lot, you bludgers!'

I'm at the ground a few hours later; I'm netting strongly and doing a number of stretches. The not out batsmen are in the change rooms, warming up, I guess by smoking cigarettes!

Eventually they're sauntering out to the middle for hostilities to resume. I am fully padded up, I have the gloves and cap on and I'm doing star jumps in anticipation of batting within the opening over.

For the next couple of hours I can barely believe what I'm witnessing. Doug is at his brilliant best; he is carving the new ball to all parts of Lancaster Park. No one is spared, particularly the great Richard Hadlee, who is conceding an average of five or six runs an over. Gus is blasting away at the other end and strikes a memorable 101 with twenty 4s and a 6. That's 86 in boundaries – given his physical condition, running between the wickets would have taken too much effort.

I'm sitting there watching this carnage and I'm thinking that if these two philistines can lacerate the attack when both have blood alcohol levels of about .25 then how many runs am I going to get completely sober? At one point, I'm moved to scream, 'Get out and give me a hit!' Eventually, Gus drags a wide one from Ewen Chatfield onto his stumps and to a rousing ovation makes his way to the pavilion. I give him a congratulatory pat on the back as I pass him but don't get too close because the stench of alcoholic fumes would put me off.

Our total has reached 7-425. This is easy . . . now for me to ice this cake. Doug stays at his end and continually crunches balls to the boundary, on his way to a career-best 250. I'm careful not to make a mistake. Two pissed humans have laid these Kiwis to waste, now for alcohol-free me! Almost at once, it's over. Doug hits one to cover, there's a fumble, he calls me through and I'm run out by 5 yards. Thanks a bloody lot! I'm making my way back to the pavilion and I have to go past Doug at the non-striker's end. He's on his haunches, giggling. I look across at him for an apology, or even some consolation. He looks up at me and says, 'Having one with us tonight, Skull?'

According to Skull: An Entertaining Stroll through the Life of Kerry O'Keeffe, Kerry O'Keeffe (ABC Books, Sydney, 2004)

THROUGH THE CARIBBEAN

*Arthur Morris on the first-ever Australian tour of
the then British West Indies, in 1955.*

This year's West Indies tour brings back many happy memories of our tour of the West Indies in 1955. Looking back, it was the most enjoyable tour I'd had.

It was the first-ever tour by an Australian team of the West Indies or, as it was then, the British West Indies and was so different from the others to England and South Africa, mainly because of our all-white

Caribbean '55: Arthur Morris (sitting, third from the left) farewelled Test cricket in the West Indies, making a century and sharing a stand of 191 with Colin McDonald (back row, extreme right) at Port-of-Spain.

associations in those two countries. This time we were guests in a predominantly coloured environment.

Beforehand there was that tiny thought lurking in our minds that our White Australia policy might cause some resentment, but that was quickly dispelled. The locals welcomed us with open arms and proved to be the most tremendously hospitable hosts one could ever wish to meet. Those islands right out of a travel brochure, Jamaica, Trinidad, Barbados, lived right up to expectation. Steel bands, calypsos, the tropical clear days mostly cooled by the trade winds were all there, plus the added attraction of good cricketers and fanatical cricket fans.

Only a month or so before we landed in Jamaica, we had been badly beaten by the MCC. Frank Tyson and Brian Statham had humbled us and eminent Australian critics had generally written us off; to quote one critic we were 'a bunch of pie eaters'. They were certain we would fail miserably against the strong West Indies. After all they had such players as 'the three W's': Frank Worrell, Everton Weekes and Clyde Walcott, plus Sonny Ramadhin and Alf Valentine on which to build a very solid combination.

The fact that we won 3–1 in this series therefore does seem hard to believe, even to us players. Certainly we were an experienced side with mighty players such as Ray Lindwall and Keith Miller but much credit must go to Ian Johnson who led the team in a very capable manner. He bowled well, the hard West Indian pitches suiting him and under his leadership the team was also extremely popular off the field.

I think our series win was helped somewhat by distances between islands and the resultant lack of communication. This lack of knowledge about players created many problems for their selectors. Add inter-island jealousies and we had something going for us. When [Glen] Gibbs from British Guiana, no relation to the off spinner, dropped me in Kingston, Jamaica, at 38 during the first Test, the crowd reacted with anger and derision. As English pressman Pat Landsberg remarked: 'it [the dropped catch] has put back Federation 10 years!'

Different playing conditions didn't help their inexperienced new boys either. Collie Smith (tragically killed in a car accident some years back) scored a brilliant century against us, in the first Test in Jamaica. He was chosen, naturally, for the second in Trinidad where he copped a pair of ducks. Collie had never seen a ball swing before; they don't in Jamaica, but they bend all over the place in humid Trinidad. Collie had never played outside Jamaica and it was of great interest to us as we saw him at practice before the match, playing down the line and not getting a touch.

The crowds added tremendously to the enjoyment of our cricket. They were usually good humoured and never quiet. They enthused over a well-bowled maiden as much as seeing 4s being hit. The din that greeted the first ball of a Test match was really something. As the opening bowler commenced his run the noise built up to a crescendo as it was delivered. By necessity, a local rule declaring the first ball of the innings a trial ball was in effect. A good one too, because no one could hear a snick or for that matter, an appeal. And I can assure taking strike in all that noise was diverting to say the least. The cries of delight when an overladen tree branch of too many cricket watchers crashed to the ground would hold the game up for several minutes. We never did find out how many spectators were lost in that manner.

Of course, the matches were interesting and full of many splendid moments. Neil Harvey was at his best, Lindwall and Miller as dangerous as ever and the opposition, particularly Worrell, Weekes and Walcott, was never dull. Out of the tour emerged perhaps the greatest all-round cricketer ever in Garfield Sobers. Certainly he is the greatest all-rounder I've ever seen. Garry played in the third, fourth and fifth Tests and although he wasn't an immediate success, his brilliant 64 in the last Test indicated we could expect great things from him in the future.

There were some very fine individual performances such as Richie Benaud's 121 in 96 minutes which included eighteen 4s and two 6s in the fifth Test. And there were Clyde Walcott's two great 100s in each innings also in the fifth Kingston, Jamaica Test.

Clyde's two 100s were superb and well deserved but an incident occurred in the second innings when he was about 60. Lindwall was bowling on this hot, still day on this rock-hard wicket when he decided to shift the one man on the fine leg boundary to the gully position. He was hoping for a mis-hit from a short one when Clyde played one of his powerful back-foot off-drives. Walcott looked down to the now-bare, short, fine leg boundary and after several balls came back on his stumps and turned one down towards the now-unmanned boundary. Unfortunately at the same time his foot slightly tilted back the off stump. The Australians appealed and the umpires, as umpires sometimes do, missed it as they watched the ball race to the boundary. What was a fella to do? Clyde figured there was only one thing to do. He calmly pulled the stump, put on the bail and resumed. Sometimes it's an advantage to be a West Indian. There was no sign of a blush and if there had been no one could have seen it!

I remember well our first island game in Trinidad, the first ball particularly. We won the toss and Les Favell playing the first ball of the match and his first on the tour – he missed the Jamaican games – promptly hit it for 6. Gerry Gomez had opened the bowling and had pitched a typical first ball outside the off stump, gently swinging away one that all respectable opening batsmen, including West Indians, would normally allow to go through to

Sobie: Multi-gifted Garry Sobers would start with the new ball before returning to bowl left-arm chinamen and googlies.

the keeper … a sighter more or less. But not for Les. The ball was struck not only over the square leg fence but out of the ground. Gerry had followed through, head down, hand going up in anticipation for the return from the keeper when he heard the 'thwack'. Even through my laughter I can still see his bewildered expression as he turned to me and said, 'What happened?' It was good to know that, on some occasions, we could surprise our West Indian friends with their own type of cricket.

Calypso Cricket, edited by Alan Davidson, story by Arthur Morris (MGA Publications, Rose Bay, Sydney, 1968)

THE START OF AN INVINCIBLE RUN

Australia's record run of 25 Tests without defeat started in a one-off international, later raised to Test status, against New Zealand in Wellington in 1945–46. The 13-man team included legendary Bill O'Reilly, then 40 and in his last summer.

The hounds of war had been thankfully leashed safely, the captains and the kings had made their legendary departures and the cricket stage was appropriately set for the Australian Board of Control to make their 1946 arrangements for a resumption of international cricket.

Their catchcry for the great occasion might well have been 'On with the Motley' to counter the grim events of a long war which had given no first-class cricket for several years.

The manner in which they organised their official tour of New Zealand, a blitzkrieg invasion that began on 1 March and finished on 2 April, gave the impression that the raising of a shaking belly laugh was their main objective.

The program called for five matches, the final one of which [later] was billed as an official Test match. New Zealand had never before, nor since, for that matter, reached the dizzy eminence of official Test competition with Australia, regardless of the fact that England had been meeting them on occasional equal terms for years past.

Billed, therefore, as an official Australian team chartered with the responsibility of our national cricket reputation in a Test encounter, this 1946 Australian side set out with the green-and-gold blazer which had the golden block letters 'ABC' embossed in the place where the Australian coat of arms on all previous official tours decorated the pockets of the proud possessors. One bright young spectator in Auckland suggested that the letters stood for 'Australia's Best Cricketers'. The team members came up, however, with many suggestions, most of them bawdy, to explain their significance.

As pay, if one might be permitted at this distant date to use such a plebian word in connection with lilywhite amateurs as Australian cricketers were supposed to be then, the Board of Control had magnanimously agreed that each player should receive one pound per day as expenses for the tour. Anything left over, of course, remained the property of the uncommonly frugal performer who could manage it.

Transport then, as now, must have been an embarrassing problem even though Sunderland flying boats were regularly crossing the Tasman on passenger flights. The team's transport was left in the capable hands of the New Zealand Air Force who took us aboard a war-weary Catalina flying boat at Rose Bay one early morn and landed us 10 hours later at Auckland.

The pioneering significance of this trip was developed importantly by the questionably enticing barbecues the team turned out from the galley aboard. But more than just a few of the senior members revealed their delight when a bottle of Bundaberg rum smuggled aboard by the vice-captain, appropriately enough, worked wonders in dispelling the cold encountered during a rostered spell in the aircraft's blisters.

Don Bradman was unable to make the tour. The great Australian batsman, to New Zealand's great sorrow, never once laid a cricket boot on the Shaky Isles. At that time it was quite uncertain that he would ever play international cricket again, although he had made an appearance against the returning Australian Services team.

The captaincy of this touring team therefore was more or less a pointer towards the immediate captaincy problems confronting this country in international cricket generally.

There were three contenders: Bill Brown, who had been skippering Queensland for several seasons; myself, who had been leading NSW; and Lindsay Hassett, who had performed with distinction in England and India in charge of the Services team.

When Brown was named captain and O'Reilly vice-captain I, for one, took it for granted that Bradman was intending to make his comeback when England toured Australia later in 1946. Had that not been his intention, I feel sure that Hassett would have been appointed to the job.

With all these side-slapping, mirth-making arrangements, the 13 players, Brown, O'Reilly, Hassett, [Sid] Barnes, [Bruce] Dooland, [Ron] Hamence, [Ian] Johnson, [Ray] Lindwall, [Keith] Miller, [Col] McCool, [Don] Tallon, [Ern] Toshack and [Ken] Meuleman, set forth. Some of the members had not yet been demobilised. Miller, I remember, wore Air Force drabs throughout. There were so many pilots amongst us that when NZ Prime Minister Peter Fraser entertained us at Wellington he was overwhelmed by the posse who demanded that we should not return by the Catalina. They were hoping, I am sure, that a Sunderland would be requisitioned when the PM said he would attend to their request. We returned on an old Dakota which took 10-and-a-half hours, too!

But to the cricket . . .

In the first match, Barnes, Miller and Hassett each got hundreds and Toshack collected seven wickets. At Canterbury it was Brown's turn for a hundred, a performance he repeated at Dunedin where two spinners, Dooland and Johnson, showed splendid form.

And by the time the Wellington Test arrived the team had moulded into such a powerful combination that a blind man could have seen it was well and truly geared to make fairly short work of anything that sparred up to it.

Lindwall went from strength to strength. His run-up grooved in, and his general bowling tactics began to crystallise. Strangely enough, the Lindwall–Miller combination did not develop fully on tour. That happened later in the year, when Hammond's Englishmen bore the full brunt of their enthusiastic ability. [Ernie] Toshack was used as Lindwall's new-ball partner. That fact is worth noting now because it was the last time that an Australian slow-medium-paced bowler was entrusted with the new ball. Such a move would be regarded as heresy these days. This team, which grouped together in Sydney, more or less as a comedy outfit, developed so startlingly that they formed the nucleus of the team which was to carry all before them for the next four years.

I took no further part in Test cricket after the Wellington Test. A 'bung' left knee saw to that. But every member of the team, with exception of the gifted Meuleman, who never got past the 12th man job in Tests after his duck at Wellington, went on to distinction

Ten of them accompanied Bradman on his record-breaking 1948 tour of England. Had Arthur Morris been available for selection for New Zealand, the show would have been absolutely complete. The magnificent left-hander's luck ran out on him when his demobilisation orders came too late to land him back from New Guinea in time.

Every member of the side was highly appreciative of the NZ hospitality that fast-moving tour but it was the Australian Board of Control who got most out of it when one considers the wealth of talent that was placed on their market by it.

A tour which began with a touch of the motley imprinted upon it proved beyond any doubt at all that greatness was a-ripening.

Australian Cricket, Bill O'Reilly (Modern Magazines, Sydney, November 1973)

STICKY DOGS

In the old days of covered run-ups and uncovered pitches, batting was perilous on an Australian 'sticky' wicket, as Denis Compton was to find.

What is an Australian 'sticky'? How does it differ from a sticky pitch in England? Those and countless questions along similar lines are asked me time and again. First I must emphasise that in England we rarely play on a really sticky pitch. The climate seldom provides the necessary conditions of torrential rain followed by scorching sun. Such weather occurs with frequency only in tropical countries.

Usually in England a rain-saturated pitch dries slowly, or at any rate reasonably so, compared with the speed at which a wet pitch dries in a hot country such as Australia. Moreover, in England a slowly drying pitch goes dead. Apart from skidding through, the ball does little out of the ordinary. Should the turf dry quickly enough under sun and wind, however, the spin bowlers find they can turn the ball sharply. Left-arm slow bowlers and right-arm off spinners come into their own. By their accuracy they can make the batsman play at nearly every ball, without being expensive.

Even so, a top-class batsman can make runs on a drying pitch. True, the conditions separate the good from the ordinary but a batsman of the calibre of, say, Len Hutton, compiles big scores.

Not so in Australia. There, on a 'sticky dog', the greatest batsman comes down to the level of the rabbit. I have played on only one such pitch, at Brisbane in 1946–47, and, although I had been warned what to expect, I was astounded. Soon after the beginning of each England innings, on successive afternoons, a violent thunderstorm broke. In the first, 2 inches of rain fell and in the second nearly 3 inches. As huge hailstones mingled with the rain and beat down on the corrugated iron small pavilion, nobody could see more than 15 or 20 yards in front of him. A few minutes after the second storm the ground lay underwater. Stumps floated on top of the lake.

In England no play would have been possible next day, but both times cricket resumed promptly the following morning, with a fierce sun burning the grass. I have never seen turf more sticky. It clung to the soles of the batsman's boots; pieces could be picked up and squeezed into little round tacky balls.

I knew at last the meaning of a 'gluepot'.

One day the first ball rose from a good length and knocked off Cyril Washbrook's cap. The next skidded along the ground; somehow Cyril managed to put his bat to it. Batsmanship was impossible. Spin was not needed, nor [was sheer] speed. The one requirement was accurate medium-paced bowling. If bowlers delivered straight half-volleys, the pitch did the rest. Either the ball stood up almost perpendicularly or shot along the ground. Naturally, Don Bradman, the Australian captain, ordered all fieldsmen to stand within a few yards of the bat to take the catches which were bound to be offered. A batsman playing correctly was nearly certain to be caught in defending himself or else bowled by a 'grub'.

I have heard many people ask how England scored 141 and 172 if the pitch was so bad. My answer is that, apart from Test matches, Australian pitches are always covered fully and that, as Australians are so inexperienced on 'sticky dogs', they did not make the best use of their opportunities. [Ernie] Toshack, for instance, bowled many short balls. If these did not rear high over the batsman's head they went through at convenient height for the hook. I am not exaggerating when I say that any two club bowlers with ability to bowl straight and to pitch well up should have run through an international side.

More true to the nature of the Brisbane sticky dog were the 66 made by Australia against England in 1928, their 58 against England in 1936, and the 58 and 98 of India against Australia in 1947.

Although the low scores do not support me, I thought that the Brisbane pitch in the first of the 1950–51 series was not as vicious as four years previously. Still, as the totals of the two sides testify, it was difficult enough on the second day when England obtained 7-68 declared and 6-30, and Australia declared at 7-32. Twenty wickets fell in just under four hours for 132!

Normally a sticky dog in Australia is worst for between two and three hours. Then, as it dries out under the hot sun, it begins to play more easily. Indeed, it can become a good batting surface again.

Australian sticky dogs are not confined to Brisbane, but touring teams often experience them there. The programs are so arranged that they visit Brisbane in December at the height of the storm period. I have been told that a Melbourne sticky is worse than anything encountered at Brisbane, though I find this difficult to believe.

Since the war, the Australians have caught England on Brisbane stickies in two Tests and India in one. England enjoyed the luck from the weather in previous Brisbane Tests and perhaps her turn will come again next time. Nevertheless, I think there can be little satisfaction in winning a Test match when the weather makes such a mockery of batting skill. The scales are weighted too heavily in favour of bowlers. Cricket surely was never meant to be a game in which ability was rendered as valueless as that.

Denis Compton's Annual, Denis Compton (Stanley Paul & Co, London, 1952)

TEST PLAYERS FOSSICK FOR DIAMONDS

*Ex-Australian spin bowler Arthur Mailey accompanied
the 1935–36 Australian team to South Africa.*

KIMBERLEY, Sunday – Members of the Australian cricket team went diamond-hunting today, when they paid a visit to the diamond fields at Sydney-on-Vaal.

After having lunched at a small hotel where the alluvial diamond millers, in their khaki shirts and shorts, gave the tables a picturesque appearance, the party visited Mr Michael Gildea's claim.

Vic Richardson and 'Chuck' Fleetwood-Smith washed a quantity of soil brought from the river by the natives. Fleetwood-Smith found a diamond weighing eight carats, worth 150 pounds. Richardson found a smaller one. Both gems were handed back to Mr Gildea, whom I suspect of having put them in the cradle intentionally. All the Australians went fossicking around the fields, expecting to pick up gems. They were so keen that when their host called them back to the hotel with the remark, 'Now, boys, there's a nice cool beer waiting for you,' the team did not budge, but continued their search for diamonds.

'I have met many Australians,' said Mr Gildea, 'but I have never seen Australians so apathetic about beer!'

Mr Gildea has had a romantic career. He left Cobargo in NSW to go to the Boer War. When that was over he tried his luck on the diamond fields. He fossicked for 18 months without success and then he accidentally stumbled across a valuable diamond. He staked a claim at the spot and has remained at Sydney-on-Vaal ever since.

The Sun, Arthur Mailey (Sydney, January 1936)

THEY REMINDED ME OF
BEES AROUND HONEY

*Maurice Turnbull, a frontline member of the 1929–30 MCC team to
Australia, on first glimpses of Sydney, The Don and the keen-as girls ...*

In this match [against NSW] we were treated to our first experience of true Australian conditions – what athletes Hammond, Tate, White and the rest of them must have been! [Don] Bradman's innings [of 157] eclipsed anything we had seen before in Australia. The others were always giving us a chance of getting them out – [Archie] Jackson and [Alan] Kippax were a little out of practice owing to illness – but Bradman played some glorious back-shots reminiscent of Charlie Macartney and hardly missed a ball at which he struck.

In his movements, build and personality he reminded us most forcibly of RWV Robins. McCabe played like a veteran after he had been missed when seven. As for [Arthur] Allsopp, his off-side strokes amazed us by their power and by the frequency with which they made contact with the ball. He was certainly out at 14, but the umpire admitted that he was watching the ball and did not see what had happened ... perhaps it was for the best, since it was this young player's first big match [he made 117 on debut].

[Alan] Fairfax struck me as being quite the best bowler for our opponents (taking four for 102).

On the Saturday night as we came off the field I got rather a thrill standing to attention for 'God Save the King' in front of more than 20,000 people and another at the way the members cheered Frank [Woolley] after his long innings [of 219]. Packed to the utmost as it was, one's impression of 'the Hill' was a favourable one, with everyone in a good humour because of the prodigiousness of the fare provided.

On the fourth day our thanks were due to Wendell Bill for being peerless as a substitute. By the way, the lunch provided for the players here is unworthy of the other arrangements ...

I shall remember Sydney not a little because of its oysters and its glorious Roman Catholic Cathedral; I lived off one for days, and visited the other more than once. Major Ken Nichol came over from Canberra to take us to *Showboat* (at which we shamefully neglected our opportunities behind the stage) and to Kensington for golf on Sunday. Then there was a dance of the younger set which our youngsters attended. We got more than we bargained for and less. Our hostess extended to us a welcome with musical honours and chevrons for the breast: ardent women wanted us to write risqué rhymes in their autograph books. They reminded me of bees around honey: no time nor inclination for philandering here. Next night Mr and Mrs Gaffney 'dined and danced' us at Romanos. They didn't have to search the town for our partners. The girls were a most eloquent tribute to the standard of Sydney's female beauty.

And all this time, we had little idea whether or not we should have to make the long journey to Brisbane. As far back as August, Lord's had complained to the New Zealand Council that the program of matches arranged for the tour in Australia was an over-strenuous one in view of the long list that was to follow. Our skipper [Arthur Gilligan] did not know exactly how the matter stood, but even when he acquainted the New Zealand Council with the low ebb of the side's physical resources, he received the following wire: REGRET

Forceful: Stan McCabe rushed to 90 in less than two hours against the MCC at the Sydney Cricket Ground in 1929–30.

CASUALTIES BUT WE CANNOT AGREE CANCELLATION OF QUEENSLAND MATCH WITHOUT AUTHORITY AUSTRALIAN BOARD – WOULD SERIOUSLY AFFECT FINANCES TOUR.

It must be made clear that the Australian Board of Control was helping along cricket in New Zealand by presenting her, after expenses had been deducted, 75 per cent of the profits on our matches played in Australia [and a full program was completed leading into the first NZ–England Test match across the Tasman].

The Book of the Two Maurices, Being Some Account of the Tour by an MCC Team through Australia and New Zealand in the Closing Months of 1929 and the Beginning of 1930, MJ Turnbull & MJC Allom, story by Maurice Turnbull (E Allom & Co Ltd, London, 1930)

CHARLIE MACARTNEY'S EPIC 345

*Sydney Smith Jr, manager of the 1921 Australians,
was an eyewitness at Trent Bridge for Charlie Macartney's
whirlwind 345 against Nottinghamshire.*

This game will live long in the memory of those who were privileged to see it, because of [Charlie] Macartney's magnificent and classic innings of 345, which eclipsed [Warwick] Armstrong's record for the highest score by an Australian player in England, 303 not out against Somerset in 1905. I must say it was the finest innings I have ever witnessed and most of those who were present were of the same opinion. Word was sent out to Macartney to go after [Archie] MacLaren's record, for first-class cricket, but unfortunately he was given out leg before wicket after playing the ball with his bat and thus MacLaren's record stands.

It was in this match that Macartney was heard to remark when he came into the dressing-room after being 200 not out, that he thought he would take his heavy bat out and have a 'dip' at them. We all wondered what 'dipping' at them meant after what we had seen. Macartney hit the ball over every blade of grass on the Trent Bridge Oval. It did not matter how the fieldsmen were placed, the ball flew between for 4 after 4. The spectators were worked up to fever heat with excitement and appreciation of perhaps the best batting they had ever witnessed.

One stroke of Macartney's will live long in the cricket history of Trent Bridge. Without any effort he played forward to a ball well pitched up, and it went flying out of the ground over cover point's head for 6. It was a perfect gem!

With the 15th Australian XI, Sydney Smith Jr (ET Kibblewhite & Co, Sydney, 1922) Macartney's unforgettable 345, the highest of his 49 first-class centuries, came in eight minutes short of four hours. Macartney was dubbed 'the Governor-General' for the contemptuous way he used to dismiss bowlers from his sight.

CRICKET WILL COST AUSTRALIANS MORE
The arrival of the first English team after the Great War was eagerly awaited ... even though the cost of seeing the games was set to substantially increase.

In consequence of the heavy all-round increases in the cost of travelling and living, it is certain that the charge for admission to matches with the English eleven will have to be substantially increased.

The expenses attached to the tour of the Englishmen have in some instances increased 100 per cent and the general cost of the tour will exceed previous tours by 50 per cent. As a fact in bringing the Englishmen to Australia, the authorities will have to incur a financial liability approaching 15,000 pounds.

In the past, Australians have been able to see Test matches from the grandstand enclosure at 2/6 [two shillings and sixpence] and from the outside ground at 1/- [one shilling]. Prices charged in England have always been much higher and they recently have been increased with a view to the Australian eleven tour next year [1921], the tariff being to the outer ground at Lord's and the Oval, 3/- and at Nottingham, Leeds and Manchester, 2/6. For admission to other portions of the grounds the rate varies from 10/6 upwards, some fans booking seats for the entire duration of the match.

It will rest with the [Australian cricket] Board of Control to decide what the increases in Australia will be. It might even be advisable for them to adopt the system of a limited number of reserve seats in the grandstand enclosure for the Test matches. For a slightly advanced fee the individual could be certain of a particular seat throughout a game. The ticket should be transferable so that in the event of the purchaser not being able to attend each day he may pass it on to a member of his family or a friend.

The value a person would derive from the reserve seat privilege would vary according to the duration of the match, but the chances are that in the long run he would have the advantage. I have an idea that the Test matches under reasonable conditions will last even longer than in the past. The batting is so strong and the bowling seems so weak.

Source unknown, 'Outfield' (October 1920)

CRICKET'S PARADISE

England's hurricane hitter Gilbert Jessop joined those to acclaim the Sydney Cricket Ground as the finest in the southern hemisphere.

'Sydney is the paradise of batsmen. It would be difficult to imagine a more perfect ground,' wrote Gilbert Jessop, after his visit with the English team in 1901–02. 'The New South Welshman with justification lay claim to the possession of the finest ground of the cricket world. As regards light and the nature of the turf it bears a closer resemblance to English grounds than either the Melbourne or Adelaide grounds. The Sydney wickets may not be better than other Australian wickets, but they do not possess their pace and consequently English batsmen prefer and are more at home on the

Sydney Cricket Ground pitches. Where the superiority of the ground over other grounds is most marked is in the general arrangements and structural improvements for spectators. Unlike in the great majority of grounds, the pavilions are not situated directly behind the bowler's arm. When the Sydney stands are filled with the youth and beauty of Australia, it is,' concluded Jessop, 'a sight to gladden even the heart of a footsore cricketer at the end of a weary day of leather-hunting.'

The Story of the Tests, England v Australia 1877–1920 (official Sydney Cricket Ground souvenir), story by Gilbert Jessop (Sydney, 1920)

'I WON'T PLAY IN SOUTH AUSTRALIA AGAIN'

Indian prince Kumar Shri Ranjitsinhji captivated crowds in England and Australia with centuries in his first appearances, teammate Gilbert Jessop claiming him to be the most brilliant cricketer in cricket's most glittering golden age.

For months before the arrival of the English cricketers, 'Ranji' was boomed as the star of the team. Press and people got the Indian fever. Drinks, boots and other articles were named after him and it was simply sickening to hear the way the name of the visitor was lauded. When they played here, he, in common with the others, was treated to the best Adelaide could boast.

Scarcely had he left the colony here he rushed into print about the South Australians in a way far from complimentary and our people naturally resented it and it was prophesised that Ranji would have a bad time when he took part in the third Test on the Adelaide Oval. He received a mild barracking and this appears to have upset his liver. Ranji may criticise to his heart's content but common Australian clay must not presume to barrack his Highness.

But it did and the result is that Ranji has declared he will never play in South Australia again. Let the Town Hall bells be tolled, drape the Oval in mourning, let all the flags in the city be half-masted, arrange with the Government for a date to be set apart for a day of humiliation. Fix up with the VCTU for a special series of prayer meetings, let the hero-worshippers go about in sack cloth and ashes for on the Adelaide Oval, Ranji will play no more – he hath said it.

Seriously, does it matter a fraction to South Australians whether a visiting cricketer taking offence at a real or imaginary slight refuses to play? The promoters may have something to say but that is his affair and theirs.

To Ranji we say:

Go bury thy sorrow, the world hath its share

Go bury it deeply, go hide it with care

Go think of it calmly when curtained by night

Go pocket thy pride and then all will be right.

Source unknown (Adelaide, 1897–98); extra research: *Ranji, Prince of Cricketers,* Alan Ross (William Collins & Sons Pty Ltd, London, 1983)

Writing in mid-tour for the Australian Review of Reviews, *Ranji made himself unpopular by backing the action of the English umpire James Phillips in the no-balling for throwing of South Australia's favourite cricketing son Ernie Jones. On return for the Test match 10 weeks later, Ranji was the target of crude barracking from sections of the crowd: 'I was at the wicket for about a quarter of an hour and during the whole of that time uncomplimentary and insulting remarks were hurled at me from all parts of the field,' he wrote. He vowed never to return ... and didn't.*

I'M RIGHT HERE THANKS DOCTOR

Alick's brother, Charlie [Bannerman] was once fielding at point close up on the treacherous wicket at Lord's. It was in fact that memorable, sensational match against the Marylebone Club [in 1878], which made all England ring with the names of Australia. WG Grace and AN Hornby were in. Seeing Charlie so close up and knowing the Lancastrian's tremendous power on the off, WG went up to Charlie and said, 'Mr Hornby hits very hard in that spot. If he lets go and gets fair hold, you might be killed.'

'Does he hit hard?' said Bannerman and didn't move.

'In Morning Dew, Round the Ground with "Felix" [Tom Horan Sr], Selections and Notes', David Morris (1995)

GEORGE ANDERSON'S DIARY

Twenty-five days in the life of Yorkshireman George Anderson, a leading member of George Parr's All-England eleven Down Under in 1863–64.

January

1st, New Year's Day: Commenced the first match at Melbourne – a very fine day and the ground filled with spectators – the largest company we ever saw – about 14,000.

2nd: AEE [All England Eleven] v Melbourne continued, about 10,000 people there today.

3rd, Sunday: Went to Dinner at Mr Farrar's – Hutchinson called for me about five and drove me round about the country.

4th: AEE v Melbourne continued.

5th: AEE v Melbourne concluded – the Eleven had six wickets to fall and about eight runs to get – myself and [William] Caffyn not out.

6th: Started at a quarter past 12 for Sandhurst – passed thro' the Diggings – passed Mount Macedon on our way – fine ride.

7th: Commenced the first day's play at Sandhurst – very rough ground.

8th: Went this morning by invitation to Latham & Watson's reef – did not go down the shaft. Match continued.

9th: Went to the Prince of Wales reef at Eaglehawk – a very hot dusty morning and heavy rain in afternoon, in which we played and got wet through – won our match very easily.

10th: Returned to Melbourne today – Parr left behind very ill from Erysipelas.

11th: Started for Ballaarat this morning and commenced the match – saw Braithwaite B Fryer and wife here.

12th: Match continued.

13th: Match concluded and left at half past 12 at night for Ararat. Travelled all night by coach and arrived at half past nine after a tremendous jolting.

14th: Commenced the match at Ararat – saw Henry Smith and Chr Simpson and family.

15th: Match concluded and the Eleven won easily – in one innings – 22 played like so many old women. Saw John Little and wife.

16th: Went out with John Little to the Western, saw Geo Kay. Dined with the 22 at night.

17th: Went to Eversley with Mr and Mrs Little and stayed all night. Most of the Eleven went fishing and shooting.

18th: Left Eversley for Maryboro' in the morning – passed thro' the amphitheatre – had invitation to stay and lunch at Avoca and met a very pleasant party – went on to Maryboro'. Everyone out to see our arrival.

19th: Commenced play at Maryboro'. Went to ball in honour of the AE [All England] Eleven this evening – nearly all there.

20th: Match at Maryborough continued. Saw Harry Court's brother.

21st: Match at Maryboro' concluded – won easily. Started for Castlemaine at night – 30 miles across the country and arrived about nine at night.

22nd: Left Castlemaine for Melbourne arriving at noon.

23rd: Received welcome letter from home and preparing for the mail for England.

24th: Sent letters and papers off to England. Went to St Kilda to tea with Mr and Mrs May.

25th: Started for New Zealand at 10 o'clock by the *Alhambra* and as soon as we got out of smooth water began to be sick . . .

Cricket's Silver Lining, edited by David Rayvern Allen, story by George Anderson (William Collins & Sons, London, 1987)

Finest ever: Dennis Lillee is chaired from the Melbourne Cricket Ground by Gary Cosier and Greg Chappell after his 11-wicket Centenary Test haul in March, 1977
Cricketer

12
FOT, RED AND OTHER SUPERSTARS

'Miller threw himself full length and took an extraordinary catch, ending up in front of the third slip. As he caught the ball, he rolled over, handed it to me and said, 'Wonder what won the two-thirty?'

HE REFUSED TO GIVE IN

Ian Chappell on Australia's finest-ever fast bowler Dennis Lillee.

'Well you can get stuffed. I'll start training as soon as I get home and I'll take five wickets in an innings five times next season.'

That's Dennis Keith 'Fot' Lillee talking. The bloke on the receiving end – well, that's me. I wouldn't have minded so much if that had been all I copped, but I had to put up with a couple of short jabs to the midriff as well. But I shouldn't really complain because I benefited next season when Lillee took 23 wickets at a cost of only 16.6 each and he took five wickets in an innings three times out of four Supertests.

The reason for the slight altercation? Well, Lillee had been talking about his poor first season of World Series Cricket and how he thought he might be finished. He then asked if I would shake him by the hand as it had all been a lot of fun.

That's when I told him I didn't shake hands with medium-pace bowlers, only quick bowlers. He retaliated with the short right first and repeated his request and after a couple of knockbacks, a couple more short rights, I then got the short soliloquy.

Incidentally, Lillee had only had an average season by his own high standards the first year – most bowlers would have been quite happy with the results.

And that is a part of the answer to Dennis Lillee's success. He has pride in his performance, he has determination, he has a tremendous capacity to work, an ability to learn, and not least of all, he has a natural ability to bowl fast. As you can judge by the story at the beginning it is not hard to motivate Dennis.

There are many things I admire about Dennis Lillee, apart from his ability to take wickets: he is a very proud Australian [and West Australian], his iron will, his boyish liking for a prank or a practical joke. And when he is in a mellow mood and his conscience is playing up with him – the way he wants to apologise for all the things he thinks he has done wrong. He is very meek and mild when he is in the latter mood, but I haven't yet seen anyone try and take advantage of that mood!

One of the lasting memories of Dennis Lillee was in the West Indies in 1973. It must have been the worst time in his life. There he was supposedly the fastest bowler in the world, unable to even play and facing the possibility that he may never have been able to bowl fast again. At worst he could have been crippled by his back injury. And all this at the ripe old age of 23.

I wouldn't have been surprised if he had come to the tour executive and asked to be sent home and I am sure in sympathy for his plight we would have allowed it.

But not once did he mention home. Instead he kept running from the motels to the grounds, 'in case my back comes good, then I will need to be fit to play in a Test'.

But he went even further than that – he offered his services as a batsman-cum-fielder in the tour matches so someone else could have a rest, as he said: 'I don't want to be a burden on the team.'

And when I thanked him for the offer and said we might think about using him as a fielder, but I wasn't too sure about his batting ability, he did what must have come hardest of all to him in those darkest days of his life – he started playing a few practical jokes. Little things like pinning a batting order up on the wall – always near to where I was changing. They would read Stackpole, Redpath, Lillee or even on one occasion: Stackpole, Lillee!

I eventually relented and opened with him in one game and he didn't stop talking about the boundary he took off the new ball, for a couple of days, but he was terribly disappointed about the way he got out. Bounced out by the fast bowler.

Just having Lillee around on that tour and seeing him make the most of a tough situation must have been worth a couple of wickets to the Australian team every time we walked on the field.

I look back at the day he walked into the Queens Park ground in Trinidad when we were in the middle of a really tight Test match. It must have been one of the saddest sights an Australian side could ever have been faced with. Dennis had gone to the hospital to undergo manipulation for his back and this had required an anesthetic. He staggered into the ground like a drunken man, still suffering the effects of the anesthetic. Again, it was typical of the man. He had refused any help to get back to the ground and had taken off under his own steam with doctors and nurses unable to dissuade him.

I am sure when we won that Test, the Australians felt they had won it for Lillee and Stackpole, our two walking wounded.

I have many other memories of the guts and determination of the man and I could easily fill a book with them. I also have many fond memories of the wickets he has taken not only with his speed, but with his guile.

He has also been a fast bowler who could take it as well as hand it out. When Lillee was batting in the second Test at Lord's recently [1981] and copped a couple of bouncers for his corner, Richie Benaud made the comment: 'You didn't see too many of those being bowled at Lillee in the early seventies.'

But Lillee accepted them as being the price you pay for ageing as a fast bowler and kept his wicket intact to remain 40 not out at the end of the Australian innings.

There must have been some very nervous fast bowlers around in Perth club cricket in the 1974–75 season; there could even have been a couple of premature retirements amongst the fraternity.

Dennis had a season off from bowling in 1973–74 and a lot of fast bowlers took that as a sign that he wouldn't bowl fast again.

Dennis didn't sit on the splice that season but set out to improve his batting. In doing so, he promoted himself up the order and copped more than his share of bouncers. I well remember his comment when next I saw him: 'Don't worry. I have all the names filed away for reference – their turn will come!'

Fast bowlers have long memories and Dennis Lillee is in the

Elephant class! It's a pity some other people don't have memories as long.

I was to read where captain Kim Hughes and manager Fred Bennett chipped Lillee about his lackadaisical attitude in the field against Middlesex, leading up to the first Test of the 1981 series. Lillee was obviously not amused and the reply was fitting: 'Have I let Australia down in a Test match?'

The answer to that is: 'No Dennis' – and I hope Australia never forgets it.

Lillee: A Testimonial, 1981–82, story by Ian Chappell (PBL, Sydney, 1981)
After his back breakdown in the West Indies in 1973, Lillee, Australia's finest-ever fast bowler, took 304 Test and 67 Supertest wickets in 73 further internationals at an average of five a match. He continued playing first-class cricket until 1988 and even at the age of 50 was still taking wickets at international level at the annual season-opener at Lilac Hill.

GREAT TOURIST, GREAT PLAYER, GREAT BLOKE

A tribute to Ian Redpath by one of his hero-worshippers, Paul Sheahan.

I vividly recall the occasion when my father and I called in to the MCG late one afternoon during the 1962–63 season. The Victorians were batting in the second innings of their match against New South Wales and there was a young lad flaying the NSW bowling – and in those days it could boast almost an entire Test attack, including the wily Richie Benaud.

I think 'Redders' made about 40 in that hand. As the shadows lengthened and the icy wind whistled through the tunnel under the outer, Dad said: 'Ian Redpath will play for Australia before long.' I took special interest in those words because he had been my idol ever since we were at school together, although we never played in the same team.

I had special cause to remember the day in 1958, the day he became my idol, when he made 112 against Melbourne Grammar School. At that time the boys in the junior school were allowed to watch some of Friday afternoon's play in the home APS matches. Because he was nearing his century, we were graciously spared the rigours of Latin for an extra half-hour. Perhaps that had something to do with my youthful idolatry!

At the time when he was establishing himself in the Victorian team, Redders lived quite close to the school and used to practise with our side when he couldn't get to Melbourne. This will bring a smile to the lips of those who have been menaced by my bowling subsequently, but I used to be able to slip the odd off spinner past him in the nets. I wouldn't like my chances now!

Hero: Ian Redpath was a hero for many, including Testman-in-the-making Paul 'Timbers' Sheahan.

To be factual and unemotional for a moment, he played his first Test against the touring South Africans in 1963–64 when Norman O'Neill was unfit and Bobby Simpson dropped down the list.

But, as so often happens, the loss of one star heralds the emergence of another. Redders took a while to fulfil the promise but no one could dispute his claims now. He made 97 in that Test and was described by John Arlott as 'a tall, slim, cool batsman, straight in defence'.

He really blossomed as a batsman of international repute after the disastrous 1966–67 tour of South Africa when he finished a clear second to Simpson in both the aggregate and the averages in the Tests. This prompted Trevor Goddard, then the Springbok skipper, to declare Ian Redpath as 'the most correct batsman in the world'; no mean praise for a man who had not yet scored a Test century.

Despite coming so close to a century in his first Test, it was to be another 27 Tests before he could look to the scoreboard with personal satisfaction – which has always been the furthest thing from his mind – and see three figures against his name. He made a slashing 132, following a duck in the first innings, against the West Indies in the fifth Test of the 1968–69 tour at the Sydney Cricket Ground. This was the same match in which Doug Walters became the first batsman to register a double-century and a single-century in the one game. But to underline Redders' consistency, he maintained an enviable average of more than 40 throughout this period.

One of my few pleasant cricketing memories of the wretched 1969–70 tour of South Africa was the way Redders handled the extreme pace and belligerence of the Springbok attack, spearheaded by Mike Procter. There will be many who may doubt what I am about to say, particularly if they have taken too much notice of the way Redders played in the first innings of the Sydney Test in this current series. But, during the 1970 tour, I was at the non-striker's end for most of the whirlwind 152 he made against Orange Free State and suffered a sunburnt roof of the mouth as I watched one particular 6-ball over sail for no less than 32 runs. In fact, his last 51 runs were scored in 12 minutes from just 15 strokes, an innings which partially helped to put the lie to the critics who maintained he was too defensive.

Perhaps Redders was fortunate to have missed the 1965 tour of the West Indies when the Australians were decimated by the fearsome pace of Wes Hall and Charlie Griffith. Certainly he had played the bouncers awkwardly in this [1975–76] series but he has only been struck one or two blows in his career, once when he ducked into a slow bouncer from Charlie Griffith that hit him on the side of the face against the 'Windies' during the 1968–69 tour. I went to see him that evening in the Royal Melbourne Hospital and he looked as if he was trying to conceal a medicine ball in his cheek, his face was so swollen. But the spirit of the man is irrepressible. He will remain one of the most doughty, courageous, dependable Test players I've ever seen.

The 1968–69 tour of Australia by the Windies turned out to be one of the most eventful in his career. One reason was that he became one of the few batsmen who has been 'Mankaded' in a Test match. Poor old Redders, I suppose he has always been a bit dreamy, but I shall never forget the look on big Charlie Griffith's face when, midway through his run-up, he realised that Mr Redpath, quite without malice or forethought, had sauntered off down the wicket. His eyes lit up and the run-up immediately changed into an uncontrollable charge; the bails were not merely lifted, the stumps were uprooted.

This happened once more in his career, to my knowledge, in a Victoria–West Australia Sheffield Shield clash. There has always been some 'needle' in these games but WA skipper John Inverarity, always the gentleman, recalled Redders after he had almost left the arena.

He has never been a glamour player in the sense of the Chappells, Dennis Lillee, Jeff Thomson and Rod Marsh. I suppose this could be due to the fact that Redders hasn't been a prolific scorer of Test centuries. Nor has he been a particularly flamboyant batsman, or drawn attention to himself by his antics, or lack of them, in the field. On only one occasion can I remember him losing his temper in the field and it occurred during a Test match in India after a run of decisions that had patently gone against Australia. At the turning-down of an unmistakable caught behind, he was moved to throw his hat on the ground, stand on it and mutter a discreet oath or two!

As for personal reminiscences, they abound. Redders has always fancied himself as a fisherman but he never fails to be out-fished by Bill Lawry, Doug Walters and latterly, Max Walker. On one rather hot day in India in 1969, a large crowd had gathered to watch the big white hunters – in the form of Bill Lawry and Ian Redpath – plying their art with fishing lines. Redders, a stickler for silence when concentrating his talents, was becoming increasingly annoyed by the cacophony from the curious crowd. At the appropriate moment, he leapt to his feet with a bloodcurdling scream of 'Charge', in a style that would have done justice to General Robert E Lee and ran straight at the onlookers! In the ensuing confusion, Redders was seen to be

Red: Ian Redpath (left) with debutant Rick McCosker approaching the Sydney Test of 1974–75. The rangy Victorian made 105 in the second innings and shared a record double-century stand with Greg Chappell.
Patrick Eagar

315

waving a bamboo pole in menacing fashion as he raced after the fugitive natives. Needless to say, the anglers were undisturbed for the remainder of the afternoon. On tour, he took the cake as the worst 'waker-up' on record. Invariably, he arose to face stone-cold bacon and eggs, having drifted back into dreamland after ordering breakfast. To get any sense out of him before the team arrived at the ground in the morning was a sheer impossibility.

Despite this, he remains one of the most imperturbable people that God ever put breath into. What a wonderful tourist he was. He used to take great pains to ensure that any newcomers to the team were never without company. Believe me when I say that homesickness, travel fatigue, jet lag, upset biological rhythms, call them what you will, are some of the greatest enemies of a touring cricketer; but Redders was always there to offer a sympathetic ear or a word of encouragement at the right time.

I suppose that the timeworn phrase 'one of nature's gentlemen' would be one of the most apt descriptions when talking of Ian. He was a touring team manager's dream: nearly always punctual, always willing to attend official functions and lend an ear to the local 'thrasher'. He never queried decisions and, above all, never brought discredit to Australian cricket.

They often say fast bowlers are frustrated batsmen, but Red fits into the reverse category. Nothing would have given him more pleasure than to have marked out a 30-metre run-up on the first morning of a Test match at the MCG on a humid day. His cricketing mates at South Melbourne say that it requires major surgery to relieve him of the ball when he makes one of his infrequent [due to first-class commitments] appearances for his home club.

But he will never live down the day at Cardiff in 1964 when umpire Jim Langridge called him for 'throwing'. Perhaps that was the fulfillment of his secret desire, to rate a mention in *Wisden* alongside such great fast bowlers as Griffith, Geoff Griffin and former colleague Ian Meckiff.

Cricketer, Paul Sheahan (Newspress, Melbourne, March 1976)
Ian Redpath finished his Test career with three 100s in his last four Tests in 1975–76 against a visiting West Indian attack which included Andy Roberts and a young Michael Holding.

THE TYPHOON

*Coronation tour newcomer Colin McDonald on
the blistering pace of Frank 'Typhoon' Tyson.*

I first experienced Frank's extreme pace at Northampton in 1953.
I'd limped in to bat with a swollen and bandaged left knee. We'd all
heard stories about his pace and there he was beginning his run-up
from just about in front of the far sightscreen. I settled over my bat
and waited. Well! His first delivery was an unexpected blur which
found the outside edge of my bat and flew at the speed of light
through the just-as-startled slips cordon for 4. The next hit my right
knee at ferocious pace plumb in front of my middle stump. I walked
off without a limp ... after all, it is difficult to limp on both knees at
the same time ...

CC, the Colin McDonald Story: Cricket, Tennis, Life, Colin McDonald (Australian
Scholarly Publishing, Melbourne, 2009)
*Colin McDonald averaged 47.66 in Tests in Australia and 39.32 overall in 47 matches
against some of the world's quickest bowling in the 1950s and early 1960s.*

THE GOLDEN NUGGET

Michael Parkinson on first meeting his hero Keith Miller.

It was while playing for the *Daily Express* I met my great hero Keith
Miller. I had first seen him when I was 10 and he came to England with
the Australian Services team [in 1945]. He was tall, broad-shouldered,
dark-haired and Hollywood handsome. He hit 6s, bowled like the
wind and caught swallows. I was smitten. When I met him at the
Express, he had retired from cricket and was employed to write about
the game. He was a reluctant member of our team. He didn't like
playing what he defined as 'comic cricket', nor did he like taking candy
from children, a fact he had amply demonstrated in times past. Playing
for Bradman's team against Essex in 1948, he walked to the wicket
with Australia well on the way to a final total of 721, let the first ball
he received hit his stumps and departed the field with the parting shot,
'Thank God that's over.' His captain was not pleased.

Bradman and Miller didn't get on. It could have been the rumour that Bradman, lately signed by the *Daily Mail,* might turn out for them that enticed Miller to play for the *Express.* The game allowed me the chance to stand next to my hero as we fielded against the *Mail.* He was at first slip and I was at second. I noticed a man near the sightscreen semaphoring Keith. This went on for an over or two before I asked my hero what was going on. 'He's a mate. He's signalling the winners at Wincanton,' he explained.

Keith Miller liked a bet.

Ten minutes later, with the semaphore man still active, the *Mail* batsman snicked a fast ball, which flew towards my right hand. I wasn't a bad fielder in those days, before the reflexes became dulled and as I started to move, there was a flash across my body as Miller threw himself full length and took an extraordinary catch, ending up in front of the third slip. As he caught the ball, he rolled over, handed it to me and said, 'Wonder what won the two-thirty?'

Parky, Michael Parkinson (Hodder & Stoughton, London, 2008)

RARE POISE AND FLAIR

*Stan McCabe was a batsman of rare gifts whose century
in the opening Test in the Bodyline summer was
simply scintillating, says teammate Bert Oldfield.*

In 1927, an official New South Wales Cricket Association side, captained by Charlie Macartney, toured the Western Districts for a week to play seven one-day matches. At Grenfell we played against the local team, which comprised many Grenfell juniors, including one Stan McCabe.

These games were mostly played on concrete pitches, covered with matting, and in this atmosphere a young McCabe revelled. Pitting his batting ability against older and more experienced bowlers, he cleverly blended his graceful stroke-play with fine footwork, which, unlike many others, he had the courage to use. His confidence impressed us all.

His performance was clearly that of a potential star and reflected well on St Joseph's College, the school where he learnt his cricket.

Next season, he was invited to play Sheffield Shield cricket for NSW at the age of 18. It was a remarkable achievement and his outstanding progress continued until, at the age of 20, in 1930, he was chosen to tour England. The side was captained by WM 'Bill' Woodfull, that capable and understanding Australian leader, in a golden era of cricket of which McCabe was very much a part.

At Nottingham, McCabe played his first Test match for Australia against England.

In this game he unfolded a delightful calmness to the ever-changing English conditions, and also an equally delightful temperament, something which he always possessed. This calmness remained with him throughout his career and a poise for stroke-play with an ease of manner, even when facing a batting collapse.

Of all his qualities, his self-control was the most impressive. It often had a valuable influence on the attitude of his teammates at awkward periods of a vital game. In fact, it is reasonable to state that his steadiness often resulted in the transformation of a match which seemed doomed to defeat and yet brought triumph to his side.

Off the field, Stan McCabe was a likeable companion, always ready to adjust himself to any circumstance. His appearance resembled that of Napoleon and duly won for him the nickname 'Napper'. As a travelling companion he freely displayed a sense of humour that aroused laughter and gaiety.

It was my pleasure to share selection with him in two Test teams which toured England, in 1930 and 1934. And then, of course, there were the many Test matches on the trying sunbaked fields of Australia, which included some less important fixtures in the outback settings of NSW.

As a batsman Stan McCabe was venturesome and refreshing. Who can ever forget his admirable, cavalier approach in the Bodyline series in 1932, when, on a Saturday in December at the Sydney Cricket Ground, [Harold] Larwood was almost invincible. The young McCabe answered this with astonishing confidence. He used his dangerous pull shots with which he frequently found the leg boundary, and even hit several 6s in his innings of 187 not out, much to the thrill of the spectators on the Hill. That unforgettable occasion remains in my memory, together with two other innings: his 232 against England at Trent Bridge in 1938, and his performance at Johannesburg, making 189 not out, in 1935.

But it was the part he played in the important Lord's Test match in 1930 that really emphasised his brilliance. England had batted cleverly to score a matchwinning total of 425 in the first innings. At a conference that evening in our London hotel, Woodfull exclaimed:

'Listen chaps, to win this important Test, we must double England's score by playing attacking cricket.' Woodfull set the example with his redoubtable innings of 155. Then came Bradman with a magnificent knock of 254 and our first-innings total finished at 6-729 (declared). England in its second innings scored 375, leaving Australia 72 runs to win.

Between the start of our second innings and the tea adjournment Australia lost Bill Ponsford, Don Bradman and Alan Kippax for 18 runs. The atmosphere was tense when Stan McCabe joined Woodfull at the crease. His captain remarked: 'Stan, it's not the pitch which caused the fall of these wickets – nor the bowling. If you feel like coming down the pitch to [Walter] Robins, do so.'

The result was that Stan, although playing cautiously, had the confidence to jump down the wicket to the slow bowler Robins several times and hit him through the covers for 4. He finished with 25 not out, in partnership with his captain, who remained 26 not out and Australia won by seven wickets.

That particular triumph illustrated Stan McCabe's invaluable temperament. From then on he played his cricket more freely and was even more polished in his execution.

He was a useful bowler in any company, which, together with valuable and remarkable catches to his credit, qualified him as a striking all-rounder. As such, he was an ornament throughout his career to the history of Australian Test cricket, which he served with distinction and dignity.

Australian Cricket, Bert Oldfield (Modern Magazines, November 1968)

A TEAMMATE TO ENVY AND ADMIRE

*Clem Hill, Australia's first great left-hander on the immortal
Victor Trumper, cricket's ultimate golden-age hero.*

Victor Trumper was the outstanding batsman on both sides in the 1902 tour of England by the Australian eleven. He went to the wicket 53 times and never failed to score. He made 2570 runs and that in a wet year. The nearest run-getter to him on our side [Hill] had 1614 to his credit. His was the highest total made in a season in England up to that time. He was a batsman by instinct and I consider him the greatest of all time.

Trumper was a most loving and unassuming champion. He never realised what a great batsman he was. There were many who were his equal on fast and fiery wickets, but there was nobody to approach him in his ability to make runs on all sorts of wickets, especially sticky ones.

No batsman ever played more for his side. In a Test at Manchester he had made a century before lunch. On resuming he was promptly dismissed [for 104]. He was disconsolate. 'I don't know how it is,' he said, 'that just when we wanted I can't make them. I never seem to do any good for the side.'

He made 11 centuries in that season and his top score was 128, but he could have made more runs. He threw his wicket away in order to give other batsmen a chance to have a hit. Of course he never did this in Tests and only in county fixtures when his side was safe. He took risks and gave the bowlers a chance. Nobody annoyed him more than the batsman who scratched around and scored from bad strokes. He was very generous to opponents.

The Englishmen would leap for joy when he was dismissed, whether he'd made a duck or 100.

He used to go for the bowlers in a most cavalier fashion. [George] Hirst had been hailed in England as a demon bowler. He came up against Trumper in a Test match. The first ball was square cut for 4. The next, which was the same kind of ball, he hit hard past mid-on to the chains, the third he pushed through the covers to the boundary and the fifth, a fast yorker dead on the middle stump, he banged round to the square-leg boundary.

Hirst turned to me in despair and asked: 'What am I to do with the next?'

I replied: 'Try a wide one to him.'

And it would have been a wide if Trumper had not chased it. No batsman could force a yorker away as confidently as Trumper could. Most of us were content to stay at home and take care not to be bowled, but he treated such a delivery almost as if it was off the wicket.

In a match in Sydney in 1903, [Wilfred] Rhodes and [Teddy] Arnold had the side tied up. Trumper made the bowlers look cheap. He made 185 not out and that, I think, was his greatest innings. One effort which ran it very close was his 74 on a sticky wicket in Melbourne in the second Test match the same year. Australia made 122, Rhodes establishing a Test match record by getting seven for 56 and eight for

68. And yet Rhodes was afraid to bowl at Trumper and kept pitching the ball wide of off stump. Can any cricketer who has played in Test matches remember a bowler of class on a wicket which suited him being afraid to bowl at the batsman?

Trumper could do anything at any time. All bowling came alike to him and he was just as likely to get a couple of 4s off the first two balls of the day as off the last two.

In later years, however, [Syd] Barnes, the great English bowler, worried him. Over and over again, Trumper left the dressing-room stating that he would have a go and try and knock Barnes off. He was determined at last to do or die. But instead there was our champion driven further and further back on to his wicket and made to play a defensive game. I have seen Barnes bowl at Trumper without an outfield.

With all his greatness, Trumper was a little superstitious. Bowlers held no terrors for him, fiery or sticky wickets did not unnerve him; but he feared if he saw some clergymen while he was going into bat he would not score. Sometime he did fail to get going after having seen them.

On one occasion in England he returned to the dressing-room and said: 'I knew I would not score with all those clergy about.'

To my surprise, I found on looking at the records that he was [also] a fair bowler. Against Cambridge he captured five for 19 and against Essex five for 33.

Trumper always wore an old Australian eleven cap when batting. It was bottle green. He was wearing it when he made 135 not out at Lord's in 1899 and he continued wearing it until he retired from Test cricket in 1912. It was faded, but he would not give it up for the many new ones he had. There was a row if one of the humorists of the team took his cap and hid it. He could make runs with any old bat. As we were beginning a county contest, an amateur bat-maker came along with an unwieldy looking piece of willow which must have weighed over 3 lb and asked the champion whether he would try it. 'Yes,' said Trumper, 'so long as it has a spring in it.' He made 100.

There was nobody in the team quicker at getting dressed. We would come from the field after the day's play, down, light our pipes and have a drink. Before most of us were out of our flannels he would have finished his bath, dressed himself, and we would hear him say, 'See you later,' and he would be off. During the 1905 tour, Victor and I had our wives with us. Mrs Hill could not understand, as she waited for me, how he could be dressed and away so quickly while I took so long.

He did not fold his clothes up neatly like most of us did, but heaved them into his cricket bag and if it did not close he would press the clothes down with his foot until it did. What a mess his clothes were in when he came to unpack.

The Sporting Globe, Clem Hill (Melbourne, February 1933)

CRICKET'S INDESTRUCTIBLE 'BIG SHIP'

J Elliott Monfries on the 'Big Ship' Warwick Armstrong, whose huge physique was once famously compared to one of the formidable, century-old Moreton Bay fig trees at the Adelaide Oval.

For sheer determination, Warwick Armstrong was unsurpassed and with the bat he could play any kind of cricket. I saw him once force two successive good length off-side balls over the fence on the Melbourne ground, both of which could have been caught by a man without moving a foot. To have done this, however, he would have had to be perched on the well-known awning in front of the public stand in the reserve!

As a bowler, Warwick, on a reasonably good wicket, could send down only 'straight leg breaks' – a straight ball from a hand action that indicated quite a lot of spin from the leg. He did, however, also have an allegedly fast ball, but this could be detected almost before he went back to bowl it. For continuous precision of one type of ball when this course was desired, he and [Hugh] Trumble were easily the most accomplished within my experience.

I remember in one match, on a perfect wicket, bowling to Reg Duff, one of the most enterprising bats Australia has produced, Armstrong sent down two successive maiden overs, every ball of which was dead on the middle and off stumps with only two men on the off side – mid-off and point. In changing ends after the second over, I said to him: 'My word, Warwick, you've got a hide bowling stuff like that to Reg with only two men on the off.'

'Well,' said he, 'did he hit me?' I didn't pursue the subject! I used to say that if I had to nominate a bowler who could shift a half-crown on the pitch more times than any other bowler, I would name Warwick Armstrong, and he, mind you, was a bowler with a leg-break action.

In the main he bowled a tempting length for a half-volley, put well out on the leg side with a heavily placed leg field.

Albert Trott, playing for Lord Hawke's team, met these tactics by reversing the position of his feet and belting the first ball from Warwick past my left ear for 4. I said to Albert: 'Have you ever hit a wicketkeeper making that stroke?'

'Yes,' he replied, 'and near killed him!' I didn't say anything, but I thought a heap and decided after that I would trust entirely to length of reach in taking the ball, as it was abundantly clear there was no mercy coming from Albert

According to the type of batsman, Warwick would vary his direction on the leg side. In a club match, Matt Ellis, one of Fitzroy's leading batsmen, told Warwick before the game began that if he bowled while he was in, he'd hit the first ball out of the ground. It so happened that Warwick was the bowler when Matt came in and I was amused at the way they smiled at one another as they passed. Knowing his man and his impetuous nature, Warwick bowled the first ball, that was to go out of the ground, so wide of the wicket that when Matt missed it and was out of his crease, I had to shy the wicket down, to have him stumped; surely a queer piece of stumping.

Not Test Cricket, Happy Reminiscences of Every Other Kind of Cricket in Adelaide, Melbourne, Sydney and Hobart, J Elliott Monfries (Gillingham & Co, Adelaide, 1950)

ROUND THE GROUND WITH 'FELIX'

Tom Horan batted at No. 3 for Australia in the very first Test match and was to continue his love affair with cricket as a long-time columnist, as 'Felix' in the Australasian.

I was quite startled the other day when a young cricketer stated that he had not heard of Sam Costick. Shades of Tom Wills, Harry Bryant, [William] Greaves, Tom Morres, Tom Wray, WJ Hammersley, George Marshall and the rest of the old ones who have passed to their account, should rise from the green turf on which ye played so well and tell the rising youth that at our manly game we never had a more consistent, peg-away bowler than old Sam – I think of the ever-memorable dinner where all the best and brightest of the time gathered in the old pavilion and made the rafters ring with laughter and with song.

I spot Ben James (rare old Ben) and the old East Melbourne identity Sam Willis, whose trout stream was stocked by the veteran, WW Gaggin. Talking of trout, there is EB Manning, brown as a berry after an outing with the famous angler and Mr Manning says, 'Not much luck; only got one, and that a small one.' Mr Trumble chaffs Harry Boyle about the number of times Harry has run men out in going for short runs.

Frank Allan, they tell me, can catch fish in the Hopkins when no one else gets a bite and I

Felix: Tom Horan Sr, a noted cricketer and cricket writer.

further learn that Frank will squat down blackfellow fashion by the riverside and never move for hours together except to take the fish off the hook.

That old lion-hitter of East Melbourne, Chas Forrester, is standing on the seat by the wall of the MCC kitchen and [Billy] Bruce and [Harry] Trott are making that fine stand and free display on the evening of New Year's Day. [Bruce made 54, Trott 95.] Charlie says, 'I want to catch an early train, but I can't miss this. I really can't. I must miss my train.'

[Frank] Iredale's easy commanding way of coming down on the ball with his late cut is very pretty to watch [he made 81]. Bob Carpenter, the famous batsman, thought Sam Cosstick one of the best bowlers he had ever met, and my own impression is that if he had been in his prime when Australian teams started going to England, he would have been one of the first chosen and would have startled the crack English batsmen on sticky wickets, with his beautiful length and whip from leg. Sam's figures in intercolonial matches for Victoria are: 2079 balls, 763 runs, 399 maidens, 78 wickets, 9.78 average – a remarkably fine result.

The Australasian, Tom Horan Sr (Sydney, 12 January 1895); reproduced from 'In Morning Dew, Round the Ground with "Felix", Selections & Notes', David Morris (1995)

AUTHOR'S ACKNOWLEDGEMENTS

It's amazing what you discover when you move. In our case, old cupboards unopened for years revealed a dozen or more scrapbooks covering Australian cricket in detail between the world wars. I was able to unearth long-forgotten stories from the old Melbourne *Herald* not only by the featured cricket writers, but by leading poet of the day CJ Dennis and by the much-loved cartoon character Ben Bowyang, both of whom were employed to go to the cricket, so huge was the fever for the game, especially whenever England visited. The famous umpire Bob Crockett assessed the fast bowlers of his time. 'The King' of old Carringbush, Jack Ryder, was interviewed about captaining his country. Clem Hill wrote a personal view of Victor Trumper. They were well-kept, fascinating volumes embellished by cigarette cards and colour posters, originally in the *Referee,* some of which have been reproduced here, in *Great Australian Cricket Stories.*

Colleagues who had given me the scrapbooks over the years said I might find something of value in them. They were right! And this anthology with a difference is the result.

Friends from near and far answered my SOS for some of their favourite contributions, Stephen Gibbs in Newcastle providing a rare interview with the ultimate golden-age legend Victor Trumper in a New Zealand boys' magazine. Mark Browning in Geelong uncovered the old 'Computer Test' match of the early '70s in which a revitalised Don Bradman made a double-century in the second innings after a rare failure in the first (not a bad effort for 63 years old!). David Studham and Trevor Ruddell at the Melbourne Cricket Club library found a rare picture of the MCG during the Bodyline Test and an unpublished manuscript of the best of Felix (Tom Horan Sr) taken from his old *Australasian* columns. David Frith, just about the ultimate historian of them all, had an input. Book-buying friends provided some of their favourite stories and readings, further fuelling my researches. The enthusiasm for the project from both sides of the globe was immense and for that I am very grateful.

Thanks to my family; I was able to hang a DO NOT DISTURB sign on my door and get away with it. I'd like to thank them in particular for readily giving up normal shared family time as I surrounded myself in newspapers and books, every now and again coming up for air and a cuppa. When I took a breather, Jessie would scan many of the little-known images which I know will truly delight.

Many others have been involved in this smorgasbord of stories which I'm hoping will provide as much enjoyment for you as it did for me in its gathering, sorting and shining. My thanks, in particular, to Colin Clowes, Graham Goulder, Alf James, Glenn McFarlane, Roger Page, Damian Melnyk, Bill Norton, Stuart Rooke, Cameron Sinclair, Ray Webster and Ken Williams for their input and helping me to stay focused as my deadline approached.

Colin McDonald, 81 years young, most graciously supplied a foreword. He's one of so many ex-Testmen only too pleased to chat about the glory days. Knowledge and reminiscences from champion players like this are truly golden. Thanks again everyone.

Ken Piesse

BIBLIOGRAPHY

ANNUALS & BROCHURES

ABC Cricket Book (Australian Broadcasting Commission, Sydney)

Australian Cricket Annual, a Complete Record of Australian Cricket in 1896–97, edited by JC Davis (George Robertson & Co, Melbourne, 1897)

Calypso Cricket, edited by Alan Davidson (MGA Publications, Rose Bay, Sydney, 1968)

Centenary Test, Melbourne, March 12–17, 1977 (official souvenir publication of the Australian Cricket Board, Sportsplan Marketing, Melbourne, 1977)

Quest for the Ashes: Ansett Australia Test Series, Official Test Program (ACP Publishing, Sydney, 1998)

The Historic Test, Australia v England, Perth, Western Australia, 11–16 December, 1970 (WA Newspapers, Perth, 1970)

The Sporting Globe Cricket Annual 1924–25: Records of the Tests, International and Interstate Games and Players, edited by EHM Baillie (Herald & Weekly Times Ltd, Melbourne, 1924)

The Sporting Globe Cricket Book 1928–29: Records of the Tests, International and Interstate Games and Players, edited by EHM Baillie (Herald & Weekly Times Ltd, Melbourne, 1928)

The Sporting Globe Cricket Book 1946–47: Records of the Tests, International and Interstate Games and Players, edited by EHM Baillie (Herald & Weekly Times Ltd, Melbourne, 1946)

The Story of the Tests, England v Australia 1877–1920 (official Sydney Cricket Ground souvenir, Sydney, 1920)

Wisden Australia

Wisden Cricketers' Almanac

BOOKS

A Game Divided, Peter McFarline (Hutchinson of Australia, Melbourne, 1977)

A Spinner's Yarn, Peter Philpott (ABC Books, Sydney, 1990)

A Wayward Genius: The Fleetwood-Smith Story, Greg Growden (ABC Books, Sydney, 1991)

According to Skull: An entertaining stroll through the life of Kerry O'Keeffe (ABC Books, Sydney, 2004)

All Out for One and Other Australian Cricket Anecdotes, Ken Piesse (Viking, Melbourne, 2005)

Ashes Diary 2005, from Victory in India to the Most Dramatic Test Series of the Century, Ricky Ponting (Harper Sports, Sydney, 2005)

At the Heart of English Cricket: The Life and Memories of Geoffrey Howard, Stephen Chalke (Fairfield Books, Bath, UK, 2001)

Australia: Its Cricket Bat, Its Kangaroo, Its Farming, Fruit and Flowers, Sir David Serjeant, MD (King & Jarrett, London, 1923)

Bowled Over, Neil Hawke (Rigby, Adelaide, 1982)

Bradman the Great, BJ Wakley (Mainstream Publishing, London, 1999 edition)

Bradmans of the Bush: The Legends & Larrikins of Australian Bush Cricket, Ken Piesse (Penguin Australia, Melbourne, 2002)

CC, the Colin McDonald Story: Cricket, Tennis, Life, Colin McDonald (Australian Scholarly Publishing, Melbourne, 2009)

Cricket Crisis, Jack Fingleton (Cassell & Company, London, 1946)

Cricket: A Little Book for Lovers of the Game, edited by SJ Looker (Simpkin, Marshall, Hamilton, Kent & Co, London, 1925)

Cricket's Enigma: The Sid Barnes Story, Rick Smith (ABC Books, Sydney, 1999)

Cricket's Silver Lining, edited by David Rayvern Allen (William Collins & Sons, London, 1987)

Denis Compton's Annual, Denis Compton (Stanley Paul & Co, London, 1952)

Dickie Bird, My Autobiography (Hodder & Stoughton, London, 1997)

Down at the Junction There's a Cricket Club: St Kilda Cricket Club, the First 150 Years, Ken Piesse (St Kilda Cricket Club, Melbourne, 2006)

First Class Cricket in Australia, Vol 1, 1850–51 to 1941–42, Ray Webster (self-published, Melbourne, 1991)

Fifty Cricket Stars Describe My Greatest Game, edited by Bob Holmes & Vic Marks (Mainstream Publishing, London, 1995)

Fight for the Ashes, CG Macartney (Findon Publications, London, 1948)

Golden Boy: Kim Hughes and the Bad Old Days of Australian Cricket, Christian Ryan (Allen & Unwin, Sydney, 2009)

Googlies: Coals from a Test Cricketer's Fireplace, Dr HV Hordern (Angus & Robertson Ltd, Sydney, 1932)

Graham Thorpe: Rising from the Ashes (CollinsWillow, London, 2005)

Great Australian Cricket Stories, Neil Marks (ABC Books, Sydney, 2002)

Hands and Heals: The Autobiography, Ian Healy (Harper Sports, Sydney, 2000)

Henry: The Geoff Lawson Story, Geoff Lawson (Ironbark Press, Sydney, 1993)

How We Recovered the Ashes, PF Warner (Chapman & Hall Ltd, London, 1904)

Kepler: The Biography, Edward Griffiths (Pelham Books, London, 1994)

Les Favell, Alan Shiell (The Les Favell Foundation, Adelaide, 1987)

Lillee: A Testimonial, 1981–82 (PBL, Sydney, 1981)

Not Test Cricket, Happy Reminiscences of Every Other Kind of Cricket in Adelaide, Melbourne, Sydney and Hobart, J Elliott Monfries (Gillingham & Co, Adelaide, 1950)

On Ya Warnie, Ken Piesse (Wilkinson Books, Melbourne, 2007)

Our Proud Heritage: A History of the South Melbourne Cricket Club from 1862, Robert Grogan (South Melbourne Cricket Club, 2003)

Out for a Duck, Kersi Meher-Homji (Kangaroo Press, Sydney, 1993)

Parade to Paradise: 101 Seasons of East Torrens Cricket and Cricketers 1897–98 to 2002–03, East Torrens CC, Peter Herbert & Geoff Sando (East Torrens Cricket Club, 2003)

Parky, Michael Parkinson (Hodder & Stoughton, London, 2008)

Phillip Blashki, a Victorian Patriarch, Gael R Hammer (Blashki & Sons, Melbourne, 1986)

Ranji, Prince of Cricketers, Alan Ross (William Collins & Sons Pty Ltd, London, 1983)

Rebuilding Your Body, Your Mind and Your Life: The Chevell Program to a Better Life, Kevin Chevell (Information Australia, Melbourne, 1998)

Richmond's 100 Years of Cricket: The Story of Richmond Cricket Club 1854–1954, Percy Taylor (CG Meehan & Co, South Melbourne, 1954)

Roy Going For Broke, Andrew Symonds with Stephen Gray (Hardie Grant Books, Melbourne, 2006)

Slasher Opens Up, Ken Mackay (Pelham Books, London, 1964)

Slats: The Michael Slater Story (Random House Australia, Sydney, 2005)

Some Statistics Concerning Cricket Casualties (Showing Batsmen Struck By Bowlers in Test Matches between England and Australia), RH Campbell (ABC, Sydney, 1933)

Stephen Fleming, Balance of Power, Richard Boock (Hodder, Moa, Beckett Publishers Ltd, Wellington, 2004)

TJ Over the Top, Terry Jenner (Information Australia, Melbourne, 1999)

Tales from the Sports Field: The best of Neil Marks (ABC Books, Sydney, 2005)

Test Cricket Certainties and Possibilities for 1928–29, MA Noble (New Century Press Limited, Sydney, 1928)

Test Match Sixes, Ross Smith (self-published, Invermay, Tasmania, 1998)

The Appeal of Cricket, Richie Benaud (Hodder & Stoughton, Sydney, 1995)

The Book of the Two Maurices, Being Some Account of the Tour by an MCC Team through Australia and New Zealand in the Closing Months of 1929 and the Beginning of 1930, MJ Turnbull & MJC Allom (E Allom & Co Ltd, London, 1930)

The Chronicles of Early Melbourne, 1835 to 1852, Centennial Edition, Vol II, 'Garryowen' (Fergusson and Mitchell, Melbourne, 1888)

The Cricketer's Weekend Book, Eric Parker (T & A Constable Limited, Edinburgh, 1952)

The Extraordinary Book of Australian Cricket, Ken Piesse (Penguin Books, Melbourne, 2009)

The History of the South Australian Cricket Association, Chris Harte (Sports Marketing Australia, Adelaide, 1990)

The Power of Passion, Justin Langer (Swan Publishing, Sydney, 2002)

The Waugh Zone, Ken Piesse (The Book Company Publishing, Sydney, 2003)

The Wit of Cricket, Ian Brayshaw (The Currawong Press, Milson's Point, Sydney, 1981)

Trumper: The Definitive Biography, Peter Sharpham (Hodder & Stoughton, Sydney, 1985)

With Bat and Ball, George Giffen (Ward, Lock & Co, London, 1898)

With the 15th Australian XI, Sydney Smith Jr (ET Kibblewhite & Co, Sydney, 1922)

With the 1930 Australians: Behind the Scenes in the Fight for the Ashes, Geoffrey Tebbutt (Hodder & Stoughton, London, 1930)

MAGAZINES

Australian Cricket (Modern Magazines, Sydney)
Australian Cricket Tourguide (Universal Magazines, Sydney)
Cricket Quarterly (Eastbourne, UK)
Cricket West (Sportscene, Leederville, WA)
Cricket: A Weekly Record of the Game (London)
Cricketer (Newspress, Melbourne)
Pavilion (Australian Cricket Society, Melbourne)
People (Sydney)
Reveille (London)
Sporting Life (Sydney)

The Bulletin with Newsweek (Sydney)
The Cricket Statistician (Association of Cricket Statisticians and Historians, Nottingham, UK)
The Modern Boy (London)
The Rugby League News (Sydney)
The Wisden Cricketer (London)
The Young Man's Magazine (New Zealand)

NEWSPAPERS
Cricket Week (International Publishing Group, Sydney)
The Age (Melbourne)
The Argus (Melbourne)
The Australasian (Sydney)
The Courier Mail (Brisbane)
The Daily Star (London)
The Guardian (Manchester)
The Herald (Melbourne)
The News (Adelaide)
The Referee (Sydney)
The Sporting Globe (Melbourne)
The Sun (Sydney)
The Sydney Morning Herald (Sydney)
The Times (London)

RADIO
Cricket on the Air: A Selection from Fifty Years of Radio Broadcasts, David Rayvern-Allen (BBC, London, 1985)
Radio Sport 927, Ken Piesse (Melbourne, March 2010)
Test Cricket 1938 National Broadcasts (Australian Broadcasting Commission, Sydney, 1938)

UNPUBLISHED MANUSCRIPTS
'In Morning Dew, Round the Ground with "Felix", Selections and Notes', David Morris (1995, copy held in Melbourne Cricket Club library)

INDEX

AUTHOR'S INDEX

STATISTICAL TABLES